MW01075056

Values in Halakha

Rabbi Aharon Lichtenstein

Values in Halakha

Six Case Studies

EDITED BY
Reuven Ziegler

Mishnat HaRAL
Yeshivat Har Etzion
Maggid Books

Values in Halakha
Six Case Studies

First Edition, 2023

Maggid Books
An imprint of Koren Publishers Jerusalem Ltd.

POB 8531, New Milford, CT 06776-8531, USA
& POB 4044, Jerusalem 9104001, Israel
www.maggidbooks.com

ISBN 978-1-59264-606-7, *hardcover*

A CIP catalogue record for this title is available from the British Library

Printed and bound in the United States

אין עושין נפשות לצדיקים דבריהם הן הן זכרונן.
ירושלמי שקלים פ״ב ה״ה

In memory of

Rav Aharon Lichtenstein זצ״ל

Whose profound teaching and inspiring deeds
continue to enrich and sustain our community

and

In memory of his devoted sister

Dr. Shoshana Avner ע״ה

A woman of valor
1931–2019

Dedicated by
The Bayer Hirt Family

Contents

Editor's Preface ix

Judaism and Humanism 1

Introduction and Biography of the Rama 1

Responsa Rama #125 12

Ma Enosh: Reflections on the Relation Between Judaism and Humanism 34

Formalism vs. Teleology: Circumvention and Adaptation in Halakha 113

Introduction and Biography of the Havvot Ya'ir 113

Responsa Havvot Ya'ir #163 119

Analysis 134

Pursuit of Self-Interest 159

Introduction 159

Responsa Havvot Ya'ir #213 164

Analysis 171

The Varieties of Halakhic Law: The Concept of *Lifnim Mishurat Hadin* 217

***Kofin Al Middat Sedom*: Compulsory Altruism?** 277

The Responsibilities of the Recipient of Charity 319

Source Index 343

General Index 361

Name Index 365

Editor's Preface

The essays before you attempt to discern the values embedded within and emerging from a variety of halakhic topics. In other words, these are studies in the axiology and teleology of Halakha, that is, the value and meaning structures of Jewish law. This enterprise entails numerous risks, which, characteristically, Rabbi Lichtenstein addresses forthrightly. Following the discussion of the risks, Rabbi Lichtenstein sets forth what may be considered a programmatic statement for this volume:

> These dangers are unquestionably real. And yet what is the alternative? Ethically – nay, religiously – speaking, none whatsoever. An automaton can respond to commands without seeking meaning in them or order among them. A fully human response relates a command to a total existential reality; and the moment such a relation is postulated, the quest for purpose becomes inevitable. If we are to grasp divine commands spiritually, indeed if we are to understand them at all in anything more than a semantic or mechanical sense, we must understand them teleologically. The contention that while mitzvot are purposeful we must act as if they weren't – because we have no surefire method of ascertaining

> their ends – emasculates one whole side of the religious life. Far from representing, *ipso facto*, an element of hubris, the attempt to interpret Halakha in categories of values constitutes a necessary phase of *kabbalat haTorah*, "the receiving of the Torah." As a dynamic participant in the dialogic process of divine revelation, man cannot and should not rest content with receiving God's message at only the most superficial of levels. Moreover, in assuming the validity of teleological interpretation, we need not rely upon our own intuition. A Torah value structure is clearly the basis of numerous rabbinic ordinances and it lies at the very heart of the concept of *lifnim mishurat hadin*. I am not at all sure that one *can* banish teleology. When barred at the door, it tends to sneak in through the window, and even professed legal literalists are apt to think and react in terms of an implicit value structure. Quite clearly, however, we *ought* not banish it – not even in the interests of theological security. When the price of security is spiritual embalming, we can hardly avoid taking some risks.
>
> The risks cannot be denied – indeed, they can hardly be exaggerated – but a meaningful set of values is too important a baby to be cast out with the bath water. Teleological interpretation can and often does entail hubris; but, given self-awareness and religious sensibility, it is fully consistent with absolute humility. Properly conceived, moreover, it is no usurpation but rather the exercise of a divinely mandated duty.[1]

Indeed, in fulfilling this divinely mandated duty, the author amply demonstrates the self-awareness, religious sensibility, and absolute humility he so avidly pursued throughout his life.

***

On September 7, 1966, the Daily News Bulletin of the Jewish Telegraphic Agency announced:

1. Below, pp. 148–149.

> Yeshiva [University] launched at its graduate center today the Israel Rogosin Center for Ethics and Human Values, a pioneering program that will focus on teaching and research into the history, philosophy and practical application of Jewish ethics. This Center, developed with the aid of a $1,000,000 gift from Israel Rogosin, will have a student body of rabbis, teachers and other qualified graduate students.[2]

Rabbi Lichtenstein served as a research fellow at the Rogosin Institute from its inception, and the first four essays in this volume were composed in the late 1960s under its auspices.[3] A glance at the bibliography of his published writings will reveal that the intersection of Halakha and ethics continued to concern Rabbi Lichtenstein throughout his career.[4] Thus, after the first four essays, this volume continues with two essays (published in Hebrew in 1972 and 1980 and translated here) that flesh out issues raised but not developed in the Rogosin essays.[5]

Several decades elapsed between the composition of the Rogosin essays and their publication. In 1968, Rabbi Lichtenstein – then a *rosh kollel* and *rosh yeshiva* at Yeshiva University in New York – was invited by Rabbi Yehuda Amital to serve as head of the newly founded Yeshivat Har Etzion in Israel, a plan that came to fruition in 1971. At that time, the four Rogosin essays were at various stages of completion, as will be noted below; one was completed and published in 2007 and the other three appear here for the first time.[6] Why were they originally set aside and why were they revived several decades later? Rabbi Lichtenstein offers insight in the "Prefatory and Explanatory Note" to the 2007 publication of the first essay in this volume:

---

2. Archived at pdfs.jta.org/1966/1966-09-07_171.pdf.
3. The latest sources cited in these four essays were written in 1968: see below, p. 34 n. 1 and p. 227 n. 29.
4. See etzion.org.il/en/RAL-bibliography.
5. See p. 209 n. 100 and p. 271 n. 175 below.
6. To be precise, "Judaism and Humanism" appears on pp. 1–112 below; pp. 34–103 of this essay were published in 2007 in *The Torah U-Madda Journal*.

Well in excess of the several years interlude between composition and publication recommended by Longinus and Cardinal Newman, this essay has been gathering dust – and, possibly, shedding interest and relevance – for almost four decades. Written as part of a broader project relating to elements of interface between Halakhah and ethics shortly before we moved to *Erez Yisrael,* it gradually lapsed into dormancy and relinquished priority. As the pressures of adjusting to the challenges of a fresh social and intellectual climate mounted, and as, concurrently, my relations to some aspects of a prior academic matrix waned, this project was deferred, as yesteryears' endeavors were overshadowed by the immediate urgency of preparing tomorrow's *shiurim*; all the more so, insofar as some of the material, although not the central and crucial issues proper, was now severed from its organic linguistic and literary audience, beyond both the grasp and reach of most Israeli readers. And so, the dust accumulated.

In the interim, however, neither time nor the religious world stood still. Hence, when the prospect of publishing this material resurfaced recently, obvious reservations suggested themselves. Were the issues still significantly relevant? Had not some been the subjects of thorough monographs? Might not some of the material appear dated, once familiar allusions now anachronistic, on the one hand, and the failure to relate to more recent expressions of the *Zeitgeist* all too evident, on the other? With respect to this particular essay, for instance, hadn't the role of classical humanism in relation to Torah Judaism, as ally or adversary, receded substantially during the past generation? And hadn't I, in a sense, preempted myself and this piece by discussions of some of its themes strewn through later writings?

Given my own uncertainty, I submitted the material to qualified readers for evaluation. I present it here – and hope, *bi-siy'atta di-shemayya,* to present related essays in the future – in deference to their favorable judgment and in response to their importunity. I presume that some of the concerns raised previously are indeed genuine, but I hope that the general audience, too, will find the material of interest and value nonetheless.

> Rather than labor under the burden of an extensive overhaul, I am presenting the essay almost intact, as originally written, the excursus on privation at the conclusion of section VI constituting the only significant change.[7] I leave the labor of overhaul and/or comparison to the individual reader. I trust he or she will not find it excessively onerous.[8]

As is clear from the above, Rabbi Lichtenstein intended to publish the remaining Rogosin essays. After some initial work on them, health reasons precluded him from completing the task. However, with the author's blessing and encouragement, and with appropriate care and circumspection, the essays are now being presented to the public.

At the time of Rabbi Lichtenstein's *aliya*, as noted earlier, the four Rogosin essays were at differing stages of preparation. The first two essays, "Judaism and Humanism" and "Formalism vs. Teleology," were the closest to completion, and required little more than transcription and copy editing. However, the next two essays, "Pursuit of Self-Interest" and "The Varieties of Halakhic Law: The Concept of *Lifnim Mishurat Hadin*," contained numerous lacunae. Though "Pursuit of Self-Interest" is a rich and resonant essay, two planned sections remain unwritten.[9] Furthermore, the original manuscript contained only brief marginal annotations in Hebrew instead of fully written footnotes in English. In the final version below, most of source citations appearing in footnotes were provided by Rabbi Lichtenstein, while the footnotes containing longer comments are reconstructed from the author's terse Hebrew notes to himself. Finally, most of the lengthy quotations of rabbinic sources were absent from the manuscript and have been added.

The first six sections of "The Varieties of Halakhic Law: The Concept of *Lifnim Mishurat Hadin*" (pp. 217–260 below) were written and

---

7. Ed. note: This excursus extends from p. 89, "With respect to dispensation," until the end of section VI on p. 92.
8. "'*Mah Enosh*': Reflections on the Relation between Judaism and Humanism," *The Torah U-Madda Journal* 14 (2006–2007), pp. 1–2.
9. These are the discussion of commercial rivalry, as noted on p. 191 n. 51, and the reexamination of the responsum of the *Havvot Ya'ir* in light of the preceding analysis, as noted on p. 216 n. 107.

edited while the author still resided in the United States, as is evident from the address appearing on the typescript. These sections were followed in the typescript by the author's outline for the remainder of the essay (p. 275 below), comprising six topics. Subsequently, the author appended two more sections in handwriting (pp. 260–274 below), covering items 1, 2, and the first half of item 3 in the outline.[10] The projected conclusion of the essay (from the second half of item 3 until item 6) remains unwritten.[11]

In addition to filling in missing sources and the like, some editing was deemed necessary to facilitate reader comprehension and clarify the development of an argument. Thus, for example, while the author divided the first five essays in this volume into numbered subsections, I provided explanatory titles to each subsection, and added further subdivisions when necessary. The titles of all essays were provided by Rabbi Lichtenstein, with the exception of "Formalism vs. Teleology" and "Pursuit of Self-Interest"; the titles of the two final essays, translated from Hebrew, were slightly modified. With minor exceptions, source references have not been updated to reflect more recent editions, nor have references been added to more recent discussions of the issues

10. It is interesting to note that in a 1978 interview with Rabbi Lichtenstein in an Israeli newspaper, the interviewer writes: "Lately, Rabbi Dr. Aharon Lichtenstein has been writing a book of Jewish thought that will include, among others, chapters on the following topics: egoism and altruism in Halakha, humanism in Halakha, *lifnim mishurat hadin* in Halakha, *ha'arama* (circumvention) in Halakha, and the like," and that Rabbi Lichtenstein was planning to publish the book in Hebrew (!) for both religious and non-religious readers. See Levi Yitzhak Hayerushalmi, "I Will Encourage My Daughter to Go to Sherut Leumi," *Maariv*, Friday, October 6, 1978 (5 Tishrei 5739), *Yamim Veleilot* Supplement, p. 24, available online at https://www.nli.org.il/he/newspapers/mar/1978/10.

11. Rabbi Lichtenstein returned to the subject of *lifnim mishurat hadin* in his celebrated essay "Does Jewish Tradition Recognize an Ethic Independent of Halakhah?" (originally published in 1975 and reprinted numerous times, including in Rabbi Lichtenstein's 2004 collection *Leaves of Faith: The World of Jewish Living* [vol. 2]). As the essay in the current volume deals exclusively with *lifnim mishurat hadin*, the treatment here is more extensive. There are two brief passages of overlap between the two essays: a quote from the *Maggid Mishneh* and the subsequent paragraph (pp. 268–269 below; *Leaves*, p. 49), and a quote from the Maharal and the comment thereon (p. 272 n. 177 below; *Leaves*, pp. 45–46).

raised. Rabbi Lichtenstein's essays, even with the lacunae noted above, are valuable contributions in themselves; therefore they are being presented as written, while the work of comparison, analysis, and expansion remains for readers to ponder and, perhaps, to contribute to Torah literature on their own.

***

Many people deserve thanks for their help in bringing this volume to print.

First, Dr. Tovah Lichtenstein provided not only support and encouragement but also helpful comments.

Yoel Weiss and Noam Shalit of the Mishnat HaRAL Foundation made sure the project moved forward and provided means for doing so.

Rabbi Elyakim Krumbein and Rabbi Michael Siev offered valuable feedback on the entire volume, and Rabbi Dr. Moshe Berger, Rabbi Dr. Judah Goldberg, and Prof. David Shatz on parts of it.

Nechama Unterman expertly proofread the volume, Rabbi Avigdor Rosensweig provided research assistance, and Tani Bednarsh prepared the indexes.

Rabbi David Strauss translated the last two chapters from Hebrew, and Yeshivat Har Etzion and Yeshiva University kindly allowed parts of this volume to be reprinted.

The following people aided at various stages of the preparation of this volume: Nadine Gesundheit, Prof. Aviad Hacohen, Rabbi Dov Karoll, Kobi Nadell, and Prof. Aaron Segal.

As always, it was a pleasure to work with Matthew Miller and the outstanding staff of Maggid Books: Caryn Meltz, Ita Olesker, Tomi Mager, and Tani Bayer.

Above all, gratitude to *mori verabbi* Harav Aharon Lichtenstein *zt"l*, from whom we continue to learn even now.

Reuven Ziegler
Nisan 5782
Alon Shevut

Judaism and Humanism

INTRODUCTION AND BIOGRAPHY OF THE RAMA

Rav Moshe Isserles – or, as he is universally known, the "Rama"[1] – played a central role in one of the most creative periods in European Jewish history – the century of Polish Jewish life extending roughly from 1550 to 1650 which established the mores and institutions of Eastern European Jewry and which produced the *Shulhan Arukh* and its standard commentaries. He was born about 1525[2] into a pious, scholarly, and munificent family in Cracow, a budding center of Jewish learning in which he subsequently spent virtually all his life. Having gained youthful renown as a prodigy, he studied under R. Shalom Shachna, an almost legendary figure who left very few writings but who trained most of the leading Eastern

1. The word derives from an acronym of the Hebrew initials of his name, preceded by the title, Rav.
2. The exact date is unknown. For a discussion and review of various suggestions, see Myer S. Lew, *The Jews of Poland: Their Political, Economic, Social and Communal Life in the Sixteenth Century as Reflected in the Works of Rabbi Moses Isserles* (London, 1944), 12–16.

European scholars of the next generation. The Rama rapidly attained a widespread reputation, and by 1550 was being consulted from various quarters on both halakhic and communal matters. Henceforth – both the exact date and the nature of his position are unclear – he assumed a post as rabbi in or of Cracow, in which capacity he served until his early death in 1572.

Living during a period in which the Jewish community was both highly organized and religiously saturated, the Rama was actively involved in almost every major aspect of civic life. This involvement helped earn him the extraordinary esteem of contemporaries, an esteem which, despite occasional controversy and the early tragic death of his first wife, enabled the Rama to lead a reasonably secure and serene life. It is through his writings, however, that he has become a household name to posterity. These covered a fairly extensive range: halakhic notes and compendia, a volume of homiletical biblical exegesis, a philosophical treatise, excursions into Kabbala, a collection of responsa, even a commentary on a medieval work on astronomy which had recently been translated from Latin.[3] By far the most significant, however, has been a relatively modest undertaking – a collection of notes which the Rama can hardly have regarded as his *magnum opus* but which have been of great historical import. The publication of R. Yosef Karo's *Shulhan Arukh* in 1565 marked the appearance – in print, moreover – of the first new comprehensive halakhic code in over two centuries. However, despite its acknowledged excellence, it suffered, as far as Eastern and Central European Jews were concerned, from one grievous defect. Having been written by a Sephardi, it generally followed the opinions and practice of the Spanish and North African tradition rather than those of the Franco-German community which had been their spiritual forebears. This defect was rectified by the Rama, who interleaved the *Shulhan Arukh* with a gloss in which he took issue with many of its decisions by citing divergent texts and customs. Hence, he adapted it for Ashkenazic purposes and enabled it to gain its subsequent dominance as the basic halakhic code. Despite its relatively ancillary nature, it is upon this achievement – for

3. The works are described by Lew, *The Jews of Poland*, 58–79, and Asher Siev, *HaRama* (Jerusalem, 1957), 39–72 [second edition: (New York, 1972), 105–180].

his role as *baal hamappa*, "the master of the tablecloth"[4] – that the Rama's reputation preeminently rests.

The collection of the Rama's responsa – representing, incidentally, only a part of those he wrote – has been published in six editions: Cracow (1640), Hamburg (1710), Hanau (1710), Amsterdam (1711), Sudylkow (1835), and Warsaw (1883; reprinted New York, 1954).[5] Except where otherwise noted, I have followed the *editio princeps* which was published by the Rama's nephew from a manuscript he had evidently prepared for publication. Parts of the following *teshuva* have also been published in translation under the title "A Radical Decision," in Solomon B. Freehof, *A Treasury of Responsa* (Philadelphia, 1963), 113–17. Reference to this translation has been made in some of the notes.

"The precepts of the Lord are right," sang the psalmist, "rejoicing the heart."[6] Or again, in a more personal vein, "I rejoice at Thy word, as one that findeth great spoil."[7] To the committed Jew, the observance of Torah and Halakha is a source of genuine joy. It is, to be sure, often demanding and even difficult. After all, the Rabbis always speak of "the yoke of the Kingdom of Heaven."[8] Yet, awareness of participation in a divinely ordained discipline – of responding, at the highest level, to a divine call – fills the Jew with a profoundly gratifying sense of engaging in what is at once the realization of God's regimen and a process of self-fulfillment.

To the *posek*, however, fidelity to Halakha may be not only difficult but agonizing. Inevitably, he is periodically confronted by situations in which Halakha comes into apparent conflict with human needs – not simply with shallow utilitarian desires, but with genuinely worthwhile needs. Under these circumstances, the process of decision can be soul-searing. The sacrifices – and they can be enormous – which he may be ready and willing to make himself, he is morally, and psychologically,

4. *Shulhan Arukh* literally means "set table"; hence, the Rama's epithet.
5. Ed. note: A critical edition was published by Rabbi Dr. Asher Siev (Jerusalem, 1971), and it is the Hebrew text of this edition that appears below. Minor modifications were made to the translation to accord with this text.
6. *Tehillim* 19:9.
7. Ibid. 119:162.
8. *Berakhot* 13a.

reluctant to exact from others. The process of decision becomes therefore – quite apart from the specific issue being decided – a moment of truth, an ethical and religious problem in its own right. Were the *posek* less committed to Halakha, less aware of his responsibility to the observance and preservation of divine law, there would be no problem. He would cut a few corners, wink at an impending peccadillo – and hand down a pseudo-*pesak*. Were he less sensitive to human need, there would, again, be no problem. He would simply pronounce, "Let the law cleave the mountain,"[9] issue a rigorous cut-and-dried decision, and let the chips fall where they may. It is the ethical and religious desire to be sensitive to both the halakhic and the human dimensions of a situation – or rather, to be sensitive to their interaction – which produces a profoundly agonizing dilemma.

The dilemma admits of no facile solution. At times, it admits of no solution at all. The conflict between personal and halakhic demands may be absolutely irreducible, the result being genuine tragedy. In tone and detail, Y. L. Gordon's poems[10] present caricatures of Halakha; but while they might be dismissed as mere anticlerical if not antinomian diatribe, the underlying problem of possible tension between law and self is very real. At other times, however, the *prima facie* conflict, while real and not merely apparent, may, through the initiative of a master *posek*, be blunted and finally transcended. Marshaling erudition and ingenuity, the sensitive scholar may exploit the element of flexibility within Halakha in order to avert personal tragedy. While remaining clearly within the bounds of the halakhic system as a whole, he combines general extenuating principles with specific personal insights in order to escape his tormenting dilemma. He strives to remain honest without being cold, to be faithful and yet related. In a word, he avoids either pole of the

9. *Sanhedrin* 6b.

10. Of the poems in this vein, the best known are *Kotzo Shel Yod,* about a woman whose life is ruined because of a minor technical flaw in a bill of divorce, and *Ashaka De-Rispak,* about a home and marriage which break up because of two grains of seed discovered in some food on Pesah, as a result of which the food itself and virtually all the utensils in the house are brusquely declared to be non-kosher by the rabbi. It might be noted, incidentally, that the "halakhic" decisions cited in both poems are highly dubious, if not, indeed, clearly erroneous.

shallow antinomy, neither sacrificing every Jew for a *din* nor every *din* for a Jew; and to this end, he draws upon every resource, personal and intellectual, at his disposal.

The following *teshuva*, written by Rav Moshe Isserles, provides a singular example of precisely such a dilemma and of a heroic attempt to resolve it. The situation concerned a young woman, a poor orphan at that, for whom, evidently with some difficulty, a match had been arranged by her father shortly before his death. Deserted by most of her relatives, the girl moved in with an uncle, to remain with him until her marriage. As the period of her engagement wore on, however, she noted indications that her relatives who, in accordance with current custom, were to supply her trousseau and dowry and arrange the wedding, were less than anxious to fulfill their responsibility. There was no sign of either dowry or wedding; only veiled rumblings transmitted through neighboring women that she should ready herself for marriage and all would soon be forthcoming. When the appointed day finally came, however, her recalcitrant relatives sought to cheat her of fully one-third of her dowry. The bridegroom, in turn, refused to go through with the wedding unless the promised sum were paid – a not uncommon stance in an era of arranged as opposed to romantic marriages.[11] No degree of remonstrance on the part of the rabbis present could move him, and it was only after lengthy haggling that he agreed to proceed. By this time, however, darkness had long set in and, the day being Friday, the Sabbath, on which no wedding may ordinarily be performed, had begun.

The dilemma was obvious. If the marriage were not performed immediately, the bridegroom might recant once more, leaving the girl poor and alone, and of course greatly embarrassed by the public ordeal. Yet the Halakha, with its frequently rigorous adherence to clocks and calendars, clearly seemed to proscribe any such performance. The Rama, who was present at the time, decided to proceed; and he personally

11. See, e.g., *Taz,* YD 192:6. Of course, from a modern perspective, the loss of this type of prospective husband may appear a blessing in disguise. However, the historical context should be kept in mind. In sixteenth-century Poland virtually any husband was deemed better than spinsterhood. Moreover, given the lower level of romantic expectation, the fact remains that many marriages which started under seemingly inauspicious circumstances turned out very well indeed.

arranged the ceremony. The decision evoked considerable criticism, however.[12] Subsequently, therefore, the Rama wrote this *teshuva*, partly by way of vindicating his personal reputation and partly by way of simply presenting a *post facto* exposition of the halakhic grounds of his action.

In developing his position, the Rama employs two general approaches, presenting both intrinsic and extrinsic arguments. He contends, on the one hand, that a Sabbath marriage under these circumstances may be inherently permissible – i.e., that this situation was simply never subsumed under the general prohibition; and he suggests three distinct possible grounds for this contention. Even assuming this to be wrong, however, he argues, secondly, that the prohibition needs to be overridden in this specific instance because of more general considerations; and he proceeds, in turn, to cite three of these. The net result is a web of arguments, each independent and yet perhaps insufficiently secure – at least in relation to this particular situation – to have been relied upon on its own, but which, collectively, justify the Rama's conclusion.

The *teshuva* opens – after a brief narrative and vindicative prologue – with a discussion of the primary relevant text: a mishna in *Beitza* and its attendant gemara. The mishna lists various acts whose performance on the Sabbath, while permitted by the Torah, was proscribed by the Rabbis. These, in turn, are broken down into two categories: neutral and mitzva actions, with the effecting of *kiddushin*, i.e., betrothal, included among the former. In commenting upon the prohibition of *kiddushin*, the gemara asks: "But is he not performing a mitzva?" It then briefly replies that the mishna may be construed as referring to a special case – that of a person who already has children – in which the element of mitzva was relatively insignificant.[13]

The question may be variously interpreted, however. The gemara may be merely objecting to the mishna's classification – the inclusion

---

12. There had been some general criticism of the Rama – e.g., by R. Hayim ben Bezalel, a brother of the Maharal of Prague – as being too lenient; see Siev, *HaRama*, 93–94. Judging from the tone of this *teshuva*'s prologue, however, it evidently evoked a storm of unusually strong protest.
13. *Beitza* 36b.

of *kiddushin* amongst forbidden neutral, rather than mitzva, actions; or it may be challenging the prohibition proper. The respective textual interpretations would, in turn, have clear legal consequences. On the first view, the gemara does not qualify the prohibition in any way. On the second, however, it concludes by confining it to special cases. Ordinarily, because of the mitzva they entail, Sabbath *kiddushin* would be fully permissible.

This text provides the raw material for the Rama's initial, internal arguments. The possible conflicting interpretations of the gemara's question had indeed been debated by the classical medieval commentaries. As generally understood, Rashi,[14] followed by almost all *Rishonim*, adopted the first; hence the accepted view that Sabbath *kiddushin* are forbidden. Rabbenu Tam,[15] however, opted for the second. The Rama's opening thrust consists of an attempt to prove, through involuted textual analysis, that Rabbenu Tam's is the superior rendering. Indeed, he argues that even Rashi's comments may be reconciled with it, so that Rabbenu Tam need not be regarded as a sole dissident overwhelmed by all other *Rishonim*; rather, the issue may be viewed as the subject of a more general controversy. However, the Rama readily concedes that this is not the way in which Rashi has been generally interpreted; and in any event, however Rashi be understood, the majority of *Rishonim* had explicitly rejected Rabbenu Tam's view.

He therefore introduces a second argument. Even barring textual support for his position and even assuming that he stands alone in the present case, Rabbenu Tam's view may be regarded as decisive because, under conditions of duress, one may rely upon the opinion of a minority – be it even a minority of one. And what, asks the Rama, could be a moment of greater duress than the situation at hand?

While expatiating upon the pressures involved in this case, the Rama veers in the direction of his second major approach – the citation of grounds which, in this specific instance, could warrant overriding the general prohibition against Sabbath *kiddushin*, even if the prohibition's existence be acknowledged. Three distinct grounds are mentioned. First,

14. Ibid., s.v. *velo mekaddeshin*.
15. Cited in *Tosafot*, ibid., s.v. *veha mitzva*, and in numerous parallel sources.

referring solely to the ordeal of the bride's public embarassment – even assuming, that is, that the groom would have consented to marriage after the Sabbath – the Rama cites the principle that the preservation of human dignity and the prevention of personal shame override rabbinic injunctions. Second, now with an eye to the possible severance of the match, he alludes to the license to violate certain laws in the interest of peace, especially domestic peace. Finally, he notes precedents setting aside certain prohibitions so that one may be enabled to undertake fulfilling the mitzva of "be fruitful and multiply."

These general considerations are discussed briefly, in almost rapid-fire order. Having cited them, however, the Rama returns to intricate analysis and to the details of the specific prohibition concerning Sabbath *kiddushin*. This sixth argument, while essentially intrinsic in character, nevertheless clearly impinges upon broader issues of general halakhic method and outlook. Hence, the Rama introduces it by citing an analogue. The argument is that since, according to the gemara,[16] Sabbath *kiddushin* were forbidden lest they be attended by some writing, their prohibition should not apply to circumstances in which no such danger exists. This, the Rama contends, is now generally the case. The prospect of Sabbath violation was only present so long as the various documents related to the wedding ceremony were ordinarily written by the groom. However now, in order not to embarrass the ignorant, these are invariably prepared by an appointed functionary, who is very unlikely to write them on the Sabbath, presumably because he is both less anxious and less harried, on the one hand, and because, as a professional, he generally draws them up long in advance of the wedding. Hence, the danger envisioned by the gemara no longer exists, and the prohibition ordained to guard against it can therefore be ignored.

This argument clearly rests upon two premises: first, that an injunction instituted to prevent a particular danger lapses with the danger itself; second, that the sole reason for prohibiting Sabbath *kiddushin* is indeed the possibility that it may lead to writing. The Rama attempts to prove the major premise – at least, with reference to the injunctions cited in this mishna in *Beitza* – by citing an analogy. The mishna also prohibits

16. *Beitza* 37a.

certain modes of clapping and dancing lest, the gemara explains, they lead to repairing musical instruments.[17] Yet *Tosafot*[18] at one point state that this injunction no longer applies, since such instruments are now generally repaired by experts; and this view has gained wide practical acceptance. As regards the minor premise, the Rama finds himself confronted by the Yerushalmi,[19] which cites another reason: *kiddushin* are forbidden because they constitute an act of acquisition.[20] He disposes of this by arguing, *de silentio*, that this reason was rejected by the Babylonian Talmud, whose authority generally overrides its Jerusalem counterpart. In our specific case, moreover, the failure of leading *posekim* to cite the Yerushalmi's reason indicates that they, too, felt it had been rejected.

To this point, the Rama has merely advanced this argument and buttressed it by a somewhat shaky syllogism. Now, he attempts to offer more specific direct proof. Once again, he resorts to analogy. Moving from *kidddushin* to divorce, he assumes, first – on the basis of a close textual reading of *Tosafot* – that divorce on the Sabbath is forbidden only if one accepts the Yerushalmi's reason for prohibiting *kiddushin* but not according to the gemara in the Bavli. Second, he contends that the presumed distinction between *kiddushin* and divorce can only be explained in one way: documents relating to the former were written by the parties involved, while the more complex bill of divorce was generally written by a professional scribe. Hence, the danger of writing on the Sabbath existed in the case of *kiddushin* but not in the case of divorce. Similarly, in our own day, there being no danger with regard to *kiddushin* either, they, too, may be permitted on the Sabbath.

With this, the presentation of the Rama's substantive position essentially concludes. The *teshuva* itself does not end here, however. First, the Rama – evidently insecure about the validity of his last argument – summarily reviews all of his previous points. Second, he feels compelled to cite and reject an entirely fresh objection – an objection

17. Ibid. 36b.
18. Ibid. 30a, s.v. *tenan*.
19. *Yoma* 1:1; p. 5b.
20. Such acts are forbidden even if no physical object is acquired; see *Beitza* 17a and *Eiruvin* 38b.

rooted in the structure of the wedding ceremony. Halakhically, the process of marriage consists of two distinct steps – *kiddushin* and *huppa*. The former, generally implemented by the groom's giving his bride money or an object of monetary value, merely effects a state of *eirusin*, betrothal. Not just an engagement, it has binding legal force and can be broken only by a bill of divorce. However, in human terms, it changes little. It does not permit the couple to live together[21] – neither as man and wife nor even, if alone, in the same home. It establishes a legal bond but not that positive unity, the cleaving and becoming one flesh which is the essence of marriage. This is effected by *huppa*, generally held to be implemented by literal cohabitation – if not by sexual relations proper, at least by entering a common home or being alone in circumstances under which such relations are possible.[22] Through *huppa*, the process of marriage is completed and the couple, no longer merely affianced but truly joined, enters fully into its state, *nissuin*, with all attendant rights and responsibilities.

This positive character of *huppa* confronts the Rama with a new difficulty. In early times, *kiddushin* and *huppa* were separated by a long interval – generally a year – during which the bride continued to live with her parents. This practice had long since been abandoned, however, so that the two were now invariably telescoped as successive phases of a single ceremony, the whole of which the Rama had of course performed. The difficulty therefore is that even if it should be conceded that Sabbath *kiddushin* are permissible, one might still entertain reservations about *huppa*; and this has indeed been contended by a number of critics. After all, they argued, acts of acquisition are prohibited on the Sabbath. If, as the Rama would have it, *kiddushin* are forbidden solely for another reason, this is not because the concept does not exist but rather because, in this case, it is inapplicable, since from one point of view, *kiddushin* may be regarded as primarily the imposition of a status and a related

21. Except, of course, for the purpose of effecting *huppa* and consummating the marriage; see Rambam, *Hilkhot Ishut* 10:1.
22. Most authorities assume that the canopy – a literal translation of *huppa* – traditionally used at weddings is only symbolic of the private residence which actually effects marriage. See *Even HaEzer* 55:1, and the summary of the various views in *Encyclopedia Talmudit*, 16:417–21.

injunction, less a taking unto oneself than a withdrawing from others. This can hardly be said of *huppa,* however. Here there is genuine giving and acquisition of rights – a procedure which, even according to Rabbenu Tam, therefore, should clearly be forbidden on the Sabbath.

The Rama acknowledges that several authorities, both contemporary and medieval – e.g., R. Yosef Karo and R. Yitzhak of Corbeil, respectively – have accepted this reasoning; yet he nevertheless goes on to reject it. He notes that a number of major sources cite Rabbenu Tam's view without introducing any distinction; that since Rabbenu Tam grounded his position on the fact that *kiddushin* relate to the mitzva of procreation, this should apply *a fortiori* to *huppa;* and that, in any event, most authorities accept the danger of writing rather than the Yerushalmi's reason as the basis for the prohibition of Sabbath *kiddushin.*

After refuting some evidence cited by proponents of this distinction, the Rama opens the concluding section of the *teshuva* with his final argument: an appeal to popular rather than to scholarly authority. He contends that the practice of arranging *kiddushin* after the start of the Sabbath has long been widespread in his area. Just how late after it has started is halakhically irrelevant, so that the *vox populi* – perhaps stimulated, as the Rama has been, by the pressure of circumstances – has evidently accepted his line of reasoning.

Finally, the *teshuva* concludes with a remarkable coda, a revealing passage reflecting both the powerful ethical impulse underlying the Rama's response and a lingering insecurity concerning its legal validity. It urges, on the one hand, that every effort be made to avoid the dilemma the Rama had been compelled to face. In the absence of any alternative, however, it gives comforting assurance that "whoever inclines to leniency has lost nothing. May he then partake in peace of Shabbat joy, and the mitzva can absolve him if his intention is for the sake of Heaven."

RESPONSA RAMA #125

My help cometh from the Lord, who maketh heaven and earth;[1] and may He save me from error.

[Lo!] I have heard behind me the sound of a great tumult[2] as some have spread word through the camp, saying, "Look after Moshe";[3] [this,] with respect to an action which was done by me recently, [namely,] that I arranged *kiddushin* beneath a *huppa* in the usual manner of which everyone knows the ritual involving the bride and the manner in which she enters the *huppa*.[4] This took place in the heart of night on a Friday evening, about an hour and a half into the night. The cause which compelled me to [do] this is known openly to all who come within the gates of our city; and here is the [story of] the action which was taken.

There was a man in the land who had lost his money and who arranged the engagement of his eldest daughter to a suitable mate. During the period of her engagement, much time elapsing before her entry to *huppa*, the father passed on to his world, leaving life for all [the rest] of Israel. The daughter remained bereft and lonely, having neither father nor mother, but only near ones [i.e., relatives] who became distant to

1. *Tehillim* 121:2.
2. *Yehezkel* 3:12.
3. A reference to *Shemot* 33:8: "And it came to pass, when Moses went out unto the Tent, that all the people rose up, and stood, every man at his tent door, and looked after Moses, until he was gone into the Tent." In applying the verse to his own situation, the Rama – also named Moses, of course – is probably alluding to the interpretation that the people's look was one of suspicion, as many were envious and suggested Moses had been gaining power and eminence at their expense; see *Kiddushin* 33b and Yerushalmi, *Bikkurim* 3:3; p. 11b.
4. The text reads *shehakol yodin seder hakalla bameh nikhnesa lehuppa,* which I think clearly refers to the general procedure concerning the bride. However, Freehof assumes the Rama is referring to this specific bride, and he translates, "All knew the state of the bride as she entered under the huppah" – a more dramatic, but (to my mind) highly improbable, rendering. [Ed. note: The Siev edition reads *lama* instead of *bameh.*]

her,[5] averting their gaze from her, with the exception of one redeemer,[6] her mother's brother, who took her into his home, as she has no closer redeemer. As the time of her marriage approached, when it was fitting to arrange a feast and [other] wedding needs, she saw no semblance of the dowry or [her] other needs. [There was] only a rumor which reached her that she should immerse herself[7] and prepare herself for the wedding as she would [then] receive the dowry. The aforementioned girl did as her neighboring women told her, and heeded them, and they covered[8] her on Friday with a veil as is customary with virgins. As evening shadows lengthened and the [Sabbath] day almost became hallowed, when her relatives were to provide the dowry, they tightened their fists and subtracted from their proper gift, so that the dowry was almost one third[9] short. The bridegroom, as well, retreated and refused to marry her under any circumstances. He paid no heed to everything which the leaders of the city said to him, [to wit,] that he should not embarrass a daughter of Israel in the interest of contemptible money. He refused to listen but, rather, like a deaf asp, stopped his ears and did not hearken to the voice of charmers[10] nor could a sage's rebuke move him. As a result, due to dissensions and disputes – as it is stated, "There is no marriage settlement into which discord is not injected"[11] – time passed and Satan's work succeeded, until the aforementioned hour arrived at which time they settled among themselves and the bridegroom agreed to enter the *huppa*. In order to avoid embarrassing a decent daughter of Israel, I arose and arranged the *kiddushin* at that hour. Now, inasmuch as some have

---

5. Freehof translates "who lived far from her." However, the context clearly indicates emotional rather than physical distance – i.e., they acted as strangers and ignored her.
6. The Hebrew word *go'el* means both a redeemer and a relative; see, e.g., *Vayikra* 25:26, *Bemidbar* 5:8, and *Ruth*, 3:9ff.
7. Halakhically, once a woman has menstruated, she may not engage in sexual relations until she has immersed herself in a ritual pool. Hence, immersion constitutes part of the prospective bride's preparation for her wedding.
8. Reading *kissu*, as in Ham., A., S., and W. However, C. and Han. have the noun *kissuy*, "a covering," an obvious error.
9. Freehof erroneously translates "at least a third."
10. See *Tehillim* 58:5–6.
11. *Shabbat* 130a.

been complaining against me, I have come to remove their complaint, to cite evidence and my reasons and explanations, and [to explain] upon what I have relied to say, "Such see and betroth."[12]

II

We read in the chapter *Mashilin*:[13] "Every act for which one is culpable on Shabbat as a *shevut*,[14] as an optional act, [or] as a mitzva, one is also culpable for on a festival.... And the following [are deemed culpable] as optional acts: One may not judge nor effect *kiddushin*, etc. And the following are [deemed culpable] as mitzva [acts]: One may not dedicate [i.e., to the Temple] nor vow a personal valuation, etc."[15] The gemara [then] asks: "'One may not judge' – But is he not performing a mitzva? This refers to a case in which a more capable person is available. 'Nor effect *kiddushin*' – But is he not performing a mitzva? This refers to a case in which he [already] has a wife and children."[16] Rashi, o.b.m., comments: "But he is performing a mitzva, [i.e.,] in order to procreate and multiply,[17] so why does he [i.e., the author of the mishna] call it an optional act?"[18] The *Tosafot* write: "The gloss[19] explains, 'And he should have listed them at the end [i.e., of the mishna] among the mitzvot'; and it [i.e., the gemara] answers, 'This refers to a case in which he [already] has a wife and children,' and therefore it is not as much of a

---

12. *Rosh HaShana* 20a. In the Hebrew, there is a pun here. The word *kaddesh* means both "hallow" (the gemara in *Rosh HaShana* deals with sanctifying the month upon the appearance of the new moon) and "betroth."
13. The fifth and final chapter of *Beitza*.
14. I.e., an act which the Torah has permitted but the Rabbis have proscribed.
15. *Beitza* 36b.
16. Loc. cit. The last phrase may mean either that one is now taking a second wife, bigamy not having yet been proscribed, or that he had previously been married, but the first reading is probably the more accurate. It should also be noted that in the latter case, the marriage would clearly be more of a mitzva; see *Yevamot* 61b.
17. The passage in *Bereshit* 1:28 – "And God blessed them; and God said unto them: 'Be fruitful and multiply, and replenish the earth, and subdue it'" – is taken both as a blessing and as a command.
18. *Beitza* 36b, s.v. *velo mekaddeshin*.
19. I.e., Rashi.

mitzva as those which are [listed] at the end. According to this [interpretation], it is possible that even when there is no one[20] more qualified than himself, one is [nevertheless] forbidden to judge. Similarly, as concerns [taking] a wife, with respect to which [the Talmud] answers that he [i.e., the individual to whom the mishna applies] [already] has a wife and children, it seems that even if he does not [already] have a wife and children it [i.e., *kiddushin*] is nevertheless forbidden." They [i.e., the *Tosafot*] [then] write, "But others[21] explain that which it says, 'But he is performing a mitzva?' [as asking:] So why did they [i.e., the Rabbis] forbid it? To this it answers that this refers to a case in which he [already] has a wife and children. However, if he does not have them, it is [indeed] permissible to effect *kiddushin*, inasmuch as one is [then] performing a mitzva."[22]

They [i.e., the *Tosafot*] discourse at length, presenting questions and answers relevant to the respective interpretations of Rashi and Rabbenu Tam – for they subsequently mention that the "others" are Rabbenu Tam – and they cite a [text of the] Yerushalmi: "R. Huna said, 'This indicates [that] those who marry[23] widows should do so while it is yet

20. All editions read *bide'ikka*, "that there is someone." However, the correct reading should clearly be *bidelekka*, and I have translated accordingly.

21. C., Han., and Ham. read the abbreviation מ"מ, which, in A., S., and W., was then written out as מכל מקום, "nevertheless." However, the correct reading should clearly be the initials י"מ, written out as יש מפרשים, "and some interpret," as is evident from the reference several lines later, שהיש מפרשים הוא ר"ת. The error resulted from the confusion of י"מ with מ"מ.

22. The text quoted by the Rama does not correspond to that of the *Tosafot* printed in the standard editions with the Gemara. The *Tosafot* were essentially collections of lecture notes and numerous variants are generally found. The standard *Tosafot* on *Beitza* were produced by students of R. Peretz; see E. E. Urbach, *Baalei HaTosafot*, 2nd ed. (Jerusalem, 1955), 479–80. Other collections are known to have been still extant in the sixteenth century, and it is possible that the Rama, who generally used the earlier *Tosafot* of Sens, may have used that collection from which R. Peretz's students evidently drew – in studying *Beitza*. I know of no extant source for this particular quotation. However, the same material may be found in paraphrase in the standard *Tosafot, Beitza* 36b, s.v. *veha mitzva*.

23. Literally, "who induct," into marriage or into their home; i.e., who are effecting *nissuin*, the legal consummation of the marriage proper, as opposed to mere *kiddushin*, betrothal.

day in order that they should not be like one who effects an acquisition on Shabbat.'"[24] The reason given there [i.e., in the Yerushalmi] is that, prior to marrying her, he [i.e., the husband] is not entitled to what she finds nor to her income; once he marries, he is entitled to both,[25] so that he may be regarded as effecting an acquisition on Shabbat. That case, too, may be construed as referring to one who already has a wife and children.[26]

Thus far, the text of the gemara and its interpretations. Now, although I am unworthy to decide, nevertheless I raise a difficulty concerning Rashi's interpretation that the [gemara's] question is only why these [i.e., judgment and *kiddushin*] are not listed at the end under the rubric of mitzva. If so, how effective is the answer that [the mishna refers to a case in which] there is a superior [judge] or that he already has a wife and children? It [i.e., the gemara] should nevertheless have rejoined that the mishna should have introduced an internal distinction [i.e., within the areas of judgment and *kiddushin*] and it should have included in its latter section [a statement] that it is forbidden to judge or marry even when a mitzva is involved. This would have been more noteworthy [i.e., than the present statement in the initial section] and would have rendered the intial statement superfluous. For if this is forbidden under circumstances of mitzva, must anything be said concerning neutral circumstances?

Furthermore, according to Rashi's interpretation, the formulation, "But he is performing a mitzva," is difficult. It [i.e., the gemara] should simply have said, "But these are [cases of] mitzva?" For the objection is only [being raised] against the *Tanna*, due to his failure to include them [i.e., judgment and *kiddushin*] among [the class of] mitzva. However, if [we understand] the question as Rabbenu Tam did, there is no difficulty. The objection concerns the performer of the mitzva: why is it

24. *Yoma* 1:1; p. 5b. Of course, the text refers only to those who marry on Friday.
25. See *Ketubbot* 65b. On most views, the husband is accorded these rights in return for supporting his wife. If she wishes, however, she can retain her income and support herself; see *Ketubbot* 58b.
26. In the ordinary case, however, the prohibition against acts of acquisition would be overridden by the mitzva entailed in marriage.

forbidden for him to act? This is clear to anyone who reads the text of the gemara closely.

Therefore, it would be possible for me to suggest that, even according to Rashi's view, it is permissible [to effect *kiddushin*] when one does not [yet] have a wife and children....[27]

However, inasmuch as the *Rishonim*, o.b.m., namely, the *Tosafot* and the *Mordekhai*,[28] cited in Rashi's name [the view] that it is forbidden under all circumstances – and they disregarded these objections which, according to my lights, I have raised against Rashi's statements – I shall continue likewise after them to assume that Rashi's view proscribes [*kiddushin* on Shabbat] under all circumstances. This also appears to be the view of the [major] *posekim* – the Rif, the Rambam, the Rosh, and the *Tur*, OH 339[29] – all of whom, o.b.m., simply state, "It is forbidden to effect *kiddushin*," without introducing any distinction. Inevitably, these *posekim*, who did not qualify their statements, either interpreted the gemara along the lines of Rashi, o.b.m., as his position was understood by the *Rishonim* o.b.m.; or, they relied on the Yerushalmi which apparently proscribes [*kiddushin* on Shabbat] under all circumstances, as will be explained. However, it does not seem likely that they relied on the Yerushalmi against our [i.e., the Babylonian] gemara, as will be explained; so they must surely have interpreted along the lines of Rashi, o.b.m.

Nevertheless, may all such worthy statements be quoted in my name[30] – [to wit,] permitting this matter under these circumstances which constituted an emergency. The girl would have been shamed had she, after her immersion, waited for the *huppa* until after Shabbat – especially so, inasmuch as it is not the custom of these localities

---

27. In the section I have omitted, the Rama suggests extraneous reasons in order to explain why, despite the fact that, as the Rama would have it, Rashi agrees with Rabbenu Tam's position, he nevertheless interpreted the gemara differently; and he also briefly seeks to prove that the *Semag* had also understood that Rashi concurred with Rabbenu Tam.
28. No such citation appears in our texts of the *Mordekhai*, *Beitza*, 697–98, which simply cite two conflicting views without mentioning Rashi.
29. See, respectively, Rif, *Beitza*, 925; Rambam, *Hilkhot Shabbat* 23:14; Rosh, *Beitza*, 5:2; and *Tur*, OH 339.
30. See *Beitza* 28a.

[for a prospective bride] to wear a veil until after Shabbat and [then] to arrange the wedding on Sunday as is the custom of the Gentiles who arrange their weddings on their holiday. Rabbenu Tam is worthy of being relied upon in a time of emergency – particularly since the discourse of the [relevant] text supports his position (and the *Haggahot Ashri,* near the end of the chapter, *Ehad Dinei Mamonot,*[31] has decided thus, in the name of the *Or Zarua*).

Rabbenu Tam has written thus in his responsum, cited by the *Semag,* "that only in a great emergency did they [i.e., the Rabbis] permit effecting *kiddushin* on Shabbat, and he would not rule thus [when applying the] Halakha in practice."[32] It would appear that in a great emergency, at any rate, it may be permitted.[33] And there can be no greater emergency than this, in which a grown orphan would have been shamed. Virtually throughout her lifetime, having been differentiated from other girls would have remained as a disgrace to her. Great is [the importance] of human dignity, in that it overrides the negative injunction of "Thou shalt not deviate from all the matters which they [i.e., the Rabbis] shall teach you"[34] in this matter which only involves a rabbinic injunction,

31. The fourth chapter of *Sanhedrin.*
32. *Mitzvot lo taaseh,* 75.
33. The Rama evidently understood Rabbenu Tam's second statement as referring to an ordinary case in which no emergency exists. The whole statement then means that while, according to Rabbenu Tam's interpretation, all first marriages should be permitted on the Sabbath, he would not rule *thus* as Sabbath *kiddushin* had only been permitted – presumably by later scholars rather than by the Gemara – very reluctantly in special circumstances. However, the statement should probably be translated "but he would not rule thus," indicating that in all cases Rabbenu Tam hesitated to implement his sole dissident position in the face of its almost unanimous rejection by others. Maharshal, *Yam Shel Shlomo, Ketubbot,* 1:2, understood the *Semag*'s statement in the second sense. Likewise, *Haggahot Maimoniyot, Hilkhot Ishut* 10:50, cites a responsum of Rabbenu Tam's to the effect that he would not actually rule that Sabbath *kiddushin* are permissible, even though he assumed this to be correct theoretically. However, in the extant text of his responsa, Rabbenu Tam explicitly states that, in special circumstances, he would actually permit Sabbath *kiddushin* in practice; see *Sefer HaYashar*: *Helek HaShe'elot VeHaTeshuvot,* ed. S. F. Rosenthal (Berlin, 1898), 48:10.
34. See *Berakhot* 19b. The term used by the gemara is *kevod haberiyyot,* which means, literally, "the dignity of the creatures," but it generally refers to people exclusively.

[established either] as a precaution lest he write, as is specified in our [i.e., the Babylonian] gemara, or because he is regarded as effecting an acquisition on Shabbat, as is specified in the Yerushalmi and as will be explained subsequently.

Apart from this, we had to be concerned in this instance lest the engagement be broken off entirely and the match severed as a result of the dissensions and disputes between them to the extent that they wanted to remove the veil from the bride's head due to the tumult of the dissensions. And great is [the importance of] peace between husband and wife[35] – and even if she is only engaged to him, one may be permissive on this ground, since she is somewhat bound to him, just as Rabbenu Tam and the Rosh wrote in their responsa with respect to an engaged woman in mourning that it is permissible [for the prospective husband] to marry her after her *shiva* period in the interest of his own procreation.[36] Similarly, in the present era, we permit, against the dictum of our Rabbis o.b.m., marrying off girls who are minors, even though they, o.b.m., said, "It is forbidden for one to give his daughter in betrothal while she is a minor, [but he must wait] until she grows up and says, 'I desire so-and-so.'"[37] The *Tosafot*[38] and later *posekim* have

The verse cited is from *Devarim* 17:11. However, the Rama – evidently quoting from memory – writes the plural *kol hadevarim*, "all the matters" (a phrase found in a similar context in *Devarim* 28:14), whereas the verse has the singular *kol hadavar*, "every matter."

35. By citing their opening words, the Rama alludes to various statements in the gemara to the effect that certain prohibitions may be violated in the interest of domestic peace. See *Hullin* 141a and parallel sources, and cf. *Yevamot* 65b.

36. Normally, a mourner may not marry for thirty days following the death of his relative. However, Rabbenu Tam and the Rosh – see, respectively, *Sefer HaYashar*, ed. Rosenthal, 23, and *Teshuvot HaRosh*, 27:5 – permit a man who has not yet raised a family to marry after only a week of mourning. It should be noted, however, that these responsa, to which the Rama alludes, only deal with a man who is in mourning and not, as the Rama suggests, with the woman likewise.

37. *Kiddushin* 41a.

38. Ibid., *Tosafot*, s.v. *asur*: "Our current practice to betroth our daughters even as minors is due to the fact that the [impact of] exile grows stronger daily, and while a man may presently have the means to give his daughter a dowry he may not have them later and she will remain a spinster forever." The Rambam, however, insisted upon the Gemara's injunction, and this was also taken by the *Shulhan Arukh*; see,

written that, in the present era, during which we are few in number, we are permissive etc. The same holds true in our case.

All this I have set before me in order to rely on the view of Rabbenu Tam (and the other *posekim* who take a permissive view) in an emergency. [However,] I say further that we may distinguish and suggest that, at present, all would agree that it is permitted. For we have studied [in the Mishna]: "One may not clap [his hands] nor dance [i.e., on Shabbat] etc."[39] The *Tosafot,* near the beginning of the chapter, *HaMeivi,* noted: "Rashi explained, 'lest he repair musical instruments.' However, for us, these [acts] are permissible. For only in their days, when people were [generally] skilled in making musical instruments, was it feasible to introduce these restrictions. As for us, however, we are not [generally] skilled in making musical instruments and it is not feasible to introduce these restrictions."[40] Indulgence in clapping and dancing on Shabbat has already become widespread everywhere – and non-Jews are even directed to play musical instruments – all because of the *Tosafot*'s statement that this ordinance is not feasible at present. The same holds true with respect to "one may not effect *kiddushin,*" of which the gemara says that the reason is "lest he write." It is well known that the [presently] prevalent custom in Israel is that the groom does not write the *ketubba* or the betrothal deed[41] himself. The reason [for this] is that we are not skilled in writing;[42] and even whoever is able to write

---

respectively, *Hilkhot Ishut* 3:19, and *Even HaEzer,* 37:8. In his gloss on the latter, the Rama cites *Tosafot's* view as the then prevalent Ashkenazic custom.

39. *Beitza* 36b. The text of the mishna includes "nor slap [his thighs]" between the prohibitions of clapping and dancing, but the Rama – again, perhaps quoting from memory – omits this.

40. Ibid. 30a, s.v. *tenan.*

41. These are different documents. The *ketubba* is a purely civil document describing and possibly effecting the civil and economic obligations devolving upon the husband whenever and however the marriage takes place. It bears no relevance, however, to effecting the marriage proper. A betrothal deed, on the other hand, is a simple self-validating statement, itself effecting *kiddushin,* that the bride is hereby betrothed to the groom. When given to the bride, it can substitute for money as an instrument of implementing *kiddushin,* with all attendant civil and religious consequences.

42. The Rama presumably does not refer to inability to write altogether. It is very doubtful that writing skills were more widespread in third-century Babylonia than

does not write [himself] in order to avoid discriminating between the skilled and unskilled. Therefore, a *hazan*[43] writes it in all cases, just as he reads the Torah for everyone for the benefit of the unknowledgeable. Hence, there is no reason to enjoin him who wishes to effect *kiddushin* lest he write inasmuch as we are unskilled therein and this writing is not incumbent upon the bridegroom. Nor need we fear lest the *hazan* write for [the purpose of arranging] the bridegroom's *kiddushin* for there is no source for such an injunction. Moreover, the *hazan*, after all, always writes the *ketubba* and the deeds of betrothal in the morning or long before entry into the *huppa* since he does not know when they will be ready with the *huppa*. Therefore, at present, there is no need to be concerned about this injunction at all.

Even if it should be rejoined that according to the Yerushalmi – which explains that the reason for this injunction is that we regard him [i.e., the bridegroom] as effecting an acquisition on Shabbat – there is no reason for distinguishing between their times [i.e., the gemara's] and the present, nevertheless, when [the Bavli is] opposed to the Yerushalmi, it seems [to me that] our gemara [i.e., the Bavli] is primary, and the *posekim* have always decided accordingly. Nor can it be argued that our gemara also acknowledges the Yerushalmi's reason

---

in sixteenth-century Poland, and the Rama probably sensed this. He rather means that people generally can no longer write the *ketubba* – now a foreign language document whose writing had become far more formal and stylized, so that the average person could not, in Hamlet's phrase, "as our statists do... write fair."

43. In modern usage, *hazan* is used to refer to a cantor exclusively. Initially, however, it referred to any communal functionary.

The precedent cited by the Rama is itself based upon another precedent. Speaking of the text whose recitation was to accompany the bringing of the first-fruits to the Temple, the Mishna says: "Initially, everyone who could recite recited, and [as for] anyone who could not recite, others recited it to him [i.e., and he presumably repeated after his prompter]. [Many then] withheld from bringing. [Hence,] it was instituted that others should recite to both one who can and one who cannot recite [himself]" (*Bikkurim* 3:7). Rabbenu Tam insisted that the same principle should be applied to reading of the Torah. In talmudic times, anyone who was called to the Torah would ordinarily read himself. Now, however, Rabbenu Tam urged that a public reader read for all, regardless of whether they could or could not do so themselves, in order to avoid embarrassing the ignorant; see *Tosafot, Bava Batra* 15a, s.v. *shemoneh*.

but that it only cited one of two [self-sufficient] reasons, as the *Tosafot*[44] there wrote concerning a similar case. For this is not feasible with respect to two reasons between which there is some substantive difference. The *Semag*[45] has also written explicitly that our gemara is at odds with the Yerushalmi with regard to the ground of this matter [i.e., the injunction concerning *kiddushin*]. Certainly, there must be a substantive difference between them, and it is that which I have presented.

It is for this reason, I think, that the Rif and the Rosh (in the chapter, *Mashilin*) did not cite the Yerushalmi's reason nor did they cite that [dictum] of "those who marry widows should do so while it is yet day." The *Tur*, [OH] 339, likewise did not cite it, for surely we hold like our gemara as opposed to the Yerushalmi, and as regards heeding the precautionary prohibition, "lest he write," the acquisition is wholly irrelevant.

(Although the Rosh in the first chapter of *Ketubbot*[46] does cite "those who marry widows should do so while it is yet day" and he writes there that a virgin, likewise, should not be brought into *huppa* on Shabbat because he [i.e., the bridegroom] acquires her with respect to her findings and her income – and the same is written in *Even HaEzer* 63[47] – nevertheless, it seems to me that since he did not cite it in its proper locus, the chapter, *Mashilin*, this matter is not truly forbidden; and this is certainly because he held that our gemara's reason, i.e., "lest he write," is primary. They only cited it in the first chapter of *Ketubbot* and in *Even HaEzer* as a mere precaution, just as they mentioned there not to arrange a *huppa* on Friday because of some remote precautionary prohibitions. Since we disregard this and do arrange a *huppa* on Friday for reasons set forth by the *Aharonim*, o.b.m. – the primary reason being that we are now in exile and it is burdensome for us to arrange a wedding independently of Shabbat[48] – perhaps we should similarly disregard this [i.e., the Rosh's citation of the Yerushalmi] and be permissive on Shabbat proper, since the primary reason is "lest he write," as has been explained.)

---

44. *Beitza* 36b, s.v. *veha*.
45. *Mitzvot lo taaseh*, 75.
46. 1:3.
47. Actually 64.
48. See the Rama's commentary to the *Tur*, *Darkhei Moshe*, EH 64:4.

By way of proof, note that the *Tosafot*, after citing the Yerushalmi, wrote: "And according to this reason that it is forbidden [for one] to effect *kiddushin* because he appears to be effecting an acquisition, it is likewise forbidden to give a *get* on Shabbat."[49] Now, why shouldn't it also be prohibited according to our gemara's interpretation that it is forbidden to effect *kiddushin* lest he write? The same holds true with regard to giving a *get*; [we should be concerned] lest he write the *get*? We should therefore infer from this as I have explained that, regarding a *get*, "lest he write" is inapplicable because it is [generally] the handiwork of an artisan and dextrous scribe who is necessary for writing the *get*, and not everyone is skilled in this. There is [consequently] no reason for concern lest the giver of the *get* write it since the giver does not ordinarily write the *get*. The same holds true, at present, with respect to writing the *ketubba* or the deed of betrothal. And although we do rely on the Yerushalmi's statements and we do not grant divorces on Shabbat – as the *Tosafot*, [in the] chapter, *HaZorek*,[50] and the Ran,[51] [in the] chapter, *Mashilin*, wrote, and as was cited by the *Tur*, *Even HaEzer*, 136 – that is because we find [this] explicitly in the *Tosefta* of the chapter, *Mashilin*,[52] which explicitly states, "it is forbidden to divorce," as was stated by the *Tosafot*, [in the] chapter, *HaZorek*. And although from the Ran, [in the] chapter, *Mashilin*, it would appear that, as concerns [giving a] *get* likewise, the reason for the injunction is "lest he write," this is not indicated by the text of the *Tosafot*. According to them, there, indeed, the reason is because of [effecting an] acquisition. Not so, however, as concerns *kiddushin*, for, surely, our gemara's reason is primary. And although from the *Tosafot*, [in the] chapter, *Mashilin*, it appears that it [i.e., divorce] was proscribed because of the Yerushalmi's reason exclusively, and that we do not read "it is forbidden to divorce" in [the text of] the *Tosefta*, we

49. *Beitza* 36b, s.v. *veha*.

50. *Gittin* 77b, s.v. *vetezil*.

51. In commenting upon 36b.

52. *Tosefta Moed*, ed. Saul Lieberman (New York, 1962), 4:4; p. 300. Some manuscripts omit the prohibition of divorce. However, others include it, and this is the text generally quoted by *Rishonim*. See Lieberman, *Tosefta KiFshutah* (New York, 1962), 1000–1001, and the references cited there.

do not accept this [contention]; for the *Tosefta* was clearly overlooked by the *Tosafot* of [the] chapter, *Mashilin*.[53]

Moreover, even if we should equate *kiddushin* to divorce completely, nevertheless it has already been established that divorce, likewise, is permissible at a time of emergency as is explained [in the] chapter, *HaZorek*. The *Tosafot*[54] [there] write that allowance has been made with respect to a mortally ill [person] so that his wife should not become involved with her husband's brother.[55] There is, then, *a fortiori*, grounds for being lenient under circumstances of mitzva – as he will fulfill [the mitzva] to procreate and multiply – which constitute, in addition, an emergency.

From all of the foregoing, it has been established that it is permissible to effect *kiddushin* on Shabbat in a case of emergency, and in which there is reason to be concerned about [personal] dignity, lest the matter lead to embarrassment and possibly result in severance of the match; and that we can rely on Rabbenu Tam who is permissive regarding this matter, as has been explained. However, many have risen up against me, challenging my position and contending that perhaps one might distinguish between *kiddushin* and entry into the *huppa*. This may be unanimously proscribed since he [i.e., the husband] thus acquires her with respect to various things regarding which a woman is acquired, so

53. The argument, as developed in this section, poses some difficulties. First, *Tosafot*'s linking of the prohibition against divorce to the Yerushalmi can be readily explained without resorting to the Rama's inference. If the Yerushalmi's reason is correct, then divorce is necessarily prohibited simply as a particular instance of acquisition not requiring a separate act of rabbinic legislation to proscribe it. However, if *kiddushin* are forbidden out of concern for possible writing, we have no broader category under which divorce is automatically subsumed out of logical necessity. *Kiddushin* are, at most, an archetype and analogue which could have led the Rabbis to ban divorce as well. This would have constituted a fresh rabbinic ordinance, however, and it is entirely possible that, for any one of a number of reasons – the relative infrequency of divorce, for instance – the Rabbis never instituted such an ordinance. Secondly, the Rama contends that divorce was proscribed solely because it entails acquisition. Yet he never explains – what surely requires explanation – how divorce is a more acquisitive act than *kiddushin*.
54. *Gittin* 77b, *Tosafot*, s.v. *vetezil*.
55. If the husband had died childless; see *Devarim* 25:5–9.

that he is considered as effecting an acquisition on Shabbat, which all agree is initially[56] forbidden. This [view] is also found in the words of the *gaon*,[57] the renowned author, in [his] work, *Beit Yosef*, on the *Tur, Orah Hayim*, the aforementioned section 339, who writes that it is forbidden to marry her [i.e., the betrothed] even on Rabbenu Tam's view; and he writes [further] that this is suggested by the words of the *Haggahot Maimoniyot*, the *Kolbo*, and the Ran, [in the] chapter, *Mashilin*.

Now, although there is no compelling force to the aforementioned words of the *gaon* that it appears from the language of these *posekim* that Rabbenu Tam held thus, but rather the *Semak*[58] added this on his own as is clear from the text of the *Semak*; and furthermore, the Ran's words can be dismissed readily[59] as he did not undertake to discuss this point at all but simply set down and transcribed the language of the *Tosafot*, and nothing concerning this matter can be inferred from his words, as is clear to anyone who studies them intelligently; nevertheless, it is proper to absolve myself from the *gaon*'s charge,[60] as one should have heeded his words on the side of stringency, especially since the *Semak* has written thus explicitly. Let me say, first, that this [apparent] leniency actually constitutes a more rigorous observance as has been established, for we had to be concerned about many pitfalls if the marriage had been held up. Secondly, that, from the *Tosafot* and the *Semag*, it appears explicitly that they do not distinguish at all between *kiddushin* and entry into *huppa*....[61]

---

56. I.e., it is a forbidden act although, should one transgress and perform it, the resultant acquisition is recognized as valid, the doctrine of *ex turpi causa non oritur actio* having rather limited scope in Halakha. [Ed. note: *Ex turpi* is a legal doctrine stating that a plaintiff will be unable to pursue legal remedy if it arises in connection with his own illegal act.]
57. I.e., R. Yosef Karo.
58. 174.
59. I.e., they do not support the *Beit Yosef*'s contention.
60. Of course, the Rama does not refer to any charge leveled at him directly by R. Yosef Karo as the latter had made no mention of him in this connection. He rather means that the position taken by the *Beit Yosef* could serve as a basis for criticizing him.
61. In the section I have omitted, the Rama quotes from *Tosafot* and the *Semag* to prove that they support his position; argues that their stature as major authorities should overrule the texts cited by the *Beit Yosef*; quotes and refutes, at some length, a contradictory inference drawn by the *Semak*; contends that since Rabbenu Tam's license

But why need I expatiate? [Just] go out and see how the people conducts itself everywhere,[62] especially in our city which has, thank God, a substantial population. Sometimes, five or six *huppas* are arranged in one Friday, continuing into the night, with no murmur or chirp [of protest]. And what difference is there between the beginning of the evening and an hour or two into the night? No distinction can be made between whether or not they have accepted Shabbat by [reciting] *Barekhu*,[63] for as regards being permissive,[64] this does not depend upon their acceptance, as Shabbat establishes itself, once darkness falls, as is stated [in the] chapter, *Arvei Pesahim*, with respect to *kiddush* and *maaser*.[65] The truth is rather that the need of the hour leads to permissiveness with respect to these things which are but rabbinic injunctions which were not instituted with regard to an emergency.

With this I started and thus I conclude[66] that certainly one should be stringent so as to be energetic before Shabbat in order to avoid coming to this. However, if everything possible was done[67] and time was consumed until darkness [fell] and there is ground for concern about

---

was grounded upon the fact that *kiddushin* relates to the mitzva of procreation, it should certainly extend to *huppa*; and insists that, in any event, as he has argued earlier, most authorities accept the danger of writing rather than the Yerushalmi's reason as the basis for the prohibition of Sabbath *kiddushin*.

The Rama's last point presents a severe difficulty. His adversaries obviously assume that all agree that acquisition is forbidden on the Sabbath and that any leniency concerning *kiddushin* can only be based on the assumption that it is not to be regarded as an acquisitive act; hence, their contention that *huppa* must certainly be prohibited. Consequently, the Rama's rejection of the Yerushalmi's statement concerning *kiddushin* does not really affect the argument in any way.

62. See *Berakhot* 45a.
63. "Bless," the opening words of the evening service summoning the congregation to prayer.
64. I.e., one can usher the Sabbath in early and thus extend its injunctions but he cannot postpone its entry.
65. Once night falls, the Sabbath takes effect involuntarily, so that one may not eat before saying *kiddush* or partake, even in small quantities, of food which requires tithing, even though, if the agricultural phase of its preparation has not yet been completed, it may be so eaten on weekdays; see *Pesahim* 105a.
66. Literally, "with this I descended and with this I ascend," a phrase found in *Pesahim* 87b, where its general import is "this is my constant concern."
67. Freehof mistranslates, "But when it has occurred, what can be done if…"

[possible] severance of the match or shame of the bride, or anything similar, whoever inclines to leniency has lost nothing. May he then partake in peace of Shabbat joy, and the mitzva can absolve him if his intention is for the sake of Heaven.

Shalom,[68]

The testament of Moshe, the son of my lord, father and master, Rav Yisrael, his memory that of a saint for the life of the World to Come,[69] known as Moshe Isserles of Cracow.

שו"ת הרמ"א סימן קכה[70]

עזרי מעם ד' עושה שמים וארץ והוא יצילני משגיאה.

אשמע אחרי קול רעש גדול אשר העבירו קול במחנה לומר הביטו אחרי משה, במעשה הנעשה על ידי מקרוב שסדרתי קידושין תחת החופה כדרך הארץ, שהכל יודעין סדר הכלה למה נכסה לחופה. והיה באישון לילה בליל שבת כשעה ומחצה בלילה. והמעשה והסבה אשר הכריחוני לזה הוא מבואר נגלה לכל באי שער עירנו, וזה המעשה אשר נעשה.

איש היה בארץ ותם הכסף ממנו ושדך בתו גדולה לבן זוגה הראוי לה. ויהי בימי שידוכיה, אשר ארך הזמן עד כניסתה לחופה הלך האב לעולמו והניח חיים לכל ישראל, ונשארה הבת שכולה וגלמודה אין לה אב ואם כי אם קרובים נעשו לה רחוקים והעלימו עיניהם ממנה, זולתי גואל אחד אחי אמה אשר הכניסה לביתו כי אין לה גואל קרוב ממנו. והיה כאשר באה בימים זמן נישואיה אשר היה ראוי לטבוח טבח והכן צרכי החופה, לא ראתה שום תמונת הנדוניא ושאר צרכים, זולתי קול אחד הבא לה שתטבול ותכין עצמה לחתונה כי יהיה לה הנדוניא. והבתולה הנ"ל עשתה כאשר צוו עליה נשים השכינות ושמעה לקולם, גם כיסו אותה ביום ו' בהינומא

68. The Rama's customary mode of signing his *teshuvot*. Freehof, evidently unaware of this, translates "for the sake of heaven and of peace."

69. A form of particular honorific reference; see *Kiddushin* 31b.

70. כל התשובות בעברית הועתקו מפרויקט השו"ת.

כדרך הבתולות. וכאשר נטו צללי ערב וכמעט קדש היום, שהיו לקרוביה ליתן הנדוניא קמצו ידיהם וחסרו ממתנת ידם הראוי להם, והיה נחסר מן הנדוניא כמעט שליש הנדוניא. גם החתן נסוג אחור ולא רצה בשום אופן לכנסה ולא שת לבו לכל הדברים אשר דברו אליו מנהיגי העיר, שלא לבייש בת ישראל מכח כסף נמאס. ולא אבה שמוע רק כפתן חרש אטם אזנו ולא שמע לקול מלחשים, ולא קול גערת חכם תנידנו. וע״י זה נמשך הזמן מכח קטטות ומריבות, כדרך שאמרו לית כתובה דלית בה תיגרא (שבת קל, א) והצליח מעשה שטן עד שהגיע הזמן הנ״ל שהשוו עצמן ונתרצה החתן ליכנס לחופה, ושלא לבייש בת ישראל הגונה קמתי וסדרתי הקידושין בזמן הנ״ל. והנה באשר מלינים עלי באתי להסיר תלונתן מאתי להביא ראיה וטעמי ונימוקי עמי ועל מה סמכתי בזה לומר כזה ראה וקדש.

גרסינן פרק משילין (ביצה לו, ב) כל שחייבין עליו משום שבות משום רשות משום מצוה בשבת חייבין עליו בי״ט... ואלו הן משום רשות לא דנין ולא מקדשין וכו׳, ואלו הן משום מצוה לא מקדישין ולא מעריכין וכו׳. ופריך בגמרא אין דנין והא מצוה קא עביד, לא צריכא דאיכא דעדיף מיניה. ולא מקדשין והא מצוה קא עביד, לא צריכא דאית ליה אשה ובנים. ופירש״י ז״ל, והא מצוה קא עביד כדי לפרות ולרבות ואמאי קרי ליה רשות עכ״ל. וכתבו התוס׳ שם (ד״ה והא מצוה קא עביד) פ״ה וה״ל למחשבינהו בסיפא גבי מצות, ומשני ל״צ דאית ליה אשה ובנים ולכך אינו מצוה כ״כ דומיא דהני דסיפא. ולפי זה יכול להיות דגם בדליכא דעדיף מיניה אין דנין, וכן גבי אשה דמשני דאית ליה אשה ובנים משמע אפילו אין לו אשה ובנים מכל מקום אסור. וכתבו וז״ל, יש מפרשים הא דקאמר והא מצוה קא עביד ואמאי גזרו כו׳, ומשני לא צריכא דאית ליה אשה ובנים אבל אם אין לו מותר לקדש דמצוה קעביד. והאריכו שם בקושיות ותירוצים לפירוש רש״י ור״ת, כי כתבו שם שהי״מ הוא ר״ת. והביאו ירושלמי: א״ר הונא, הדא אמרה הני דכנסין ארמלין צריך לכנסן מבע״י שלא יהא כקונה קנין בשבת, ומפרש התם טעמא דעד שלא קנה אינו זכאי במציאותיה ולא במעשה ידיה משכנסה זכה בכולם ונמצא כקונה קנין בשבת, וההוא נמי איכא לאוקמי בשיש לו אשה ובנים, עכ״ל הגמרא עם הפירושים שבה.

והנה אע״פ שאיני כדאי להכריע מ״מ קשה לי על פירש״י, דהקושיא אינה רק למה לא חשיב אלו בסיפא גבי מצוה דא״כ מאי משני בדעדיף

מיניה או בדאית ליה אשה ובנים, דמ"מ ה"ל לאקשויי דלחלק וליתני בדידיה וליחשב בסיפא ג"כ אין דנין ואין מקדשין אפילו במקום מצוה דהוי רבותא טפי ולא הוי צריך למתני רישא כלל, דהשתא במקום מצוה אסור במקום רשות מבעיא. ועוד קשה לפירש"י דקאמר והא מצוה קא עביד ולא הל"ל רק והא מצוה נינהו, דהא הקושיא אינה רק על התנא דלא חשיב להו גבי מצוה. אבל אם הקושיא כר"ת ניחא, דהקושיא על העושה המצוה אמאי אסור לעשות וזהו מבואר למדקדק בלשון הגמרא.

ולכן היה אפשר לי לומר דאף לדעת רש"י מותר כשאין לו אשה ובנים...

אמנם מאחר שהראשונים ז"ל, דהיינו התוס' (ביצה לו, ב ד"ה והא מצוה) והמרדכי (שם פ"ה סימן תרצז) כתבו בשם רש"י לאסור בכל ענין ולא השגיחו לקושיות אלו שהקשיתי על דברי רש"י לדעתי, אמשך ג"כ אחריהם להאמין שדעת רש"י לאסור בכל ענינים. וכן נראה דעת הפוסקים הרי"ף (ביצה פ"ה) ורמב"ם (פכ"ג מהל' שבת הלכה יד) והרא"ש (ביצה סי' ב) והטור סי' של"ט (באו"ח), שכתבו כולם ז"ל סתם אין מקדשין ולא חילקו בדבריהם. הנה לא ימלט שהפוסקים שסתמו דבריהם פירשו הגמרא שלנו כדרך רש"י ז"ל כפי הבנת הראשונים ז"ל דבריו, או שסמכו על הירושלמי דמשמע שאוסר בכל ענין כמו שיתבאר. אך אינו נראה דסמכו על הירושלמי נגד גמרא שלנו כמו שיתבאר, ובודאי פירשו כדרך רש"י ז"ל.

מ"מ כל כי הני מילי מעליותא לימרו משמאי (ע"פ יבמות פ, א וכתובות סח, א) להתיר הענין בכה"ג, שהיה שעת הדחק והיתה הבתולה מתביישת אם תמתין עם החופה אחר טבילתה עד לאחר השבת. גם כי אינו מדרך המקומות לילך בהינומא עד אחר השבת ולעשות הנישואין ביום ראשון, כדרך האזרחים שעושין נשואיהם ביום חגם. וכדאי הוא ר"ת לסמוך עליו בשעת הדחק, כ"ש שהסוגיא דשמעתא מוכח כדבריו. וכן פסק בהג"ה אשר"י סוף פרק אחד דיני ממונות בשם א"ז וכן כתב ר"ת בתשובתו והביאה הסמ"ג (לאוין עא - עה בסוף הלכות יו"ט) כי בדוחק גדול התירו לקדש בשבת ולא היה מורה כן הלכה למעשה עכ"ל. משמע מיהו דבדוחק גדול יש להתיר. ואין לך דוחק גדול מזה, שהיתה יתומה גדולה מתביישת והיה לה לקלון כל ימיה, כמעט לשנותה מכל הבתולות.

וגדול כבוד הבריות שדוחה לא תעשה (ברכות י״ט, ב) דלא תסור מכל הדברים אשר יורוך (בדברים יז, יא), בדבר הזה שאינו אלא איסור דרבנן, גזירה שמא יכתוב כמו שמפרש בגמרא שלנו (ביצה לז, א) או משום דהוי כקונה קנין בשבת כדמפרש בירושלמי, וכמו שיתבאר לעתיד.

מלבד דהוי לן למיחש בכאן שלא יתבטלו השידוכין לגמרי ויתבטל הזיווג מכח הקטטות והמריבות שביניהם, עד שרצו להסיר ההינומא שעל ראש הכלה מכח ניצוח הקטטות, וגדול השלום בין איש לאשתו (חולין קמא, א) ואפילו אינה אלא משודכת אליו יש להקל מכח זה דהוי קצת אגידא ביה, כמו שכתב רבינו תם והרא״ש בתשובותיהם (בשו״ת הרא״ש כלל כז סי׳ ה; ור״ת מובא במרדכי מועד קטן סימן תתצ) לענין אבלה המשודכת אליו, שמותר לכנסה אחר ז׳ שלה מכח פריה ורביה דידיה. וכן אנו מקילין נגד דברי רבותינו ז״ל בזמן הזה להשיא הקטנות, אע״פ שאמרו ז״ל אסור לאדם שיקדש בתו כשהיא קטנה עד שתגדיל ותאמר בפלוני אני רוצה (קידושין מא, א) וכתבו התוס׳ והפוסקים האחרונים, דבזמן הזה שאנו מתי מעט אנו מקילין וכו׳. וה״ה בנדון זה.

כל זה שמתי נגד עיני לסמוך על דברי רבינו תם ושאר פוסקים המתירים בשעת הדחק. ועוד אני אומר דיש לחלק ולומר דבזמן הזה לכ״ע שרי, דהא תנן אלו הן משום שבות אין מטפחין ולא מרקדין וכו׳ וכתבו התוספות ריש פרק המביא (ביצה ל, א ד״ה תנן) פירש״י שמא יתקן כלי שיר ומיהו לדידן שרי, דדוקא בימיהם שהיו בקיאים לעשות כלי שיר שייך למגזר, אבל לדידן אין אנו בקיאים לעשות כלי שיר ולא שייך למגזר עכ״ל. וכבר פשוט היתר הטפוח והרקוד בשבת בכ״מ ואף מצווים לכותים לנגן בכלי שיר והכל הוא מטעם דברי התוס׳ דלא שייך גזירה זו בזמן הזה. וה״ה בענין אין מקדשין, דאמרינן בגמרא הטעם שמא יכתוב וידוע המנהג פשוט בישראל שאין החתן כותב בעצמו הכתובה או שטר אירוסין, והוא מטעם שאין אנו בקיאים בכתיבה. ואפילו מי שיודע לכתוב אינו כותב שלא לחלק בין בקיאים לשאינן בקיאים, ולכן כותבה בכל מקום החזן כמו שקורא בתורה לכל אדם לתקנת שאינו בקי. ומעתה אין לגזור על המקדש שמא יכתוב, מאחר שאנחנו אינן בקיאים ואין מוטל על החתן כתיבה זו. ואין לחוש שהחזן יכתוב משום קידושי החתן, דגזירה כזו לא מצינו. ועוד שהרי החזן כותב כל פעם הכתובה ושטרי האירוסין

בשחרית או זמן רב קודם הכניסה לחופה כאשר אינו יודע מתי יהיו מוכנים עם החופה, ולכן אין לחוש בזמן הזה לגזירה זו כלל.

ואף אם נאמר דלפי דברי הירושלמי, דפירש טעם הגזירה משום דהוי כקונה קנין בשבת אין לחלק בין זמן הזה לבימיהם, מ"מ נראה דגמרא דידן עיקר נגד הירושלמי וכן פסקו הפוסקים תמיד. ואין לומר דגמרא דידן אית לה נמי טעמא דירושלמי אלא דנקט חדא מתרי טעמי, וכמ"ש שם התוס' על כיוצא בזה (שם לו, ב ד"ה והא מצוה קא עביד) דזה לא שייך בב' טעמים שיש נפקותא ביניהם. וכן כתב הסמ"ג (לאוין עא) בהדיא, דגמרא דידן פליג על הירושלמי בטעמא דמילתא ובודאי יש נפקותא ביניהם והיא זאת שכתבתי.

ונראה דלהכי לא הביאו הרי"ף והרא"ש דברי הירושלמי, ולא כתבו ג"כ ההוא דהלין דכנסין ארמלין צריכין למכנסי מבע"י ולא כתבו הטור סי' של"ט ג"כ, דודאי קי"ל כגמרא דידן נגד הירושלמי וליכא נפקותא בקנין לחוש לגזירה שמא יכתוב. (ואע"ג דהרא"ש פ"ק דכתובות (סימן ג) הביא הלין דכנסין ארמלין צריך למכנסי מבע"י, וכתב שם דה"ה דאין להכניס בתולה לחופה בשבת משום דקונה אותה למציאותיה ולמעשה ידיה וכ"כ בא"ע סי' ס"ג מכל מקום נ"ל מדלא הביאו אותה במקומה פרק משילין דלית בדבר איסור ממש. ובודאי היינו משום דס"ל דטעמא דגמרא דידן עיקר דהיינו שמא יכתוב, ולא הביאו אותה פ"ק דכתובות ובא"ע אלא משום הרחקה בעלמא, שלא לעשות חופה בשבת כמו שכתבו שם שלא לעשות חופה בע"ש משום גזירות רחוקות. ומאחר שאין אנו חוששין ועושין חופה בע"ש מטעם שכתבו האחרונים ז"ל, והעיקר משום שעכשיו אנו בגלות וטריחא לעשות נישואים בלא שבת, אפשר שה"ה שאין חוששין בזה להקל בשבת מאחר דטעם שמא יכתוב הוא עיקר וכמו שנתבאר.)

ותדע, דהרי התוספות (ביצה לו, ב ד"ה והא מצוה) לאחר שהביאו הירושלמי כתבו וז"ל: ומהאי טעמא דאין מקדשין לפי שנראה כקונה קנין אסור כמו כן לתת גט בשבת עכ"ל. והשתא אמאי לא יהא אסור ג"כ לפירוש הגמרא שלנו שאין מקדשין שמא יכתוב וה"ה לתת גט שמא יכתוב הגט. אלא ש"מ כדפרישית, דבגט לא שייך שמא יכתוב שהוא מעשה ידי אומן וסופר מהיר הצריך לכתוב הגט, ואין כל אדם בקיאים בו וליכא למיחש שנותן הגט יכתבנו מאחר שאין הנותן רגיל לכתוב הגט.

וה״ה בכתיבת הכתובה ושטר אירוסין בזמן הזה. ואע״ג דסומכין על דברי הירושלמי ואין מגרשין בשבת, כמו שכתבו התוספות פרק הזורק (גיטין עז, ב ד״ה ותיזיל) והר״ן פרק משילין (ביצה פ״ה על הרי״ף דף כ) והביאו הטור בא״ע סימן קל״ו, היינו משום שמצינו בהדיא בתוספתא דפרק משילין דקתני בהדיא אין מגרשין, וכמו שכתבו התוס׳ פרק הזורק. ואע״ג דבהר״ן פרק משילין משמע דגם בגט הטעם שאסור משום שמא יכתוב, מדברי התוס׳ לא משמע כן, ולדבריהם אולם שם הוא טעמא מטעם קנין, אבל לא גבי קידושין דודאי טעמא דגמרא דידן הוא עיקר. ואע״ג דמתוספות פרק משילין נראה דמטעם הירושלמי דוקא נאסר ולא גרסינן בתוספתא אין מגרשין לא קי״ל הכי, דודאי התוספתא היתה נעלמת מפי דברי התוס׳ דפרק משילין. ועוד, דאף אם נשוה קידושין לגירושין לגמרי מ״מ הרי כבר נתבאר דאף בגירושין במקום הדחק שרי, כמו שמבואר פרק הזורק. וכתבו התוס׳ דבשכיב מרע הקילו דלא תפול קמי יבם, כ״ש דיש להקל במקום מצוה שמקיים פריה ורביה והוא שעת הדחק. מכל הנ״ל נתבאר שמותר לקדש בשבת במקום הדחק ובמקום שיש לחוש לכבוד שלא יבוא הדבר לידי כסופא ואפשר לבא לידי ביטול הזיווג, ולסמוך על ר״ת המיקל בדבר וכאשר נתבאר.

אמנם רבים קמים עלי וסליקו רעיוני עלי באולי יש לחלק בין קידושין לכניסה לחופה דאפשר שהוא לכ״ע אסור, דהא קונה אותה לכמה דברים שהאשה נקנית להם והוי כקונה קנין בשבת שהוא אסור לכתחילה לכ״ע. וכן נמצא בדברי הגאון המחבר הגדול ספר ב״י בטור או״ח סי׳ של״ט הנ״ל, דכתב דאסור לכנסה אף לדברי ר״ת, וכתב דכן משמע מדברי הגהות מיימוני הכלבו והר״ן פרק משילין. והנה אע״פ שאין הכרח בדברי הגאון הנ״ל דמשמע מדברי הפוסקים הנ״ל שר״ת ס״ל הכי, אלא שהסמ״ק הוסיף דבר זה מדעתו כמבואר בדברי הסמ״ק גם יש לדחות בקל דברי הר״ן כי לא ירד לדבר מזה כלל, רק כתב והעתיק לשון התוס׳ ולא משמע מדבריו כלום מדבר זה כמבואר למשכיל בדבריו מ״מ נכון להסיר מעלי תלונות הגאון, שהיה לחוש לדבריו להחמיר גם כי הסמ״ק כתב כן בפירוש. ואומר חדא, כי באמת קולא זו חומרא היא כאשר נתבאר, שהיה לחוש לכמה קלקולים אם היו מעכבים הנישואין. שנית, כי מן התוספות והסמ״ג נראה בהדיא שאין מחולקין כלל בין קדושין לכניסה לחופה...

ומה לי להאריך פוק חזי מה עמא דבר (ברכות דף מה, עמוד א) בכל מקום, ובפרט בעירנו אשר יש בה קיבוץ עם ת"ל ולפעמים עושים ה' או ו' חופות ביום אחד ונמשכים עד הלילה ואין פוצה פה ומצפצף. ומה לי בתחילת הלילה או שעה או ב' בלילה, דאין לחלק בין קבלו שבת בענין ברכו או לא דאין תלוי בקבלתם להקל, דשבת מעצמו קבעה משחשיכה כדאיתא פרק ערבי פסחים לענין קדוש ומעשר (פסחים קה, א.) אלא האמת שצורך השעה מביא להקל בדברים אלו שאינן אלא איסור דרבנן, ובמקום הדחק לא גזרו. ובהא נחיתנא ובהא סליקנא דודאי יש להחמיר להיות זריזין קודם השבת שלא יבוא לידי כך. אבל אם כבר נעשה מה שאפשר לעשות ונטרפה השעה עד שחשיכה, ויש לחוש לפירוד הזיוג או לביוש הבתולה וכיוצא בזה הסומך להקל לא הפסיד, ויתענג לשלום בעונג שבת אח"כ. ויכולה המצוה לכפר עליו אם כוונתו לש"ש, ושלום.

נאום משה בן לא"א מורי ה"ר ישראל זצלה"ה, נקרא משה איסרלש מקראקא.

MA ENOSH: REFLECTIONS ON THE RELATION BETWEEN JUDAISM AND HUMANISM

I. What is Humanism?

What is the relation between humanism and Judaism? A question so central to a basic understanding of a Torah *Weltanschauung* bears examination in any age. And yet, it has, additionally, a special relevance to our own. The prevalence of humanistic winds currently blowing through general religious thought[1] makes it imperative that this partially neglected problem[2] be presently treated from a halakhic perspective.

[References to and translations of R. Joseph B. Soloveitchik's *Ish HaHalakha* and *Kol Dodi Dofek* have been updated to reflect the most recent English editions of those works.]

1. See, e.g., Roger L. Shinn, *Man: The New Humanism, New Directions in Theology Today*, vol. IV (Philadelphia, 1968).
2. Many specific elements are of course discussed in connection with other problems in works dealing with Jewish thought as a whole. However, I know of no adequate study of the subject in its entirety – nothing comparable, for instance, to the fairly substantial literature on Christian humanism that has been published during the last forty years. Mendel Hirsch's *Humanism and Judaism*, trans. J. Gilbert (London, 1928), is almost exclusively concerned with the problem of universalism and the Jewish view of Gentiles; and it is, in any event, more apologetics than exposition. Hans Kohn's *L'Humanisme Juif: Quinze Essais sur le Juif, le Monde et Dieu* (Paris, 1931), sweeps a wider arc but is more historical than analytic and focuses, moreover, upon very recent history. It is also, to say the least, unsympathetic to traditional Judaism. R. Samuel Belkin, *In His Image: The Jewish Philosophy of Man as Expressed in Rabbinic Tradition* (London, 1960), contains much useful material and many valuable insights but deals with far too many subjects to be able to treat any of them exhaustively. Harris H. Hirschberg, *Hebrew Humanism* (Los Angeles, 1964), raises fundamental problems and cites numerous texts but does not quite come to grips with the essential issues. Erich Fromm, *You Shall Be as Gods: A Radical Interpretation of the Old Testament and Its Tradition* (New York, 1966), does deal with our problem at some length and has the merit of treating the Bible and the rabbinic tradition as a unit. However, it presents a distorted one-sided view, relying excessively upon hasidic stories, ripped out of their religious and historical context, to shore up its central thesis. Finally, some of Buber's writings and the voluminous literature on them have some bearing upon some aspects of our problem; see, e.g., *A Believing Humanism*, trans. and ed. M. Friedman (New York, 1967), esp. 117–22,

It cannot be treated, of course, without answering a prior question, "'What is Humanism?' a question within whose murky depths," according to a recent writer, "whole libraries might be sunk without affording a foothold."[3] Historically, humanism has indeed presented, even at its most self-conscious, a multifaceted appearance. During the Renaissance, it was as much a literary and educational gospel as a social and political program.[4] In our own century, whether in league with religion or in militant opposition to it, it has often stressed social activism. Nevertheless, even at the risk of seeming rash, I think that, for our philosophic purposes, we can formulate a terse working definition: humanism is a worldview which values man highly. If this be the case, however, it becomes immediately apparent that our initial question is not one but several. For in this formulation, "values" must be understood in two senses, both as "appraises" and as "cherishes." The two are of course radically distinct. While the second is frequently grounded in the first – friendship, as Aristotle noted, is generally dependent upon appreciation – they are by no means identical. Achilles respected Hector but had no concern for his welfare, while Sonia worried over Raskolnikov but could have had but scant esteem for him.

With respect to man, however, humanism both appraises and cherishes him highly. Hence, philosophically and historically, it revolves around two foci. The first is the nature of man. Humanism affirms the dignity, the uniqueness – to a point, even the virtue – of man. Factually, it holds that man is endowed with a singular character; normatively,

---

and "Hebrew Humanism," in *Israel and the World* (New York, 1948), 240–52. But these, again, are of course not written from a halakhic perspective.

3. G. K. Hunter, *John Lyly: The Humanist as Courtier* (London, 1962), 13.
4. Just how narrowly literary was the focus of Renaissance humanism is a matter of dispute. Some scholars would regard Paul Oskar Kristeller's judgment that "Renaissance humanists were also interested in human values, but this was incidental to their major concern, which was the study and imitation of classical Greek and Latin literature" (*Renaissance Thought: The Classic, Scholastic, and Humanistic Strains* [New York, 1961], 120–21), as too extreme. See, e.g., Myron P. Gilmore, *The World of Humanism*, 1453–1517 (New York, 1952), 204–28, and Douglas Bush, *The Renaissance and English Humanism* (Toronto, 1939), who argue for a somewhat broader conception. No one would question, however, that literary interests were a major concern.

that he must realize his distinctive dimension, or rather, his distinctive potential. The basis for these affirmations may vary. In their medieval and Renaissance form – from John of Salisbury through Pico and Erasmus to Hooker and Milton – it was predominantly religious. In their modern form, as exemplified by, say, Babbitt, Camus, or Dewey, it is often secular. The scope of the affirmations may likewise vary. Secular humanism is, in one sense, relatively restricted. Its preoccupation with man is unrelated to any grand vision of man's objective place within the universe. It accepts the naturalist's view that man is merely an insignificant speck of cosmic dust. From such a perspective, the centrality of man is purely moral and subjective. It can be accepted only by consciously averting one's gaze from cold reality and focusing one's attention upon an infinitesimal portion of the universe.

Religious humanism, by contrast, often makes the most sweeping cosmological claims. In one sense, of course, the religious position *per se* – especially that of revealed religion – assumes man's special status as the one creature capable of relating intelligently to God. To this extent, religion is, by definition, more humanistic than secularism; in positing a transcendental dimension to his existence, it assumes a nobler view of man. Many religious humanists go much further, however. They regard not only their own systems but the objective universe itself as being anthropocentric. Among Renaissance writers, for instance, statements that man is the very focus of the creation, that the entire cosmos exists but to serve him, are almost clichés. Whatever the form, however, the primary humanistic thesis is the same. Against radical Augustinian and Calvinistic pessimism on the right and all modes of naturalism on the left, the humanist insists that man is presently endowed with a unique exalted character, be its source transcendental or natural; that his primary duty consists of realizing his distinctive dimension; and that through the exercise of his rational and moral faculties – and through that alone – he has the capacity to attain his potential.

The second focus, related to and yet distinct from the first, concerns the destiny of man – insofar as he can affect it – rather than his nature. The issue here is not what man is, nor even what he can become, but the degree to which human life should be geared to the satisfaction of man's needs and desires. Whatever his worth, to what extent should man be collectively concerned with his own mundane well-being? From a secular perspective, such a question makes very little sense. The answer is, obviously, as much as possible, provided, of course, in the spirit of John Stuart Mill, that these are not confined to the hedonistic or sybaritic but include spiritual desiderata as well. From a religious perspective, however, which regards mankind as having not only rights but responsibilities, it is not only relevant but crucial. Man's relation to God entails obligations to Him, so that energies which might have been channeled toward the advancement of purely human welfare are expended in the service of God. In this sense, therefore, the religious point of view is, by definition, less humanistic than the secular; and the American Humanist Association is correct in regarding supernaturalism as its sworn enemy. If it is indeed true, as Corliss Lamont would have it, that

> Humanism is the point of view that men have but one life to lead and should make the most of it in terms of creative work and happiness; that human happiness is its own sanction and requires no sanction or support from supernatural sources; that in any case the supernatural, usually conceived of in the form of heavenly gods or immortal heavens, does not exist; and that human beings, using their own intelligence and cooperating liberally with one another, can build an enduring citadel of peace and beauty upon this earth,[5]

then of course religious thought can have no truck with it. However, while such absolute "humanism" cannot be countenanced – of course, from a religious point of view, a philosophy grounded in so limited a view of man's nature and his aspirations is not humanistic at all – varying degrees of concern for human welfare are clearly possible. Even within a religious framework, one can speak of relatively more or less humanistic points of view. As regards both foci, then, we may validly ask: In what sense, and to what extent, should Torah Judaism be regarded as humanistic?

5. *The Philosophy of Humanism*, 4th ed. (New York, 1957), 11.

In dealing with this, as with almost every major problem of religious philosophy, a number of answers are clearly possible. These are not matters of simple dogma, to be settled by reference to catechetical formulations; and, in actual fact, Jewish thought has certainly advanced a significant variety of attitudes and emphases concerning them. Maharal's worldview was more anthropocentric than Rambam's, and Rabbenu Bahya's more ascetic than Rav Kook's. Nevertheless, one can speak of a broad central position. Above all, one can look to a common objective element to help define the limits of discourse. This element is preeminently the Halakha. Reference to halakhic texts and categories will not necessarily delineate the nuances of various positions. Indeed, as regards our first problem, the nature of man, one might be hard put to find halakhic texts which deal with it directly. While the native Jewish tradition regarding this question is central to the whole of Halakha, it is so pervasive as to be implicit rather than expressed. Nevertheless, as regards both foci, the Halakha, as the very essence of Judaism, enables us to recognize the bounds of legitimate Jewish thought.

II. The Nature of Man

Judaism has regarded the nature of man in the light of a basic antinomy. On the one hand, man is a noble, even an exalted being. His spiritual potential and metaphysical worth are rooted in his *tzelem Elokim,* "the image of God" with which his Creator has invested him. The phrase is doubly significant. It describes man's metaphysical essence, on the one hand, and it suggests a kinship on the other.[6] "Beloved is man that he is created with an image. Particular love is manifested to him in that he is created in God's image, as it is said, 'For in the image of God He made man.'"[7] Man was imbued with a transcendental spark – endowed with

6. Some, particularly mystics, tend to link both aspects and speak of a partial consubstantiality. However, thinkers who have stressed the elements of divine transcendence have criticized such claims severely. This was one of the Gaon of Vilna's principal criticisms of *Hasidut.*
7. *Avot* 3:14. See commentaries, ad loc., many of whom see the particular love as consisting in the fact that man has been told he had been created in the divine image. See also the textual variants in the Vilna edition of the Mishna.

personality, intelligence, and freedom – because divine grace destined him for a special relation with itself. Individually and collectively, man is therefore the object of particular Providence, and, as a spiritual being, a subject capable of engaging his personality in a dialectical community with God.

Faith in the essential worth of man, independently considered, is basic to Judaism. As regards his relative cosmic position, however, the tradition has harbored conflicting views. Thus, Maharal placed man at the very apex of creation,[8] while Rambam insisted the angels were ontologically superior.[9] Similarly, Rambam[10] strongly rejected the notion, often cherished by humanists, that the universe as a whole exists solely in order to serve man. Just as God willed the existence of man, so He willed that of other beings, each for its own sake. None, in Tennyson's phrase, "but subserves another's gain."[11] Yet numerous texts expound the very position the Rambam rejects. The Midrash, for instance, repeatedly discusses the creation in strikingly anthropocentric terms. After the fall, it depicts God as stating: "Did I not create animals and beasts solely for man? Now that man has sinned, what need have I of animals and beasts?"[12] Man is the culmination because he is the pinnacle of creation, "created after everything so as to rule over everything."[13] According to R. Shimon b. Elazar, even the higher animals "were but created in order to serve me."[14] For, as *Avot DeRabbi Natan* put it, "a single man is worth the [entire] creation."[15]

However, despite differences that have existed concerning these issues – and they are certainly of momentous importance – the basic thesis has always remained central. Whatever man's position relative to

8. See his commentary on *Avot, Derekh Hayim*, 3:14; also in *Kitvei Maharal MiPrague*, ed. A. Kariv (Jerusalem, 1960), II, 54. See also Kariv's introduction, I, xxiii–xxxii.
9. *Guide for the Perplexed*, III:13.
10. Ibid.
11. *In Memoriam*, 54:12.
12. *Yalkut Shimoni, Bereshit*, 57.
13. *Bereshit Rabba*, 19:5. The remark is part of an argument attributed to the serpent, but the midrash clearly accepts his facts and would only reject the concluding inference.
14. *Kiddushin* 82a.
15. *Avot DeRabbi Natan*, ed. S. Z. Schechter, 2nd ed. (New York, 1945), A-text, 31; p. 46a. Cf. *Sanhedrin* 37a and 38a.

the universe as a whole is, there can be no question about the absolute and ultimate worth of his own existence. Judaism has not assumed man's natural goodness.

> Our Rabbis taught: "The evil inclination is hard [to bear], since even his Creator called him evil, as it is written, 'For the inclination of man's heart is evil from his youth.' R. Yitzhak said: Man's evil inclination renews itself against him daily, as it is written, 'Every imagination of the thoughts of his heart was but evil every day.'"[16]

But Judaism has always insisted upon man's natural worth – upon the sanctity as well as the dignity of human personality.

On the one hand, then, man is regarded as a majestic and exalted being. And yet, on the other, we are confronted by the radical pessimism of *Kohelet*: "For that which befalls the sons of men befalls beasts; even one thing befalls them; as the one dies, so dies the other; yea, they have all one breath; so that man's preeminence over the beast is naught, for all is vanity."[17] For devotees of biblical criticism, it would of course be easy to dismiss this apparent contradiction on historical grounds, to regard the conflicting statements as the contrasting expressions of individual personalities or the *Zeitgeist* of different periods. Not only easy, however, but facile. The Rabbis, in any event, thought otherwise. They insisted on incorporating both attitudes in adjacent passages of one of the oldest and most august of our standard prayers, the *Ne'ila* recited at the end of *Yom Kippur*:

> What are we? What is our life? What is our goodness? What our virtue? What our help? What our strength, what our might? What can we say to Thee, Lord our God and God of our fathers? Indeed, all the heroes are as nothing in Thy sight, the men of renown as though they never existed, the wise as without knowledge, the intelligent as without insight. For the multitude of their actions

16. *Kiddushin* 30b. The verses cited are from *Bereshit* 8:21 and 6:5, respectively.
17. *Kohelet* 3:19.

> is empty and the days of their life vanity in Thy sight; and man's preeminence over the beast is naught, for all is vanity. Yet, from the first Thou didst single out man and acknowledged him [as worthy] to stand in Thy presence.…[18]

Quite apart from its allusion to the element of divine grace – one of the central motifs of Yom Kippur and one whose role within Judaism is often greatly underestimated – the import of the passage is clear. In and of himself, man is simply a part of the natural world and, as such, of little ultimate consequence. However, inasmuch and to the extent that he relates to God, he assumes immense significance. As Rambam[19] noted in commenting on this passage, this relation is initiated through an act of grace. There is no ground here for vainglorious arrogance. It is God who invests human life with meaning – first, by electing man in the act of creation proper, and then by maintaining community with him. Once established, however, the relation radically alters the very fiber of human personality and existence. "Why did he [i.e., the psalmist] call the Holy One, blessed be He, the king of glory?" asks the Midrash. "Because He imparts glory to His adherents."[20] Through his election, man becomes unique not only as the passive object of special Providence but as a creative spiritual being. In all spheres of activity, he realizes himself as a person rather than as an individual object. Even apart from his religious relation, narrowly conceived, his life attains a genuinely meaningful dimension. It is only through that relation, however, that his *sui generis* character develops. Of man on his own[21] one can only say, "Man's preeminence over the beast is naught, for all is vanity."

This antinomy finds vivid biblical expression in the eighth psalm:

> When I behold Thy heavens, the work of Thy fingers, the moon and the stars which Thou hast established – What is man, that

18. *High Holiday Prayer Book*, ed. P. Birnbaum (New York, 1959), 971.
19. *Guide*, III:13.
20. *Shemot Rabba* 8:2, and numerous parallel texts cited in *Yad Yosef*, ad loc.
21. Of course, having been created, he never is fully on his own. I speak only of a theoretical possibility, the secular view of man and the world, although that view is false even as an account of the secularist's own state.

> Thou art mindful of him? And the son of man that Thou thinkest of him? And[22] that Thou hast made him but little lower than the angels, and hast crowned him with glory and honor; hast made him to have dominion over the works of Thy hands, and put all under his feet: sheep and oxen, all of them, yea, and the beasts of the field; the fowl of the air, and the fish of the sea, whatsoever passes through the paths of the seas? O Lord, our Lord! How glorious is Thy name in all the earth!

Harvard people remember part of this passage as the subject of an interesting local incident. Before leaving for summer vacation, members of the department of philosophy once selected Protagoras' "Man is the measure of all things" as the inscription for a new building. Upon their return, they discovered that President Eliot had substituted "What is man that Thou art mindful of him?"[23] One cannot understand the Jewish position, however, without seeing the entire passage – or rather, without regarding it as a unitary whole; without seeing man both as he might be independently, naked in his natural insignificance, and as he exists through his relation to God, invested with majesty and power.

The whole of Halakha rests upon this vision. As a normative system, it is grounded upon one cardinal premise: human freedom and creativity. And as an experienced reality, it trumpets forth, in turn, one central message: human freedom and creativity. It does not merely posit this doctrine as a metaphysical principle. It envisions freedom, at every level and in every sphere, as a pragmatic *modus operandi*.[24] It makes one

22. The current J.P.S. translation – as well as numerous others – have "yet" instead of "and" at this point. On this reading, the opening rhetorical question has been concluded and the rest of the chapter goes on to state – and to marvel over – the fact that, despite his presumed insignificance, God has granted man such stature. There is nothing in the text to suggest such a turn, however, and I am convinced the rest of the psalm (until the last verse) should be read as an expansion of the earlier question. The enumeration of God's favors reinforces the question, but its focus remains human existence rather than, as in the other version, divine action.
23. The incident is cited in Douglas Bush, *Science and English Poetry: A Historical Sketch, 1590–1950* (New York, 1950), 137.
24. Of course, the freedom exists within a normative framework. It constitutes, in large measure, freedom to achieve specified ends rather than unbridled autonomy. A

persistent demand: Choose. Decide. As a pervasive legal system, Halakha posits Jewish existence at the plane of maximal consciousness and decision.[25] The Jew is insistently called upon to exercise intelligence and rational will – to act, that is, as an active subject rather than as a passive object. He is impelled to regard himself – and, in turn, to regard and to treat his fellow man – as an agent rather than a patient, not as a thing but as a person. Perhaps no single distinction runs through halakhic thought more persistently than that of *heftza* and *gavra*, "object" and "subject," the inchoate natural world and the creative human spirit which, like its Creator, strives to give that world meaning and purpose.[26]

The Halakha's emphasis upon man as a creative and responsible agent stands, above all, stubbornly opposed to any naturalistic ethics. It assumes man's *sui generis* character; and it insists that, because of his character, he cannot resign from a life of moral and religious decision. He may rise or fall, but he cannot sit still. There is no opting out. The decision to withdraw would itself be an ethical – or rather, an unethical – decision. From the perspective of the Jewish view of man, to live "naturally" is to be true to only one side of human nature – and, hence, to be false to the whole of it. As A. S. P. Woodhouse noted in a similar connection:

> Nature, said Renan, knows nothing of chastity. And of nature on her sub-human level, this statement (as Spenser would agree) is perfectly true. She knows no more of chastity than she does of temperance and continence, of friendship, of justice, of courtesy or constancy or magnanimity. She does not know them because

radical antinomian might complain that I am misusing the word. I have no desire to enter upon a logomachy but I think the essential point is clear.

25. In its fullest measure, Halakha exists within the specific covenantal framework of Judaism. However, on a more limited scale, its essential conception of man and his potential is thoroughly universal.

26. The terms proper do not appear very frequently in *Hazal*, but the concepts, particularly as elicited by more recent *Aharonim*, are pervasively latent. For a discussion of the Halakha's concern with creativity at the highest level, see R. Joseph B. Soloveitchik, *Halakhic Man*, trans. Lawrence J. Kaplan (Philadelphia, 1983), 99–137. Cf. also his *Kol Dodi Dofek: Listen – My Beloved Knocks*, trans. David Z. Gordon (New York, 2006), 1–7, 52–71.

> she does not need them, having her own sure law, adequate to each level of existence. But this does not mean that the human virtues are unnatural. On the contrary, they are natural in a double sense: because they belong to the nature of man, and because nature, adequately conceived, is seen to furnish their base and to lend them her sanction.[27]

It is precisely by transcending his undisciplined psychological and biological self that man both realizes his own distinctive dimension and finds his place within universal Nature.

Of course, Halakha, in its fullest sense, is not the only alternative to naturalism. But it *is* the Jewish alternative; and it can be fairly stated that it rests upon the Torah's view of man. Judaism has placed such enormous emphasis upon normative living – and implicitly, therefore, upon human freedom – because it has envisioned such an existence as a means of realizing the potential inherent in *tzelem Elokim*. Man can, of course, seek to abdicate his responsibility. But to the extent that he moves in this direction, he betrays his own nature and divests his life of significance. At the limit, "The preeminence of man over the beast is naught, for all is vanity."

As regards the first focus, then – the conception of the nature of man – Judaism is very much within the mainstream of religious humanism. Or rather, it constitutes one of its primary fountainheads. What we have seen as the traditional Jewish position closely resembles so much that was commonplace among, say, Renaissance humanists precisely because they drew so heavily upon it.[28] Cultural historians

---

27. "Nature and Grace in *The Faerie Queene*," *ELH*, XVI (1949): 217. Cf. John Stuart Mill's posthumous essay, "Nature," in *Nature, the Utility of Religion and Theism* (London, 1874).

28. For an incisive summary of their views concerning this question, see Theodore Spencer, *Shakespeare and the Nature of Man*, 2nd ed. (New York, 1955), 1–50; and, for a full account, Herschel C. Baker, *The Dignity of Man* (Cambridge, Mass., 1947), with full bibliography. From a Catholic perspective, see Francis Hermans, *Histoire Doctrinale de L'Humanisme* Chrétien (Paris, 1948). For a more critical discussion, see Gordon W. O'Brien, *Renaissance Poetics and the Problem of* Power (Chicago, 1956).

sometimes glibly speak of Christian humanism as the product of Judaic abnegation blended with Graeco-Roman pride.[29] The sense of man's nihility is traced back to the Bible and awareness of his potential and accomplishments to a chorus from *Antigone*. The fact of the matter is, however, that both elements are central to the Jewish tradition *ab initio*.[30] In terms of emphasis there is perhaps room for contrast. Job's vision is obviously different from Prometheus' and we have no tradition paralleling Protagoras'. As regards the central antinomy, however, both poles are deeply imbedded within the historical Jewish consciousness. It shares Pico's view of human greatness and it has plumbed the depths of Swift's savage despair. At bottom, it regards man, with Pascal, as "*ni ange ni bête*, neither angel nor beast,"[31] because he is both, not only *in potentia* but in actual fact. "If [a man] is worthy," says the Midrash, "he is told, 'You were prior to ministering angels.' If not, he is told, 'An insect preceded you, a worm preceded you.'"[32]

It should not be assumed that the Jewish view of the nature of man simply coincides with that of Christian humanism. No Jew could have written the latter parts of *In Praise of Folly*. We do not speak of God as "the divine fool" nor could we readily identify our own "folly" with

29. Levi A. Olan, "On the Nature of Man," *C.C.A.R. Yearbook*, LVIII (1948): 255–71, reverses this process. He argues that the Jewish view of man and the world has led to a sense of his greatness and importance, and hence to all liberal and socially progressive movements, while the Greek view, as represented by platonic otherworldliness, leads to Pauline [sic] notions of human degradation and neglect of social issues. I think this, too, is erroneous. It overstresses one side of the Jewish tradition to the exclusion of others and it thoroughly misrepresents the Greek position. For one thing, Platonism does not constitute the whole of Greek thought. Furthermore, even as regards Plato proper, his transcendentalism regards man more as limited and imperfect than as positively corrupt. The idea and ideal of deiformity – see, e.g., *Theatetus* 176a – is very much alive for him and subsequently played a crucial role within the Platonic tradition. And certainly – as both his *Republic* and *Laws* clearly attest – Plato did not neglect social issues.
30. For a generally sound and lucid account of the tradition as it appears in the Bible, see William A. Irwin on "Man," in *The Intellectual Adventure of Ancient Man*, H. A. Frankfort et al. (Chicago, 1946), 255–63.
31. *Pensées* (Paris,1950), 128; no. 358.
32. *Bereshit Rabba*, 8:1; cf. *Sanhedrin* 38a. The midrash literally refers to chronological precedence at the time of creation but axiological priority is no doubt also intended.

Him. The doctrine of the incarnation enables a Christian to ground his humanism upon premises which a Jew must regard as nothing short of idolatrous. In this sense, it is perfectly true that Christian humanism resulted from the conjunction of Greek and Jewish thought; or perhaps indeed, as Toynbee would have it, that Christianity itself developed out of the injection of Hellenic "man-worship or Humanism" into Judaism.

> For the Jews, this revolutionary Christian doctrine of God's incarnation was a blasphemous importation into Judaism of a myth that was one of the most damnable of all the errors in hellenic paganism. This was a betrayal of everything that Judaism had achieved in a long and arduous struggle to purify and elevate man's vision of God's nature, and no orthodox Jew would have been capable of it.[33]

Needless to say, in this regard, nothing has changed during the last two millennia. At bottom, any Jewish humanism must reject one dimension of its Christian counterpart. Christian thinkers are fully aware of this dimension. "*L'humanisme Chrétien,*" writes a Catholic scholar, "*est d'abord une spiritualité axée sur le dogme de l'incarnation.*"[34] Maritain, in pleading for an "integral" humanism, suggests that "such a humanism, which considers man in the wholeness of his natural and supernatural being, and which sets no *a priori* limit to the descent of the divine into man, we may call *the humanism of the Incarnation.*"[35] That being the case, Judaism – which does set an "*a priori* limit to the descent of the divine into man" – must, in part, reject it.

Moreover, Christian humanists often instinctively think in terms that are relevant but not quite as central for their Jewish counterparts. The problem of the nature of man actually involves two issues: 1) man's inherent metaphysical character and status and 2) his psychological

33. Arnold J. Toynbee, *Hellenism: The History of a Civilization* (New York, 1959), 16.
34. "Christian humanism is first and foremost a spirituality based on the dogma of the Incarnation." Hermans, *L'Humanisme Chrétien,* IV, 59. See also IV, 87–95.
35. Jacques Maritain, *Scholasticism and Politics* (Garden City, 1960), 18; the italics are Maritain's.

tendencies within his actual historical situation. As regards the first, the Jewish position and that of Christian humanism largely coincide. As regards the second, however, one often encounters significant divergence. While humanists represent the Pelagian strain within Christianity, they nevertheless – partly, in spite of themselves – often employ the categories of depravity and grace in a manner distinctly foreign to Judaism. Nevertheless, in its broad outlines, Jewish anthropology does have much in common with Christian humanism;[36] and sensitivity to important differences of tone and emphasis as well as substance should not blind us to this fact. Above all, they share the concurrent vision of man's complex dual nature: the grandeur of what Milton called "the human face divine" and the animality of the two-footed beast.

III. The Torah's Concern for Human Welfare

Whatever be the Torah-halakhic view of the nature of man, our second focus – the degree of concern for human welfare – poses an entirely different question. In a sense, of course, the two problems are related. Insofar as one assumes the majesty and dignity of man, he presumably becomes less prone to otherworldliness. Respect for human personality would naturally lead to concern for satisfying all its needs and for the fullest development of the total environment within which it finds both realization and self-fulfillment. Historically, this has no doubt generally occurred. An obvious instance is provided by modern secular humanism, with its consuming passion for exploring and exploiting the human potential of what Wordsworth called "the very world, which is the world / Of all of us, – the place where, in the end, / We find our happiness,

36. It does seem to me, however, that the element of rationality, which Werner Jaeger – see his *Humanism and Theology* (Milwaukee, 1943), 15–19 – and others have seen as the focus of the humanistic view of man, is not quite so central within the halakhic tradition. It is important but not quite the linchpin. As far as Rambam's view is concerned, however, the interpretation of much-disputed passages in his *Guide*, I:1–2, would be crucial. See also Reinhold Niebuhr, *The Nature and Destiny of Man* (New York, 1943), I, 6–14, who argues that the classical view emphasized human rationality while the biblical tradition stressed rather the capacity for self-transcendence.

or not at all!"[37] Religious parallels can readily be cited, however. In his *De dignitate hominis*, for instance, the Florentine humanist Giannozzo Manetti writes: "Just as the force, the reason, and the power of man, for whom the world itself and all the things of the world were created, are great, straight, and admirable, so we must judge and believe that the mission of man consists in knowing and ruling over the world made for him, as well as over all things which we see established in this immense universe."[38] Or again, as More's example particularly manifests, one can hardly challenge G. K. Hunter's statement that sixteenth-century English humanists "sought to turn religious ideals and energies towards the amelioration of life in this world and to achieve an order in this life corresponding to the religious vision of man's worth."[39] Nor can we seriously doubt that the eudaemonistic element in Greek culture – what Jaeger called "the innate Greek belief in the value of this world, their confidence that they could bring 'the best state,' 'the best life' into being here and now"[40] – is directly related to its profound confidence in man himself.

Nevertheless, despite their prevalent psychological link, these two questions have no necessary logical connection. One could conceivably entertain the highest estimate of man's worth and yet be relatively unconcerned with "the amelioration of life in this world." And I would agree with Professor Bush that it is "very misleading" to assume "as an unquestionable fact that humanism and related words signify a turning from heaven to earth, from medieval theology and otherworldliness to this mundane world which the classics have taught men to enjoy."[41] The crucial question turns on the conception of human welfare. Inasmuch as man consists of body and soul, his well-being must presumably be defined with reference to both. Or rather, if we are to speak from a religious perspective, it may be defined purely in terms of the latter, physical well-being becoming relevant only insofar as it contributes to spiritual

37. *The Prelude*, 11:142–44.
38. Cited in Giuseppi Toffanin, *History of Humanism*, trans. Elio Gianturco (New York, 1954), 198.
39. *John Lyly*, 13.
40. Werner Jaeger, *Paideia: The Ideals of Greek Culture*, trans. Gilbert Highet (New York, 1943), II, 4.
41. *Renaissance and English Humanism*, 54.

development. Given certain conceptions of the relation between body and soul, therefore – if it should be assumed, for instance, that one can only grow at the expense of the other and that a rigorous asceticism is essential to spirituality – there is no logical contradiction whatsoever between the most exalted notions of human nature and destiny and the most extreme forms of otherworldliness. In the history of Western thought, Neoplatonism furnishes an excellent example of this combination. Plotinus could, on the one hand, regard himself as virtually divine, a temporarily miscast demigod; and yet, on the other hand – or perhaps, for that very reason – Porphyry writes that he "seemed ashamed of being in the body."[42] Or, to take a recent Jewish example, R. Yosef Yosel Hurwitz, the founder of the Nowaredok school of *musar*, entertained the most exalted conceptions of man's intrinsic worth and yet counseled radical forms of asceticism and renunciation.[43]

Hence, the Torah-halakhic conception of the nature of man suggests no definitive answer to our second question: How much weight has Judaism assigned man's realization of temporal happiness? To what extent has it recognized the value of satisfying his physical and emotional needs? The answer to this question must rather primarily be sought – apart from explicit biblical or aggadic statements of attitude – in areas of Halakha which either define or reflect a perspective upon man's relation to the mundane. Such an inquiry should concern itself, in turn, with two distinct elements. The first might be called the normal or fundamental Halakha, the moral and religious demands imposed by the Torah as a program for human life under ordinary circumstances. The second concerns whatever provisions the Halakha has made for superseding its usual norms in emergency situations in which these conflict with essential human needs.

With regard to either element, but especially the first, it becomes immediately apparent that any answer must be largely relative. It all

42. *On the Life of Plotinus and the Arrangement of His Work*, in *Plotinus: The Ethical Treatises: Being the Treatises of the First Ennead with Porphyry's Life of Plotinus*, trans. Stephen Mackenna (London, 1917), 9.

43. See his *Madregat HaAdam*, 3rd ed. (Jerusalem, 1964), 1–27. It should be noted that the question of the nature of man constituted one of the primary concerns of the *Musar* movement as a whole.

depends on one's standard and expectations. As compared with medieval Christianity, Judaism is singularly mundane; as compared to most contemporary versions, it is rather otherworldly. Beside Abelard or Anselm, the halakhist appears almost secular; beside Harvey Cox, he is very much the *religieux*. Much also depends on one's perspective. To outsiders accustomed to a relatively unfettered existence, the minutiae of halakhic living can seem terribly onerous. A devout Episcopalian once ate supper at our home and expressed amazement that one could be constantly aware of the laws concerning washing, blessings, and so on without being wholly overwhelmed. To those acclimated to its regimen, however, the demands of Halakha, comprehensive though they be, are fully compatible with a reasonably comfortable life. Indeed, aided by the marvels of modern technology, some are now so thoroughly inured as to feel no discomfiture whatsoever. Nevertheless, if we eschew judgmental and comparative epithets, an exposition of the fundamental Jewish attitude can be readily formulated.

Like seventeenth-century Anglicans, modern Jews often pride themselves upon possessing a eudaemonistic *via media* – a humanistic religion which avoids the Scylla of secular liberalism on the left and the Charybdis of Christian asceticism on the right. While this claim is often shallowly entertained and its value insufficiently analyzed (what value is there in mediacy *per se*?), it is nevertheless securely grounded. The humanistic strain is reflected in what the Halakha both says and avoids saying. In a positive sense, it finds expression in the overriding emphasis upon *hesed*, usually translated as "goodness" or "mercy" but truly denoting a total complex of empathy and action deriving from concern for the welfare of others. Transcending mere paternalism and demanding not only charity but *caritas*, *hesed* entails genuine personal involvement with the needs of my fellowman, rich or poor. Its centrality is reflected in numerous mitzvot, ranging from various tithes for the poor through interest-free lending to wedding celebration,[44] and is, at times, explicitly stated: "R. Elazar said: What is the implication of the

44. See *Sukka* 25b and commentaries, a number of whom assume that during the week following the wedding, participants in the festivities are exempt from performing other mitzvot if these concur or interfere with their celebration.

text, 'It hath been told thee, O man, what is good, and what the Lord doth require of thee – to do justly, to love mercy, and to walk humbly with thy God.' 'To do justly' refers to justice; 'to love mercy' to acts of *hesed*; 'and to walk humbly with thy God' to attending to funerals and dowering a bride [for her wedding].'"[45] The Torah as a whole is seen as framed by the concept: "R. Simlai expounded: The Torah begins with an act of *hesed* and ends with an act of *hesed*, for it is written, 'And the Lord God made for Adam and for his wife coats of skin and clothed them'; and it ends with an act of *hesed*, for it is written, 'And He buried him in the valley.'"[46] And it frames the Torah precisely because it is so intimately related to its essence and purpose. Hillel's statement – in answer to a prospective proselyte who wanted to be taught the whole Torah while standing on one leg – expressed it most radically: "What is hateful to you, don't do to your fellow – that is the whole Torah. The rest is its commentary; go and study it."[47]

The drive to *hesed* has two motive springs. One is the obligation to imitate divine attributes and actions. Commenting on the verse, "To go in all His ways,"[48] the *Sifre*, after noting that these are the thirteen attributes of merciful grace cited in a theophanic passage in *Shemot* 34:6-7, goes on to apply this point within a more specific context:

> "Whosoever will be called by the name of the Lord shall be spared." How is it then possible for a person to be called by the name of the Holy One, blessed be He? But [this means] as the Omnipresent is called gracious and compassionate, so you be gracious and compassionate and give gifts of grace to all. As the Holy One, blessed be He, is called righteous ... so you be righteous. As the Holy One, blessed be He, is called merciful ... so you

45. Ibid. 49b. The verse cited is from *Mikha* 6:3.
46. *Sota* 14a. The verses cited are from *Bereshit* 3:21 and *Devarim* 34:6.
47. *Shabbat* 31a. I am here assuming the obvious literal meaning of the text. Rashi, s.v. *de'alokh*, presents both this interpretation and another – that the fellow alluded to is God, with the odious thing being disobedience. Cf. also Ramban, *Shemot* 15:26.
48. *Devarim* 11:22.

> be merciful. In this sense, it is said, "Whosoever shall be called by the name of the Lord shall be spared."[49]

Or, to put it more concretely:

> What is the meaning of the text, "Ye shall follow the Lord your God"? Is it, then, possible for a human being to follow the *Shekhina*? Has it not been said, "For the Lord thy God is a devouring fire"? But [this means] walk after the attributes of the Holy One, blessed be He. As He clothes the naked…, so you also clothe the naked. The Holy One, blessed be He, visited the sick…, so you also visit the sick. The Holy One, blessed be He, comforted mourners…, so you also comfort mourners. The Holy One, blessed be He buried the dead…, so you also bury the dead.[50]

The second spring is the obligation to love another. This commandment – singled out by R. Akiva as a "central principle in the Torah"[51] – was cited by Rambam as the halakhic basis of the very acts of *hesed* subsumed by the Gemara in *Sota* under imitation of the ways of God, *imitatio viarum Dei*. After presenting a catalogue of such acts that have been ordained as rabbinic commandments – besides those cited in *Sota* it includes other kindnesses to the dead and their memory, escorting guests, and arranging and celebrating weddings – he concludes: "These constitute acts of *hesed* [to be] performed in person for which no limit can be prescribed.[52] Although all these commands are of rabbinic origin, they are included in 'And thou shalt love thy neighbor as thyself.'"[53] Rambam evidently means that these acts manifest love to one's fellow and as such are to be subsumed under a general biblical

49. *Sifre, Ekev*, 49. The verse cited is from *Yo'el* 3:5. Cf. *Shabbat* 133b and Rambam, *Hilkhot De'ot* 1:6.
50. *Sota* 14a. The verses cited are from *Devarim* 13:5 and 4:24, respectively. In this and the preceding selection each point is buttressed by a proof-text. I have omitted these, however.
51. *Sifra, Kedoshim*, 4:12.
52. See *Pe'ah* 1:1.
53. *Hilkhot Evel* 14:1. The verse cited is from *Vayikra* 19:18.

injunction; but that, as specific objects of a particular commandment, their status is only of rabbinic origin. The Torah, speaking of a subjective emotional relation, formulated a general principle which is both realized and reflected through the performance of various acts of *hesed*. Over and above this, the Rabbis have singled out some of these acts and have posited them, at the objective plane of action, not only as instances of a broader category, but as definite categories in their own right.[54] Be this as it may, however, Rambam's formulation emphasizes a second normative dimension of *hesed* – the interpersonal. In extending empathy and aid to others, the Jew therefore strives in two directions. At one level, he moves toward the fulfillment of his own spiritual personality. At another, he improves the lot of his fellow man.

This intersection of two orders of mitzvot, duties to God and man respectively, is no accident. It reflects halakhic faith that religious self-fulfillment imposes social obligations, on the one hand, but that, on the other hand, social action cannot have ultimate meaning unless it draws upon and relates to a transcendental source. The reciprocal interaction of the "ethical" and the "religious" – at a legal and not only at a philosophic plane – reflects the fact that the Halakha can never reconcile itself to their divorce. And it invests *hesed,* as a quality and as a mitzva, with its singularly Jewish character.

The importance attached by the Halakha to helping the needy – be they rich or poor[55] – reflects the profoundly Jewish spirit of compassion and commiseration for the weak and the downtrodden. In a very real sense, this spirit constituted our specific contribution to the classical world. Graeco-Roman culture knew much of friendship and something of love but relatively little of compassion. At the same time, this spirit is rooted in an awareness of the significance of man's temporal needs, physical as well as psychological. This awareness is most strikingly manifested in a different context. Among incidents which can be regarded as visitations of divine chastisement, the Gemara cites the most pedestrian frustrations: "if a man had, for example, a garment woven for

54. See also *Sefer HaMitzvot,* "Principles," 1.

55. As opposed to *tzedaka* ("charity"), the obligation to do *hesed* includes helping the rich as well as the poor. See *Sukka* 49b.

him to wear and it does not fit him"; "if a drink was to be served hot and was served cold or vice-versa"; "even if his shirt gets turned inside out"; "even if he puts his hand into his pocket to take out three [coins] and takes out but two."[56] But the same sensitivity, although expressed in less dramatic terms, constitutes the basis of the Torah's emphasis upon *hesed*.

The humanistic strain is likewise evident in a major halakhic omission. As a moral and religious regimen, the Halakha demands a great deal; but its discipline contains little which can be regarded as purposively ascetic. Of mortification it knows almost nothing,[57] of monasticism even less. The emphasis is rather upon a discipline of choice and direction. Man's basic physiological and psychological drives are recognized as healthy, but they are channeled and chastened by being integrated into a harmoniously ordered discipline. He is encouraged to eat well – hearty meals are an integral aspect of Sabbath and festival celebration[58] and often conjoined with "rejoicing before God"[59] – but never at will. He is commanded to indulge his sexual appetite – at most, celibacy is permitted in only the rarest of instances[60] – but not indiscriminately. With respect to the social and economic order, likewise, man is commanded to lead a full and productive life – "as the Torah was granted through

56. *Arakhin* 16b.

57. Fasting does, of course, have halakhic significance. Quite apart from several set fast days, it is regarded as a mitzva at times of crisis and is specifically linked to repentance; see Rambam, *Hilkhot Taaniyot* 1:1–2. Nevertheless, it is not conceived as part of a mortifying regimen and remains poles removed from hairshirt and sackcloth. There is, however, a secondary tradition – not, strictly speaking, halakhic – of ascetic mortification stemming from the *hasidei Ashkenaz*, medieval Franco-German pietists. See, e.g., R. Eliezer of Worms, *Sefer HaRoke'ah* (Warsaw, 1880), 8–11; and see R. S. J. Zevin, *HaMo'adim BaHalakha*, 6th ed. (Jerusalem, 1957), 65–66.

58. See *Shabbat* 118b–119a and *Pesahim* 109a; Rambam, *Hilkhot Shabbat* 30:7–10, and *Yom Tov*, 6:16–20. Yom Kippur is, of course, an exception, but its celebration, too, entails a worldly aspect; see *Shabbat* 119a. See, however, also, the controversy between R. Yehoshua and R. Eliezer as to whether festival celebration must include both Torah study and physical pleasures or whether one may devote himself exclusively to one or the other; see *Pesahim* 68b and cf., with respect to the Sabbath, Yerushalmi, *Shabbat* 15:3.

59. See, e.g., *Devarim* 12:18, 14:26, and 27:7.

60. This is based, in part, upon the need for procreation but not exclusively so. See *Yevamot* 62b and Rambam, *Hilkhot Ishut* 15:3 and 15:16.

a covenant, so was labor granted through a covenant"[61] – but he is enjoined, even with respect to the economic sphere, from becoming *homo economicus*, an agent whose decisions are guided solely by secular considerations. The basic goal is *kedusha*, not the suppression but the sanctification of world and self, and the primary means is the organization of experience around a divinely ordained normative order. This ideal links seemingly disparate areas. Rambam included laws concerning sexual behavior in the "book of holiness" – together with those governing ritual slaughter and proscribed foods – rather than in the book dealing with marriage and divorce. Raavad lumped the laws of sexual abstinence following menstruation together with a whole slew of mitzvot: injunctions concerning modes of plowing or sowing, tithes, *tzitzit*, circumcision, wearing *shaatnez* garments, blessing before and after eating, observance of Sabbath and festivals, and numerous others – all having been given "in order that man should know that he has a Creator governing him."[62] In ethical areas, the individual norms are generally ethical in character; in other areas, they may be, relatively speaking, almost arbitrary. The ideal of *kedusha* is all-pervasive, however.

The Halakha does occupy, therefore, a middle ground between secular utilitarianism and Christian asceticism. On the one hand, it not only omits but positively decries excessive self-denial:

> R. Elazar HaKappar Berabbi said: What is the point of the words: "And make an atonement for him, for that he sinned regarding the soul"? Regarding what soul did this [Nazirite] sin unless by having deprived himself of wine? Now can we not base on this an argument *a fortiori*: If a Nazirite who deprived himself only of wine is already called a sinner, how much the more so one who deprives himself of all matters?[63]

A remark cited in the Yerushalmi is even more emphatic: "R. Hizkiya [in the name of] R. Kohen in the name of Rav: 'A person is destined

61. *Avot DeRabbi Natan*, A-text, 11; p. 22b.
62. *Baalei HaNefesh*, ed. J. Kafach (Jerusalem, 1965), 15.
63. *Bava Kamma* 91b. The verse cited is from *Bemidbar* 6:11.

to render judgment regarding everything that he has seen and not partaken thereof.'"[64]

One could no doubt cite seemingly conflicting sources – students of the *Mesillat Yesharim*[65] will recall Ramhal's attempt to reconcile evidently disparate texts – and it is more than likely that within *Hazal* proper, and in the *Rishonim* certainly, we may encounter varying degrees of humanistic world-acceptance. One version of a celebrated text presents this divergence explicitly. Expanding upon the mishna, "And all your actions should be for the sake of Heaven,"[66] the *baraita* of *Avot DeRabbi Natan* comments:

> Like Hillel. When Hillel would go somewhere, people would ask him, "Where are you going?" "I'm going to do a mitzva." "What mitzva, Hillel?" "I'm going to the toilet." "Is this, then, a mitzva?" "He said to them: yes – in order that my body should not degenerate." [Or again,] "Where are you going, Hillel?" "I'm going to do a mitzva." "Which mitzva, Hillel?" "I'm going to the bathhouse." "Is this, then, a mitzva?" "He said to them: yes – in order to clean my body. By way of proof – look. If as regards icons which stand in royal palaces, the government pays their appointed polisher and cleaner a salary annually, and moreover, he is placed among the nobles of the kingdom – we, who were created in [divine] image and form, as it is said, 'For in the image of God He created man,' *a fortiori*!" Shammai would not say thus, but rather: "Let us perform[67] our duties with this body."[68]

Professor Lieberman's comment that "Shammai did not permit physical enjoyment except with the sense of one who is being gratified against

64. *Kiddushin* 4:12.

65. See chapter 13.

66. *Avot* 2:12.

67. Reading *naaseh*, as in a manuscript cited in Schecter's notes, rather than *yaaseh*, as in his printed text.

68. B-text, 30; p. 33b. Cf. *Vayikra Rabba* 34:3, which quotes essentially the same text but without Shammai's concluding dissent.

his will"[69] may overstate Shammai's dissent; but, in any event, a difference in attitude is clearly discernible.

Or, to cite a later example, the difference is perhaps reflected in two radically divergent interpretations of R. Yehuda HaNasi's deathbed statement: "Master of the world! It is revealed and known before You that I have labored in Torah with my ten fingers and have not derived pleasure even with a small finger. May it be Thy will that there be peace in my rest."[70] *Tosafot*[71] and a number of other commentators take this as a testament of lifelong renunciation. Rashi,[72] however, understands R. Yehuda HaNasi to be stating that he has not received mundane reward commensurate with the deserts of the effort expended by even one finger. Again, an element of otherworldliness is clearly present in such statements as, "R. Yehuda HaNasi says: Whoever takes upon himself pleasures of this world, the pleasures of the World to Come are withheld from him, and whoever does not take upon himself the pleasures of this world, the pleasures of the World to Come are given to him";[73] or, "Rav said: The world was but created for Ahav b. Omri and R. Hanina b. Dosa – this world for Ahav b. Omri and the next world for R. Hanina b. Dosa."[74]

Nevertheless, while these differences should not be minimized, I do not believe they erode the fundamental halakhic position. By and large, these statements concern shading and emphasis within a commonly accepted framework; and while some may sound starkly ascetic when regarded in isolation, we should not lose sight of the normative context which they take for granted and upon which they seek to provide a perspective. It was Shammai, after all, who, when he noticed a fine food on Sunday, would already set it aside for the Sabbath[75] – hardly an ascetic practice; and it was of R. Yehuda HaNasi and Antoninus that the Gemara relates that "winter or summer, lettuce, cucumbers, and radishes

69. R. Saul Lieberman, *Tosefta KiFshuta* (New York, 1955), I, 56.
70. *Ketubbot* 104a.
71. Ibid., s.v. *lo*.
72. Ibid., s.v. *velo*.
73. *Avot DeRabbi Natan*, A-text, 28; p. 43a.
74. *Berakhot* 61b.
75. See *Beitza* 16a.

were never absent from their table."[76] The primary halakhic attitude clearly discourages a rigorously ascetic posture. In some instances – as that of a fair-haired dandy who became a Nazirite in order to overcome his narcissism[77] – allowance might be made for special circumstances. Obviously, ascetic practice must ultimately be judged in the light of its motivation.[78] But these are rather the exceptions. Ordinarily, the Halakha places the Jew very much within a worldly milieu. At the level of personal piety, it instinctively assumes a framework of participation rather than renunciation; at the level of public policy, it assumes the last of what Tawney called "four main attitudes" – the first three are asceticism, indifferentism, and zeal for some particular or final reform – "which religious opinion may adopt toward the world of social institutions and economic relations."[79] Its attitude is one which "may at once accept and criticize, tolerate and amend, welcome the gross world of human appetites, as the squalid scaffolding from amid which the life of the spirit must rise, and insist that this also is the material of the Kingdom of God."[80]

But no – it goes further. The Halakha does not merely regard the mundane order as "squalid scaffolding" from which spiritual life may emerge. The mundane is itself one facet of the spiritual life – not just an arena within which spirituality may grow but, insofar as it is the subject of numerous commandments, the very fabric of halakhic living. It is not just a preliminary to religious existence but, when governed by the relevant mitzvot and halakhot, one aspect of it. For if the

76. *Avoda Zara* 11a. Antoninus was one of the Antonine emperors and a close friend of R. Yehuda HaNasi's. In the light of this and similar factual accounts, the contrasting attitudinal statements cited earlier should presumably be understood to refer to the quality and motivation of worldly consumption rather than to actual abstinence. The "enjoyment" abjured is the sybaritic pursuit of pleasure for its own sake rather than physical indulgence.

77. See *Nedarim* 9b. Upon concluding the period of his vow, the Nazirite would cut off all his hair.

78. See *Tosafot, Bava Kamma* 91b, s.v. *ela*, who suggest that when properly motivated, a Nazirite may be regarded as both holy, with respect to his goals, and a sinner, with respect to the means he employs to attain them. See also Rambam, *Hilkhot Nedarim* 13:23–24 and *Hilkhot Nezirut* 10:14.

79. R. H. Tawney, *Religion and the Rise of Capitalism* (New York, 1947), 22.

80. Ibid., 23.

Torah regards the world positively, on the one hand, it does not, on the other hand, simply leave the Jew free to mind his own store. It makes both general and specific demands, it formulates priorities, and it posits both a mode and a direction for man's exploitation of nature. Standing firmly upon its middle ground, it places pleasure within an eternal as well as a temporal framework. But perhaps we would do better to call it a third ground. Avoiding either pole of James' familiar dichotomy, the world-rejection of the sick soul and the world-acceptance of the healthy-minded, the Halakha has adhered to what C. E. Raven has justly described as "the more profound concept of world-redemption."[81] "Halakhic man," writes its leading contemporary expositor, "...fights against life's evil and struggles relentlessly with the wicked kingdom and with all the hosts of iniquity in the cosmos. His goal is not flight to another world that is wholly good, but rather bringing down that eternal world into the midst of our world."[82] Not content with the integration of the secular and the religious into a single harmonious scheme, the Halakha demands their interpenetration. The sacred must not only relate to the profane but – even as the two remain distinct – impregnate it. Halakha proclaims the central truth that while religion is, in one sense, an area of experience, in another sense it frames all experience, inasmuch as it concerns man's relation to God, the ground and goal of life itself. It is not only a quantitative but also a qualitative aspect of existence, and, as such, impinges upon every area. "All human activity," Rambam insisted, "is subsumed under *yirat shamayim*, 'the fear of Heaven.'"[83]

IV. The Need for Sacrifice

In one respect, therefore – its concern with man's mundane welfare – the Halakha is thoroughly humanistic. In others, however, it is not – at least, not in the sense in which secularists generally use the term. For one thing, its ritual aspect imposes demands which contribute little to man's temporal well-being. If the Halakha has eschewed asceticism *per se,* it has

81. *Natural Science and Christian Theology* (Cambridge, UK, 1953), II, 39–40.
82. R. Soloveitchik, *Halakhic Man,* 41.
83. *Teshuvot HaRambam,* ed. J. Blau (Jerusalem, 1960), 715.

nevertheless established norms which, at a practical level, often achieve almost the same effect. Positive commandments divert energies and resources from worldly tasks; negative injunctions may limit indulgence to the point of hardship. Neither aims directly at self-flagellation – a crucial point, philosophically. Practically, however, observance of mitzvot may necessitate severe self-denial. The Rabbis had no illusions on this score. In discussing the controversy concerning the interlude between Pesah and Shavuot – the Sadducees contended that it began on the Sunday following the first day of Pesah while the Pharisees held that the Torah's "on the morrow after the Sabbath"[84] referred to the second day of Pesah – the Gemara reports an interesting exchange. Challenged by R. Yohanan b. Zakkai, one Sadducean elder grounded his position upon the Torah's presumed compassion:

> Moses our master was a great lover of Israel and, knowing full well that Shavuot lasted only one day, he proceeded to establish it on the day after the Sabbath so that Jews should enjoy themselves for two [successive] days. [R. Yohanan b. Zakkai] quoted the following verse to him: "It is eleven days' journey from Horev unto Kadesh-Barnea by the way of Mount Seir." If Moses our master was [such] a lover of Israel, why, then, did he detain them in the wilderness for forty years?[85]

As his students pointed out to him, R. Yohanan's answer was more a flippant riposte than a serious reply. Nevertheless, it reflects a deeply ingrained awareness that both the pursuit of the normal halakhic regimen and, particularly, unswerving commitment at occasional moments of crisis can produce genuine hardship.

The oft-used phrase, "the yoke of mitzvot,"[86] not to mention common experience, attests to this point readily. The Gemara does occasionally refer to a principle that "the Torah has consideration for the money of Israel," but always within a context of sacrifice and obligation.

84. *Vayikra* 23:11.

85. *Menahot* 65a. The verse cited is from *Shemot* 1:2.

86. See, e.g., *Yevamot* 47a and *Berakhot* 13a.

Indeed, the specific instances would strike a utilitarian pragmatist as perfectly ludicrous. In one case, the principle is applied to explain why the censer used in the Temple during the year, as opposed to Yom Kippur, was silver rather than golden.[87] In another, it justifies purchasing grain rather than flour for use in preparing regular votive offerings; the former may contain impurities but it is also cheaper.[88] These savings attest to a nice sensitivity to human loss. But they are minor modifications within a program of substantial expense, and as such will hardly excite humanitarian liberals. Clearly, if the Halakha rejects outright asceticism, it has no hesitation about demanding personal sacrifice. It requires, for instance, that a Jew abandon all his property rather than actively transgress a single injunction.[89] It no doubt envisions ultimate human happiness even at the secular plane. The Bible is full of this theme and, in several places, the Talmud cites the verse "Her [i.e., the Torah's] ways are the ways of pleasantness" to establish a halakhic point.[90] But its attainment could well entail much self-denial along the way.

Secondly, far more than the particular sacrifices it requires, the very existence of Halakha rejects one aspect of humanism. As an objective normative order, Halakha shifts the center of authority from man to the law. To be sure, man plays a crucial role in interpreting and, to a point, even in shaping the law. But so long as he remains honestly committed to the system, he is no longer a final arbiter. The human element is thus diminished twofold. On the one hand, man is no longer vested with the power of ultimate decision. On the other hand, human comfort is discarded as the normal ground of decision. Not the realization of human desires but conformity to the divine law – attendant hardship notwithstanding – becomes the central objective. Special circumstances may justify limited dispensations. Ordinarily, however, the keynote is obedience rather than convenience.

87. *Yoma* 44b.

88. *Menahot* 76b.

89. See *Yoreh De'ah* 157:1.

90. *Mishlei* 3:17. See *Yevamot* 87b; *Sukka* 32a; and cf. *Tosafot, Yevamot* 2a, s.v. *ve'ahot,* and *Pesahim* 39a, s.v. *ve'eima.*

In one respect, this shift resembles the subjugation of inclination to the moral law that lies at the heart of Kantian ethics. In reality, however, the halakhic demand goes much further. The sacrifice it requires – in principle, and occasionally in practice – is not only natural inclination but moral judgment proper. As Kierkegaard so clearly perceived, the *Akeda* involved Abraham's ethical instincts as well as his son. The halakhic system thus compromises human autonomy far more than Kant's.

Nor can the halakhic demand be equated with the sacrifice of self-will – in a sense, the very sacrifice of self – that all spiritual religion urges upon its adherents. Dante's *e la sua volontade è nostra pace* – "and His will is our peace" – or Tauler's negation of selfhood posit an ideal and point a direction. They legislate little at the level of detail. The Halakha, however, with its comprehensive scope, impinges upon the minutiae of human activity. With respect to the ordinary Jew as well as the most spiritual, it is no mere general principle but a universal presence. The sacrifice of self-will that it exacts from every Jew is not, as with the mystics, just an ultimate goal. It is, albeit in a more limited mode, a point of departure.

To be a Jew means giving up something of one's autonomy. Covenantal commitment, at Sinai or later, is not so much the acknowledgment of the moral law or the assumption of specific obligations. It is, first and foremost, an act of submission. The Jew accepts not just the law but the King, not only the mitzva but the *Metzaveh*. "Why," asks the Mishna with respect to the order of the paragraphs in *Shema*, "does the portion of *Shema* precede that of *vehaya im shamo'a*? In order that he [who recites] should first accept the rule of the Kingdom of Heaven and then the rule of mitzvot."[91] This is the crux of the precedence of *naaseh*, "we shall do," to *venishma*, "and we shall hear,"[92] which the Rabbis saw as being so basic to Israel's acceptance of the Torah. Virtually by definition, however, such precedence entails some loss of autonomy. Indeed, the Rabbis refer to it as the *modus operandi* of the angels,[93] who, in Jewish thought, are generally regarded as lacking free will. Hence, the Gemara

91. *Berakhot* 13a.
92. See *Shemot* 24:7.
93. See *Shabbat* 88a.

even speaks of future mitzvot, such as Purim, as having been accepted in the desert.[94] Covenantal commitment constitutes a blank check.

The Torah itself defines Israel's position in the clearest of terms. "For they are My servants, whom I brought forth out of the land of Egypt."[95] This bondage is not just the terminus of a passionate religious quest. It is the ground of the Jew's fundamental relation to God, the point of departure for his spiritual life. Christianity has often denigrated this relation, contrasting the sonship of the new dispensation with the indentures of the old. Judaism, however, has insisted that we can be God's children only if we are His servants, and that this entails not only service but servitude. Bondage is not a propaedeutic preliminary to spiritual adulthood. It is a permanent pole within the dialectic of the religious life. On Rosh HaShana, Jews implore God, "Be it as sons, be it as servants,"[96] and small wonder. The term *eved*, servant-slave, is used in the Bible repeatedly to describe Moses, David, Abraham, and numerous others; and the threefold imagery of bondsman, subject, and son recurs throughout Scripture, the Talmud, and the *siddur* with reference to Israel's relation to God. To be sure, this bondage is regarded as the highest privilege and is defined, even in a narrow legal sense, as an asset.[97] The gift of Torah is regarded as an act of merciful grace. "R. Hananya b. Akashya used to say: The Holy One, blessed be He, wished to render Israel more worthy. Therefore, he provided them with much Torah and [many] commandments."[98] Nor is the Jew's commitment regarded as incompatible with genuine freedom. On the contrary, the Rabbis insisted that "there is no free man but he who engages in the study of Torah."[99] For, as Berdyaev noted, "Exteriorization is the source of slavery, whereas freedom is interiorization. Slavery always indicates alienation, the ejection of human nature into the external."[100] Covenantal commitment,

94. See *Shevuot* 39a.
95. *Vayikra* 25:42.
96. *High Holiday Prayer Book*, 383.
97. See *Ketubbot* 11a.
98. *Makkot* 23b.
99. *Avot* 6:2.
100. Nicolas Berdyaev, *Slavery and Freedom* (New York, 1944), 60. Of course, Berdyaev's own attitude was radically anti-halakhic; see ibid., 82–92, and his autobiographical

however, is the very opposite of such alienation. It constitutes man's turning as subject, from the objectified external to the source of being and his sole and ultimate repose. But it is bondage nonetheless, and we overlook this at our peril.

Much of this probably has a somber Calvinistic ring. It will fall harshly on ears accustomed to a more liberal and humanistic view of Judaism. But I don't see how the Torah view of the Jew's relation to God can be accurately portrayed in any other terms. It is almost ludicrous to speak of Judaism as an anthropocentric religion. Judaism is humanistic in its vision of man's worth, its concern for his well-being, and its positive approach to all aspects of his existence. But it harbors no illusions about man's servile position, a position he occupies not as a punishment for some Original Sin but simply as his natural condition; or, at a higher level, as the result of his covenantal commitment. Judaism never transposes the Creator and the creature; does not confuse means and ends; always remembers that the temporal welfare of man and society is but valuable as an instrument of attaining eternal salvation; and it inexorably asks Prospero's question – "My foot, my tutor?"[101] A Halakha that intones, "'And thou shalt love the Lord with all thy heart, and with all thy soul' – even if He takes away thy soul,"[102] can be nothing but theocentric. As if profound religion could be anything else.

Even in its worldly aspect, therefore, the Halakha is radically different from the "secular" religion now in vogue in certain Protestant circles. It is different not only from the "theology of blasphemy" (as it has been aptly titled), the blend of confused claptrap and disguised atheism currently heralding the new dawn of human dominion. The halakhic attitude is different even from that of a figure like Bonhoeffer, whose profound faith and saintly sensibility experienced God as a living presence but who felt that, for the average man at any rate, God would now only be relevant incognito, as it were. Bonhoeffer saw himself on the verge of an age in which man would no longer approach God best by seeking Him consciously within a religious mold, but rather simply

---

Dream and Reality (New York, 1962), 56 ff.

101. *The Tempest*, I, ii, 469.

102. *Berakhot* 61b. The verse cited is from *Devarim* 6:5.

by finding Him through immersion in the secular order, through active devotion to improving the lot of mankind. In a passage that has been worn threadbare with quotation he suggested that

> the time when men could be told everything by means of words, whether theological or simply pious, is over, and so is the time of inwardness and conscience, which is to say the time of religion as such. We are proceeding toward a time of no religion at all: men as they are now simply cannot be religious any more.... Religious people speak of God when human perception is (often just from laziness) at an end, or human resources fail: it is in fact always the *Deus ex machina* they call to their aid, either for the so-called solving of insoluble problems or as support in human failure – always, that is to say, helping out human weakness or on the borders of human existence. Of necessity, that can only go on until men can, by their own strength, push those borders a little further, so that God becomes superfluous as a *Deus ex machina*.[103]

Or again:

> Is it not true to say that individualistic concern for personal salvation has almost completely left us all? Are we not really under the impression that there are more important things than bothering about such a matter? (Perhaps not more important than the matter itself, but more than bothering about it.) I know it sounds pretty monstrous to say that. But is it not, at bottom, even biblical? Is there any concern in the Old Testament about saving one's soul at all? Is not righteousness and the kingdom of God on earth the focus of everything...? It is not with the next world that we are concerned, but with this world as created and preserved and set subject to laws and atoned for and made new.[104]

103. Dietrich Bonhoeffer, *Letters and Papers from Prison* (London, 1959), 91, 93.
104. Ibid., 94.

What Bonhoeffer anticipated – clearly, with rather mixed emotions – some of his popularizers – often, with far less spiritual sensitivity – have positively trumpeted. Dr. Cox's paean to megalopolis barely stops short of naming the post-religious age the eschatological.[105] The Jew stands on wholly different ground, however. Bonhoeffer's analysis is grounded upon a Christian, and especially a Lutheran, outlook to which it has a special relevance. Its central premise is a salvific conception of religion, and it conditions man to see God primarily as a savior rescuing him from the morass of his own impotence. To the Jew, however, God is as much a commander as a redeemer, perhaps even more so. Hence, for one thing, increased mastery over his environment, while it may have serious spiritual repercussions, will exert a less decisive impact upon him than upon the Christian. More important, however, God's commanding posture vitiates the antithesis between religion and activism. For what God commands is not merely the contemplation of one's religious navel. It is – at least, much of it is – action; and a great deal of that action entails laboring in "worldly" vineyards.[106] It is perfectly true, as R. Kook has noted,[107] that the Bible – and the Halakha as well – does not place exclusive or even direct primary stress upon individualistic striving for personal salvation. The Torah is equally concerned with forging a sacral society. "The ideal of halakhic man," as R. Soloveitchik has written, "is the redemption of the world not via a higher world but via the world itself, via the adaptation of empirical reality to the ideal patterns of Halakha."[108] And this adaptation has its public aspect. "Halakhic man's

105. See Harvey Cox, *The Secular City*, rev. ed. (New York, 1966), 95 ff.

106. It might be added that not only the problem but the limits of the proposed solution are different for the Jew. "Being with God in the world" has, in one sense, a far more immediate ring for the Christian than it can have for him.

107. See R. Avraham Y. Kook, *Orot*, 2nd ed. (Jerusalem, 1961), 109–15. R. Kook notes and laments the fact that, in the post-biblical period, and especially in the Diaspora, the individualistic element became so much more prominent among Jews. It should be emphasized, however, that R. Kook's periodization is not premised upon the presumed contrast between biblical and halakhic Judaism sometimes postulated by non-traditional historians. R. Kook of course envisioned both elements as parts of an organic unity. He is rather lamenting a shift, within that single framework, from a broader to a narrower focus.

108. *Halakhic Man*, 37–38.

religious viewpoint is highly exoteric.... The ideal of eternal life is not the private domain of a small spiritual elite or some particularly gifted individuals, but is the public domain of all Israel."[109]

Precisely, however, because his religion impels him normatively to establish an ideal "secular" order, the Jew need not – indeed, cannot – abandon it so that he may improve the world. In Rabbi Professor Twersky's words, he acts "for the sake of humanity *because* of religious conviction and obligation."[110] Judaism thus diverges sharply from the position outlined by Bonhoeffer and since championed by exponents of the secular city.[111] With them, it regards secular activity as related to man's quest for God; it sees the temporal order as an instrument of its own transcendence; and it stresses social involvement as an integral aspect of the spiritual life. However, Judaism does not consider activism as a possible substitute for religion. It regards it as a part – but only a part – *of* religion. It does not suggest that we abandon our conscious and even formal quest for God in the hope that we may find Him all the better as we strive to improve the temporal human condition. Instead, it demands that we commit ourselves to Him and then consecrate the mundane by imposing God-given categories upon it. Not content to accept the secular world on its own terms, it attempts to permeate our experience of it with religious awareness. Improving the human condition is important, but not self-sufficient; and it is not to be considered in isolation. The social and economic sphere is not only a milieu for raising the standard of living, essential as that may be. It is one arena among many for implementing divine law as part of a heroic effort to embrace

---

109. Ibid., 42.

110. R. Isadore Twersky, "Some Aspects of the Jewish Attitude toward the Welfare State," *Tradition*, V (1963): 143; my italics. See, generally, 139–45, and references; and see also R. Walter S. Wurzburger, "Pluralism and the Halakha," *Tradition*, IV (1962): 221–39, who argues – rather convincingly, I think – that the Halakha generally encourages an activist rather than a quietist relation to the world.

111. For a sharp reaction to Cox's book proper, and especially to some of its statements concerning Judaism, see Steven S. Schwarzschild, "A Little Bit of a Revolution?" in *The Secular City Debate*, ed. Daniel Callahan (New York, 1966), 145–55; and cf. Cox's equally acerbic reply, 183–85.

the totality of experience within a harmonious order consecrated to God and pervaded by consciousness of Him.

To the modern secularist, the effort may occasionally appear naïve. He is accustomed to think of finance much as he thinks of mechanics; and he regards the market as the dominion of little but economic muscle and human avarice. He may admire, in Tawney's words, "the endeavor to draw the most commonplace of human activities and the least tractable of human appetites within the all-embracing circle of a universal system,"[112] as a noble albeit futile experiment; and, in reflecting upon its history, he may agree that "it had in it something of the heroic, and to ignore the nobility of the conception is not less absurd than to idealize its practical results."[113] But he may find it difficult to repress a smile. The Jew is in dead earnest, however. He feels the sanctification of all of life can be attained and must be attained. And he feels this is best done by remembering God rather than ignoring Him.

In one respect, I am of course oversimplifying. The halakhic life is not a neat two-step affair: commitment and acceptance followed by mechanical implementation. It is a dialectical process. The world is not just a *mise-en-scène* in which pre-fabricated personalities routinely apply preconceived orders. It is, in Keats' phrase, "the vale of soul-making."[114] The ethical life – of which social involvement is an essential ingredient – does indeed both enrich man and bring him closer to God. All the more so, however, to the extent that he acts, in Milton's words, "as ever in my great Task-master's eye."[115] Activism and religious commitment, far from being opposed, reinforce and sustain each other. "I have set the Lord always before me."[116] This verse, cited and glossed by Rama in the very opening codicil of the *Shulhan Arukh,*[117] epitomizes the whole of Judaism.

---

112. *Religion and the Rise of Capitalism*, 58.
113. Ibid., 60.
114. *The Letters of John Keats, 1814–1821,* ed. H. E. Rollins (Cambridge, Mass., 1958), II, 102; April 21, 1819.
115. "How Soon Hath Time…," 14.
116. *Tehillim* 16:8.
117. OH 1:1.

Finally, the traditional Jew parts company with the champions of the secular city in yet another respect – as regards not only the mode of approaching the world but also the value ultimately attached to it. He is earnest; ideally not dour, but dead earnest nonetheless. Yet, there is a point beyond which he cannot take the vicissitudes of human life as seriously as the professional humanist. There is a level at which, in attitude although not in practice, he transcends the world after all. Even on his mundane side, he goes no further than Dunbar's pithy prescription: "Man, please thy Maker, and be merry, / And give not for this world a cherry."[118] With R. Eliezer, he cannot but wonder at those who "put aside life eternal and occupy themselves with life temporal."[119] Not that he neglects "life temporal." He knows that, on the one hand, "one hour of spiritual repose in the World to Come is finer than all the life of this world," yet, on the other hand, "one hour in penitence and good deeds in this world is finer than all the World to Come"[120] – and "good deeds" includes a passionate concern with improving man's temporal condition. He realizes that the transient is not only transitory but transitional. Yet the very fact that the world derives its significance precisely from its transitional character, from being a "vestibule" rather than a "palace,"[121] must alter the Jew's perspective. In the religious life, perspective is all-important.

V. Halakhic Dispensations: *Pikuah Nefesh*

The scope and limits of Judaism's concern for man's secular welfare are best seen through an analysis of the basic framework of what might be called the normal or fundamental Halakha. They may also be seen, however, by a study of the extent to which the Halakha has sanctioned exceptional deviations from its ordinary norms. The very concept of

118. Quoted in C. S. Lewis, *The Four Loves* (London, 1963), 84.
119. *Beitza* 15b.
120. *Avot* 4:22.
121. See *Avot* 4:21. Of course, the Mishna there deals with the plane of personal existence. At a universal plane, history may no doubt have greater intrinsic significance. Still, the basic distinction I am making holds up. For a characteristic statement, see Ramban's preface to *Torat HaAdam* (Jerusalem, 1955).

deviation poses a crucial difficulty – a difficulty amply illustrated by a striking quotation. "The Catholic Church," wrote Newman,

> holds it better for the sun and moon to drop from heaven, for the earth to fail, and for all the many millions who are upon it to die of starvation in extremest agony, as far as temporal affliction goes, than that one soul, I will not say, should be lost, but should commit one venial sin, should tell one wilful untruth, though it harmed no one, or should steal one poor farthing without excuse.[122]

Contemporaries may find it difficult to believe that this sentence was not written by a virulent critic of Roman Catholicism but rather by one of its leading nineteenth-century spokesmen – indeed, by one of its most *liberal* spokesmen, and, *mirabile dictu*, in a work addressed to Anglicans, at that. It may seem more incredible still that when the statement was attacked by Charles Kingsley, Newman deliberately repeated and defended it.[123] The very harshness of the dictum serves, however, to point up the dimensions of the problem to which, in context, it addresses itself. The difference between temporal and eternal bliss is one of kind rather than duration. As the metaphysician holds that timeless eternity is not to be confused with infinite time, so the moralist contends that no amount of mundane joy can equal a single grain of transcendental bliss. Since he "regards this world, and all that is in it, as a mere shade, as dust and ashes, compared with the value of one single soul," he "considers the action of this world and the action of the soul simply incommensurate, viewed in their respective spheres."[124] The difference between

---

122. John Henry Newman, *Lectures on Certain Difficulties Felt by Anglicans in Submitting to the Catholic Church* (London, 1850), 199.

123. Interestingly enough, Kingsley, although he does twit Newman for writing in a manner "shocking to plain English notions," criticizes the passage not so much because of its extreme nature as because it is inconsistent with Newman's position that lying is sometimes permissible. See his pamphlet, "What, Then, Does Dr. Newman Mean?" in *Newman's Apologia Pro Vita Sua: The Two Versions of 1864 and 1865, Preceded by Newman's and Kingsley's Pamphlets*, ed. Wilfrid Ward (Oxford, 1913), 46; and cf. Newman's reply on p. 339.

124. *Lectures on Certain Difficulties*, 199.

them being qualitative rather than quantitative, no measure of physical or emotional good can compensate for even the minutest spiritual evil. Hence, once a normative duty has been established, it becomes inviolate. Moral and religious law defines principles of right and wrong, and henceforth – except insofar as that law itself provides for dispensations – these can be sacrificed to nothing.

Given its premises, Newman's position, paradoxically harsh as it may seem, is grounded upon an inexorable logic. The Church is right in insisting that it "would rather save the soul of one single wild bandit of Calabria, or whining beggar of Palermo, than draw a hundred lines of railroad through the length of Italy or carry out a sanitary reform, in its fullest details, in every city of Sicily, except so far as these great national works tended to some spiritual good beyond them."[125]

The premises need not be granted, however. These are – apart from the generally religious conception of man and the universe – primarily two: first, that specific normative absolutes exist; and second, that the moral law itself does not provide for their abrogation under emergency conditions. The first premise, its prestigious history notwithstanding, has come under considerable contemporary attack, even from religious quarters – precisely, in part because its application often seemed to produce excessively harsh results. To a humanitarian temper, Kant's discussion of the *notlüge,* "the necessary lie" – whether, for instance, I may falsely deny to a potential murderer that his intended victim is in my home – is surrounded by an air of unreality. It seems not only doctrinaire but downright silly. From a Jewish point of view, however, the existence of normative absolutes is beyond question. They are the very substance of the revelation manifested in the Torah; some, perhaps even antecedent to it.

The second premise is quite another matter, however, and – from a halakhic perspective – thoroughly inadmissible. The Halakha has recognized several grounds which justify – at times, even require – the violation of its normal standards. These may be subsumed under two broad categories: one consists of specific elements that, in accordance with fairly rigorous formulae, may override certain norms; the other

125. Ibid.

consists of more general extenuating factors, perhaps a bit amorphous in character, which allow for dispensations due to extraordinary circumstances. The first may be described as an ingredient determining the basic law governing a situation; the latter, as an escape hatch providing temporary relief from it. In a sense, one set of elements enters into the formulation of fundamental Halakha; another – still halakhically sanctioned, of course – permits deviation from it. Both, however, override ordinary normative demands out of sensitivity to the humanitarian dimensions of a given situation, and both, in this sense, reflect the humanistic aspect of Halakha.

Of the elements subsumed under the first category, *pikuah nefesh*, "the preservation of life," is both the most obvious and the most comprehensive. With but several significant exceptions, all halakhic injunctions, positive or negative, are set aside when they entail a possible loss of life.[126] The danger may be neither likely nor immediate, but so long as it can reasonably be said to exist, even in a remote sense, it suspends all ordinary halakhic duties. Or rather, in dangerous circumstances *pikuah nefesh* itself constitutes the highest duty. Saving a life can hardly be a matter of option. "The quick one," says the Yerushalmi, "is praiseworthy; whoever is asked [i.e., whether one may proceed with a violation], repugnant; and he who [pauses] to ask [i.e., whether he may proceed], like a murderer."[127] Or as Rambam put it: "It is forbidden to hesitate with Sabbath violation as regards a dangerously ill person, for it is said 'which a man shall do them [i.e., the mitzvot] and live by them,' and not that he shall die by them. Hence you learn that the laws of the Torah are not a [source of] destruction in the world but of lovingkindness, compassion, and peace in the world."[128] Even martyrdom, on Rambam's view[129] – except when fully mandatory – is absolutely forbidden and tantamount to suicide.

---

126. See *Sanhedrin* 74a–b; Rambam, *Hilkhot Yesodei HaTorah* 5:1–3.

127. *Yoma* 8:5. The authority whose opinion was sought is evidently criticized for not having educated the public previously.

128. *Hilkhot Shabbat* 2:1. The verse cited is from *Vayikra* 18:5.

129. See *Hilkhot Yesodei HaTorah* 5:4. Many *Rishonim* disagree; see, e.g., *Tosafot, Avoda Zara,* 27b, s.v. *yakhol.* Even on their view, however, one may only choose death rather than "transgression" when coerced to choose by an oppressor. Under such circumstances, he fulfills the mitzva of *kiddush Hashem* by suffering martyrdom.

The precedence of *pikuah nefesh* over other duties rests on one of two grounds. One is the biblical verse cited in the passage I have quoted from Rambam. The second is a rational, almost actuarial, consideration of the net long-term effects of saving a life in danger: "'And the children of Israel shall keep the Sabbath.' The Torah said: Profane for his sake one Sabbath, so that he may keep many Sabbaths."[130] While either source ordinarily constitutes a sufficient rationale, the two are conceptually poles apart. The first affirms the primacy of one value over another – of preserving human life over observing ritual laws. Hence, it reflects, to however limited an extent, a humanistic concern. The second merely calculates that, even in the interest of ritual observance proper, its temporary abrogation is in order. Normally, of course, the more incisive thrust of the first reason would obviate the need for the second. There are, however, situations to which only the second may be relevant. Ramban[131] cited the second justification, for instance, as the basis of his contention that *pikuah nefesh* extends to a fetus even before the fortieth day of conception, although, for other purposes, such a fetus is not yet regarded as a "life." Or again, the possible extension of "preservation" to include not only saving a person from physical extinction but from spiritual death as well – from insanity or apostasy,[132] for instance – may very well depend upon the validity of the second ground. Finally, it is entirely possible that the Gemara felt specifically constrained to advance this reason with respect to the Sabbath because the Scriptural "and he shall live by them" might not have applied to it. In view of its gravity – "the Sabbath and idolatry are, each of them, equal to all the other mitzvot of the Torah,"[133]

In the absence of coercion and resistance, however, no authorities would permit dying rather than, let us say, eating non-kosher food.

130. *Yoma* 85b. The verse cited is from *Shemot* 31:16.

131. *Torat HaAdam*, 11. Cf. also Rambam, *Hilkhot Mamrim* 2:4.

132. R. Hayyim Soloveitchik regarded both as constituting *pikuah nefesh*. I know of no written source concerning insanity. As to apostasy, see *Orah Hayim* 306:14 and commentaries. I cite R. Hayyim's view as I have heard it from his grandson, R. Joseph B. Soloveitchik. I do not know for certain, however, whether his decision was based upon the reason I have suggested; upon the fear that insanity might lead to actual physical danger; or, finally, upon the idea that insanity *per se* is a kind of spiritual death.

133. Rambam, *Hilkhot Shabbat* 30:15.

and its rejection, insofar as it implies a denial of the creation and providence, is regarded as a form of apostasy[134] – Sabbath violation might conceivably have been included among the exceptions to *pikuah nefesh*. Only the pragmatic self-interest of Sabbath proper, as it were, sanctions the extension of the concept to it.

In light of this distinction, I believe the dual source may be salient in another significant context, with respect to the thorny issue of the inclusion of Gentiles in the category of *pikuah nefesh*. As regards the first source, the response to a question of *pikuah nefesh* may very well be positive.[135] With respect to the second, however – i.e., the possible suspension of Sabbath observance at one point in order to facilitate and engender much fuller observance subsequently – this factor obviously only obtains with respect to the community which has been covenantally charged with *shemirat Shabbat*. Hence, on this view, discussions in the Gemara and subsequently regarding the suspension of halakhic norms in the interests of the *pikuah nefesh* of Gentiles have focused upon Shabbat, as it would be clearly permissible in the case of other prohibitions.[136]

VI. Halakhic Dispensations: *Kevod HaBeriyyot, Shalom, Tzaar*

The preservation of life constitutes the most obvious ground for abrogating halakhic norms, but it is by no means the only one. Preserving something of its quality – the maintenance of personal dignity or domestic peace, specifically – constitutes another. Logically enough, the dispensation provided by these factors is far narrower than that deriving from *pikuah nefesh*. While mortal danger suspends all but a handful of laws, the preemptive power of *kevod haberiyyot* or *shalom* is more limited in scope. The precise limits are in dispute. As regards the former, the generally accepted view – based upon the conclusion of the discussion in

134. See *Hullin* 5a and Rashi, s.v. *alma*.

135. This may depend on the semantic nuances of the term *adam*, as it appears in the Torah. See *Sanhedrin* 59a, *Yevamot* 61a, and *Bava Kamma* 38a.

136. I have limited these remarks to one aspect of the topic. Fuller discussion would of course include far more evidence, textual and historical, as well as the analysis of relevant halakhic and hashkafic variables.

a gemara in *Berakhot* – is that it only suspends rabbinic ordinances or, at most, permits the passive violation of biblical precepts.[137] The Yerushalmi, however, cites opposing views as to whether *kevod haberiyyot* may even sanction the active violation of *deoraita* commandments.[138] Indeed, in another passage the Yerushalmi evidently assumes that the principle certainly can override commandments of the Torah – at least, when the honor of a public is at stake.[139]

Rambam takes a somewhat median position. He writes that "*kevod haberiyyot* does not override a negative injunction which is [explicitly] expounded in the Torah."[140] His phrasing clearly suggests that *kevod haberiyyot* would override norms which, while not explicitly formulated in the Torah, are derived therefrom through certain exegetical and hermeneutical principles. This view is in line with his general position[141] that such norms, while generally enjoying full biblical force, nevertheless are, for some purposes, weaker than those expressly stated. Finally, the most restrictive view is that of Rabbenu Hananel,[142] who holds that not even all rabbinic ordinances can be overridden. Only those which are wholly novel and which, lacking a *deoraita* background or archetype, in no way constitute an extension of a biblical norm may be set aside in the interests of *kevod haberiyyot*.

As regards *shalom*, the situation is, if anything, even more murky. There is no full-blown talmudic discussion suggesting guidelines for its dispensation. There is no doubt, however, that this very fact, plus the limited nature of the specific applications we do encounter, clearly indicates that this principle's range is also relatively restricted. These applications are varied. There is, first, a matter of priority. Confrontation

---

137. *Berakhot* 19b–20a. See also *Shabbat* 81b and 94b.
138. *Kilayim* 9:1; p. 40b.
139. *Berakhot* 3:1; p. 24a.
140. *Hilkhot Kilayim* 10:29.
141. See, e.g., *Hilkhot Shevuot* 5:7, as explained by *Hiddushei HaRan, Shevuot* 23b; and, for a possible theoretical basis, *Sefer HaMitzvot*, "Principles," 2. The import of the latter passage is in dispute, however. See commentaries, ad loc., and *Siftei Kohen*, HM 33:1. Cf. also *Teshuvot HaRambam*, II, 631–33; and see J. J. Neubauer, *HaRambam Al Divrei Sofrim* (Jerusalem, 1957).
142. Cited in Ramban, *Torat HaAdam*, 37–38.

between two norms may take one of two forms. Either the fulfillment of one requires direct violation of the other, as when a positive commandment can only be realized by breaking a negative. Or the conflict may be indirect, as when the allocation of time or resources to meeting one need necessitates ignoring another. At the level of priority, the Gemara states that a mitzva related to maintaining peace takes precedence over another which does not. If only a single candle is available, for instance, it should be used for the Sabbath rather than for Hanukka.[143] Going beyond this, the Yerushalmi[144] perhaps assumes that the preservation of domestic peace proper, quite apart from any mitzva related to it, justifies the neglect of rabbinic commandments. Thus, a fiancé may visit his prospective in-laws although he must therefore forgo burning his *hametz*.

These are marginal instances, however, and provide little insight concerning when, if ever, the threat to domestic or communal peace warrants the direct violation of halakhic norms. Such violation is apparently sanctioned by numerous texts stating that one may lie – or, as another version has it, should lie – in the interests of peace.[145] Indeed, the rabbis ascribe such prevarication to God Himself. For when Sarah questioned the prediction of her pregnancy, she thought, "After I am waxed old shall I have pleasure, my lord being old also?" Yet, in the very next verse we read that God asked Abraham, "Wherefore did Sarah laugh, saying: 'Shall I of a surety bear a child, being old?'"[146]

143. See *Shabbat* 23b.

144. *Pesahim* 3:7; p. 23b. This text is not wholly conclusive because perhaps it deals exclusively with a person who had already begun such a visit and who is then not required to cut it short. See, analogously, Rambam, *Hilkhot Hametz UMatza* 3:9, and cf. *Zevahim* 100a. Furthermore, it is conceivable that the obligation to burn *hametz* and the prohibition against keeping it apply only when one possesses it willfully. If he is aware of its existence but cannot, for some reason, destroy it, perhaps he is not merely regarded as duty-bound but not held accountable due to extenuating circumstances. He is not subsumed under these norms at all. See Rambam, ibid., 3:8, and *Kesef Mishneh*. If this be true at a *deoraita* level, it may also apply to the rabbinic commandment to burn *hametz* even after one has disavowed it. In that case, this text may have no universal implications.

145. See *Yevamot* 65b; *Sifre, Naso,* 42; *Vayikra Rabba,* 9:9 and analogues cited there in *Yad Yosef*. Cf. also *Sota* 41b and Yerushalmi, *Pe'ah* 1:1; p. 4b.

146. *Bereshit* 18:12–13.

Nevertheless, one may question whether the principle implied here will apply equally to other transgressions. If popular morality be any guide, certain forms of lying are regularly granted a license we should hardly accord other legal or moral violations. Indeed, so-called "white" lies are not regarded as lies at all, just a social amenity. Nor is this notion merely popular. Despite recent outcries against the "Sylvester doctrine" and the subsequent development of the "credibility gap," the idea that a government or an individual often has the right or even the duty to sacrifice literal truth to other interests has a long and honorable history. Readers of Newman's *Apologia* will recall the body of Catholic and Anglican casuistic literature that he marshals in support of this doctrine;[147] and there is no question that the Halakha had, long before, already advanced this position. The *locus classicus* is, of course, the celebrated controversy between the disciples of Shammai and of Hillel concerning the proper procedure at wedding feasts:

> How does one dance [i.e., and sing] before the bride? Beit Shammai say: "The bride as she is." Beit Hillel say: "Beautiful and graceful bride!" Beit Shammai said to Beit Hillel: "If she is lame or blind, does one say of her: 'Beautiful and graceful bride'? But the Torah said, 'Keep yourself far from any false matter.'" Beit Hillel [then] said to Beit Shammai: "According to you, if one has made a bad purchase in the market, should one praise it in his eyes or deprecate it? Surely, one should praise it in his eyes. Hence, the Sages said, 'A man's disposition toward people should always be pleasant.'"[148]

As usual, Beit Hillel's opinion prevailed, and its underlying principle is reflected in a number of relevant texts. Even the most honest – to whom one may return a lost object on the basis of their mere recognition without any identifying marks whatsoever – are presumed to lie in response

147. See 360–71 and especially Note G. on "Lying and Equivocation," 436–63.

148. *Ketubbot* 17a. The verse cited is from *Shemot* 23:7. It should be added that *Tosafot*, s.v. *kalla*, comment that, even according to Beit Shammai, one should either be silent or cite other praises but certainly not present the insulting truth.

to certain questions. If extended lavish hospitality, for instance, they may lie about it to those who would then beat a quick path to their host's door; or if asked about details of their sexual life, they may not only parry the question but, where the interests of modesty require, answer it falsely.[149] Moreover, a number of incidents cited in the Talmud clearly reflect the implementation of Beit Hillel's principle.[150]

Hence, the gemara which states that "it is permissible to alter [a statement] in the interest of peace" must be regarded an insufficient basis for extending this license to other transgressions. To date, no responsible authority has suggested that one may violate biblical or even rabbinic ordinances in order to enliven a wedding feast or prevent unwanted guests from taxing a former host. Evidently, a measure of disingenuousness is tolerated and even encouraged because it is not regarded as lying at all, truth and truth-telling being somewhat flexibly defined. As a recent writer put it, "Here" – he is speaking of God's "prevarication" to Abraham –

> it is not a matter of overriding truth in the interests of peace, as the Sabbath is overridden by *pikuah nefesh* or injunctions concerning impurity by public sacrifices. Here we have a different insight into the concept of truth. God's name is peace and His stamp is truth,[151] and between the name and the stamp there can be no contradiction, else it constitutes a forgery. The truth, however, lies in "and I have aged." There is psychic truth and lip-truth or the truth of mere fact. Genuine truth is always the psychic.[152]

As Newman put it, "It is not more than a hyperbole to say that, in certain cases, a lie is the nearest approach to truth."[153]

149. See *Bava Metzia* 23b–24a. See also Rif and Tosafot, s.v. *ushpiza*, who discuss the relation of this text to that of *Yevamot* 65b.

150. See, e.g., *Pesahim* 5a (but note the very relevant controversy between Rashi and *Tosafot* there), *Shabbat* 129a, and *Sanhedrin* 11a.

151. See *Shabbat* 10b and *Berakhot* 13b.

152. R. Avraham Hen, *BeMalkhut HaYahadut* (Jerusalem, 1959), I, 294–95.

153. *Sermons, Chiefly on the Theory of Religious Belief* (London, 1844), 343.

Injunctions narrowly defined in purely physical terms are not as amenable to being stretched, however; and with respect to them, one may validly raise a question as to whether they may indeed be overridden in the interest of *shalom*. Rama thought they certainly could.[154] Partly on the basis of the gemara concerning white lies but primarily on the strength of an aggadic text, he states unequivocally that even *deoraita* injunctions may be violated in order to attain social or domestic harmony. His only hesitation is that this may apply only to commandments "between man and God," not to those "between man and man." He concludes, however, that the latter, too – the case at issue involved slander – are included. However, the failure of other *posekim* to develop this principle suggests, *de silentio*, that Rama's perspective may be a minority view. The limits of the dispensation provided by *shalom* therefore remain shrouded in uncertainty.

Whatever the precise limits, however, it is clear that, in one sense, the scope of *kevod haberiyyot* and *shalom* is much more restricted than that of *pikuah nefesh*. And yet, in another sense, it is far broader. Concern for dignity or tranquility may not be as decisive a consideration but it applies to an immeasurably greater number of situations. It is not often that literal life or death hangs in the balance. The fracture of personal worth or social harmony may be a daily occurrence. We should remember that the Halakha has been extremely sensitive to all forms of embarrassment. There are even laws prohibiting the disgrace of inanimate objects. According to one interpretation, we cover the *halla* while making *kiddush* over wine, "so as not to shame the bread."[155] Not, of course, because of some primitive animism, but because the Halakha's concern for respect and dignity has been so wide-ranging. People concerned about shaming bread have a reminder not to insult their fellows. Commenting on the verse, "Neither shalt thou go up by steps unto Mine altar, that thy nakedness be not uncovered thereof,"[156] the *Mekhilta* comments: "Now, this is an *a fortiori* matter. If, with respect to stones which have no sense for better or for worse, the Holy One, blessed be He, said,

---

154. *Teshuvot HaRama*, 11.

155. *Mordekhai, Pesahim* 100b (in the *Tosefet MeArvei Pesahim* section).

156. *Shemot* 20:23.

'Do not treat them disdainfully' – your fellow who is in the image of He who spoke and the world came into being, certainly you should not treat with disdain."[157] Given this kind of sensitivity, events impinging upon dignity and peace may be common indeed.

This very frequently sharpens the problem posed by *kevod haberiyyot* and *shalom*. It is, quite simply, the problem of definition. Whatever the difficulties attendant upon defining the nature and scope of *pikuah nefesh*[158] – and they are formidable – they seem almost elementary when compared to the challenge presented by concepts so broad and so amorphous as "personal dignity" and "peace." In this context, *shalom* does not denote solely the avoidance of war. That would naturally come under *pikuah nefesh*. *Shalom* here includes the avoidance of strife; or, to put it in more positive terms, social or domestic harmony. Hence, the number of situations in which either factor might be somewhat affected is almost limitless. Yet, some limit must clearly be set. No legal system could long survive if it regarded even slight impact upon human dignity or interpersonal harmony as sufficient justification for overriding its norms. So the nagging question persists: Where can we draw the line?

Unfortunately, basic halakhic sources here provide only limited guidance. At most, they supply us with raw material but not with definitions proper. As regards *kevod haberiyyot*, the Gemara cites only a few instances: ensuring prompt and proper burial of a corpse; personal hygiene and dignity as related to the function of excretion; and the avoidance of disrobing in public.[159] These are all fairly drastic circumstances. Collectively, they would set a standard restricting the license of *kevod*

157. *Yitro, Masekhta DeBaHodesh*, 11.

158. These concern primarily two questions: 1) the extent, if any, to which a mortal danger need be clear, immediate, and specifically related to a particular individual or group; 2) the possibility, if any, that any cause of public physical injury comes under *pikuah nefesh*, although no potential loss of life is apparent – either because we fear, statistically, that one person may die after all or, although this is logically difficult, because mass injury proper constitutes *pikuah nefesh*. These are, of course, basic and highly relevant issues but they deserve full independent discussion and cannot be treated within the confines of this essay, let alone in a footnote.

159. See *Berakhot* 19b; *Shabbat* 81b and 94b; *Eiruvin* 41b; and *Menahot* 37b.

haberiyyot to very few situations indeed. Nevertheless, it is possible that the concept may be construed more broadly.

Rashi, in any event, evidently did. The Gemara in *Hullin* states: "A man should not open [for a guest] casks of wine which are to be sold by the shopkeeper, unless he informs the guest of it.... If, however, the purpose is to show the guest great respect, it is permissible."[160] In commenting upon the passage, Rashi notes: "It is permissible – for great is *kevod haberiyyot*."[161] The halakha cited in the text could of course be interpreted otherwise. Inasmuch as the injunction concerns the element of deception, it is confined to deception motivated by self-aggrandizement. If, however, one engages in the practice not in order to ingratiate himself but in order to enhance the position of another, it is innocuous. The problem is analogous to that of complimenting someone, in which case the motivation – whether it be ingratiation through flattery or supporting someone else's ego – makes a crucial ethical and halakhic difference. However, Rashi's quotation of the precise formulation used in the texts concerning *kevod haberiyyot* strongly suggests that he interpreted this gemara by reference to that general concept rather than in purely local terms.

Nor is the reason hard to find. The legal underpinnings of the license of *kevod haberiyyot* are nowhere clearly formulated in the Talmud. It is ordinarily assumed that it is grounded upon the Rabbis' legislative authority with respect to their own injunctions.[162] Inasmuch as these are their own creation, they could of course provide as they saw fit for their occasional suspension. As regards *deoraita* injunctions, their passive violation could be sanctioned by the principle – exemplified, for instance, in our not blowing *shofar* when Rosh HaShana falls on the Sabbath – that "the Rabbis have the authority to uproot a law of the Torah in a case of abstention."[163] As for their active violation, which such rabbinic authority could not sanction – it cannot, indeed, be licensed by

160. *Hullin* 94a.
161. S.v. *mutar*.
162. In *Berakhot* 19b, Rashi himself, s.v. *kol mili*, offers this explanation.
163. *Yevamot* 90b.

kevod haberiyyot. Rashi,[164] however, cites a different source – a principle initially qualifying the mitzva of returning lost property but potentially having more universal relevance. On the basis of a somewhat unusual construction found in a verse, the Rabbis comment that despite the injunction, "Thou mayest not hide thyself [i.e., so as to avoid returning lost objects],"[165] there are times when one may hide himself. One of the instances cited is "if he [i.e., the finder] is an elder and it is not in accordance with his dignity."[166] Clearly, if the license of *kevod haberiyyot* is derived from this source, be it even solely by analogy, it must extend far beyond prompt burial or avoiding nudity.

Rambam likewise extends the bounds of this license. After establishing the principle that a *kohen* "may defile himself with a rabbinically ordained impurity for *kevod haberiyyot*," he goes on to exemplify: "For instance, if a mourner enters a *beit hapras*,[167] everyone may follow him there in order to console him."[168] The implications of this example fall

164. *Shabbat* 81b, s.v. *shedoheh*. Cf. *Turei Even*, *Megilla* 3b.
165. *Devarim* 22:1.
166. *Berakhot* 19b.
167. A field in which a grave has been plowed up.
168. *Hilkhot Evel* 3:14. This halakha is, of course, found in *Berakhot* 19b and does not originate with Rambam. However, the Gemara does not relate this dispensation to *kevod haberiyyot* specifically. One might, for instance, see it as deriving from the mitzva of comforting mourners. Secondly, it only mentions the dispensation with reference to *beit hapras* whose impurity, inasmuch as it is grounded upon uncertainty, may be weaker than that of other rabbinic sources of defilement. In this case, therefore, the prohibition may be initially and internally circumscribed rather than overridden by an extraneous factor. This view is buttressed by the fact that a *kohen* may enter a *beit hapras* – or places of similar status – whenever this is essential to the performance of a mitzva; see *Semahot* 4:25–26 and *Avoda Zara* 13a. Rambam, however, while, at the beginning of this halakha, he restricts the license cited in *Semahot* to the category of *beit hapras*, permits defilement by *all* rabbinic impurities in order to comfort the mourner. Hence, he felt virtually constrained to invoke the general principle of *kevod haberiyyot*. It should be noted, further, that he similarly goes on to include all rabbinic defilements in a third dispensation granted to recover property unjustly expropriated by Gentiles. The *baraita* in *Semahot* included this license in one catalogue with defilement for the purpose of mitzva. Rambam, however, inasmuch as he evidently gave the two dispensations different scope, was careful to formulate them separately. It might be added, finally, that the Yerushalmi, evidently reading *mipnei kevod haam*, assumed the text in *Semahot*

short of Rashi's, but they still go well beyond the more extreme instances noted earlier. Similarly, in another context – while urging a judge to be restrained in disciplining recalcitrant defendants or offenders – Rambam appears to be thinking in fairly broad terms: "Whatever [he does], let all his actions be for the sake of Heaven. And let him not regard *kevod haberiyyot* lightly; for it overrides rabbinic prohibitions."[169] The context clearly suggests that Rambam is cautioning against all forms of unnecessary abuse; and this seems, in turn, to suggest a fairly broad conception of the license rooted in *kevod haberiyyot*.

Just how far we should go remains in question, however. Several tentative guidelines come to mind readily. First, personal dignity must be significantly, albeit briefly, fractured, rather than merely ruffled. Secondly, genuine dignity must be involved, not superficial vanity. The avoidance of any and every frivolous hurt can hardly override an injunction. It can only be overridden when one has the halakhic and ethical right to be sensitive or feel threatened. Having suggested these guidelines, however, one immediately realizes that they are, inevitably, so ambiguous as to offer little definitive guidance. The key terms, "significantly" or "genuine," can take their place among the amorphous hobgoblins – "reasonable doubt," "frequent occurrence," and the like – haunting the practical implementation of law. Moreover, quite apart from the ambiguity of the criteria, the phenomena involved, sensitivity and personal dignity, are so subtle and complex as to defy precise evaluation. Nevertheless, as general guidelines, these criteria may at least help point a direction.

Finally, a third possible criterion may be suggested. Perhaps some distinction should be made between situations involving others and those confined to oneself. Of course, Judaism has never subscribed to the currently popular view that ethics is restricted to interpersonal relations. "By morality," a Gifford lecturer once wrote, "I mean what is meant in common speech, the behaviour of men in society."[170] The Jew, however, would rather agree with Henry More, the seventeenth-century

permits the *kohen* to follow the crowd through a defiled path, out of deference to it, rather than vice-versa; see *Berakhot* 3:1; p. 24a.

169. *Hilkhot Sanhedrin* 24:10.

170. H. H. Henson, *Christian Morality* (Oxford, 1936), 29.

Cambridge Platonist, that "political society…by no means is the adequate measure of sound morality, but there is a moral perfection of human nature, antecedent to all society."[171] The maximal realization of the dignity and sanctity potentially inherent in a human personality is itself an ethical imperative of the highest order. Nevertheless, actions impinging upon another impose a special obligation. Lying is forbidden; but insofar as it affects one's fellow, it becomes doubly abominable, pertaining to both *bein adam laMakom* ("between man and God") and *bein adam lahavero* ("between man and man"). Thus, Rambam cites the prohibition against misleading others twice, once in the section on ideal personal attitudes and conduct and again in the section concerning sales.[172]

It is therefore entirely possible that in defining *kevod haberiyyot* and the license granted by it we should employ different yardsticks, depending on whether or not a situation impinges upon the sensibilities of one's fellow. The cases cited in the Gemara do not involve the feelings of others. Avoiding nudity and insuring privacy and cleanliness in excretion are purely personal; and burial, while it concerns another, concerns him only as a passive object rather than as a sentient subject. Hence, since the question is purely one of treating human personality *per se* with respect rather than adversely affecting others, the impact upon *kevod haberiyyot* must be fairly severe. However, where the prospect of hurting another is also present, as in the cases noted in Rashi and Rambam, it is conceivable that the principle may be much more broadly defined.

One may perhaps find sanction for such a distinction in a statement of Rosh. The Gemara in *Berakhot* states that "if one finds *shaatnez* in his garment, he takes it off even in the street. What is the reason? 'There is no wisdom nor understanding nor counsel against the Lord,' wherever a profanation of God's name is involved, no respect is paid [even] to a teacher."[173] Inasmuch as continued wearing would constitute

171. In John Norris, *The Theory and Regulation of Love, A Moral Essay in Two Parts: to which are added, Letters, Philosophical and Moral, between the author and Dr. Henry More* (London, 1694), 147.

172. See *Hilkhot De'ot* 2:6, and *Hilkhot Mekhira* 18:1.

173. *Berakhot* 19b. The verse cited is from *Mishlei* 21:30.

an active violation, the principle of *kevod haberiyyot* is ineffectual. The Yerushalmi,[174] however, relates that R. Ammi reproached a student who had informed his fellow that he was wearing a *shaatnez* garment. Rosh resolves the contradiction by suggesting that "when one finds *shaatnez* in his [own] garment, 'There is no wisdom nor understanding nor counsel against the Lord,' and he must remove it even in public. However, a person who sees *shaatnez* in his fellow's garments – and the wearer does not know of it – should not inform him in public before he reaches his home; for, because of *kevod haberiyyot,* one should not deter him [when he is] unwitting."[175] The distinction may turn on the quality of the transgression – whether it be willful or unwitting.[176] It is equally conceivable, however, that Rosh is distinguishing between two levels of *kevod haberiyyot,* the individual and the interpersonal. If so, his comment may provide some guidance in applying this somewhat elusive principle.[177]

With reference to the license provided by *shalom,* we are confronted by a virtually identical situation. How great must the threat be and how much amelioration must the violation of a norm produce in order to legitimize a dispensation? It seems inconceivable that norms may be freely violated in order to enhance the beatitudes of Tennyson's *Enoch Arden*. Nor does it seem likely they may be readily set aside in order to effect slight improvement in what would in any event remain an explosive situation. What guidelines can one employ, then?

As with *kevod haberiyyot,* I'm afraid we are driven back upon ambiguities. The particular case discussed by Rama concerned a heated controversy which embroiled a whole community and threatened its very fabric; the proposed remedy – which, incidentally, failed – would have resolved it entirely. Without necessarily requiring quite this much, one must nevertheless presume – if, for no other reason, simply *de silentio,* because this factor is not cited by Rama more frequently – that injunctions can be overridden only when the threat to peace, on the one hand,

174. *Kilayim* 9:1; p. 40b.

175. Commentary on *Kilayim* 9:4.

176. See *Yoreh De'ah* 303:1 and 372:1.

177. Of course, even if this interpretation be correct, Rosh is dealing with the scope of *kevod haberiyyot* rather than its definition. Nevertheless, his view would support the distinction in principle.

and the impact of the violation, on the other, are both measurably significant. The stability, perhaps the very existence, of an institution or a relation – and of one worth preserving – should be at stake before such a drastic measure can be considered. This criterion is admittedly vague. It permits – or rather, requires – *ad hoc* application on a primarily subjective basis. But, as with *kevod haberiyyot*, it is difficult to imagine a more precise definition.

One major qualification does suggest itself, however. The quest for amity can justify overriding norms only when the source of friction is not itself a halakhic issue. If a domestic or social quarrel can be patched up by temporarily overriding a specific law, it is conceivable that a dispensation may be in order. Such a dispensation in no way undermines the authority of Halakha as a whole. Rather, on the basis of that very authority, it momentarily suspends one section in favor of another. However, when friction is rooted in a direct challenge to the validity of Halakha, it is inconceivable that its proponents should always back down in the interests of irenicism. From the biblical period down, Jewish history affords ample evidence that, when necessary, the Torah community has fought rather than submit. Nor could it have been otherwise. With the Halakha itself under attack, to yield rather than risk possible schism is to adopt the most naïve form of pacifism. In effect, it entails knuckling under to the threat of force or blackmail – allowing the Halakha's desire for peace to be exploited to the point of eroding its very foundations. As such, concessions become clearly unconscionable. There are times when the Halakha's concern with peace may itself require a struggle. "Whatever is written in the Torah," says the Midrash, "was written for the sake of peace; and although wars are cited, the wars, too, were written for the sake of peace."[178] This is not to suggest that a battle must be waged around every issue. At times, compromise may be not only acceptable but desirable. Religiously, ethically, and/or tactically, the game is not always worth the candle. All I am suggesting is that any decision concerning resistance or accommodation must be based

---

178. *Tanhuma, Tzav*, 3. Of course, such a principle can be invoked for totalitarian purposes, and one needs to guard against its abuse. But there are times when it is unquestionably valid.

on a number of halakhic and tactical factors – communal context, the nature and motivation of the opposition, and so on – and with an eye to the long-range realization of ethical and religious ideals. It cannot be imposed as an absolute halakhic imperative, "better yield than quarrel."

Our attempt to define *kevod haberiyyot* and *shalom* has not arrived at a truly precise formulation, one which could be readily applied at a practical level. Whatever the exact definitions, however, one point seems fairly clear. The dispensations warranted by these factors have not been sufficiently recognized. Wherever any reasonable line may be drawn, we have collectively strayed far on the side of caution. Precisely because these concepts are so amorphous and their application so potentially sweeping, *posekim* have generally been reluctant to resort to them as grounds for overriding halakhic norms. Their reluctance is thoroughly understandable. Inasmuch as these concepts lend themselves to widespread and dangerous abuse, one naturally tends to stifle even their legitimate application. No doubt, in the modern period particularly, as organized attempts at the irresponsible manipulation of Halakha have actually materialized, the urge to tone down elements that, in reckless hands, could undermine its entire structure has become almost irrepressible. One suspects that, in some instances, even where the primary basis for a decision has been *kevod haberiyyot* or *shalom*, a *posek* has preferred, wherever possible, to advance narrower formal or technical grounds rather than encourage the use and potential abuse of general dispensations.

Nevertheless, this conservatism, however laudable in motive and intent, is not without its own dangers. Elements such as *kevod haberiyyot* and *shalom* are central to a Torah *Weltanschauung*, a fact to which their legitimate and limited role in suspending certain halakhic norms clearly attests. Yet the reluctance to permit them to play that role tends to downgrade their position. The result is twofold. First, there is a danger that in situations in which they ought to be decisive, so that certain usual norms actually should be overridden, they may not be invoked. The wrong decision might thus be handed down; after all, relevant technical grounds for arriving at the same conclusion are not always available. This possibility is, in itself, a matter of grave concern. We should bear in mind that in situations in which *kevod haberiyyot* or *shalom* can legitimately suspend a norm, such suspension is not merely permissible but mandatory. Moreover, the reluctance to invoke a dispensation tends to feed upon itself. Once it has fallen into relative disuse, one is understandably reluctant to apply it more broadly lest he rock the boat – or lest he be accused of rocking the boat. Even R. Hayyim Soloveitchik, despite the immense prestige he enjoyed as the foremost halakhic master of the early twentieth century, came under criticism for extending the concept of *pikuah nefesh* beyond what had then been its prevalent range.

Secondly, quite apart from possible specific errors, there exists a potentially graver danger. The axiological centrality of *kevod haberiyyot* or *shalom* as the moral and religious basis of large tracts of Halakha may be seriously undermined. The dispensation provided by them is not a mere technicality, nor is their application an exercise in legal mechanics. It is grounded in – and hence serves to sharpen and to heighten the awareness of – their position as fundamental Torah values. This point is clearly emphasized in the basic relevant texts. The Gemara does not merely state – as it does in comparable cases elsewhere[179] – that *kevod haberiyyot* overrides the usual norms in certain situations. It states, rather, "Great is human dignity, so that it overrides a negative precept of the Torah."[180] Even more emphatically, Rambam, in the final words of the book of "Seasons," on the Sabbath and the festivals, states that Sabbath candles[181] take priority over Hanukka candles "for the sake of household peace, seeing that even a divine name might be erased in order to make peace between husband and wife. Great is peace, as the whole Torah

179. See, e.g., *Yevamot* 3b ff. where the Gemara simply states that a positive commandment overrides a negative. Cf., however, Ramban, *Shemot* 20:8.

180. *Berakhot* 19b. The passage can alternatively be translated "since it overrides," in which case the dispensation of *kevod haberiyyot* would prove its greatness rather than be explained by it. In either case, however, the juxtaposition of the two parts of the statement remains significant.

181. I cite these in accordance with Rashi's interpretation of the referent in the Gemara's discussion, possibly buttressed by its overall context, which deals with a parallel question concerning the relative priority of *kiddush* wine. However, no mention of the candles' identity appears in Rambam, and he may very well have subscribed to the view of Ritva that the Gemara deals with ordinary weekday candles, employed for the potential goal of illumination. Of course, in that case, the force and weight of *shalom* is even more sharply emphasized.

was given in order to bring peace upon the world, as it is said, 'Her ways are ways of pleasantness, and all her paths are peace.'"[182] Consequently, the failure to invoke these dispensations in any but the most extreme cases cannot but erode their position – and popular awareness of that position – as central values within the Torah-halakhic order. No committed Jew can regard such a prospect lightly. Some margin of safety is perhaps advisable. But must it be as large as we have tended to maintain?

This is not to suggest that dispensations grounded in *kevod haberiyyot* and *shalom* be bandied about with abandon. Certainly, the risks inherent in applying them cannot be ignored. I do, however, wish to point out the risks inherent in the opposite course, in the direction of extreme caution; to emphasize that we have collectively perhaps – I should rather say, probably – strayed too far in that direction; and to suggest that, in this area, we should be well advised – nay, religiously obligated – to reassess our current thought and practice. The price we are paying for caution may be excessive; and, in any event, we need to ask whether we have the halakhic right to pay any price at all. The concepts of *kevod haberiyyot* and *shalom* are not personal property.

With respect to dispensation, we have dealt heretofore with the familiar factor of acute crisis, when personal survival is at stake, and with less prominent and less crucial elements of a more social and communal cast. We cannot leave this topic, however, without noting, however cursorily, a complex of cognate factors, whose comprehension and detailed treatment lie beyond the scope of this essay, but which are in need of acknowledgment nonetheless.

Broadly speaking, these may be subsumed under the umbrella rubric of "privation" – an omnibus term which I take to denote a wide range of deficiencies, maladies, and other assorted hardships or misfortunes, but not confined to the harsher associations of suffering, nor including mere nuisance or annoyance. In searching for a halakhic equivalent, I note that while specific aspects of privation can be readily identified as halakhic entities, no general correlative comes to mind readily. The apparent implication that no such category exists seems almost self-evident, and it is clearly of relevance to our discussion.

182. *Hilkhot Hannuka* 4:14. The verse cited is from *Mishlei* 3:17.

To be sure, some data can be marshaled, and, as to a term, we may ponder the rough equivalency of *tzaar*. The term denotes either pain or anguish, and is multifaceted with respect to the source and etiology of either. However, for our purposes, it is hardly adequate. Unquestionably, its relation to certain aspects of privation is amply clear. The most obvious example – in a sense, contiguous with *pikuah nefesh* and yet distinct from it – is that of medical need. At the extreme, some authorities have virtually accorded some instances the status of actual *pikuah nefesh*. Thus, major *posekim* were divided about the status of possible loss of limb,[183] while others, making the surprising leap from the quantitative to the qualitative, held that the prospect of injury in a public venue should be classified as a mode of mortal danger.[184] In more moderate situations, defined as those of a *holeh she'ein bo sakkana*, "a sick [patient] in no life-threatening danger,"[185] the scope of the license to override halakhic norms is both in dispute and, differentially formulated, subject to several variables. What is not in dispute, however, is the clear fact that the basis of leniency is not an overarching mantra of *tzaar*, but, rather, specific local factors. A similar pattern emerges if we analyze the area of financial distress, reinforcing the impression we have noted.

There are some exceptions, but, to the best of my knowledge, they, too, are isolated and marginal. The Gemara in *Ketubbot* 60a cites an instance in which even an act that is proscribed *mideoraita* may be performed in order to relieve pain if performed abnormally, in which case the prohibition is reduced to the level of a *derabbanan*, as *bimekom tzaara lo gazru rabbanan*. But the very textual isolation of the license, as well as its being cited regarding a specific case, suggest that here, too, we confront a focused dispensation rather than an overall formulation. Such a formulation is perhaps reflected in a gloss of Rama in *Hilkhot Shabbat* wherein he permits, in situations of *tzaar*, untying knots when

183. See the range of views cited in *Shulhan Arukh*, OH 328:17, all of which prohibit *deoraita* violations in order to save an organ, and *Siftei Kohen*, YD 157:3, who is inclined to permissive resolution of this question.

184. See *Shabbat* 42a, and the discussion regarding the view of the *Geonim*, cited in the *hiddushim* of Ramban and his successors, ad loc.

185. See *Shulhan Arukh*, OH 328:17.

unraveling is only proscribed *miderabbanan.*[186] Since in this case his explanatory assertion, *debimekom tzaara lo gazru,* nowhere appears in the Gemara, one can only presume that Rama expanded and extrapolated the citation from *Ketubbot* into a general principle. Even here, however, the isolated application and the absence of any comprehensive assertion mitigate this impression.

In another context, Rama apparently recognized the impact of *tzaar* as grounds for leniency with respect to far more critical decisions. Grounding himself upon a *teshuva* authored by the fifteenth-century Italian *posek* R. Yosef Colon (Maharik), he writes that a child is not obligated to abstain from the choice of a mate if his parents object to it.[187] In Maharik's responsum,[188] this conclusion is theorized in light of the assumption that one is not obligated to incur significant financial loss in order to support his parents, and, hence, *a fortiori,* that he need suffer no psychological privation, *vekhol sheken tzaara degufa.*[189] However, as the *tzaar* in this case would be considerable, we can only infer license in comparable circumstances. At the very least, then, we cannot employ sweeping generalities and need to acknowledge correlation between levels of *tzaar* and the scope of any *hetter* based upon it.

The need for a differential approach in any consideration of license based upon *tzaar* seems self-evident *per se,* and it is reflected in a distinction drawn by *Rishonim,* for instance, between pains of illness and pangs of hunger.[190] And yet, even allowing for such differentiation, the status of privation as the basis of dispensation is more limited than might have been anticipated from a humanistic perspective. Unlike the analysis of the more axiologically laden elements of *kevod haberiyyot* and

186. See ibid. 317:1.

187. See ibid. YD 240:25.

188. See *She'elot UTeshuvot HaMaharik,* 167.

189. The limitation is of both a local and of a more general character. Specifically, a child is not legally obligated to cover his parents' expenses if they have the means to do so themselves; see *Kiddushin* 32a. Generally, while one is required to sacrifice all his assets rather than violate a negative *deoraita* prohibition, there is a limit of a fifth of personal assets which must be sacrificed in order to avoid the failure to perform a positive mitzva.

190. See *Tosafot, Ketubbot* 60a, s.v. *gone'ah yonek.*

shalom, I am inclined to assume that this excursus regarding *tzaar* has rather shed light upon the Halakha's alternate mien – which demands and challenges, which persists in urging servitude and sacrifice, which bespeaks denial of human desire and inhibits aspiration, even, at times, positive aspiration. It certainly illuminates the facet that is so graphically manifested in a gemara in *Sukka*. In the wake of a discussion of the impact of the principle that one who is engaged in performing a given mitzva is, concurrently, exempt from others upon assorted dispensations granted with respect to *sukka,* the gemara ponders the status of a mourning *avel* during *shiva*. After citing a view that the mitzva is incumbent upon him, the gemara goes on to query that this should be presumably self-evident, inasmuch as the general halakhic regime is binding upon him. In response, the gemara explains why the *din* required exposition and formulation. The reason given is that inasmuch as a *mitzta'er,* one who is in a state of *tzaar,* is exempt from sitting in a *sukka,* a grieving *avel* should likewise be exempt as he, too, is in *tzaar*. Hence, there was need to clarify that the analogy does not hold. "It is only the onset of external *tzaar* [which exempts]; here, however, the *tzaar* is self-induced. He ought to have calmed himself."[191] The concluding demand unquestionably raises the bar rather high. That, too, however, is an aspect of the halakhic complex.

VII. Halakhic Leniency Due to Straitened Circumstances

To this point, we have gauged the Halakha's humanism – as regards its concern with man's worldly welfare – on the basis of two criteria: the fabric of the fundamental halakhic order, the complex of rights and duties of which it is constituted; and the factors, at once humanistic and halakhically normative, which suspend, in part or in whole, the usual demands of that order. It can also be measured, however, by a third criterion: the

191. Rashi, *Sukka* 25a, s.v. *tirda direshut,* explains that the mitzva of *avelut* is confined to external actions, so that any emotional component is purely voluntary and ought therefore to have been controlled. Ramban, however, on the basis of *Sanhedrin* 46a, held that anguish was the very essence of grief, a position much expanded and expounded by the Rav, *z.t.l.* On his view, it is presumably the excess of grief which should be restrained.

extent, if any, to which halakhic standards may be compromised as a concession to personal or even financial difficulty. This factor should not, of course, be confused with the second. The recognition accorded *pikuah nefesh* or similar elements entails neither compromise nor concession. These elements override certain injunctions simply because, even from a purely legal standpoint, they carry greater weight. Their power is grounded in the fact that, occasional confrontation between opposing norms being inevitable, the Halakha had to formulate principles of priority. When these elements override an injunction, they do so as one halakhic norm preempting another, and not as a humanitarian factor transcending, as it were, the Halakha. Hence, in cases of conflict, the precedence of these elements is mandatory and not merely optional. When critics accused R. Hayyim Soloveitchik of excessive laxity because of his sweeping application and broad definition of *pikuah nefesh,* he replied that he was not, Heaven forfend, lax as regards prohibitions. He was just exceedingly scrupulous as regards *pikuah nefesh.*[192] Of those who were visibly chagrined when they had to violate the Sabbath in order to avert possible danger, he would ask whether they were equally upset over the "violation" involved in Sabbath circumcision. Both, he would argue, have been not only permitted but mandated, and, as regards either, twinges of residual guilt are thoroughly baseless. Similarly, with reference to the Mishna's statement that between the sections of *Shema,* "one may give greeting out of fear and return it out of respect,"[193] the Hafetz Hayim would insist that one not only may interrupt but must.[194] *Kevod haberiyyot,* again, is not merely optional.

By contrast, the principle to be explored presently – that normative standards may be compromised in straitened circumstances – does concern the clash of human and halakhic factors. It suggests that, within limits, extraneous factors may validly intrude upon halakhic judgments; that, for the *posek* or his respondent, non-normative considerations may properly enter into normative decision. Clearly, however – as regards the respondent, certainly – the consideration of such factors must be,

192. See R. S. J. Zevin, *Ishim VeShittot* (Tel Aviv, 1952), 59.
193. *Berakhot* 13a.
194. I have been told this by R. Joseph B. Soloveitchik.

at best, a matter of license. If one may, as a concession to his condition, take certain liberties, these can hardly be elevated into duties. And even if one argues correctly that it is the Halakha itself which has sanctioned these liberties – so that they be rightfully regarded as grounded in principle rather than convenience – it has sanctioned them only as such, as an option of which one may avail himself rather than as an imperative duty. Hence, the humanistic moment implicit in such permissiveness must be regarded as more significant than that reflected in *pikuah nefesh* or *kevod haberiyyot*. Whereas they constitute particular halakhic concepts relevant to specific areas of Halakha, this principle represents a broad flexibility within the halakhic process generally; and whereas they remain genuinely internal elements, it can, in a very real sense, be construed as an extraneous factor.

With respect to such a principle, one may ask three primary questions. First, does it exist? Secondly, if so, what is its basis? And, finally, what are its limits?

There can be little doubt of its existence. The Talmud sets down certain guidelines concerning situations governed by unresolved halakhic controversies: if the case involves a biblical ordinance, one should heed the more rigorous view; if a rabbinic, he may assume the more lenient.[195] Yet, in a number of instances,[196] the Talmud states that, under conditions of stress, one may rely upon the less stringent opinion, even if it be a minority view – evidently, even if the question involves a biblical injunction.[197] Similarly, with reference to many disputed issues cited in the *Shulhan Arukh*, Rama's gloss accepts the more rigorous view but with the accompanying proviso that in cases of *hefsed merubbeh* ("substantial

---

195. *Avoda Zara* 7a.

196. See, e.g., *Nidda* 6a–b and 9b; *Eiruvin* 46a; and *Shabbat* 45a.

197. This last point has been disputed. The cases cited in the Talmud are inconclusive. However, inasmuch as he does not qualify, one would assume that Rashba's statement concerning such license covers *deoraita* injunctions as well; see his *Teshuvot*, I, 253. But cf. *Siftei Kohen*, YD 242 (concluding discourse), who argues the practice is only legitimate with respect to rabbinic ordinances, and who contends, moreover, that Rashba should be understood in a similar vein. See also *Encyclopedia Talmudit*, s.v. "*Halakha*," IX, 260–1 and n.

loss") it may be ignored.[198] In many *teshuvot*, likewise, one sees leading *posekim* straining, sometimes without success, to ameliorate the effect of halakhot whose impact, in a given instance, might be excessively harsh.[199] Circumstances may clearly license a degree of leniency.

But what is the halakhic basis of such license? That the basis must indeed be halakhic is beyond question. No committed halakhist can seriously countenance the simplistic socioeconomic interpretation that, under pressure, the Halakha just periodically capitulates. For one thing, the image – or rather the reality – of Halakha and its masters which he envisions simply does not correspond with this theory. For another, if *posekim* or their constituents have always been bent, consciously or subconsciously, upon adjusting the Halakha to suit social or economic needs, they have certainly made a terrible botch of things. In one area after another, they have "modified" one injunction only to leave untouched a dozen far more stringent. Pressures of circumstance no doubt make themselves felt, but they generally operate within halakhic limits and to the extent that they are accorded halakhic recognition. Interpretations of the Halakha's past – or projections of its future – that ignore its fundamental objectivity distort its very essence. Least of all, will the halakhist accept the contention that, under pressure, the Halakha *should* capitulate.

We are confronted, once again, by Newman's dictum. Despite its terrifying severity, it expresses one ineluctable truth. Given the conception of an absolute religious law, no degree of purely temporal bliss or suffering can compensate for the slightest sin – except insofar as the legal system itself has provided for such compensation. In that case, the prospective "sin" is of course neutralized, perhaps even transmuted into a virtue. Barring this, however, utilitarian considerations count for nothing. Where the law has stood rigid, an individual can claim no inherent right to transcend it, simply because the cost is too great. To many, this fact is no doubt sufficient reason for rejecting absolute religious law. Given the conception, however, this conclusion seems inevitable. What *a priori* limit can be set to the sacrifice which religion can rightfully demand?

---

198. See, e.g., *Yoreh De'ah* 36:16, 39:2, 39:13, 69:2, 92:4, 108:1–2, 135:1.

199. See, e.g., *Teshuvot Rav Akiva Eiger*, 85; *Noda BiYehuda* (1st ed. YD 48, 57, and 61).

For the Jew, therefore, it is Halakha and Halakha alone that determines what it can exact from him. Hence, if straitened circumstances can justify a degree of leniency, the rationale must be grounded in – must, in a sense, constitute – a halakhic principle. This rationale is based upon two premises. The first is the obvious desire and duty to employ every possible means to assist those in need. This obligation, rooted and expressed both in specific precepts and in the omnibus drive toward *imitatio viarum Dei*, is not confined to charity or social action. It impinges upon the process of *pesak* as well. In cases of genuine difficulty, the imposition of possibly needless burdens is not merely neutral. It violates the letter as well as the spirit of Halakha. Or, to put it more positively, within the limits of flexibility, the exercise of ingenuity in an effort to relieve potential hardship becomes a matter of the highest duty. Of course, ingenuity alone does not suffice. It can only be used in conjunction with erudition and commitment, and the number of those possessing the religious and intellectual qualifications for halakhic decision can never be very large. For those endowed with them, however, sensitivity to the human as well as the legal dimensions of a situation is imperative. It is, of course, easier to be cautious and to take refuge in presumed ignorance; hence, the Rabbis' statement that "the power of leniency is greater,"[200] because, as Rashi explained, the lenient *posek* "relies upon his knowledge and is not afraid to permit while the power of those who forbid proves nothing as everyone can be rigorous even with respect to the licit."[201] But the first-rate *posek*, jealous as he is in guarding the tradition, is also driven by a sense of responsibility to his straitened respondent; and to the extent that he can employ scholarship to reconcile their respective interests, he feels duty-bound to do so.

The obligation to compassionate leniency is imposed by *caritas*. The opportunity is provided by a pluralistic conception of Halakha. So long as Halakha is defined in purely monistic terms, every text being subject to only one correct interpretation and every problem amenable to only one solution, it is difficult to justify such leniency. However, the

200. *Beitza* 2b.
201. Ibid., s.v. *dehetera*.

Rabbis interpreted Halakha in somewhat more flexible terms. "R. Abba stated in the name of Shmuel," says the Gemara in *Eiruvin*,

> For three years there was a dispute between Beit Shammai and Beit Hillel, these asserting, "The Halakha is in accordance with our views," and those asserting, "The Halakha is in accordance with our views." A *bat kol*[202] then issued, pronouncing: "These and these are the words of the living God, but the Halakha is in accordance with the rulings of Beit Hillel."[203]

This famous albeit somewhat enigmatic dictum can only mean that, at the primary level, the Rabbis recognized a pluralistic dimension within Halakha. The rational interpretation of texts or concepts is not governed by the principle of the excluded middle. Where a number of reasonable alternatives are present, none can be categorically rejected. For the scholar who conscientiously arrives at it, each alternative – simply by dint of it being a reasonable possibility – is considered right. For that situation to obtain, the scholar must be a genuine authority and he must sincerely interpret according to his best lights. Given those elements, however, his understanding of Halakha becomes for him, at the primary normative level, the Halakha. This concept is not to be confused with the conundrum of relativistic subjectivism. The scholar who acts upon his interpretation is not just charitably viewed as being, at worst, an unwitting and therefore innocent "sinner." He is regarded as being correct – objectively correct.

This implication was clearly recognized by the Tosafists. "The French Rabbis o.b.m. asked," writes Ritva,

> "How is it possible that 'these and these are the words of the living God' if one proscribes and one permits?" They answered that when Moses ascended on high to receive the Torah he was shown, concerning each and every matter, forty-nine grounds for proscription and forty-nine for license. He asked God about

202. A semi-oracular voice.
203. *Eiruvin* 13b.

> this and He said that the issue should be placed in the hands of the Sages of Israel in each and every generation and the decision should be theirs.[204]

This conception raises obvious metaphysical and epistemological questions; but these lie beyond the confines of this essay. Our present concern is rather with practical corollaries deriving from it. One is that a qualified scholar who has become honestly and fully convinced of one interpretation may safely ignore conflicting alternatives.[205] So long as he remains convinced – and provided that none of the principles governing decision in case of controversy apply – he can, by definition, do no wrong. Hence, the Gaon of Vilna could refuse to wear two pairs of *tefillin* in order to heed conflicting opinions concerning their specifications.[206] Once such a principle were countenanced, he argued, one would have to pay equal homage to all possibilities. As regards *tefillin*, this would entail wearing sixty-four pairs – a practice no one had yet suggested. This *reductio ad absurdum* points out the inconsistency of those who do heed one dissenting view; but it does not yet explain the Gaon's own position. Nor can his reluctance be ascribed to common indolence. It was rather rooted in the conviction that those who, like himself, were thoroughly convinced of one position could safely ignore other points of view. Within the limits of rational halakhic discourse, certainty confers *ipso facto* legitimacy.

The second corollary is, in one sense, the obverse of the first. If, on the one hand, the convinced *posek* can ignore alternatives, then, on the other hand, the uncommitted *posek* – while he is ordinarily bound by various canons of decision – can, when ethical considerations warrant,

---

204. *Hiddushei HaRitva, Eiruvin* 13b.

205. See *Hullin* 116a and *Teshuvot HaRashba*, I, 253. It is conceivable, however, that such license would only extend to the convinced scholar proper and to those who, residing in his town, are subject to his authority. It may not apply to others, even if they choose to make inquiry of this scholar. See *Pesahim* 51b; *Eduyot*, 5:7; and Yerushalmi, *Berakhot*, 1:1; p. 6b. Cf. also *Yevamot* 14a ff.

206. This practice is mentioned – with reference to a disagreement between Rashi and Rabbenu Tam – in *Orah Hayim* 34:2. For the Gaon's view, see Asher Hakohen, *Orhot Hayim* (Jerusalem, 1819), sec. 14 (often printed in *Siddur HaGra*).

strain after any reasonable option in order to arrive at a favorable conclusion. So long as he is not convinced that a given position is wrong, he may ground a decision upon it. He does so secure in the knowledge that, for those who are committed to it, this position constitutes conclusive halakhic truth; and that, even for the indifferent, its mere possibility confers legitimacy. "These and these are the words of the living God." The *posek* need not be absolutely sure that a given contention is right and therefore universally applicable. But so long as his logic has not discarded it as a live option, the imperative drive to compassionate action impels him to draw upon it in an ethical emergency.

In straining after occasional leniency, the *posek* has recourse to various processes. He may strike out on his own – offering novel textual interpretations, redefining concepts, or introducing hitherto overlooked distinctions. Or he may draw sustenance from authorities whose views had not become the standard *pesak* but which had not been categorically demolished. Overruled but not moribund, these views can be brought into play under conditions of duress. No canon of decision is clearer than that of majority: "An individual versus a group – the Halakha is like the group."[207] And yet: "Worthy is R. Shimon" – or any other legitimate authority – "of being relied upon at a time of emergency."[208]

This procedure has – and clearly must have – certain limits. Not every minority opinion is cast into limbo. Some are rejected with utter finality. In the first place, some issues concern matters of fact and error rather than analytic interpretation; and of these, as Rashi pointed out,[209] one can hardly say that a number of views are legitimate. Secondly, halakhic pluralism is operative at a primary level of individual confrontation with the raw material of Halakha. At this purely theoretical plane, all reasonable options (however that be defined) are equally open. The opinions of Beit Shammai are as much a part of the corpus of Torah as those of Beit Hillel. Certainly, whoever engages in their study is fulfilling the mitzva of *talmud Torah* equally. At a secondary level, however, one must make a choice – and the practical halakhic code incorporates the

207. *Berakhot* 9a.
208. Ibid.
209. *Ketubbot* 57a, s.v. *ha*.

one and excludes the other. "These and these ...," but "the Halakha is in accordance with the rulings of Beit Hillel." Hence, to the extent that they are bound by precedent and tradition, later *posekim* can only draw upon prior minority statements which have not been formally and definitively rejected. We do not, for instance, find *Rishonim* citing minority views mentioned – and implicitly rejected – in the Mishna.[210] Whatever its limitations, however, the fundamental validity of this process is clear, and it reflects one dimension of halakhic humanism.

The extent to which this dispensation is invoked will undoubtedly vary with the individual *posek*. As with *kevod haberiyyot* and *shalom*, terms like *she'at hadehak* ("a moment of pressure") or *hefsed merubbeh* ("substantial loss") are somewhat ambiguous. Attempts have indeed been made to define the latter in fixed quantitative terms; but one is inclined to agree with the conclusion of the author of *Har HaKarmel* that "it has no fixed figure whatsoever. Everything depends upon the judgment of the *posek*, with respect to the time and the period, and the person who would incur the loss. If the loss would be substantial for him, it is considered *hefsed merubbeh*."[211] Such a formulation clearly allows for considerable latitude in the definition and application of the concept. Confronted by a situation in which the "normal" Halakha comes into conflict with a genuine human need, two *posekim*, both working within strictly halakhic limits, may produce diametrically opposed decisions. Differences in attitude, temperament, and emphasis may lead the one, compassionately responsive to the personal dimensions of the problem, to accept a broader construction of "emergency" and to strain generally

210. See *Nidda* 9b where the Gemara states that, in an emergency, R. Yehuda HaNasi could have relied upon the minority view of a *Tanna*, but not if that view had been formally rejected. As regards post-talmudic *posekim*, however, the fact that a position had been cited in the Mishna as a minority view would itself be tantamount to its rejection and would therefore close that particular option. For them, the principle I've been discussing would therefore be operative with reference to decisions handed down by other post-talmudic *posekim*. See, however, *Or Zarua*, II, 306, who does seem to apply it to minority views of *Tanna'im* as well; and cf. *Shiltei HaGibborim*, *Shabbat*, 48a (in Alfasi). See also *Siftei Kohen*, YD 242, and R. A. Y. Kook, *Shabbat HaArez*, 3rd ed. (Jerusalem, 1951), intro., 41–44. Cf. also *Or Zarua*, *Sanhedrin*, 67.

211. Cited in *Pithei Teshuva*, YD 31:2. With respect to *she'at hadehak*, see *Tosafot*, *Nidda* 6b, s.v. *bishe'at*.

after any factor which may possibly support a lenient decision; while the other, primarily imbued with a sense of responsibility to the truth of the tradition, may be inclined to very limited recourse to dispensations and will perforce hand down a rigorous decision.[212] Such variation is not an indictment of halakhic objectivity; nor does it imply that the process can be extended *ad infinitum*. It merely attests to the presence of an element of flexibility within Halakha and to the fact that, within certain limits, this flexibility – its definition proper being in occasional dispute – produces varied decisions.

The modern temper is, of course, on the side of the angels. Whatever its general feral tendencies as regards the application of religious law, it is all in favor of compassion. We should, however, beware of glib judgments. The *posek* who adopts a more rigorous stance is not being insensitive to human needs. Rather – if I may paraphrase Julius Caesar – he loves not man the less but Torah more. Yet, on the other hand, we should not minimize the difference in approach and emphasis. Any serious study of the corpus of responsa clearly reveals it. However, the full discussion of this issue would require a monograph – probably several – analyzing the approaches implicitly and explicitly adopted in the responsa of leading *posekim*. If it were grounded upon an awareness of the moral and religious dimensions of the problem and did not merely rely upon facile sociological and pseudo-psychological interpretation, such a study could make a significant contribution to our present understanding of Halakha. Here, even while noting that its scope has often varied, I simply content myself with sketching the legal and philosophic basis of this humanistic halakhic strain.

VIII. The Limits and Nature of Halakhic Humanism

In the final analysis, the Halakha cannot satisfy the demands of the radical secular humanist. For its humanistic strain is, although not muted, nevertheless counterpoised; or rather, as the committed Jew prefers to think, counterpointed. Judaism holds with Plato that "God ought to be

212. See *Hullin* 49b; but see also *Tosafot*, s.v. *Rav*.

to us the measure of all things, and not man, as men commonly say."[213] It subscribes, in consequence, to Carlyle's "Everlasting Yea" – "love not Pleasure; love God."[214] No doubt, when it is a question of alleviating suffering – especially of others – rather than seeking pleasure, the problem assumes a different aspect. And yet the focal issue remains the same. The heart of the halakhic message is that, at one level, the Sabbath was made for man: "The whole Torah was given in order to bring peace upon the world, as it is said, 'Her ways are ways of pleasantness, and all her paths are peace.'"[215] At another level, however, man was made for the Sabbath: "If you have learned much Torah, do not plume yourself, for it is for that purpose that you were created."[216] The Jew profoundly believes that God's law was given for man's good – and he acts and is bound to act upon that belief. But he does not flinch even when it induces pain. Obedience would mean little if it were purely selective. Yet obedience is the least which the Jew, both as a created spiritual being and as the recipient of divine Torah, owes and proffers to God. His assessment of what he is ready to give is made in the light of the ultimate knowledge that "even the whole world," as the Yerushalmi would have it, "does not equal [in value] one item of the Torah."[217]

It is often difficult to impart this message to the modern Jew – even to the avowedly believing Jew. While renunciation is not the central motif of Halakha, it is, at times, an inevitable by-product; and to a mind deeply engaged in the pursuit of secular happiness, any call for withdrawal strikes an almost Oriental note. The Halakha, despite its profound reverence for life and its activist orientation, must occasionally proffer Carlyle's advice: "The fraction of life can be increased in value not so much by increasing your numerator as by lessening your denominator. Nay, unless my algebra deceive me, unity itself divided by zero will give infinity."[218] However, in an age caught up in a revolution of rising expectations, such advice is neither lightly given nor lightly taken. It is,

213. *Laws*, 716.
214. Thomas Carlyle, *Sartor Resartus* (London, 1908), 145; II, ix.
215. Rambam, *Hilkhot Hanukka* 4:14.
216. *Avot* 2:9.
217. *Pe'ah* 1:1; p. 4a.
218. Carlyle, *Sartor Resartus*, 144; II, ix.

in fact, difficult to convey this message today without appearing – sometimes even to oneself – grossly callous. Largely pragmatic in character, contemporary Western culture does little to cultivate respect for law generally or for an absolute Halakha specifically; and modern men and women, as remote from Aquinas and Hooker as from Rambam, and primarily oriented to the attainment of utilitarian desiderata, often simply cannot see how a formal or technical element can be permitted to block an otherwise desirable step. Moreover, it is precisely the ethically sensitive who are frequently most dismayed. It seems inconceivable to them that one could not, at the very least, wink here and cut a corner there; and rigorous adherence to standards, accompanied by exhortations to sacrifice, may strike them as cold indifference. Yet, if there is one quality thoroughly absent from Halakha, it is callousness. From a perspective of commitment, halakhic demands, while often exacting, have a genuinely positive character. There is profound joy – even in worldly terms – in halakhic living; but its necessary concomitants are courage and faith.

The *posek*, finally, is confronted by a further difficulty. In applying Halakha for others, he is often caught between two imperatives, truth and *hesed*. The renunciation which, for him, would represent fortitude can, when demanded of others, reflect cold indifference. Hamlet's dictum, "Since no man knows aught of what he leaves, what is't to leave betimes?"[219] is as true for others as it is for myself. And yet, as a principle of conduct in dealing with one's fellow, such a philosophical perspective can produce frightful cruelty. Caught within this ethical and religious dilemma, the *posek* strains after every possible dispensation. But when ultimately confronted by the authority of the law, he submits – and, with honesty and commiseration, he asks others to submit. In his heart of hearts, he senses that it is here, in the consecration of man and society to God, that genuine humanism lies.

IX. Returning to the Rama

The concepts developed in the body of this essay enable us, finally, to formulate its coda – the succinct analysis of the *teshuva* to which it is

219. V, ii, 233–34.

appended. Their relevance need hardly be emphasized. Both in the prologue and the body of the *teshuva*, the Rama's straining after a lenient decision is writ large. And small wonder. If one must classify, the Rama should certainly be included within the more humanistic wing of *posekim*. The tenor of his thought is clearly revealed in his major philosophical treatise, *Torat HaOla*. In the very opening chapter, we are told that "the world in its totality is called a sanctuary on high."[220] Every generation is urged to regard itself as "the whole world for whom it had been created."[221] The Rambam is criticized for having minimized the formal similarity between man and God.[222] Perhaps most strikingly, the Rama writes, with respect to "all the mitzvot that appear in the Torah," that "most are [concerned with] physical needs and interpersonal conduct. And although they also benefit the soul, nevertheless their primary benefit is also [sic] reflected in the [area of] needs of [other] people and of physical needs."[223]

The Rama is, first and foremost, a *posek*, however. In the context of a *teshuva*'s halakhic decision, therefore, his humanism cannot be unbridled. Not one to dismiss formal or ritual demands lightly, he presents a phalanx of arguments to explain why these demands may not apply to the situation at hand. To this end, he appeals to both narrow and broad halakhic grounds. The broad grounds are those we have considered *in extenso*: *kevod haberiyyot* and *shalom*; to which the Rama adds a principle – suggested to him by analogy with another halakhic area – that the need for procreation may suspend certain norms. The narrow grounds are three contentions specifically related to the halakhic area under discussion: 1) that perhaps a number of authorities permit Sabbath *kiddushin* for a childless person; 2) that even if this view was Rabbenu Tam's alone, a sole dissenter may be relied upon "in a pinch"; 3) that inasmuch as the reason for their prohibition no longer applies, Sabbath *kiddushin* are now universally permissible. The respective

220. *Torat HaOla* (Prague, 1833), I, i; p. 19a.
221. Ibid., IV, xxxii; p. 139a.
222. Ibid., II, ii; pp. 10–11. The Rama goes on to stress the idea of deiformity and, in this connection, quotes the story of Hillel and the mitzva of washing one's face.
223. Ibid., III, xxxviii; p. 48.

arguments are all fraught with significant difficulties, and the very fact that the Rama marshaled a whole array perhaps suggests he was not absolutely certain of any. We might do well, in conclusion, to examine some of these difficulties briefly.

The problems attendant upon *kevod haberiyyot* and *shalom* require no further elucidation. The ambiguity surrounding their definition explains both the Rama's ability to appeal to them, on the one hand, and his reluctance to rely upon them exclusively, on the other. As for the third general ground, the mitzva of procreation, it is nowhere clearly recognized as a broad principle overriding certain normative categories. The Rama attempts to infer it by analogy from a specific instance in which it does set aside the particular prohibition of marriage during the first thirty days of mourning. However, even that case is somewhat in dispute;[224] and, in any event, the whole procedure is clearly a bit precarious.

As to the more specific arguments, the first – that not one but a number of *Rishonim* permit Sabbath *kiddushin* for the childless – hinges upon an unconventional and slightly forced reading of Rashi. Moreover, as the Rama acknowledges, even if his reading be accepted, this position would only be saved from being a solitary opinion. It would still, however, constitute a minority view. The next argument – that even if Rabbenu Tam alone subscribed to this view, his solitary dissent may be relied upon in an emergency – is more clear-cut. Nevertheless, as we have seen, the scope of its underlying principle is somewhat indefinite. The recurrent problem of definition should presumably present no difficulty here. The circumstances described by the Rama clearly constitute a genuine emergency. However, the question of the extent to which

224. See Rambam, *Hilkhot Evel* 6:5; Ramban, *Torat HaAdam*, 99–100; and *Yoreh De'ah* 392:1–2, all of whom make no allowance for all childless mourners to marry during the first thirty days of mourning. They mention such a dispensation only with respect to the case specifically cited in *Moed Katan* 23a – mourning for a wife. This fact clearly suggests the allowance is not due to the overriding of an injunction but to an initial qualification within it. Even if we accept the permissive view of Rabbenu Tam and the Rosh, this may very well still be the nature of this license. If so, however, the Rama has no precedent. It might be added that a secondary analogy cited by the Rama – the marriage of minors – also presents little support. It is, again, a matter of controversy and the prohibition involved is less definitive than that relevant to the Rama.

one may legitimately appeal to generally rejected opinions persists. In dealing with *hefsed merubbeh,* the Rama himself restricted the practice considerably. Responding to charges that he had been excessively lax by citing far too many instances in which one could accept lenient opinions in case of substantial loss, he insisted that he had applied this principle only in cases which were "fully permissible according to the [fundamental] Halakha but concerning which recent *posekim* o.b.m. were inclined to strictness. Therefore, I wrote that where it is not feasible [i.e., to be strict], the matter may be restored to its basic [licit] status; and we find that [both] early and late scholars have acted similarly."[225] To be sure, much greater allowance might be made for a truly unusual emergency, especially if, as in this case, it entails personal rather than purely financial loss. While the license of *hefsed merubbeh* is no doubt to be subsumed under the general category of *she'at hadehak,* it by no means exhausts it. Nevertheless, one cannot entirely dismiss the possibility that, over the years, the particular dissent relevant to this *teshuva* has been rejected with finality, so that it cannot be invoked even in an emergency.

Evidently guarding against such a prospect, the Rama introduces his final narrow argument. He contends, first, that Sabbath *kiddushin* were only proscribed in order to guard against possible violation in connection with them; second, that such danger no longer exists; and finally, that the rabbinic prohibition therefore no longer applies. The first two premises concern matters of fact and, on the basis of talmudic texts and current experience, respectively, are thoroughly tenable. The

---

225. *Torat Hatat* (Petrokov, 1903). See Siev, *HaRama,* 93–94. It is clear from the Rama's statement here that he regarded *hefsed merubbeh* as a traditional principle rather than as his own invention. Siev, however, quotes – and evidently accepts – a statement by Rav Tza'ir that "this principle, which occupies of course a very honored position in *pesak,* is an innovation instituted by the Rama. No previous scholar preceded him in this regard" (p. 94n). The facts support the Rama, however. Quite apart from the fact that the specific term, *hefsed merubbeh,* is cited earlier in this connection – see, e.g., *Teshuvot HaRashba,* I, 253 – the principle is not novel at all but simply a particular application of the more general concept of *she'at hadehak* which of course appears in the Talmud. See also *Encyclopedia Talmudit,* s.v. *hefsed merubbeh,* X, 36–37. It is true, however, that the Rama invoked *hefsed merubbeh* with much greater frequency than his predecessors; and it is this practice which brought him under criticism.

last concerns a matter of legal theory and presents major difficulties. It apparently contradicts the basic dictum that "every matter decided by a council requires another council in order to rescind it."[226] Within a legal system, laws which have been formally promulgated by legislative authority – assuming that they were constitutionally valid to begin with – can only be nullified by similar or superior authority. They cannot be summarily dismissed by a judge who happens to regard them as anachronisms. The Rama bases his argument upon *Tosafot*'s analogous statements that the prohibition against certain forms of dancing – initially instituted to guard against possible repair of musical instruments – no longer applies. However, in the talmudic phrase, "The guarantor is [himself] in need of a guarantor."[227] That statement has itself been challenged on these very grounds.[228]

The Rama would no doubt answer that he is not nullifying an existing law at all. He is merely contending that its authors had never intended it to apply to present circumstances to which its authors' motivation has little relevance. Such a contention is occasionally advanced in halakhic discourse concerning rabbinic injunctions;[229] in some cases, it seems almost obvious. Yet, as a general principle to be consistently applied in interpreting Halakha, it hardly seems acceptable. In the first place, it presents formidable practical difficulties. The latitude such a principle would necessarily offer to almost rampant subjectivism poses a clear threat to halakhic stability. Readers of Orwell's *Animal Farm* will recall his merciless satire of those who would qualify laws so as to exempt their present situation from them; and while Napoleon and Squealer limited laws whose purpose had not been stated, the danger is considerable even where it has. Secondly, the tendency to identify the motive and its substance, the "why" and the "what" of an injunction, while it appeals

226. *Beitza* 5b.

227. *Sukka* 26a.

228. See *Beit Yosef*, OH 339. In *Shulhan Arukh*, OH 339:3, R. Yosef Karo prohibits such dancing and the Rama glosses that the practice is now indulged in without rabbinic protest, because protest would probably be ineffectual. He then concludes by citing *Tosafot*'s view and adds that it is perhaps the reason the practice has become widespread.

229. See, e.g., *Shabbat* 95a; *Eiruvin* 104a.

to the realistic pragmatist, clearly runs counter to the primary trend of halakhic thought. Whatever role be assigned to teleology in Halakha, it can hardly be regarded as its sole operative principle – as regards either biblical or rabbinic injunctions. *Hametz* which had been owned by a Jew during Pesah is rabbinically forbidden even after Pesah as a penalty for its previous possession. Yet, the Rambam,[230] among others, states that even if it had been possessed under duress, it is forbidden. Certain Gentile food products are rabbinically forbidden lest their consumption lead to intermarriage. Yet, as the Rashba explained in a *teshuva*, they may not even be purchased from monks.[231] One reason given for the prohibition against the purifying immersion of vessels on the Sabbath is that one may be led to extract the water they have absorbed. Yet, it includes stone vessels.[232] The substance of a rabbinic injunction is clearly not identical with its impulse. Not all such injunctions were similarly instituted. In some cases, these two elements are more closely intertwined than in others. In one instance, the form and content of a rabbinic prohibition may virtually coincide with its reason and telos: it applies only when its cause is relevant. In another, the prohibition may have been flatly formulated, in which case the purpose of the law and its substance may overlap. In a third, the nature and scope of the injunction may be in dispute. And no doubt, an analysis of this issue with reference to the whole range of rabbinic ordinances would prove a valuable subject for a monograph.[233] Certainly, however, one cannot assume any equation

---

230. *Hilkhot Hametz UMatza* 1:4. However, this view is not unanimous.

231. *Teshuvot HaRashba*, I, 248. By way of explanation, he cites both the point I am making and the possibility that the reason for the prohibition may be indirectly relevant in the case of monks, too. His primary ground is the first, however.

232. See *Beitza* 18a.

233. For a cursory discussion, see Moshe Silberg, *Kakh Darko Shel Talmud* (Jerusalem, 1961), 60–65. It should be noted that we should not confuse two types of situations: 1) injunctions whose initial reason is still applicable to some cases but not to the one at issue; 2) those whose motive is no longer relevant at all. The first turns on the question of defining the initial nature and scope of the ordinance; the second may also involve assumptions concerning the need for formal revocation of officially promulgated injunctions. See also *Kaftor VaFerah*, ch. 5; *Peri Hadash*, YD 116; *Hiddushei HaMe'iri, Beitza* 5b; and *Tosafot, Avoda Zara* 2a, s.v. *asur*; 15a, s.v. *emur*; and 57b, s.v. *le'afuki*.

a priori; and with respect to ordinances – such as those treated here by the Rama – which are presented in a mishna without qualification or explanation, one would normally presume it likely that they were instituted across the board. Would we contend that Sabbath horseback riding, proscribed lest the rider shear vegetation, be permitted in the desert? At the very least, the burden of proof would seem to lie with the Rama.

This argument, too, then, is fraught with difficulty; and in the final analysis, the Rama's reasons, either singly or in combination, are far from absolutely convincing. They render a lenient decision possible, but that is about all. It remained for the Rama's humanistic compassion to make that decision definitive. He applied it, interestingly enough, not only as regards this isolated instance, but as a broad rule covering all similar cases. When the *Shulhan Arukh* states that Sabbath *kiddushin* are prohibited, the Rama glosses:

> And some permit effecting *kiddushin* for one who has no wife and children, and perhaps the induction into *huppa* is likewise permissible. And although we do not accept this view, nevertheless we rely upon it in a moment of crisis, for great is *kevod haberiyyot*. Thus, it is customary that sometimes, when the parties had been unable to reach agreement concerning the dowry before nightfall, the *huppa* and the *kiddushin* are made on Friday night, since they had already been prepared for the meal and the wedding and there would be shame for the bride and groom if he were not to induct [her] then. Nonetheless, initial care should be taken to avoid reaching this point.[234]

It is essential, however, that both the letter and the spirit of the *teshuva* be clearly understood. The Rama does not merely let his humanistic instincts ride roughshod over Halakha. He does not even rely solely upon

234. OH 339:4. With reference to the Rama's final comment, it is interesting to note that subsequent to the incident involved in our *teshuva* – and no doubt in light of the furor caused by it – the community instituted an ordinance that weddings no longer be held on Fridays in Cracow. When a Friday wedding was deemed necessary, the parties arranged it on the outskirts of the town.

some of its more general principles to transcend a specific injunction. He presents solid grounds, within this area of Halakha, for leniency. As both the early part of the *teshuva* and the text of his gloss make clear, the heart of the decision was one central point: since *kevod haberiyyot* was involved, one could legitimately regard the case as an emergency in which one could rely upon Rabbenu Tam's permissive dissent. The primary legal basis was Rabbenu Tam's position; more general factors justified the Rama's recourse to it.

I particularly emphasize this aspect because none of this might have been guessed from the thoroughly misleading presentation of the *teshuva* set forth in Freehof's *A Treasury of Responsa*.[235] The impression

235. Pp. 113–17. Possibly determined to make the *teshuva* live up to its assigned title ("A Radical Decision"), Freehof presents it in the following form: After his own introduction, we are given, under the heading, "Text," a translation of the Rama's prologue, followed by sections of the body of the *teshuva* interleaved with a few editorial comments. The first such section – in the absence of any qualifying note, one of course presumes it to be continued translation, but it is only a paraphrase – describes the primary text in Beitza, breaking off after presenting Rashi's interpretation. After a brief note explaining, in very general terms, what the Rama contends in the omitted portion, the "text" skips over to a translation of the section on kevod haberiyyot, followed in turn by a greatly abbreviated paraphrase – again passed off as translation of the text – of the section stating that the prohibition against Sabbath kiddushin may no longer apply, as its cause no longer exists. Freehof then adds a parenthetical note, "After discussing these various ways in which old rabbinic restrictions were set aside under changed circumstances, he [i.e., the Rama] concludes as follows:" and he ends his presentation by translating the last few lines of the *teshuva*.

The overall impression is, of course, perfectly clear. First, the omission of all its technical parts – perhaps justified by an appeal to a general reader – removes the legal nitty-gritty from the *teshuva*. Second, the total omission of Rabbenu Tam's interpretation of the gemara in Beitza – it is mentioned in neither the "text" nor the notes and one only learns that Rabbenu Tam took a lenient view, presumably of course solely because of an emergency – emasculates the very heart of the decision. Third, the hesitancy with which the Rama advanced his final suggestion is conveniently omitted. A distinction which the Rama clearly threw out as only a tentative possibility – it is not even mentioned in his gloss in Shulhan Arukh – becomes, in what is presented to us as translation, an almost causal certainty: "After all, the prohibition (against marriage on Sabbath) is only a rabbinic decree to keep us from writing the marriage documents…." Moreover, in the next editorial comment, we are blandly informed that "then Isserles goes on to show that there

we get from Freehof is that, like a good humanist, the Rama felt that, in a pinch, rabbinic injunctions could simply be given cavalier treatment; or, at most, that his only halakhic ground was *kevod haberiyyot*. This with respect to a *posek* who would not give the back of his hand to a minor custom – "Nor should a man depart from the custom of the town even with regard to the tunes or the *piyutim* which are recited there,"[236] the Rama writes concerning High Holiday prayers – let alone to a definitive halakha. Just how accurate the impression is, any reader of the *teshuva* can judge for himself.

In one sense, it is quite true that the *teshuva* is radical in nature. Precisely because he was so profoundly committed to the letter and the spirit of Halakha, any departure from its normal dictates constituted, for the Rama, a sharper break than far more sweeping changes might represent for those less deeply committed. Inasmuch as the Rama did not regard a rabbinic Sabbath ordinance as a straitjacket to be snapped or a stumbling block to be hurdled, its confrontation with *kevod haberiyyot* posed not only a legal but an axiological issue. To this extent, any decision to "violate" one in the interests of the other necessarily assumed a somewhat radical character. However, this should not lead us to misconstrue his total approach. Although his glosses upon the *Shulhan Arukh* introduced many prohibitions R. Yosef Karo had excluded, the Rama

are a number of such rabbinic decrees which we no longer observe; for example, the decree against dancing...." The fact of the matter is, of course, that the Rama makes no such general statement; and that the only decree he goes on to discuss is that against dancing – precisely because it was formulated in the same mishna with that concerning kiddushin, suggesting that, unlike numerous other rabbinic decrees, this group was not instituted flatly, but was imposed subject to relevant circumstances. Finally, a sweeping and thoroughly disingenuous general statement ("After discussing these various ways in which old rabbinic restrictions were set aside under changed circumstances...") and some, to say the least, dubious translations ("The rabbinical prohibitory decrees were not meant to apply in times of emergency") round out the picture.

236. OH 619:1. *Piyutim* are prayers which are not part of the basic standard text but which were composed and adopted in some communities as addenda for special occasions.

The overall role of custom – with attendant dangers of rigidity and stagnation singled out by Bagehot – require full treatment, with reference both to Halakha generally and to the Rama specifically. But this lies beyond my present purpose.

was not quite the heartless rigorist castigated by some nineteenth-century *maskilim*. We should remember that in many cases he was primarily presenting local Ashkenazic custom in an effort to preserve the integrity of the community; that he introduced many key lenient provisions as well; and that, in any event, he was often attacked simply because he had come to embody the whole Eastern European halakhic tradition against which the *Haskala* rebelled. Neither, however, was he a humanistic radical determined upon bending Halakha at will to serve purely human ends. He was simply an honest and compassionate man who saw that halakhic decision often entails, in the Hegelian sense, an element of tragedy; and who knew that if, in the popular Yiddish phrase, *Es ist schwer zu sein a Yid*, "It is difficult to be a Jew," it is far more difficult to be a *posek*.

Formalism vs. Teleology: Circumvention and Adaptation in Halakha

INTRODUCTION AND BIOGRAPHY OF THE *HAVVOT YA'IR*

Rav Ya'ir Hayim Bacharach (1638–1702), one of the leading *posekim* of the early modern period, was born the scion of a celebrated rabbinic family. His father, like Rav Ya'ir Hayim after him, served as rabbi of the historic city of Worms; his great-great-grandfather was the Maharal of Prague; and the family included numerous noted scholars, among them R. Isaiah Hurwitz, author of the famous ethico-halakhic treatise, *Shenei Luhot HaBrit*. Throughout his life, Rav Ya'ir Hayim was sorely beset by continual tribulation: his childhood was spent in the shadow of the Thirty Years' War and the Chmielnicki massacres; his last years, starting with Louis XIV's capture of Worms in 1689, found him, sick and impoverished, in recurring flight from French oppression; and the intervening period was marked by a variety of troubles, ranging from decimation of the Worms community in a plague to the rampant spread of Sabbateanism. There were personal disappointments as well: after succeeding his father as rabbi of Worms in 1670, he was forced to step down for a while; what was to have been a *magnum opus* – the manuscript of a commentary on *Orah Hayim* (one of the four sections of the *Shulhan Arukh*) – had to be shelved when it was preempted by the appearance of what subsequently became the standard commentaries.

Adversity notwithstanding, Rav Ya'ir Hayim nevertheless lived a rich and productive life. Perhaps in part because of the Maharal's influence, he had an unusually wide range of interests. He studied astronomy, geometry, and philosophy. Although vigorously opposed to popular dissemination of the Kabbala, he sought to master its arcane wisdom. He wrote pietistic verse and a historical treatise; and, unlike many contemporaries, he often cited secular sources. However, Rav Ya'ir Hayim's primary interest, by far overshadowing all the rest, was Halakha; and in the course of a career which straddled Germany and its environs and during which he served as rabbi of several renowned communities, he became one of its acknowledged masters.

Methodical to the point of precision, Rav Ya'ir Hayim was a prolific writer. Apart from voluminous commonplace books – divided, strikingly enough, into sections on Halakha, Aggada, philosophy, pietism and ethics, and matters of general interest,[1] and miscellaneous minor treatises – he wrote a number of works on both the methodology and the substance of Halakha. Relatively little of this has been published, however – some having been lost, some remaining in manuscript. Of the published writings, by far the most important is the collection of *teshuvot*, or responsa, *Havvot Ya'ir*, a work whose title casts some incidental light upon its author's singularity. The title appears to be simply a biblical phrase selected because it includes the author's name. However, in the preface we are told that, among other things, it is intended to perpetuate the memory of Rav Ya'ir Hayim's paternal grandmother, a pious and

1. Descriptions of some of these commonplace books and interesting gleanings from them may be found in D. Kauffmann, *R. Jair Chajjim Bacharach, 1638–1702, und seine Ahnen* (Trier, 1894), 86–107.

learned woman who had influenced him profoundly. Her name having been Hava, the title is to be regarded as a German (a Yiddish) possessive, "Hava's Ya'ir," a designation presented as a fitting appellation for the author whom she had so strongly impressed. It is from this collection that the following two responsa are drawn. The translation is based upon the text of the *editio princeps* (Frankfurt, 1699), whose publication was supervised by the author.

The following *teshuva* looks through both ends of the telescope. Its immediate subject is a specific situation involving a complex of narrow legal problems. Yet its broader implications impinge upon a wide range of profound moral and religious issues. Indeed, the very dual nature of the *teshuva* provides a striking example of the interaction, if not the coalescence, of morality and law within the halakhic ethic.

The specific case involved is quite simple. A group of textile dealers, finding it almost impossible to abide by the rigorous halakhic injunctions against *hassagat gevul*,[2] unfair competition, were presented with an ingeniously simple solution: Let them all agree to permit any and every mode of competition. Advance consent having been granted by all injured parties, there would be, legally speaking, no future injury. Hence, the compact would absolve all members of the group from transgressions relating to their business practices. Under the protective umbrella of mutual consent, they could thus pursue their competitive enterprises with a clear conscience. Provided, that is, that the compact receive halakhic sanction; and for this they turned to Rav Ya'ir Hayim Bacharach.

The broader implications of this solution are fairly obvious. Quite apart from the immediate question of the scope of halakhic business ethics – more the point of departure of this *teshuva* than one of its substantive issues – the proposal raises basic problems of attitude and approach to Halakha as a whole. Fidelity to the spirit as well as the

2. The phrase literally means "removal of boundary" and is derived from the verse, "Thou shalt not remove thy neighbor's landmark which they of old times have set" (*Devarim* 18:14). In its primary sense, the term refers to territorial annexation. By extension, however, it includes all forms of infringement and, hence, of illegal competition.

letter of Halakha; recognition of both ethical and legal dimensions of religious norms; evasive circumvention under stress of economic pressure; above all, defining the extent to which prior consent can neutralize social halakhic injunctions – all are, in some measure, clearly related to the case at hand.

The *Havvot Ya'ir* rejects the proposal unequivocally; and, in doing so, he deals with both its narrower and its broader aspects. He rejects it on three grounds – or rather, at three levels. First, he chastises his respondents on general principle – partly ethical and partly religious. He reproaches them for seeking to enact a plan which, while possibly eliminating technical infractions, would greatly increase turbulent dissidence and internecine strife – i.e., the very ethical evils which the laws of *hassagat gevul* should presumably reduce; and he predicts that the final result will be out and out plunder. Moreover, even granting the basic legal soundness of the proposal, it might still lead, incidentally, to outright halakhic violations. Once put into effect, it would exceed any intended temporal or spatial bounds. On the one hand, the aggressiveness engendered by a permissive atmosphere would become second nature, ineradicable even after the compact had lapsed; and, on the other hand, the legalized license prevailing within this group would quickly infect members of other communities. The parties to the compact would thus be *hotim umahati'im*, both sinning themselves and inciting others to sin.

Moving beyond moral reproach and general principle, the *Havvot Ya'ir* finds, secondly, that, even from a purely legal perspective, the compact does not attain its ostensible purpose. Mutual consent cannot sanction ethical and religious wrong. Notwithstanding any compact, whatever the Torah has forbidden as being socially disruptive and inherently unethical, or has forbidden out of its concern for the economic interests of every Jew, remains in a strict normative sense, a transgression. Guilt is not amenable to the absolution of prior consent.

Finally, the compact is examined and found wanting at a third level – that of legal validity. The argument is not only ethically and religiously repugnant. It is not only that, even assuming the legal validity of the compact, *hassagat gevul* remains forbidden – not only as a generally unethical act but as a specific and definite sin. The compact is perhaps also technically void.[3] Hence, whatever damage might have been due an injured party without the compact shall continue to be collected in its spite. *Hassagat gevul* remains fully actionable.

The grounds for possible nullification are two. The first is *asmakhta,* the concept that commitment grounded upon misconception – even where the terms are clearly understood and no fraud is involved – is regarded as error and is therefore not binding. In its primary form, this concept applies to cases of self-delusion, as when a debtor, fully confident of his ability to repay a loan by a specified time, might commit himself to make a penalty payment to his creditor should he fail to do so.[4] However, the Rambam[5] also applied it to a boundless open-ended commitment wherein one does not and cannot be fully aware of the future cost or implications of his commitment; and the *Havvot Ya'ir* contends that, in principle, this view may very well be regarded as unanimous. He argues that those who rejected the Rambam's view[6] only quarreled with his definition of boundlessness. Where consent has been given to a truly unfathomable commitment – as in the present case – all would argue that it had no binding force.

The second ground is that of *davar shelo ba laolam,* the halakha that nonexistent things cannot be involved in transactions.[7] Just as such objects cannot be sold, so, the *Havvot Ya'ir* contends, as yet nonexistent claims cannot be renounced. Hence, the proposed compact must be declared null and void. For while it is true that the sale of a *davar shelo ba laolam* can be validated once the object comes into existence and is subsequently acquired by the purchaser, this has no bearing upon the present case. The sale is then valid only because, the prior argument not

3. Halakhically, these are independent questions. A transaction may be forbidden and nonetheless valid; see *Hoshen Mishpat* 208.
4. The example is taken from *Bava Batra* 168a. The other major primary sources are *Sanhedrin* 24b–25a, *Nedarim* 27b, *Bava Metzia* 48b, 66a–b, and 73b, and commentaries; see also *Hoshen Mishpat* 207.
5. *Hilkhot Mekhira* 11:16.
6. As, for instance, the Raavad, ad loc.; see also the sources cited in *Beit Yosef, Tur,* HM 207.
7. See *Yevamot* 93a–b, the various sources cited there, and commentaries; also, *Hoshen Mishpat* 209.

having been repudiated, current acquiescence is regarded as consent which, with respect to the newly existing object, can now take effect. The principle that there can be no transaction involving nonexistent objects is therefore not breached, for in this case the purchaser retains the object only because we presume consent after it came into being. Hence, as regards the proposed compact, it could only have some legal validity with respect to any infractions which were not preceded by its repudiation. Silence could then be construed as continued consent and, therefore, as acquiescence in what had become an existing reality. However, repudiation at any time would nullify the compact with regard to all future violations. Subject to this limitation, the proposal would of course fall short of its aim, so that the *Havvot Ya'ir,* in effect, uses the argument of *davar shelo ba laolam* as a ground for its rejection. Moreover, he suggests that in the present case, the principle of presumed continued consent is inapplicable. Such a presumption has merit only when the later situation, to which there had been prior consent, had been anticipated accurately. The initial meaningful consent can then be said to continue in force and to become relevant once the situation materializes. However, the excesses of entrepreneurial zeal – graphically portrayed – are such that they cannot be genuinely anticipated and accepted.[8] There having been no true initial consent, it cannot, of course, be said to continue.

The vivid description of various shady practices serves as a fitting prelude to the *teshuva*'s summary conclusion: "Therefore let my soul be no party to their plot, for they shall not be absolved as regards either human or, certainly, Heavenly judgment. Let him who hears listen and him who can cease cease, for I have written what, in my humble opinion, seems correct."

8. This contention, of course, also reinforces the previous argument of *asmakhta*.

RESPONSA HAVVOT YA'IR #163

Question: A group of textile dealers who study daily under a scholar agreed that any complaints which should arise among members of the group concerning *hassagat gevul* in the area of sales should be presented to their master who instructs them daily in matters of Aggada. Now, inasmuch as complaints have proliferated and the expense of their adjudication has become burdensome, their *gabbai,* the most outstanding and pious among them, has advised them [as follows]: "Why should you lose the fees for rulings and the time wasted in quarrel[1] – apart from [the fact that there are] secret acts [of violation whereby it is] unrevealed to his fellow that one has infringed upon him by speaking to his clientele or by maligning his goods, in which case he is, at any rate, culpable in the eyes of Heaven?[2] Since it is impossible to repair this breach, as all have become rooted in this evil, let us rather agree to permit all forms of *hassagat gevul* among ourselves, and we shall remit[3] to each other any financial loss which may have been caused by our fellow. Thus, civil complaints will be put to rest and divine judgment will be quieted."

They asked their master whether they have the authority to do this and whether they are thus living up to their religious obligation. He answered them that he was an interested party inasmuch as he had occasionally derived financial benefit from their disputes; but that "nevertheless – I shall present my opinion to you in writing, and you may show it to any learned authorities that you may select. If I shall have spoken

1. This translation is based upon the Frankfurt text which reads *biluy hazeman hameriva,* a somewhat unusual form of the construct. The Lemberg edition reads *biluy hazeman hamerubbeh,* "much waste of time," a more normal construction.
2. Literally, "duty vis-à-vis Heaven." The term generally refers to duties which, while legal rather than merely pietistic in character, nevertheless, even when they involve and impinge upon another individual, are regarded as obligations vis-à-vis God rather than one's fellow. Their precise moral and religious character may vary in different contexts. See, for instance, the contrasting nuances of *Bava Kamma* 56b, 114a (according to the interpretation of Ramban, *Milhamot Hashem,* ad loc.), and 118a.
3. Ed. note: In this context, "remit" means to release from guilt or penalty.

properly, abide by my ruling; if not, do as you wish"; and he wrote and presented to them accordingly.

It seems to me that although you acted badly [by engaging] in *hassagat gevul*, and [indeed] the *posekim* have spoken of this – that sometimes he [i.e., the violator] is liable to pay, sometimes it is [classified under] acts which, in the interests of peace, are [regarded as] robbery,[4] and sometimes he is [only] called an evildoer,[5] but, in all instances, there is, at the very least, a transgression; nevertheless, your last action, if you should maintain your resolve to legitimize it [i.e., *hassagat gevul*] by remission, is worse than the former. For undoubtedly, as a result of its being [regarded] by you as lawful,[6] turmoil, strife, recrimination, and desecration of [God's] name[7] will increase manifold from what had been heretofore, until your homes will be filled with iniquity. And if you should introduce this novel institution – or rather, this corruption[8] – for a [limited] period, undoubtedly, when the time limit will expire, the habit will remain and will become a permanent and incurable nature. Moreover, [you should refrain] lest others elsewhere shall also learn from you and tradesmen will be instructed by your corruption, and you shall be both sinners and the instigators of sin. O! Would that I were governor, *parnas*, and leader! I would punish the members

4. I.e., it does not come under the strict legal definition of robbery, but nevertheless has been forbidden by rabbinic ordinance as if it did, their motivation being a desire to maintain social peace. See *Gittin* 59b.
5. I.e., although an act may not even come under the aforementioned rabbinic injunction concerning what, in the interests of peace, is regarded as robbery, its perpetrator may nevertheless be described as an evildoer, inasmuch as his action may be ethically reprehensible. See *Kiddushin* 59a.
6. The text, *sheye'aseh lakhem hetter*, may either mean that it actually will become permissible or that it will come to be regarded as being permissible – i.e., indulgence will inure them to the legal and ethical import of the principle of *hassagat gevul* generally (see *Kiddushin* 40a: "R. Huna said, 'Once a man does wrong and repeats it, it is permitted him.' It is permitted him! Can you really think so? – But it becomes to him as something permitted.")
7. The injunction of *Vayikra* 22:32, "And ye shall not profane My holy name," includes all actions which diminish respect for, and commitment to, God and His Torah; see *Yoma* 86a and Rambam, *Hilkhot Yesodei HaTorah* 5:11.
8. A slight play on the two meanings of the term *takkana* – a new institution and an improvement.

of this group for such an evil plan, in accordance with their capacity [to accept punishment] – and all others might hear and fear.

However, since you did not seek moral chastisement but law and judgment whether this arrangement suffices to remove it [i.e., their practice of *hassagat gevul*] from [the category of] indirect robbery; therefore I say that, as regards [the letter of] Torah law as well, it is wholly insufficient, and even with respect to civil law,[9] they shall not be absolved through such an arrangement. Likewise, all those who permit one another to do an action which the Torah has proscribed, such as theft, profiteering, or *hassagat gevul*, apart[10] from [the fact] that the doer of all these will not be absolved from divine judgment, inasmuch as it is contrary to the order of the world and its conduct. And this was the sin of the generation of the flood: "And the earth was full of plunder." It [i.e., the text] calls it plunder because none of them was absolved, [and each] was like a plunderer who gives money.[11] And although one might contend that [the situation] there was different, as they did not remit, who says so? In my opinion, due to their habit, they did not care at all, for it does not say of them, as with respect to Sodom, that their outcry arose before Him, blessed be His name.[12]

9. Literally, "human laws." "Human" does not describe the source of the laws but rather their domain. The contrasting phrases, *dinei adam* and *dinei shamayim*, refer to two levels of Halakha, both of which derive from the same source but whose legal and normative character differ. The former entails civil obligation, and violation is normally actionable. The latter, although it may deal with social situations, imposes purely religious obligation. Both make binding legal demands, however, and therefore go beyond the purely moral dimension discussed earlier in the *teshuva*.

   The term *din*, finally, may mean either law or judgment. I have translated it variously, depending on the context.
10. The text reads *demilvad*, "that apart," but I presume the initial "*de*" is erroneous.
11. The text is a bit obscure here, and quite possibly corrupt. I believe the general sense is as follows. The *Havvot Ya'ir* notes that the verse speaks of *hamas*, "plunder," rather than *gezel*, "robbery." The distinction between the terms is explained in *Bava Kamma* 62a: while both take property forcefully, the *hamsan* gives the owner compensation, whereas the *gazlan* does not. The *Havvot Ya'ir* assumes that expropriation with compensation was socially permitted among Noah's contemporaries – and it was this rather than outright theft which prevailed – and yet the Torah calls it plunder, indicating that consent did not produce absolution.
12. See *Bereshit* 18:21.

Furthermore, we have studied in the Mishna: "He who injures himself, even though he is not permitted [to do so], is not liable."[13] And why shouldn't he be permitted, since he remits to himself? [Because,] nevertheless, the Torah has objected and has declared, "And you shall take heed for your souls."[14] As regards property as well, it has objected in many instances with [the prohibition], "Thou shalt not destroy."[15] Thus, they have also said: "He who chops down his plants, even though he is not permitted etc."[16] Also, the entire discourse about [he who tells another] "Tear my cloak, break my vessel or my hand or my leg"[17] deals only with the liability to pay or the lack of it. However, it is certainly prohibited and the permission of one's fellow is of no avail with regard to this. [Just] go and infer from usury, in which the debtor remits to the creditor and gives him voluntarily, and yet the Torah has forbidden it to the creditor and even to the debtor.[18] [Indeed,] we find also that the Torah has [even] been concerned about the vessels of an evildoer, as our Rabbis of blessed memory taught in connection with house plagues.[19]

Therefore, since this action [i.e., *hassagat gevul*] is wrong[20] and bitter *per se*, regardless of whether or not there is remission, let it remain [proscribed] in its bitterness. [For it is] like a debtor and a creditor who argue together to litigate in a secular Gentile court and to remit any differential between its ordinances and Torah law.[21] Another analogue

13. *Bava Kamma* 90b. The possible "liability" is discussed in *Tosafot*, ibid. 91b, s.v. *hahovel*.
14. *Devarim* 4:15. In context, the verse refers primarily to avoiding spiritual danger. By extension, however, it is taken to refer to physical danger as well.
15. *Devarim* 20:19; see also Rambam, *Hilkhot Melakhim* 6:10.
16. *Bava Kamma* 90b.
17. Ibid. 92a.
18. See Rambam, *Hilkhot Malveh VeLoveh* 4:13.
19. The allusion is to the comment of the *Sifra*, *Metzora*, 5:12, on the verse in *Vayikra* 14:36, stating that before the priest enters a plagued house in order possibly to condemn it, all vessels should be removed so that they may be spared. The *Sifra* comments that although the plague is regarded as a punishment for sin (see Ramban, *Vayikra* 13:47), nevertheless the Torah sought to save the sinner's vessels.
20. The Hebrew term *ra* actually lies somewhere between wrong and evil. It is, however, considerably sharper than its literal but flaccid English equivalent, "bad."
21. I.e., wherever recourse may be had to a rabbinic court, it would be forbidden to bring litigation before a Gentile court, even if both parties agree. See Ramban, *Shemot* 21:1, and *Hiddushei HaRan*, *Sanhedrin* 2b.

is the Rabbis o.b.m.'s statement, "You shall not steal with the intent of repaying twofold,"[22] even though the victim certainly remits to him [i.e., the thief], as was stated by the *Tur* and the *Shulhan Arukh*, at the beginning of [HM] 348. Similarly, with respect to property damage, as was stated by the *Sema*,[23] at the beginning of [HM] 378.

Let us now, therefore, consider the legal question,[24] whether this arrangement suffices so that if one [of them] infringed upon his fellow in such a manner that [barring the compact] it would turn out that he would be liable to pay or that he should be called an evildoer, whether this arrangement will be effective in removing his liability. *Prima facie*, it seems that it is effective, just as we hold with reference to the law of *asmakhta*, that, although even an unqualified *kinyan*[25] is ineffective, nevertheless, in the case of two dice players [we say that] inasmuch as each is anxious to acquire he also transfers, as is stated at the conclusion of the lengthy note, HM 207:13.[26] This idea was [also] employed

---

22. *Bava Metzia* 61b.
23. These are the initials of one of the earliest major commentaries on *Hoshen Mishpat*, the segment of the *Shulhan Arukh* which deals with civil law. Its full title is *Sefer Me'irat Einayim*. The author, Rav Yehoshua Falke (?–1614), was recognized both as an outstanding halakhic authority and as one of the communal leaders of Eastern European Jewry.
24. The immediately preceding part of course also deals with legal issues. However, heretofore the question had been whether entering into it was permissible. Henceforth, it becomes whether the compact is valid. Should litigation ensue, it is of course the latter question which would be relevant. In this sense, one is, at this point, becoming more deeply enmeshed in the legal issues.
25. This term, in its broadest sense, may mean ownership or property; in a narrower sense, any mode of acquisition; in a still narrower sense – probably intended here – the specific mode of *kinyan sudar*, "acquisition via a scarf." In this mode – first described in *Rut* 4:7 – one party to the transaction, be it either exchange or commitment, hands the other an artifact, usually a handkerchief or scarf. This act serves as a symbolic expression of will which makes the proposed transaction binding.
26. Dice playing, as presumably all modes of gambling, should, *prima facie*, be classified under *asmakhta* (see introduction). However, the Gemara in *Sanhedrin* 24b cites opposing views with regard to this. In seeking to explain why dice playing might not constitute an *asmakhta*, Rabbenu Tam – cited in *Tosafot*, ad loc. – advanced the concept that *asmakhta* was confined to unilateral commitment. However, in bilateral situations, wherein each party may not only lose but win, the prospect of winning engenders genuine commitment. Each is willing to pay the price of possible loss

by the *Sema* 209:2–3, and from there it would, *prima facie*, appear that [it applies] even to [commitment concerning] something whose identity and amount are wholly unknown.[27] In such a case, one might say that even the opponents of the Rambam who held that [obligation even with] *kinyan* is ineffective with reference to an unknown, [might accept his view]. All later authorities disagreed with him, as is stated by the *Beit Yosef* in *Shulhan Arukh*, [HM] 60:2 and at the end of 207, [but] that was with reference to something whose general identity is known, such as board,[28] so that it may be appraised on the basis of donation. And even if the donation was not specified but he simply said [to someone] that he would provide for him all his life, nevertheless this is known approximately according to nature – "the days of our years are threescore and ten, etc."[29] Similarly, "that which I shall inherit from Father"[30] can be appraised and estimated approximately. This resembles the case of the known species of 209:1[31] in contradistinction to "all the contents of

in order to attain possible gain. It is this concept, subsequently cited by many later sources, that is alluded to here.

27. In the following section, the *Havvot Ya'ir* develops a twofold argument. 1) In principle, everyone may very well accept the Rambam's view that unfathomable commitment constitutes *asmakhta*. Those authorities who challenged his specific statement were only rejecting his criteria of the unfathomable. 2) Rabbenu Tam's concept, that reciprocity eliminates *asmakhta*, would not apply to the case of unfathomable commitment. It can apply only to a situation such as dice playing wherein the stakes are known and the delusion is confined to the contingency of the commitment; each of course hopes he will never pay. However, when the *asmakhta* derives from the fact that the very subject of the commitment – rather than the prospects of honoring it – is unknown, reciprocity only compounds the confusion. The *Sema* did not make this last distinction, and the *Havvot Ya'ir* goes on to challenge him on this point, albeit diffidently.
28. The Rambam formulated his position with reference to the specific case of a person who committed himself to feed or clothe someone else for a fixed period of time.
29. *Tehillim* 90:10.
30. See *Bava Metzia* 16a, where the Gemara states one cannot sell his future inheritance *in toto* because it does not yet belong to him. Evidently, however, its identity and value being unspecified presents no problem.
31. The *Shulhan Arukh* there states that a transaction involving a known species but an unspecified quantity is valid. However, if even the species is unknown as, for instance, if the contents of a house or bag are sold sight unseen – the transaction is invalid.

this house etc.," 209:2, with respect to which we find no opposition and everyone agrees that it [i.e., obligation] is ineffective.

Nevertheless, even in such a case, if neither [i.e., the buyer nor the seller] knows, it [i.e., the sale] is effective, as was stated by the *Sema*.[32] However, although I am unworthy of challenging the *gaon*, the author of the *Sema*, nevertheless I say, after begging his forgiveness,[33] that his position is not irrefutable. Rather, even if the seller also does not know what is in the house – as, for instance, if he himself also had simply bought it thus with its contents and resold it to another – the sale is equally invalid, because, in any event, the purchaser does not truly consent to buy something whose identity cannot be determined by any estimate, as is written there, "whether hay or gold."[34] The Rambam, because he holds that dice playing constitutes *asmakhta*, compares [a sale of] "the whole contents of the house"[35] to it. However, those who hold that it [i.e., dice playing] does not constitute *asmakhta* will say that [sale of] "the whole contents of the house" is certainly inferior. Just note: We are compelled to say that dice playing is superior even to [a transaction concerning] something whose kind is known but whose amount

32. 209:3. The *Sema* contends that in a case in which two people would exchange their total assets blindly, or if, in the present case, the seller also was ignorant of the contents of the house, the transaction would be valid, since there is reciprocal pot luck.

33. This phrase, while sometimes used *pro forma*, generally expresses genuine humility. It should not be confused with the almost truculent contemporary equivalent, "begging your pardon."

34. HM 209:2.

35. The Rambam (*Hilkhot Mekhira* 21:3), in formulating the halakha that sales of wholly unknown objects are invalid, explains that the purchaser's will is not truly engaged, "since he does not know what is in it [i.e., the container], whether hay or gold, and this is nothing more than dice playing." The *Havvot Ya'ir* suggests that this equation only holds true for the Rambam. Inasmuch as he holds – in the *Havvot Ya'ir*'s view – that dice playing constitutes *asmakhta*, the comparison was sufficient to invalidate such a sale. However, those who hold that dice playing does not constitute *asmakhta* would reject the comparison. Even on their view, pot luck sales would be invalid.

Whether the Rambam actually classified dice playing under *asmakhta* has been questioned. See *Hilkhot Eidut* 10:4, and *Hilkhot Gezela VaAveda* 6:7, and commentaries.

is indeterminate. The latter requires, in any event, a *kinyan*,[36] whereas dice playing requires no *kinyan*. Perforce, this is because on each and every occasion how much one will give to the other is definitely known, whether or not the money is placed on the board before them.[37] It would only constitute an *asmakhta* nonetheless because each imagines that he will win; so with respect to this, the anonymously cited[38] view that [the transaction is valid] because both obligate themselves, is effective.

Therefore, the Rama made no comment upon the Rambam's words [cited] in *Shulhan Arukh* 209:2, because – as the *Sema* also stated – he accepted his decision, although not his reasoning.

Similarly, in the *Terumat HaDeshen*'s[39] case, cited in the note at the end of [HM] 203, of two who exchanged [their total assets], it can also be said that some sort of limited appraisal is possible on the basis of conjecture, as we may disregard what we find as an oddity, "there is that pretendeth himself rich etc."[40]

Nevertheless, I am not worthy to challenge the *Sema*, and therefore, although in my humble opinion the arrangement of the members of this group which certainly concerns a wholly indeterminate and unappraisable matter – for who can measure future trades – is invalid even if each agrees to transfer; nevertheless, according to the *Sema* who did not make this distinction,[41] so that, in his view, the principle that since each hopes to win he assents to transfer is effective even in [the case of] "the whole contents of this house" – if, for instance, the seller did not know

36. I.e., a formal *kinyan sudar* in order to validate the commitment.
37. The allusion is to the view, here rejected, that obligations resulting from dice playing are only valid when the players have the money at stake before them – either because the commitment is the more intensely earnest so that pure will, devoid of any formal vehicle, can then effect obligation; or because the board on which the money rests can serve as the vehicle of the actual transfer of the money – if it belongs to both of them – since one's property can "acquire" whatever rests upon it. See *Tosafot, Eiruvin* 82a, s.v. *amar*; *Haggahot Maimoniyot, Hilkhot Eidut* 10:5; and *Hoshen Mishpat* 207:13, and commentaries.
38. By the Rama, HM 207:13.
39. A collection of responsa by R. Yisrael Isserlein, ca. 1390–1460.
40. *Mishlei* 13:7. The rest of the verse reads: "There is that pretendeth himself poor, yet hath great wealth."
41. I.e., between various types of *asmakhta*.

as well – then, as regards the aforementioned group, it is also effective; and if it [i.e., such a compact] was made and one of them infringed upon the other, the latter has no claim upon him. However, even according to the *Sema*, a *kinyan* is, in any event, required, and it would also be necessary for each of the members of the group to effect a *kinyan*. As to dice players not requiring a *kinyan*, we may say that this is because the money is immediately available;[42] see the lengthy note, 207:13.

Moreover, even if it should be conceivable that, when each hopes to gain, a *kinyan* can effect the transfer of even something which is wholly indeterminate because this principle negates all [*asmakhta*], nevertheless this *kinyan* [i.e., that proposed by the group] may be invalid for another reason. For perforce the nature of this *kinyan* is but that of renunciation [by each] of a claim and a right that he will have in the future vis-à-vis his fellow. [It is therefore] similar to a testament of renunciation of a wife's property which is invalid [when made] before betrothal, inasmuch as it [i.e., the object being renounced] is as yet nonexistent and is not in his possession.[43] [In such a case,] even a *kinyan* is ineffective, as was stated by the *gaon*, our master, Rav Gershon,[44] who inferred this from the responsa of the Ran; see [supra] responsum 50. Here, likewise, how can he renounce that which his fellow will owe him as a result of *hassagat gevul* in the future? And there, *asmakhta* – which might lead us to apply the concept of "inasmuch as he wishes to acquire" – is not the reason, but rather that a *kinyan* is invalid with respect to something which is nonexistent.

Nor can it be objected that there we hold that if he [i.e., the purchaser] took [the object] we do not requisition it from him, as is stated in the Gemara in the chapter on usury, at the end of 66, and likewise

42. See, however, supra, n. 24.

43. The category of *davar shelo ba laolam* includes both physically nonexistent objects and those which may exist but are not the property of the seller at the time of the transaction. The general concept is that one cannot transact with reference to the future that which he could not validly effect at present.

44. Rav Gershon Ashkenazi, the author of *Avodat HaGershuni*, a collection of responsa. The text of some of his exchanges with Rav Ya'ir Hayim – one of which is mentioned here – were included in the *Havvot Ya'ir*.

in the *Tur* and *Shulhan Arukh*.[45] For there the reason is that since it became known to the seller that this one [i.e., the purchaser] was eating the produce and he acquiesced inasmuch as he had not yet changed his mind, so this constitutes remission. This is evident in the Gemara there and Rashi[46] interpreted thus explicitly. Here, however, if it will become known to one member of the group that his fellow has been trespassing upon his rights and he will immediately complain against him, he will certainly be able to withdraw his remission concerning a nonexistent matter. And prior to this [i.e., the *hassagat gevul*], there is no question but that even if he agreed, via a [binding] *kinyan sudar*, to renounce his claim upon his fellow over his having infringed upon him in any way whatsoever, nevertheless whoever so wishes can reverse himself. For even he who says that one can transfer a nonexistent thing, nonetheless holds that one can reverse himself prior to its coming into existence.[47]

Moreover, our situation is inferior to all matters which have no bound or limit and to all the *asmakhtot* in the world. For not only because of the amount of the damage whose kind is unknown and cannot be estimated; but also the act of *hassagat gevul per se* has [various] aspects and modes and improper[48] actions, varying one from the other in notoriety. For one goes to the home of his fellow's client and says to him that he should buy from him and he will give him more cheaply;

---

45. *Bava Metzia* 66b; *Tur*, HM 209; *Shulhan Arukh*, HM 209:4, respectively.
46. Ibid. and Rashi, ad loc. The point being made is that the prior consent is not even partially valid. It should not be viewed as conferring even the option of unopposed seizure. Rather, so long as it is not repudiated, it is regarded as being constantly repeated, and at any given moment the current implicit repetition is valid with regard to the present.
47. Rav Ya'ir Hayim assumes that both R. Huna and R. Nahman, who dispute whether the seller of a *davar shelo ba laolam* can reverse himself prior to its coming into existence (see *Yevamot* 93a), basically agree that one can sell a *davar shelo ba laolam* but differ about this one detail. Others have held that they disagreed about the principle proper; still others, that both would agree that those who hold that one can sell a *davar shelo ba laolam* certainly reject any possibility of reversal. The question is rather whether even those who regard such sales as invalid agree that they do take effect if unrepudiated prior to the object's coming into existence.
48. The phrase "*asher lo yaasu*" could mean either actions which "are not done" or "ought not be done."

one speaks to him when he happens to encounter him; one signals him when he is in his fellow's store; one buttonholes him while he is passing and drags him to his store. There are some who exaggerate the price line of their fellow['s goods] by saying that he overcharges in all his sales; others denigrate his goods, [saying] that they are very old and on the verge of rotting; others attribute a flaw to them, that they were eaten by moths and insects, or that they are not new but painted over. So that he who remits may say, "It never occurred to me that my fellow would harm me to this extent, that I should remit to him." Even if he had said [i.e., at the time of the agreement] "in any manner," he can say, "Such and such I never imagined that a member of the covenant[49] [i.e., a Jew] would do."

Therefore, let my soul be no party to their plot, for they shall not be absolved, either as regards human, or, certainly, divine judgment. Let him who hears listen and him who can cease cease, for I have written what, in my humble opinion, seems correct.

The statement of the preoccupied Ya'ir Hayim Bachrach

שו"ת חוות יאיר סימן קסג

שאלה חבורת מוכרי כסות שלומדים ג"כ בכל יום אצל בר אוריין ותיקנו שכל משפטים שיפלו בין איש לרעהו מבני חבורה מענין השגת גבול בענין המכירה יבואו לדין לפני רבם המגיד שיעור בדברי אגדה בכל יום. ומפני שנתרבו המשפטים והוכבד עליהם הוצאות הפסקים יעץ להם גבאי שלהם והוא הגדול והירא אלהים שבהם מה לכם לאבד מעות הפסקים עם בלוי הזמן המרובה מלבד הנסתרות שלא נגלה לרעהו מה שהשיג זה גבולו לדבר עם מערופי' שלו ולגנות סחורות חבירו דחייב מיהו בידי שמים ואחר שא"א לתקן פרצה זו שכבר נשרשו בחטא לכן נסכימה יחד להתיר בינינו השגת גבול באיזה אופן שיהיה ונמחל זה לזה הפסד ממון שגרם לו חבירו ובזה ינוח דין שלמטה וישקוט דין שלמעלה. ושאלו לרבם אם יש בכחם לעשות זה ואם יצאו י"ש בכך והשיב להם רבם כי הוא נוגע בדבר מפני שהיה לו הנאת ממון לפרקים ע"י מחלקותם ומ"מ אכתוב לכם דעתי בכתב ותראוהו

49. The phrase *ish brit* could mean either "a Jew" or "a friend."

למי שתרצו ליושבי על מדין אם יפה דברתי שמעו בקולי ואם אין עשו כטוב בעיניכם וכך כתב ונתן בידם. נראה לי כי אף אם הריעותם אשר עשיתם בהשגת גבול ודברו בו הפוסקים שלפעמים חייב לשלם ולפעמים הוי גזל מפני ד״ש ולפעמים נקרא רשע ובכל אנפי איסורא מיהו איכא. מ״מ המעשה האחרון אם יגמר דעתיכם להתירו ע״י מחילה קשה מן הראשון דבלי ספק ע״י שיעשה לכם היתר תגדל המהומה והמריבה והמגערת והחילול השם כמה כפלי כפלים מאשר היה בראשונה עד כי ימלאו בתיכם חמס. ואם תעשו תקנה או קלקלה זו לזמן בלי ספק יעבור זמן המוגבל וישאר ההרגל ויעשה טבע קיים בלי תרופה. גם פן ילמדו מכם גם במקומות אחרי׳ ובעלי משא ומתן דילפינן ממקלקלת׳ והייתם חוטאים ומחטיאי׳ ומי יתנני קצין עם פרנס ומנהיג היתי מעניש לבני חבורה על מחשבה רעה כזו כפי יכולתם והנשארים ישמעו וייראו.

ומפני שאין מבוקשכם תוכחת מוסר רק דין ומשפט אם מספיק תיקון כזה להוציאו מידי אבק גזל. לכן אני אומר כי גם לענין דין תורה אינו מספיק כלל ולא ינוקו בתיקון כזה אפילו בדיני אדם וכן כל המוחלים זה לזה לעשות מעשה שאסרה תורה כגון גניבה ואונאה והשגת גבול דמלבד דלא ינקה מדין שמים כל עושה אלה מצד שהוא נגד ישוב העולם והנהגתו וזה היה חטא דור המבול כי מלאה הארץ חמס קראו חמס מפני שאין נקי מהם ה״ל כחמסן דיהיב דמי ואע״פ שי״ל שאני שם דלא מחלי מאן יימר ולדעתי להרגילם לא קפדו כלל דלא נאמר בהו כמו גבי סדום דצעקתם באה לפניו יתברך שמו. ותנן במשנה החובל בעצמו אע״פ שאינו רשאי פטור ולמה לא יורשה שהרי מחיל לנפשי׳ מ״מ הקפידה תורה ואמרה ושמרתם לנפשותיכם וגם על הממון הקפידה מבל תשחית בכמה גוונא וכן אמרו הקוצץ נטיעותיו אע״פ שאינו רשאי וכו׳ וכן כל ההוא סוגיא דקרע את כסותי שבר את כדי או ידי ורגלי לענין חיוב ופטור דתשלומין מיירי מ״מ אסור הוא ולא מהני בזה רשות חבירו. צא ולמד מרבית דלוה מחיל למלוה ויהיב ליה מדעתי׳ ומ״מ אסרה תורה למלוה ואפילו ללוה ומצינו שהתורה חסה על פכים של רשע כדרז״ל על נגעי בתים.

לכן מפני שהמעשה רע ומר מצד עצמו בין מחיל בין לא מחיל ישאר בתמרוריתו כמו לוה ומלוה שמסכימי׳ יחד לדון בערכאותיהם ולמחול על מה שיצא במשפטיה׳ נגד דין תורה וכן דמי לזה מ״ש רז״ל לא תגנבו ע״מ

לשלם תשלומי כפל אע״פ דודאי מחיל לי׳ הנגנב וכמ״ש טור וש״ע ר״ס שמ״ח וכן בנזק ממון כמ״ש בסמ״ע ר״ס שע״ח.

ומעתה נבא לדינא אם מספיק תיקון זה לענין שאם השיג אחד גבולו של חבירו באופן שהיה יוצא חייב בתשלומין או שיקרא רשע אם יועיל התיקון הזה להפקיע ממנו חיובו ולכאורה נראה דמועיל כמו דק״ל בדין אסמכת׳ אע״ג דאפילו קנין סתם לא מהני מ״מ גבי שנים שמשחקין בקוביא אגב דכל חד בעי למיקני ג״כ מקני כמ״ש סוף הג״ה ארוכה בח״מ סי׳ ר״ז סי״ג. והשתמש בסברא זו הסמ״ע ר״ס ר״ט ס״ק ב׳ ג׳ ומשם לכאורה מוכח דאפילו דבר שאינו ידוע כלל מה וכמה דבכה״ג י״ל דאפילו לדעת החולקים על הרמב״ם דס״ל דאין קנין חל על דבר שאין לו קצבה וחלקו עליו כל האחרוני׳ כמ״ש הב״י בש״ע סי׳ ס׳ ס״ב וס״ס ר״ז היינו בדבר שמיהו ידוע ענינו כמו מזונות שאפשר לשומו לפי הזמן ואפי׳ לא נתן קיצבה לשנים רק שיפרנסנו כל ימיו מ״מ ידוע לפי הטבע בקרוב ימי שנותינו בהם שבעים שנה וגו׳ ובכה״ג מה שאירש מאבא אפשר לשום ולהעריך בקרוב ודמי למינו ידוע דבר״ס ר״ט מש״כ כל מה שיש בבית זה וכו׳ שם ס״ב דלא מצינו בו חולקים וכ״ע ס״ל דלא קני.

ומ״מ גם בכה״ג אם אין שום אחד יודע קנה כמ״ש בסמ״ע. מיהו אע״פ שאינני כדאי להשיג על הגאון בעל הסמ״ע מ״מ אני אומר אחר בקשת המחילה שאין דבריו מוכרחין רק אפילו גם המוכר ג״כ אינו יודע מה בבית כגון דאיהו גופי׳ קנאו כך עם מה שיש בו ומכרו לאחר ג״כ לא קנה מפני שעכ״פ הלוקח לא סמכה דעתו לקנות דבר שאין מינו ידוע בשום אומדנא כמ״ש אם תבן אם זהב ומפני שהרמב״ם ס״ל דמשחק בקוביא ה״ל אסמכת׳ מדמה כל מה שיש בבית זה אליו אבל לאותן דס״ל דלא הוי אסמכת׳ יאמרו דודאי כל מה שיש בבית זה גרע. ותדע דע״כ צ״ל דמשחק בקוביא עדיף אפילו מדבר שמינו ידוע רק שאינו מסויים דעכ״פ בעי קנין כדמוכח שם מש״כ משחק בקוביא דלא בעי קנין וע״כ מפני שממש ידוע כל פעם ופעם כמה יתן אחד לחבירו הן שמונח לפניהם על הדף או לא רק דמ״מ ה״ל אסמכת׳ מצד שכל אחד סבר להרויח ובזה מהני סברת י״א מפני ששניהם מתנין ולכך לא הגיה רמ״א שום דבר על דברי הרמב״ם בש״ע סי׳ ר״ט ס״ב דס״ל כוותי׳ בדינא ולא מטעמי׳ כמ״ש גם הסמ״ע וכן

שנים שהמרו דבת"ה הובא בהג"ה ס"ס ר"ג י"ל דשייך בו שומא קצת לפי דעת נוטה ואין ראיה ממה שמצינו ע"צ הזרות יש מתעשר וגו'.

מ"מ אין אני כדאי להשיג על הסמ"ע ולכן אע"פ שלפענ"ד תיקון של בני החבורה דה"ל ודאי דבר שאין לו קצבה ואומדנא כלל כי מי יכול למוד משא ומתן שיבא אחר זמן ולא קני אפילו כל חד בעי למקני מ"מ לדעת הסמ"ע שלא חילק בזה ולדעתו סברת מה שכל אחד רוצה לקנות מקני מועיל גם בכל מה שיש בבית זה כגון אם גם המוכר לא ידע וא"כ גם בחבורה הנ"ל מועיל ואם נעשה והשיג אחד גבול חבירו אין לחבירו עליו כלום. האמנם גם לדעת הסמ"ע צריך עכ"פ קנין והיה צורך שגם בני חבורה יקבלו קנין כל אחד. והא דמשחקין בקוביא א"צ קנין י"ל מפני שהמעות מוכני' עי' בהג"ה ארוכה סי' ר"ז סי"ג.

ועוד דלו יתכן דע"י קנין מועיל אפילו הקנאת דבר שאין לו קיצבה כלל בדכל חד בעי ליקני דסברא זו מבטלת כל אסמכתות. מ"מ מצד אחר י"ל דאין הקנין חל שהרי ענין הקנין הזה ע"כ אינו רק כסילוק מתביעה וזכות שיהיה לו להבא על חברו כענין שטר סילוק מנכסי אשתו שאינו מועיל לפני האירוסין מפני דה"ל דבר שעדיין אינו בעולם ואינו ברשותו ואפי' קנין לא מהני כמ"ש הגאון מוהר"ר גרשון שהוכיח כן משו"ת הר"ן עיין תשובה נ' דכ"ט ע"א ה"נ האיך ימחול זה מה שעתיד חבירו להתחייב לו ע"י השגת גבול והתם לאו טעמי' משום אסמכתא דנימא ג"כ סברת איידי דבעי ליקני רק דאין הקנין חל על דשלב"ל.

ואין לומר הא ק"ל שם דאי תפס לא מפקינן מיני' כבגמ' פרק הריבית ס"ד ס"ו וכ"כ טור וש"ע ששם הטעם מפני דנודע להמוכר שזה אוכל פירות ושתק דאכתי לא הדר ביה ה"ל מחילה וכן מוכח שם בגמ' וכ"פ רש"י בהדיא מש"כ פה אם יודע לאחד מבני חבורה שחבירו עבר עליו הדרך ותיכף יקבול עליו ודאי מצי למיהדר ביה על מחילת דשלב"ל.

ומקמי הכי לית דין ולית דיינא דאפילו קבלו בק"ס להסתלק מתביעתו לחבירו על שהשיג גבולו באיזה אופן שיהיה מ"מ כל מאן דבעי מצי למיהדר ביה דאפילו מ"ד אדם מקנה דשלב"ל מ"מ ס"ל דמקמי שבא לעולם יכול לחזור בו. ומה גם נדון זה דגרע מכל דברים שאין להם גבול וקצבה ומכל אסמכתות שבעולם כי לא לבד מצד סך הנזק שאין מינו ידוע וא"א לשערו גם מעשה השגת גבול עצמו יש בו בחינות ודוגמות

ומעשי׳ אשר לא יעשו שניין דא מדא לגריעות׳ כי יש הולך לבית מערופי׳ של חבירו ומדבר עמו שיקנה אצלו ויתן לו בזול ויש מדבר עמו בפוגעו בו ויש רמוזי רמז לו בהיותו בחנות חבירו ויש תופס בו בעברו ומושכו לחנותו ויש מגדילי׳ שער דמי סחורה שמוכר חבירו באמרם שמוכר כל סחורתיו ביוקר משוויים ויש מוציאי׳ לעז על סחורותיו כי ישן נושן הם וקרובי׳ לבלות ויש מטילי׳ בהם מום שאכלם עש וכנימה ואינם חדשים רק צבועים באופן דמצי המוחל למימר כולי האי לא עלתה דעתי שיעשה חבירי רעה שאמחול לו אפילו אמר בכל אופן מצי למימר כזאת וכאלה לא חשבתי שיעשה איש ברית לכן בסודם אל תבא נפשי כי לא ינקו מזה לא בד״א כ״ש בד״ש והשומע ישמע והחדל יחדל כי הנלפענ״ד כתבתי.

נאם הטרוד יאיר חיים בכרך

ANALYSIS

I. The Need for Adaptation

"Every man," said Coleridge, "is born an Aristotelian or a Platonist."[1] As regards ethical theory, it can be said with equal justice that every man is – albeit not necessarily born – an absolutist or a relativist. No question of ethical thought – impinging, to be sure, upon much outside its pale – is so basic as that of the relative or absolute nature of ethics. Whether terms like right or wrong or good and evil refer to mere consensus rooted in social convenience or are grounded in ultimate metaphysical reality – this is the alpha and omega of moral philosophy.

Historically, the Jewish position on this question has been unmistakably clear: radical and unequivocal commitment to absolute truth and absolute values. It has entailed certain difficulties, however. In one sense, to be sure, it is the ethical relativist who faces the more arduous challenge. Lacking both an anchor and a polestar, he can have neither operational stability nor ultimate direction. He not only strives to walk according to his best light but must also create it – *ex nihilo*; yet, inasmuch as he is wholly unfettered, his task is fundamentally far easier. The relativist is blessed with the *virtu* of his defects: mobility, adaptability, the capacity for confronting a changing order and responding to it flexibly. The absolutist, normally operating through the application of universal moral principles to individual situations, has no such latitude. Striving to apply various categorical imperatives – and both unable and unwilling to rely excessively upon mere intuition or desire – he is hard put to relate his ideal ethical system to concrete reality.[2]

1. *Table Talk of Samuel Taylor Coleridge*, ed. Henry Morley (London, 1884), 102; July 2, 1830.
2. The current allure of "situational ethics" derives precisely from the fact that it strives to have the best of both worlds. Its fusion of a semblance of absolutism concerning ends and general relativism with respect to means attempts to satisfy both the ultimate craving for permanent anchor and the desire for mobile response to specific problems. The nature of the difficulty involved in this attempt may be illustrated by the fact that the best-known exposition of this ethic, Joseph Fletcher's *Situation*

How much more difficult, however, is the ethical challenge confronting the halakhist. Working within a legal, rather than a purely philosophic, framework, in making ethical judgments he must often refer back to detailed laws as well as to a teleological and axiological structure; and this renders his task doubly exacting. The fissure that time inevitably creates between elements of the ideal halakhic system and the particular reality to which they initially related; special circumstances surrounding a specific case even when the overall scene has remained unchanged; the difficulty of employing a legal system – whose demands may, in the nature of things, often be minimal – as a general guide to ethical conduct; the interplay of technical and substantive elements within Halakha – all severely task the ethical insight of the halakhist on the one hand and his intellectual capacity on the other. All, moreover, present an implicit demand for a degree of flexibility. In one situation or another, each factor offers a mutely eloquent testament to the need for a measure of adaptation in relating the halakhic system to a given ethical reality.

So long as adaptation takes the form of addition – either through the expansion of the halakhic corpus proper, as with rabbinic ordinances, or through the superimposition of other ethical elements, as with the observance of *lifnim mishurat hadin*, "[that which lies] beyond the line of the law"[3] – it presents relatively little difficulty. However, when it involves countermanding the fundamental Halakha, the prospect of adaptation poses some basic questions. First, has the Halakha recognized the legal validity of such change, and, if so, what are its mechanics? Second, even if the quest for adapting or circumventing a halakhic

---

Ethics (Philadelphia, 1966), has been followed in short order by his *Situation Ethics: A Casebook* (Philadelphia, 1967). See also Kenneth W. Underwood, *Protestant and Catholic* (Boston, 1957), 317–21, and from a different, although not wholly unrelated, perspective, Emil Brunner, *The Divine Imperative*, trans. Olive Wyon (London, 1937), 82–93. See, finally, the incisive remarks of Eugene B. Borowitz, "On the New Morality," *Judaism*, XV (1966): 329–36.

3. In one sense, this element is itself an aspect of Halakha rather than something which lies beyond it; see *Bava Kamma* 100a and *Bava Metzia* 83a. Nevertheless, it can be distinguished as a dimension of Halakha separate from the legal corpus narrowly conceived; and it is in this sense that it is cited here.

norm is legally valid, under what circumstances, if any, can it become morally and religiously legitimate?

II. Public and Private Adaptation

Adaptation is possible at two levels, the private and the public. It can result from either stipulation and agreement or promulgation and legislation. With respect to the halakhic validity of the former, the Gemara cites conflicting views:

> If one says to a woman, "You are betrothed to me on the condition that you have no claim upon me for food, clothing, and regular cohabitation,"[4] she is betrothed but his condition is void. These are the words of R. Meir.
>
> R. Yehuda says: With regard to an economic matter, his condition is valid.[5]

R. Yehuda's view subsequently prevailed and the Gemara speaks of stipulations that a given transaction not be governed by the laws concerning profiteering; that a particular loan not be nullified by the Sabbatical year; or that a bailee assume more or less than his normal responsibility.[6] The legal basis of such private circumvention – or rather, negation – of some halakhic norms is fairly clear. It is essentially proprietary. As an interested and involved party, an individual has the power to waive rights accruing to him through a given law. Hence, although the Halakha has defined the rights and responsibilities of a given relation – be it of husband and wife or depositor and bailee – in one set of terms, mutual agreement

4. According to the prevalent interpretation of the phrase *she'era kesuta ve'onata* (*Shemot* 21:10), the Torah has imposed these obligations upon a husband. See *Ketubbot* 47b and Rambam, *Hilkhot Ishut* 12:1–2.
5. *Bava Batra* 126b. Most authorities assume that the condition is only valid with respect to food and clothing, sexual satisfaction being regarded as a matter of normative duty rather than a personal privilege subject to remission. See commentaries ad loc. and Rambam, *Hilkhot Ishut* 12:6–7.
6. See *Bava Metzia* 51a, *Makkot* 3b, and *Bava Metzia* 94a, respectively.

can define them in another. Through the joint exercise of their prerogative, interested parties can, in effect, construct new halakhic entities.[7]

A somewhat different mode of overriding the normal Halakha – apparently unrelated to the controversy between R. Yehuda and R. Meir[8] – is indicated by a mishna in *Bava Kamma*:

> If one says [to his fellow], "Blind my eye, sever my hand, break my leg," he [i.e., the subsequent assailant] is liable. "On the understanding that you will be exempt," he is [nevertheless] liable. "Tear my cloak, break my vase," he is liable. "On the understanding that you will be exempt," he is absolved.[9]

The underlying basis of this last stipulation is again proprietary. Nevertheless, there is a radical distinction between the sort of stipulation discussed here and that debated by R. Yehuda and R. Meir. Their case concerns an attempt to reshape, in effect, a halakhic entity. An individual wishes to enter a halakhic category but to reconstruct it so that it should no longer entail the usual consequences or implications. He would create a marriage that would require no wifely support, or a loan that would transcend the Sabbatical framework. No such reconstruction is attempted here, however. The prospective victim has neither the power nor the desire to place vandalism or assault on an entirely new footing. Even in relation to himself, he does not seek to create, in a positive sense, some new contractual or legal state. He simply wishes to absolve his future assailant from a specific penalty. This is not so much reconstruction as remission. It does not create a new nexus of rights or duties but merely excludes a particular punishment. Such absolution is closer to pardon than to contract; and the fact that it precedes rather than follows an action does not change its essential character.

---

7. This prerogative is only relevant to the initial establishment of a halakhic relation. Consequences which flow more or less automatically from a normal relation are not subject to stipulation. Thus, one could not give a gift on the condition that the recipient's heirs not inherit it. See *Ketubbot* 83a–84a and commentaries.
8. See, however, *Tosafot, Ketubbot* 56a–b, s.v. *harei*.
9. *Bava Kamma* 92a.

The distinction between these two private modes of countermanding halakhic norms is, in many respects, crucial. Nevertheless, both share a common basis: proprietary rights. At the public level, however, the legal basis of deviation is entirely different. It is grounded upon the authority of legislation – the right of a community, acting through various organs, lay or rabbinic, to establish its own principles of conduct.[10] To be sure, this right is circumscribed in important respects. While a community can institute its own ordinances, recognize new modes of contract, expand the class of torts, or restrict the rights of ownership, it cannot dismiss an injunction or obligation ordained by the Torah. It can neither permit slander nor renounce *tefillin*. Nevertheless, within these limits, communal legislation has considerable scope. So long as it does not abrogate the halakhically mandatory, it can not only add to Torah law but reverse it. The community can do little if anything to alter Torah laws that impose duties. It can, however, drastically revise those conferring powers; and it can, of course, ordain either duties or powers of its own. "And this has been customary," as the Rashba noted, "in all holy [i.e., Jewish] communities, and no one ever doubted this."[11]

III. The Justification for Circumvention

The outlines of the legal issue thus appear reasonably clear. A grasp of the possibility and the mechanics of overriding primal Halakha only serves, however, as a prelude to the moral and religious question: When, if ever, is such circumvention justified? Even if legal authority for change exists – so that deviation may be said to have halakhic sanction – ought it be enacted?

At least two major objections might be raised. First, inasmuch as we would be substituting human for divine legislation, we would be left with poorer law. Second, quite apart from the objective merits of

10. See *Gittin* 36a–b; *Bava Kamma* 116b; *Bava Batra* 8b–9a, and commentaries thereon. See also *Teshuvot HaRivash*, 399; *Teshuvot HaRashba*, 1:769 and 4:185; HM 2:1, 231:28, and *Pithei Teshuva* thereon; and the essays on jurisprudence in *HaTorah VeHaMedina*, I (1949): especially that of M. Z. Neriyah, "*Takkanot beit din vetakkanot tzibbur*," 50–57.
11. *Teshuvot HaRashba*, 4:185.

the respective laws, the substitution *per se* entails an act of rebellion. Revision implies usurpation. Even if the halakhic authority for change absolves us from outright revolt, we are, at best, staying within the letter of the legal corpus, but clearly violating its initial spirit – or, at least, the spirit of one of its components.

The answer must, of course, be yes. Else, in suppressing all change, we opt for total ossification; and it is inconceivable that we should really insist on the complete stultification of all spiritual thrust. But it is a qualified yes. At least three basic distinctions should be recognized.

First, the ethical and religious texture of the Halakha's legal fabric is not uniform. While the Halakha, as a legal corpus, specifically proscribes or requires numerous actions or institutions, it is often silent or permissive in areas where, from a total Torah perspective, it can hardly be assumed to be neutral. The reason for such permissiveness may vary. Although spiritually deplorable, a course of action might be either ignored or even explicitly allowed as a concession to human frailty, at either the individual or the social level. Viewing man from a realistic rather than a rigorous perspective, the Halakha, without countenancing either, has sometimes granted license to the lesser of two evils. At times, the Rabbis taught, "The Torah has but spoken vis-à-vis the evil inclination,"[12] providing one outlet for a base passion, lest it seek an even more corrupt channel. Or, at the other end of the spectrum, a worthy action may not have been required because it represented, at the time, too high a rung on the ordinary individual's ladder of perfection; because it belonged, in Lon Fuller's phrase, to the "morality of aspiration" rather than to the "morality of duty."[13] Whatever the reason, however, an attempt to revise this sector of Halakha – when religiously motivated and grounded in ultimate commitment to Torah values – can hardly be construed as usurpation. It does not breach the halakhic ethic but expands it. Regardless of their legal validity, however, no religious sanction could be granted attempts to dilute the ethical and spiritual content of Halakha by revising laws which, while not absolutely obligatory

12. *Kiddushin* 21b.

13. See Lon L. Fuller, *The Morality of Law* (New Haven, 1964), 5–15. This distinction is, of course, a central aspect of the difference between *din* and *lifnim mishurat hadin*.

and therefore legally subject to change, clearly aim at raising our ethical sights rather than merely making peace with the natural man within us. Individuals may be legally competent to waive the injunction against profiteering; but, ordinarily speaking, the waiver can hardly enhance their spiritual growth.

Nevertheless, even in dealing with the hortatory, as opposed to the permissive, segment of Halakha, two further distinctions should be kept in mind. The first concerns the nature of the change rather than its subject. Stipulation or legislation effecting halakhic change may merely revise the laws governing a given reality; or, it may, as a dynamic factor, transform that reality proper. A compact transforming private into public or jointly owned property may exempt it from numerous halakhic categories. Such "circumvention" need not constitute evasion, however. So long as the change in circumstances is genuine and not a mere paper transaction, the revision does not evade Halakha but avoids it.

To be sure, even the avoidance of normative situations may be questioned. While one can free himself of certain mitzvot by steering clear of the circumstances to which they apply, such an escape is hardly the hallmark of a genuinely religious personality. "Why," asked R. Simlai, "did Moses our master desire to enter *Eretz Yisrael*? Did he then need to eat of its fruit? Or did he need to sate himself from its bounty? Rather, Moses said thus: 'Many mitzvot were commanded to Israel which can only be fulfilled in *Eretz Yisrael*. Let me enter the land so that all of them should be fulfilled by me.'"[14] Hence, as the Rosh noted in citing this midrash, while one can avoid the mitzva of *tzitzit* by wearing garments with less than four corners, a *yerei shamayim*, "one who fears Heaven," will not engage in this practice.[15] As the Rambam put it: "Although a person is not obligated to buy himself a [four-cornered] garment and to clothe himself in it so that he may put *tzitzit* on it, it is not proper for a pious person to absolve himself from this mitzva. Rather, he shall always strive to be clothed in a garment requiring *tzitzit* in order that he may

14. *Sota* 14a.
15. *Tosfei HaRosh, Nidda* 61b.

fulfill this mitzva."[16] Nevertheless, this type of circumvention is radically different from attempts to revise the halakhot governing the situation subsumed under them. More a failure to realize one's spiritual potential than an outright neglect of duty, it can be far more easily extenuated by the force of circumstance.

The third distinction turns on the dialectic tension between the formal and normative aspect of Halakha, on the one hand, and its axiological and teleological aspect on the other; and it involves, in essence, recognizing the legitimacy of accommodating, within certain limits, the former to the latter. Accommodation may take one of two forms. It may consist of the evasive use of loopholes and legal fictions; or, wherever feasible, of outright amendment. In the one case, while its letter is preserved, the spirit of a specific law is sacrificed in the interests of the spirit and values of the Law as a whole. In the other, even the letter of a law may be abandoned. In both cases, however, circumvention results from the need for accommodating the formal to the teleological element of Halakha.

That accommodation might occasionally appear not only worthwhile but essential should be fairly obvious. As a system of law – although it is, to be sure, much more than that – Halakha inevitably produces certain anomalies. A legal corpus addresses itself, almost by definition, to the general and therefore ordinary case. Yet, the unusual circumstances surrounding a specific situation may direct the application of a given law against the very ethical and equitable purposes it was presumably designed to promote. Moreover, historical changes in the social or economic structure of a community may render a statute self-defeating in even the ordinary case.

---

16. *Hilkhot Tzitzit* 3:11. See also, as regards the mitzva of *tzitzit*, *Menahot* 41a. Cf., however, *Tosafot*, *Arakhin* 2b, s.v. *hakol*. Of course, one should distinguish between mitzvot which, while optional, nevertheless involve a *kiyyum*, i.e., the positive realization and fulfillment of a religious commandment, and others, such as the laws governing divorce, which simply prescribe a procedure for a wholly neutral course of action. A lesser distinction might be made between consciously avoiding situations with which one would be ordinarily confronted and failing to reach out to encounter normative obligations.

Hence, the desire to circumvent primal halakhic norms – whether through the evasive use of loopholes and legal fictions or through the invocation of personal or collective authority to override a law – can be variously grounded. Circumvention may simply be motivated by a selfish and utilitarian desire to avoid the ethical and religious burden imposed by a particular norm. However, it can also derive from a desire for greater ethical and religious fulfillment; and this in one of two ways.

First, where special circumstances or historical change have turned a mitzva on its teleological head, circumvention – or, when halakhically possible, amendment – of its formal aspect may be necessary in order to further the purposes of that mitzva proper. Thus, although the Torah forbids all forms of interest, one might justifiably endorse the evasive use of the legal loophole – actually, the legal fiction – of the *hetter iska,* an arrangement whereby the creditor shares in the risks attendant upon the use of the money, which is then regarded as an investment rather than a loan.[17] Presumably, a primary purpose of the prohibition is to aid the poorer classes by affording a relatively underprivileged debtor protection against a rapacious creditor. Moreover, as Tawney noted in an analogous connection, "Its character had been given it in an age in which most loans were not part of a credit system, but an exceptional expedient,"[18] and in which loans were generally sought only under the strain of necessity. Within the modern economic climate, however, interest need no longer be the symbolic pound of flesh extracted by a greedy moneylender from a hard-pressed borrower. The advent of capitalism, with its vastly expanded role for money, and the pegging of general interest rates at levels incomparably lower than those prevalent in the ancient or medieval world, have taken the ethical bite out of the ordinary loan.

---

17. The Gemara deals with *iska* which entailed genuine risks to the creditor – he and the debtor shared more or less equally in any profit or loss which accrued from the investment – and which apparently was not intended as a ploy to evade the injunction against taking interest; see *Bava Metzia* 68b–69a and 104b–105a. Subsequently, however, the arrangement became hedged in by numerous qualifications, all of them limiting the potential loss of the creditor to the point where it became more of a paper reality than a live possibility.
18. R. H. Tawney, *Religion and the Rise of Capitalism* (New York, 1947), 45; see also 38–54.

Antonio could still counsel: "If thou wilt lend this money, lend it not / As to thy friends – for when did friendship take / A breed for barren metal of his friend?"[19] The modern borrower is only too happy to find a friend willing to grant a loan at moderate rates. A total ban on interest would choke off avenues of credit, producing severe economic hardship for the very classes the injunction sought to protect. Hence, one may rightly feel that, on balance, evasion in these circumstances is fully justified. To be sure, it would be best if creditors could be gotten to continue to lend without interest, so that other purposes of the mitzva – growth in altruism, for instance – might likewise be fulfilled. Failing this, however, one can find circumvention ethically and religiously satisfactory. "What of evading?" the Yerushalmi asks. In reply, it cites a precedent: "And did not R. Tarfon, the father of all Israel, evade?"[20] It then goes on to cite an incident in which he had employed a legal fiction of paper marriages in order to alleviate the hunger of several hundred women.

Instances such as these entail the use of circumvention within a given body of Halakha in order to enable it to meet its own presumed purpose. A second group may swing a wider arc, however, in that it may involve the necessary sacrifice of the teleological aspect of one mitzva to the axiologically superior needs of another. It may be clear that an evasive technique does not help but hinders the attainment of the purposes of a particular mitzva. And yet its use may be deemed necessary in order to facilitate the fulfillment of broader or more basic aims. Hillel's introduction of the *prozbul* – a declaration made by the creditor which in effect overrides the cancellation of debts by the Sabbatical year[21] – is a perfect example. Whatever the purposes of *shemittat kesafim* – increasing social equality and distributive justice, turning from attachment to property to religious commitment, and so on – they are clearly not enhanced by

19. *Merchant of Venice*, I, iii, 133–35.

20. *Yevamot* 4:12. The Yerushalmi deals with a specific technical case but its comment clearly has broader implications. For a fairly full listing of the instances of legal evasion cited in halakhic sources and a discussion of its legal limits, see *Encyclopedia Talmudit*, s.v. *haarama*, IX, 697–713. Moshe Silberg, "*Haarama al hahok*," in *Kakh Darko Shel Talmud* (Jerusalem, 1961), 26–44, cites the major cases and includes a brief discussion of the philosophic aspects of the problem.

21. See *Shevi'it* 10:3–4 and *Gittin* 36a–37b.

the *prozbul*. And yet Hillel, confronted by the hard fact that rigorous adherence to the law was deterring the extension of credit, exercised his authority for amendment in order to achieve other goals. On the one hand, the door which was slamming shut in the face of borrowers had to be opened. On the other, potential creditors' violation of the Torah's injunction against precisely this type of reluctance had to be stopped.[22] The optimum solution would, of course, have been to educate people to lend despite possible cancellation of the loan. Realizing that this ideal was currently unattainable, however, Hillel had to settle for second best. And second best meant circumvention – sacrificing the values inherent in *shemittat kesafim* to the need for preserving the economic stability of the borrower and the spiritual integrity of his lender.

IV. The Premises and Risks of Halakhic Teleology

The assumption that there may occasionally be justification for the halakhic subordination of one mitzva – and of the moral and religious values realized through it – to the greater axiological demands imposed by others[23] clearly rests, as noted, upon a dual conception of the Halakha: as a legal and formal construct on the one hand and as a teleological and axiological system on the other. While this conception is open to radical question – it has certainly not gone unchallenged – I think it clearly represents the primary strain within the tradition. It is grounded upon three related premises.

The first premise is the rationality of the divine will, the assumption that God's will is not the subject or the result of arbitrary desire but

22. In citing Hillel's innovation, the Mishna states that "when he observed people refraining from lending to one another, and thus transgressing what is written in the Torah, 'Beware, lest there be a base thought in your heart,' he instituted the *prozbul*" (*Shevi'it* 10:3). This could be interpreted to mean that his purpose was the prevention of sin rather than the satisfaction of an economic need. It need not be so interpreted, however; and in any event, one need hardly be a Marxist to assume that the economic factor – in this case, itself a religious element – provided a major stimulus to Hillel's motivation.

23. The subordination need not be based exclusively on the relative importance of the two mitzvot. Quantitative elements and possible future consequences – in short, a sort of felicific calculus – might also figure.

is governed by absolute ethical and ontological truth. In the history of Western thought, this problem has traced a long and tortuous path. In its seminal form, it was clearly formulated by Plato. An early dialogue reports a discussion between Euthyphro and Socrates as to "whether the pious or holy is beloved by the gods because it is holy, or holy because it is beloved of the gods."[24] Subsequently, the question divided Aquinas from Occam among the Scholastics, Hooker from Perkins in the sixteenth century, and Hobbes from Bramhall in the seventeenth; and it is far from being a dead issue today. Its perennial relevance can be readily understood. On the one hand, many – particularly those who experience God primarily as power – are loath to accept the limitations upon divine freedom implicit in the rationalist position. Even when the point is softened by the contention that the truths which circumscribe (*mutatis mutandis*) God's actions are of His own essence and therefore do not constitute an external constriction, the fact remains that some limit is being acknowledged. On the other hand, particularly for those who experience God primarily as love or justice, the notion of capricious divine will totally divorced from absolute ethical and metaphysical moorings seems repugnant, if not indeed repulsive.

As regards the basic Jewish position concerning this problem, it seems irrevocably clear. As one of the Cambridge Platonists noted, it is definitely implied in the question posed by Abraham prior to the destruction of Sodom – "Shall the judge of all the earth not do justice?"[25] – or, for that matter, by the whole of the book of Job. It is explicitly formulated in a halakhic precept, R. Yehuda's statement that while one may, under certain circumstances, interrupt between the various sections of *Shema,* one may never interrupt between its concluding phrase, "I am the Lord your God," and the first words of the following blessing, "True and firm." "What is R. Yehuda's reason?" the Gemara explains. "Because it is written, 'And the Lord God is truth' (*Yirmiyahu* 10:10)."[26] Probably the best-known statement of the concept occurs in a celebrated passage in the Yerushalmi: "R. Elazar said: [The Greek proverb states,] 'On the

24. *Euthyphro* 10a–b.
25. *Bereshit* 18:25.
26. *Berakhot* 14a–b.

king the law is not binding.' Ordinarily, when a human king issues a decree, if he chooses, he obeys it, otherwise [only] others obey it; but when the Holy One, blessed be He, issues a decree, He is the first to obey it."[27] Clearly, the Yerushalmi should not be understood to mean merely that God obeys His own laws out of deference or as an example to subjects upon whom He has imposed them. Rather, it is grounded upon a profound conviction of the order and rationality pervading His very essence.

The assumption of a rational and moral divine will renders possible (although by no means necessary) a second premise – the purposive character of mitzvot. From a voluntarist perspective, every command is simply the expression of an arbitrary wish, and one can hardly speak of absolute meaning or ultimate purpose, much less of a total axiological structure. Voluntarism is, after all, simply divine relativism. Once a transcendent rational will is posited, however, the conception of commands as being not only so much drill or exercise but rather directed to the realization of a meaningful desideratum becomes not only tenable but probable. Not, to be sure, indisputable. One might still, paraphrasing Austin, regard mitzvot as simply the command of an ontological superior, self-contained orders designed to attain nothing beyond their own fulfillment and the habit of obedience they incidentally inculcate. And on such a view, all mitzvot being not only fully equal but, in a sense, identical, one could hardly speak of a teleological hierarchy or of subordinating the maximal realization of one mitzva to that of another. Nevertheless, assuming a divine will governed even to the point of limitation by its intrinsic rationality and goodness, it surely seems likely – if not, indeed, ethically (albeit not logically) certain – that its commands relate to the realization of spiritual value. Within a moral universe charged with potential meaning and purpose, it would be strange indeed if God's commandments aimed at nothing more than obedience for its own sake.

It *is* certain, at any rate, that Judaism has traditionally assumed the purposefulness of mitzvot – of all mitzvot. The distinction between

27. *Rosh HaShana* 1:3. For a brief discussion of this text, see Saul Lieberman, "How Much Greek in Jewish Palestine," in *Studies and Texts: Volume I, Biblical and Other Studies*, ed. Alexander Altmann (Cambridge, Mass., 1963), 126–29.

mishpatim and *hukkim*, rational and suprarational commandments, which looms so large in medieval Jewish thought, is of no relevance here. It refers solely to their respective relations to human reason, a *hok* lying beyond its range while a *mishpat* could have been discovered even if it had not been revealed. It thus corresponds roughly to the Thomistic distinction between the *revelatum* and the *revelabile*;[28] and as such, bears some relation to the tradition of natural law. It says nothing, however, of the intrinsic rationality of mitzvot. When Rashi, possibly drawing upon a gemara,[29] defined *hukkim* as "royal decrees with no reason for them,"[30] the Ramban – as much by way of explanation as of criticism – commented:

> It was not their [i.e., the Rabbis'] intention that the decree of the King of kings should, at any point, be without reason, for "Every word of God is pure" (*Mishlei* 30:5). Rather, the *hukkim* are [as] decrees which the king has ordained in his kingdom without revealing their purpose to the people; and the people do not enjoy them but question them in their hearts and accept them [only] out of fear of the government. Similarly, the *hukkim* of the Holy One, blessed be He, are the secrets which He has in the Torah, which the people do not consciously enjoy as [they do] *mishpatim*. All, however, are [endowed with] proper reason and perfect purpose.[31]

The final premise is that a teleology of mitzvot not only exists but can be discerned. Unless one can legitimately assume that man can grasp, if not God's purposes, at least the purposes of God's commands, the abstract concept of a normative value structure will be of little relevance

28. See Etienne Gilson, *Le Thomisme* (Paris, 1947), 20–25, and *Reason and Revelation in the Middle Ages* (New York, 1938), 69–84.
29. See *Yoma* 67b.
30. Commentary to *Vayikra* 19:19.
31. Commentary to *Vayikra* 19:19. The same position has been taken by the Rambam, *Guide* III:26, who then proceeds to attempt to find some sort of rationale for a number of mitzvot, including *hukkim*. See also Ramban, *Devarim* 22:6; and cf. C. S. Lewis, *The Problem of Pain* (London, 1940), 88–90.

either in relating mitzvot or in defining, at an operative level, the degree and mode of their fulfillment. Such a premise poses obvious difficulties. The mere attempt to puzzle out divine purpose smacks of an element of hubris – "Canst thou find out the deep things of God? Canst thou attain unto the purpose of the Almighty?" (*Iyyov* 11:7) – and the suggestion that necessarily hazardous guesses, even if they happen to be right, serve as an instrument of legal interpretation or as a guide to practical conduct, may even seem positively brazen. Secondly, one might of course just happen to be wrong. Thirdly, while law constitutes a rigorously defined area based on reasonably specific principles and sources, the definition of values is both nebulous, on the one hand, and speculative, on the other. Finally, even assuming its intrinsic validity, the right to interpret divine purposes – and to act on the basis of such interpretation – is a dangerous implement to place in fallible human hands. The temptation to overreach in order to accommodate interpretation to one's social and psychological needs is an ever-present danger – a danger of which the *Musar* movement and modern psychology have made us especially aware but which was notorious enough even in earlier periods. This process is particularly insidious, however, in the definition of values. Inasmuch as we are not concerned with the explication of a text or a normative system but with the elucidation of a set of ethical and religious categories, there is far greater danger that we may impose rather than elicit. One might go so far as avoiding the halakhic dialectic entirely. Rather than wrestle with the conflicting claims of the formal and teleological aspects of Halakha, one might simply subordinate the former to the latter *in toto*. Fused with personal ethical intuition, the more appealing elements of Halakha can become the basis for an axiological framework which could then be used to justify jettisoning less palatable elements as being anachronistic or irrelevant. Failure to meet subjective standards of value could become sufficient ground for dismissing various norms as having been intended for only one set of conditions and not our own; and as we might find it increasingly convenient – I use the term in an ethical, rather than a utilitarian, sense – to exorcise one mitzva after another, we would shortly find that we had, in effect, usurped the role of legislator.

These dangers are unquestionably real. And yet what is the alternative? Ethically – nay, religiously – speaking, none whatsoever.

An automaton can respond to commands without seeking meaning in them or order among them. A fully human response relates a command to a total existential reality; and the moment such a relation is postulated, the quest for purpose becomes inevitable. If we are to grasp divine commands spiritually, indeed if we are to understand them at all in anything more than a semantic or mechanical sense, we must understand them teleologically. The contention that while mitzvot are purposeful we must act as if they weren't – because we have no surefire method of ascertaining their ends – emasculates one whole side of the religious life. Far from representing, *ipso facto*, an element of hubris, the attempt to interpret Halakha in categories of values constitutes a necessary phase of *kabbalat haTorah*, "the receiving of the Torah." As a dynamic participant in the dialogic process of divine revelation, man cannot and should not rest content with receiving God's message at only the most superficial of levels. Moreover, in assuming the validity of teleological interpretation, we need not rely upon our own intuition. A Torah value structure is clearly the basis of numerous rabbinic ordinances and it lies at the very heart of the concept of *lifnim mishurat hadin*. I am not at all sure that one *can* banish teleology. When barred at the door, it tends to sneak in through the window, and even professed legal literalists are apt to think and react in terms of an implicit value structure. Quite clearly, however, we *ought* not banish it – not even in the interests of theological security. When the price of security is spiritual embalming, we can hardly avoid taking some risks.

The risks cannot be denied – indeed, they can hardly be exaggerated – but a meaningful set of values is too important a baby to be cast out with the bath water. Teleological interpretation can and often does entail hubris; but, given self-awareness and religious sensibility, it is fully consistent with absolute humility. Properly conceived, moreover, it is no usurpation but rather the exercise of a divinely mandated duty.

Beyond hubris, there is the possibility of error. This is naturally always present, but we should regard it as a spur to humility and caution, not as a total brake upon decision. A healthy conservatism should certainly restrain us from being swept away by ephemeral elements, from interpreting merely to suit the *Zeitgeist*, and from reducing all to mere probabilism; but it should not stifle us completely. We cannot have infallibility. However, as Newman insisted, between that and probabilism, there lies certitude;[32] and in the valid exercise of a genuine mode of interpretation, we have both the right and the duty to rely upon it. The only alternatives are Pyrrhonism and passivity.

The third difficulty – the paucity of guidelines – should be viewed from a similar perspective. Subjectivism need be no more operative here than in human life generally. With its objective legal corpus serving as ballast, a teleology of Halakha could derive from the interplay of revelation and tradition, on the one hand, and individual conscience, on the other. A measure of diversity would no doubt result; but, again, no more than is necessary or, for that matter, desirable.

Finally, the danger of overreaching – of using teleological interpretation not to grapple with Halakha but to eviscerate it – poses a genuine threat. "Why," asked R. Yitzhak, "were the reasons of Torah laws not revealed?"

> Because in two verses reasons were revealed and they caused the greatest in the world [i.e., Solomon] to stumble. It is written, "He shall not multiply wives to himself,"[33] whereon Solomon said, "I will multiply yet not turn away." Yet it is written, "And it came to pass, when Solomon was old, his wives turned away his heart [after other gods]."[34] Again, it is written, "He shall not multiply horses to himself,"[35] whereon Solomon said, "I will multiply and not cause to return." Yet it is written, "And a chariot came up and went out of Egypt for six [hundred shekels of silver]."[36]

And yet, even this should not deter us. The fact that the Torah generally refrained from revealing the grounds of mitzvot does not necessarily

---

32. See John Henry Newman, *An Essay in Aid of a Grammar of Assent* (New York, 1955), 181–94.
33. *Devarim* 17:17. The verse continues, "that thy heart turn not away."
34. *I Melakhim* 11:4.
35. *Devarim* 17:16. The verse continues, "nor cause the people to return to Egypt, to the end that he should multiply horses; forasmuch as the Lord hath said unto you: 'Ye shall henceforth return no more that way.'"
36. *I Melakhim* 10:29. The entire quotation is from *Sanhedrin* 21b.

militate against *our* seeking them. Where we might have been misled by revealed explanations, we can learn to be wise enough and humble enough not to be dazzled by our own. The essential point is that we avoid confusing the legal scope of a mitzva with its presumed reasons; or, to put it differently, that we do not confuse human with divine motivation. Whatever God's reasons for commanding us, the mere fact that we *have* been commanded is sufficient reason for us. A gemara in *Rosh HaShana* illustrates the halakhic attitude perfectly:

> R. Yitzhak said: Why do we sound the horn on Rosh HaShana? Why do we sound?! The All-Merciful has told us to sound! Rather, [he means] why do we sound a *terua*? [Why] sound a *terua*?! The All-Merciful has proclaimed a "memorial of *terua*"! Rather, [he means] why do we sound a *tekia* and a *terua* sitting [i.e., independently of any *Amida* prayer] and [then again] sound a *tekia* and a *terua* standing [i.e., during the recital of the *Musaf* prayer]?[37]

At one level, the question is not even answered. It is simply ignored as illegitimate. Whatever the value of *shofar* – and how many sermons have sought to explore it? – it does not constitute the ground of our obligation nor can it serve as a condition of our observance. Awareness of this point prevents the jettisoning of mitzvot and, at the same time, sets up the dialectic tension between the formal and axiological aspects of Halakha. It does not, however, preclude teleological inquiry entirely. Such inquiry remains essential, ethically and theologically, simply in order that we deepen and broaden our understanding of Torah; and

---

37. *Rosh HaShana* 16a–b. The general question of the legitimacy and advisability of seeking reasons for mitzvot (not to be confused with rationalizing them) has been a matter of long-standing controversy; see Yitzchak Heinemann, *Taamei HaMitzvot BeSafrut Yisrael*, 4th ed. (Jerusalem, 1959), I, 11–36. One might also mention a recent brief comment by David S. Shapiro, "The Ideological Foundations of the Halakha," *Tradition*, IX (1967): 100 and 116n.

it is relevant, practically, as a guide to the legitimate circumvention or adaptation of the fundamental Halakha.[38]

V. Returning to the *Havvot Ya'ir*

Against this background, we can turn, in conclusion, to reexamine the *Havvot Ya'ir's teshuva*. The *teshuva* clearly considers the moral as well as the legal aspects of its subject; it asks both whether the proposed compact can be implemented and whether it should. As regards the question of validity, no fundamental objections are raised. R. Ya'ir Hayim does cite possible grounds for invalidating the proposal but these – *asmakhta* and *davar shelo ba laolam* – are essentially extraneous. The fundamental right to override the halakhot concerning *hassagat gevul* is clearly recognized. Its precise basis is not spelled out, although it is presumably proprietary. The controversy between R. Meir and R. Yehuda is obviously of little relevance here; the compact's proponents were not attempting to create a new halakhic entity but to evade the penalties of an existing one. The principle of remission is, however, quite relevant, and the mishna applying it to torts is cited in the *teshuva*, albeit more by way of proscribing the compact than of conceding its validity.

With respect to the second major mode of halakhic adaptation, communal legislation, the *teshuva* is strangely silent. In an almost syndicalist vein, the Gemara specifically extends this concept to non-governmental bodies such as federations of tradesmen or laborers who are empowered to legislate with respect to their own affairs. This extension should presumably include the textile dealers involved in our case.

38. It should be noted that one position cited in the Gemara went further: "R. Shimon, who interpreted the reason of the [Torah] verse," qualified a number of laws in the light of their presumed purpose; see, e.g., *Bava Metzia* 115a, *Kiddushin* 21a and 68b, *Gittin* 49b. In practice, this principle was generally not employed to challenge the basic relevance of a halakha to its broad field of application but to deal with relative minutiae, exempting particular sets of circumstances. Nevertheless, as a principle, it constitutes a considerable extension of the scope of teleological interpretation. However, this position was challenged by contemporaries (see loc. cit.) and subsequently rejected. See also *Tosafot, Gittin* 49b, s.v. *verabbi*, who state that R. Shimon's adversaries only rejected his use of teleological interpretation to qualify the law proper, but certainly accepted the validity of such speculation *per se*.

Perhaps the *Havvot Ya'ir* accepted the view of some *Rishonim*[39] that while the power of legislation extends to specialized groups, they must nevertheless be community-wide in scope. A group might be confined to barbers but it must include all the barbers within a given social or political unit.[40] More likely, however, this right was not invoked because it is restricted by a major qualification. It may only be exercised by non-governmental bodies in the absence of superior political or religious authority.[41] When such an authority exists – as it probably did in the textile dealers' town – its approval must be obtained for all legislation. In our case, R. Ya'ir Hayim obviously considered such approval

39. See the commentaries of Ramban and Ran, ad loc., and *Teshuvot HaRashba*, 4:185.
40. Within the context of the concept of communal legislation, the Gemara (*Bava Batra* 9a) mentions a compact made by some butchers. As cited by some *Rishonim* – e.g., Rabbenu Gershom, Ramban, and Ran, ad loc. – the text specifically states only two were involved. Others – e.g., *Yad Rama* and Rosh, ad loc., and Rashba, *Teshuvot* 4:185 – read "[there were] some butchers" with no mention of the number. The first reading would seemingly weaken if not refute the contention that a legislating body must be community-wide in scope. However, the Ramban read "two" and advanced his position nonetheless, apparently assuming the town had no more butchers and that as long as a group included all the eligible members within a community, the number, no matter how small, was irrelevant.

    The general problem of the limits of the authority of non-governmental bodies over their members has many modern applications. Cf. Fuller, *Morality of Law*, 123–29, and the references cited there.
41. The Gemara, ibid., speaks somewhat ambiguously of *adam hashuv*, "an important person." However, R. Yosef ibn Migash – cited in *Shitta Mekubbetzet* and by numerous commentaries, ad loc. – insisted the qualification applied only to an individual who was both a religious and a political leader, and this view was accepted by most *Rishonim*; see *Yad Rama*, Rashba, Ritva, and Rosh, ad loc., and Rambam, *Hilkhot Mekhira* 14:11, as understood by *Maggid Mishneh*. This position would seem to derive logical support from the Ramban's explanation of the need for the consent of the *adam hashuv* (see his *Hiddushim, Bava Batra* 9a). He contends that it is rooted in the fact that while the ordinances of a trade or labor organization are initially purely internal in character, their ramifications may affect the broad public interest adversely – e.g., a price rise may result. Hence, the consent of a religious authority would not suffice. Agreement would have to come from a duly selected public political figure. It might be noted, finally, that the Rivash (*Teshuvot*, 399), pursuing this line of reasoning, held that the qualification of *adam hashuv* applied only to ordinances instituted by non-governmental groups but was irrelevant to ordinances passed by the citizenry as a whole or its representatives.

inconceivable. Hence, he was compelled to treat the proposed compact at a purely individual level.

At this plane, however, the basic legality of the compact is reasonably clear. Its morality is another question – one on which R. Ya'ir Hayim has some rather strong feelings. He regards it as evasion at its worst – an attempt both to outflank the letter of the law, and to ride roughshod over its spirit. Moreover, the evasion would be attended by no compensatory spiritual gain. It would help realize neither the values envisioned by the law of *hassagat gevul* nor any other significant Torah-halakhic goals. On the contrary, the resultant rapacity would impoverish its victims, on the one hand, while brutalizing its agent, on the other. Here was a clear instance of circumvention for which no moral or religious justification could be found.

Judging from the background of this particular compact and the motives ascribed to its proponents, one is inclined to agree. And yet, if the issue is to be generalized, certain questions inevitably arise. The primary thrust of the halakhot concerning *hassagat gevul*[42] is quite clear: restraint of excessively aggressive and acquisitive instincts, on the one hand, and protection of established property rights, on the other. However, the ethical relevance of these halakhot is more obvious in some contexts than in others. Within a rural society, its trade primarily local and its economy relatively stagnant, the intrusion of a competitor can normally be regarded as a personal aggression. More likely than not, it entails the direct confrontation of two individuals, the stronger (as he imagines) retailer and sharper merchant seeking to supplant the weaker, with little social benefit attendant upon the substitution. Within an industrialized urban society, however – or, to be more specific, within a capitalist economy – the picture is radically different. For one thing,

42. I have not ventured to discuss these in detail as this would take us rather far afield. It should not be assumed, of course, that all forms of modern competition are, in the absence of any consent circumventing it, forbidden by the Halakha. It can be fairly stated, however, that, as they have been traditionally formulated and applied, the laws of *hassagat gevul* would proscribe much which a capitalist economy takes for granted and which may, indeed, be essential to its existence. It might be mentioned that the basic halakhot concerning *hassagat gevul* were discussed by the *Havvot Ya'ir*, 42–44.

the impact – in a sense, even the nature – of the competition itself differs. While it may involve a direct clash between small businessmen or a supermarket chain's driving the corner grocery into bankruptcy, it may just as well entail the relatively impersonal competition of manufacturing and merchandising giants, each striving to gain a share of a broad national market. In such circumstances, no family enterprise is threatened with extinction. The stakes are a few cents per share on an earnings statement rather than personal economic survival; the participants are not the entrepreneurs proper but executive hierarchies. Hence, both the suffering and the greed may be significantly mitigated.

Secondly, under such circumstances, the evils of *hassagat gevul* may at least be balanced by compensatory social benefits. Needless to say, competition has been the lifeblood of modern industrial progress. It has not only generally provided better products but, in many cases, has expanded the total market so that instead of one firm's crippling another, both have, albeit unwittingly, jointly developed a broader base which they could then share mutually. In any overall view of the merits of competition, these factors can hardly be ignored. To be sure, it may still be contended that the possibly intensive social and economic suffering of a few is too great a price to pay for a better universal mousetrap. We are here confronted by one aspect of the problem of technological dislocation with which the modern world has wrestled since the advent of the Industrial Revolution. Yet the point remains that in any attempted solution, the positive contribution of competition cannot be ignored. It would be a bit paradoxical if we were to dwell with infinite care upon the just distribution of the current economic pie and at the same time neglected means of enlarging it.

Under modern conditions, therefore, a compact – or, for that matter, tacit consent – permitting certain forms of *hassagat gevul* could have a very different character than it had for the *Havvot Ya'ir*. Certainly, Jewish ethics cannot possibly countenance a blanket Darwinian sacrifice of the weaker tradesman to the stronger; and no responsible thinker could wish a return to the "rugged individualism" of the nineteenth century. But the alternative need not be the vested entrenchment of the seventeenth. Within a changed economic order, a different axiological perspective becomes essential. It is indeed possible that, even at the formal halakhic level, some of the laws concerning *hassagat gevul* do not govern many contemporary situations. They may be hedged with qualifications – perhaps the very points we have been discussing – which would render them inoperative under certain modern conditions. Be this as it may, however, at the level of values, certainly, vibrant competition must often be regarded in a positive light. The possible use of legitimate authority to adapt the halakhot concerning *hassagat gevul* thus becomes a live ethical and religious option.[43] The question may not be "whether?" but "how?" and "how far?"

It is by no means an easy question. A proper balance between restraining avarice and protecting individuals, on the one hand, and stimulating growth and providing incentive, on the other, cannot be readily or permanently achieved. Not only the evaluation of details but even the determination of emphasis and the allotment of priorities may be in dispute. The difficulty is clearly illustrated by a controversy in the Mishna concerning two related matters: "R. Yehuda says: A shopkeeper must not distribute parched corn or nuts to children, because he [thereby] accustoms them to come to him; and the Sages permit it. Nor may he reduce the market price;[44] but the Sages say, 'He is to be remembered for good.'" Strikingly enough – and somewhat against the modern capitalist grain – the Gemara takes R. Yehuda's statement at face value and only feels compelled to explain the position of his opponents: "What is the Rabbis' reason? – Because he can say to him [i.e., one shopkeeper to his fellow], 'I distribute nuts, you [go and] distribute plums.'"[45] And again, "What is the Rabbis' reason? – Because he eases the market."[46] In our day, these issues are infinitely more complex – not only because

43. It should be emphasized that even in the absence of the specific laws regarding *hassagat gevul*, the Torah's injunctions against coveting and plotting to acquire other people's property – see *Shemot* 20:14 and *Devarim* 5:18, and Rambam, *Hilkhot Gezela VaAveda* 1:9–11 – would still prohibit many excessively competitive practices. However, being largely subjective and more elusive in nature, they may sometimes not provide as great a deterrent as more rigidly objective restraints.
44. "To sell more cheaply because he induces [customers] to come to him and thus constricts his fellow's livelihood" (Rashi).
45. *Bava Metzia* 60a.
46. Loc. cit.

the contemporary stakes are far greater and our economy so much more interdependent, but also because the techniques of bait advertising and loss-leader price cutting are so much more sophisticated. But the heart of the matter – the question of primary direction and emphasis – remains the same. From the perspective of halakhic ethics, we are continually confronted by the same persistent question: To what extent should we allow the progress of civilization to lead us back to the law of the jungle?

Pursuit of Self-Interest

INTRODUCTION

Moral and political philosophy knows few hardier chestnuts than the perennial problem of the relation of the individual and the community. Multifaceted, the problem presents itself in different, even in contrasting, contexts. It may concern mutual rights or mutual responsibilities; the demarcation of bounds or the resolution of conflict; the interaction of either pervasive impact or direct confrontation. Whatever the aspect, however, it is basic to the appreciation of one of the major areas of ethical thought – social morality.

The following *teshuva* deals with one dimension of this problem: the right of an individual to pursue his own ends when such pursuit entails a potential threat to communal welfare; or, to put it in more contemporary terms, the degree to which an individual need consider the public interest in determining his own course. The particular case evidently involves a certain Levi who has fallen upon hard times financially and seeks to recoup by emigrating temporarily to warmer economic climes. Unfortunately, however, his prospective destination has already absorbed a substantial number of apparently refugee Jews, much to its government's chagrin, and various punitive measures have been periodically announced in order to stop and, indeed, to reverse the influx. These measures may not necessarily have been motivated by outright antisemitism. During the last years of the seventeenth century, Louis XIV's expansive foreign policy plunged much of Western and Central Europe into war, with many Jews – so often the first to suffer – being consequently uprooted. The resultant migration may have caused genuine social dislocation or economic hardship in countries to which the refugees fled. Whatever the motivation, however – and latent antisemitism certainly cannot be ruled out as a factor – the government's decrees were tantamount to an edict of expulsion, and the respondent is naturally very much concerned about them. One gathers – although the *teshuva* does not quite say so explicitly – that as long as the status quo is maintained quietly, these measures are not very vigorously enforced. They merely constitute a statutory Damocles' sword. However, the arrival of fresh immigration – possibly, even of a single immigrant – might aggravate the situation by calling attention to it, thus leading the government to invoke and enforce restrictive measures. Hence, apart from the potential impact upon the economic opportunities of the present inhabitants – this point is not really raised in the *teshuva* – Levi's entry could threaten the community with the danger of various sanctions. The question is therefore raised:[1] Halakhically, may Levi emigrate to this locale?

The *Havvot Ya'ir*'s *prima facie* reaction is negative. Inasmuch as the *Mordekhai* states that villagers already residing near a town should move if their continued residence poses a possible danger to the town,[2] then, *a fortiori*, one could not enter a community if his entry entailed

1. The identity of the respondent is not mentioned in the *teshuva*, but evidently it is not Levi.
2. The specific case – cited not in the *Mordekhai* proper but in *Haggahot Mordekhai, Kiddushin*, 561–2 – concerns a demand made by the Duke of Lothair from the Jewish community under his rule that it deal with Jews living in villages under lesser feudal lords – i.e., that it compel them to return to live under his hegemony, which they had apparently left. Should the community fail to do so, he threatened to expel all its members.

potential *hezzek rabbim*, "public harm."[3] The analogy – and the initial response superficially based upon it – is quickly rejected, however; and this for three reasons. First, the concept of "public harm" presupposes a public. This term, the *Havvot Ya'ir* suggests, can apply only to a community, a stable and reasonably permanent social entity. However, the group potentially threatened by Levi's immigration is itself comprised of recent arrivals – essentially a ragtag conglomeration of basically transient persons who have descended upon this locale from various places and who are residing there temporarily until they can reestablish themselves.[4] This is not so much a community as a collection of individuals, less a social entity than a multitude of single units; and the laws concerning "public harm" may not apply.

Secondly, in the *Mordekhai*'s case, the enjoined villagers were not subject to clear and definite loss. It was not certain that they would suffer financially if they moved;[5] and even if they did incur some losses, they could probably obtain restitution from the established local authorities. In the present case, however, Levi will suffer certain loss for which, given the haphazard civil and legal structure of the affected group, he will never be reimbursed.

Finally, in the *Mordekhai*'s case – as well as in a case discussed in the gemara upon which the *Mordekhai* had based his decision[6] – the public harm was reasonably clear and definite. The principles governing that situation, therefore, cannot apply to another in which the potential danger, while a distinct and foreseeable possibility, is nevertheless neither certain nor perhaps even probable. The *Havvot Ya'ir* argues, *a priori*, that it is inconceivable that it should be forbidden for each and every person to attempt any venture which might, conjecturally, cause public harm; and he buttresses this argument by citing a recent precedent. A

3. In its primary semantic sense, the term *hezzek* refers to physical damage. However, by extension, it often denotes financial loss as well.
4. Evidently, the antecedent and permanent Jewish community – if there was one – was under no sanction.
5. The *Havvot Ya'ir* is apparently thinking only of the financial loss. The social hardship attendant upon dislocation, while very real, may not have been regarded as legally actionable.
6. *Bava Batra* 21b.

wealthy Jew had sued a functionary of a provincial governor before a sort of national supreme court in Heidelberg. Other Jews, fearful of reprisals by that governor, begged the plaintiff to withdraw his suit. At no point, however, did they – or halakhic authorities who were consulted – challenge his legal right to proceed with it.

In light of these distinctions, the *Mordekhai* is rejected as a relevant proof-text, and Levi's right to immigrate to his chosen site is upheld. Having staked out his basic position, the *Havvot Ya'ir* proceeds to adduce proofs to support it. In doing so, however, he underscores a point which had been barely implied previously but which now emerges as the heart of the argument. The proof consists of the citation of certain actions – payment of excessive ransom or encouraging prisoners to flee, for instance – which are enjoined halakhically because they may lead to some public harm, repeated raids to capture prisoners in the one case or reprisals against them in the other.[7] Nevertheless, the *Havvot Ya'ir* insists, the individual prisoner involved may certainly do all in his power to attain maximum personal safety, in disregard of the possible consequences to the public. It is this distinction between acting for oneself and acting for others – and not just the previous qualifications concerning the nature of the public or the certainty of private or public loss – which now becomes crucial.[8] An outsider would perhaps have no right to assist Levi at the risk of inducing certain communal dangers. For Levi himself, however, the identical course of action is fully permissible.

The last third of the *teshuva* is then devoted to the discussion of this distinction – partly to adducing proof, partly to refuting apparently contrary evidence, and partly to introducing one major qualification: a person beset by an existing source of active harm may not, even indirectly, divert it to someone else. This is not deemed applicable to the present case, however, and the decision affirming Levi's right to immigrate is allowed to stand.

---

7. See *Gittin* 45a.
8. It is not clear whether this distinction is superimposed upon the preceding – so that the individual involved may act only when at least one of the three previous conditions is met, and a third party not even then – or is independent of them. The continuation of the *teshuva* would appear to suggest the former.

In style and texture, this *teshuva* presents somewhat of a contrast to most of the *teshuvot* in the *Havvot Ya'ir*, of which our previous selection[9] is rather typical. Particularly when dealing with so crucial and complex a problem, these tend to be quite full and comprehensive, if not, indeed, dense. The relatively sparse – although, perhaps, therefore more translucent – character of this *teshuva* is explained, in part, by its concluding lines: "Due to our many sins, I am unable to embellish my remarks by the adornment of authors, [i.e., reference to] the Talmud and earlier authorities, as I have no book whatsoever in my possession." The cause of this destitution provides an interesting concluding sidelight to the *teshuva*. While fleeing from successive waves of French invaders, R. Ya'ir Hayim was forced to abandon his library – which his wife eventually sold at an apparent discount[10] – so that this *teshuva* was written on the basis of memory. In one sense, this fact serves to dramatize R. Ya'ir Hayim's erudition. In another, by reminding us that it was written by a refugee, it adds a significant dimension to the *teshuva* proper.

9. See the chapter "Formalism vs. Teleology" above.
10. For the details, see the autobiographical notes – a gloss on the manuscript of *Mekor Hayim*, R. Ya'ir Hayim's unpublished commentary on *Orah Hayim* – published and discussed in Alexander Marx, "Some Notes on the Life of R. Yair Hayyim Bacharach," in *Essays in Honour of the Very Rev. Dr. J. H. Hertz*, ed. I. Epstein et al. (London, 1943), 307–11.

RESPONSA HAVVOT YA'IR #213

With reference to your first question, as to whether Levi has the right to go to dwell there for two years in order to venture [to provide] for himself, or whether he should refrain out of concern lest public harm result therefrom (i.e., because many Jews [already] reside[1] there and also[2] the government objects very strongly and, upon its orders, it has often been announced in the synagogue that they [i.e., the Jewish residents] should move from there, upon pain of punishment and/or fine, so that this venturer is stirring up and reviving the matter [anew]): *prima facie*, it would appear that it is forbidden *a fortiori*. For individuals who dwell in villages are enjoined to move their residence if there is a fear of public harm as it is written in the *Mordekhai*,[3] cited by Rama in his

1. The Hebrew term *mitgorerim* may mean either simply reside or reside temporarily, especially as an alien. In this case, the latter is probably intended.
2. This literal rendering of *gam* leaves open the possibility that a second objection is being introduced, of which the first – possibly based on the potential loss of economic opportunity for present residents – is wholly independent. This seems very unlikely, however, as no such independent point is developed in the *teshuva*. The flow of the argument is probably meant simply to elucidate the very general statement already made.
3. Inasmuch as this text is so central to this *teshuva*, it might best be cited *in extenso*:

   With respect to the Duke of Lothair who demanded of the Jews that they should deal with those Jews residing in his villages under petty princes so that they [i.e., the villagers] should return to him and if not he will expel them [i.e., the whole Jewish community] entirely – it seems to me that the duke has the power to expel them all [so that, consequently,] even though these [i.e., the villagers] say, "Let my soul perish with the Philistines" [i.e., that they may as well stay put and then let all be expelled together; see *Shofetim* 16:30], it is of no avail. Rather, we compel them over a trait of Sodom [i.e., causing loss to others at no gain to oneself; see *Bava Batra* 12b] to return to him. Moreover, there is some basis to the duke's statement, for "the government's law is law" [i.e., is accorded halakhic weight; see *Gittin* 10b]. If those Jews [i.e., the villagers] have some claim because of the loss incurred in moving from their place, they should argue this later after they have removed the public harm. Until then, however, they have no right to claim anything so that the matter shouldn't be delayed, as it is [like] the pot of a group of partners neither [cold nor warm]. This can be proven from the chapter, *Lo Yahpor* [see *Bava Batra* 24b], where it says [i.e.,

note upon *Hoshen Mishpat* 155:22. Hence, [it is] certainly [forbidden] to undertake a venture for one's private need if it entails public harm. However, upon further scrutiny, [it becomes clear that] no proof whatsoever can be adduced from there; [and this] for many reasons. The first concerns [the particular circumstances of] this case. For it may be said that "public harm" refers solely to a community, a city, or the members of a commonwealth who have banded together. Such is the case of the threshing floor and tree adjoining the city[4] discussed in the Gemara and of the citizenry discussed in the aforementioned *Mordekhai*. However, these migrants who come from different villages and towns and take up temporary residence in a community are [to be] regarded as individuals.

Secondly, even if one should assume that they are defined as a public, [we must] nevertheless [consider another point]. Certainly, in the *Haggahot Mordekhai*'s case, the villagers had no clear and definite loss. Moreover, were they to suffer a loss, they could demand restitution from the prince's subjects, as these probably have *parnasim* and leaders, so that, in any event, the injured parties could demand restitution. This is evident and elucidated there proper and [can also be inferred] from the source of this law [the halakha] that he chops down the tree [first] and they make restitution [later]. It is otherwise in our case, however. If [Levi] will refrain from venturing and will thereby sustain a substantial loss, from whom will he seek compensation? For those [Jewish] residents are stray individuals, and they have no common organization whatsoever.

---

with reference to the statement of the Mishna concerning someone who has obstructed the entrance to a city by planting a tree there]: "'If the city came first, he must chop it down without [receiving compensation], and if the tree came first, he chops it down and [the city] compensates him' – But let him say [i.e., in the latter case], give me money first and then I shall chop?" And it [i.e., the Gemara] concludes because [the situation resembles that] of a jointly owned pot [i.e., one which tends to be tepid because each partner, not being the sole owner, neglects it and relies upon the other; here, likewise, a public matter will not be attended to as promptly as a personal one, and meanwhile the danger persists]. (*Haggahot Mordekhai, Kiddushin* 561–62)

4. Both of which must be removed when they constitute a threat to a city; see *Bava Batra* 24b.

A third reason consists of a clear and evident distinction. [This ruling applies] only in a case such as that of the tree or the threshing floor in which the loss is known and certain; or, similarly, in that of the *Haggahot Mordekhai*, in which the lord issued a decree which, as the declaration of a sovereign ruler, will undoubtedly be executed. It would be very different, however, [to say] that it should be forbidden for every individual to venture and to serve his own interest lest some loss should thereby result to an individual or a group. This is counter to reason and inconceivable. Shall we, then, enjoin a wealthy person from giving a New Year's gift to his lord out of fear that he [i.e., the lord] might be cross with the other wealthy members of the community?

While considering this halakha, I recalled an incident.[5] A [Jewish] nobleman once brought suit in the High Court at Heidelberg against a subordinate of the lord of a Pfalzian province. As a result, all the Jews of that entire country became apprehensive and were gripped by fear, particularly those living under the jurisdiction of that lord, for it was in his power to oppress them at any time. Consequently, they vehemently and tearfully implored this nobleman that he should try to settle with him, as the lord had already threatened to avenge himself upon the Jews; and they agreed to reimburse part of his loss. However, they could not have told him that, according to law, he must give up his claim in order to avert their loss. Even if, be it forfended, there had been fear[6] of expulsion, they could not have imposed such a demand against the nobleman, and they were told this by great Torah authorities.

The proof [may be derived] from what we hold in the Gemara in *Gittin*[7] that we should not pay exorbitant ransom for captives. The reason is – as set down in *Yoreh De'ah* 252 – in order that potential captors should not be attracted. Nevertheless, we hold[8] that one may ransom himself for any sum that he wishes.

5. An inversion of the Gemara's statement about Phineas: "He saw the incident and recalled the halakha" (*Sanhedrin* 82a).
6. The term *hashash* may mean either anxiety or danger. Both are probably intended here.
7. 45a.
8. Ed. note: See *Tosafot*, ad loc., s.v. *delo*.

Similarly, while we hold[9] that we do not abet prisoners in escaping lest there be retaliation against the others, it is nevertheless certain that an individual who can escape may do so and he need not consider [consequences to] the others. Or again, it is not forbidden to store commodities – even though the resultant rise in prices certainly harms the public – except in *Eretz Yisrael* or in a predominantly Jewish community, and then, only such objects as are necessary for sustaining life, as stated in *Hoshen Mishpat* 231.[10]

One may also infer thus from [the story of] the payment for a crown of the first chapter of *Bava Batra*,[11] in which he [i.e., R. Yehuda HaNasi] told them they may flee although a loss thus resulted to those who remained; and this law is cited in the note upon *Shulhan Arukh* [HM], 163.[12] Nor can it be objected, from there, subsection 6, that with respect to taxes all are regarded as partners,[13] as is well known to scholars.[14]

---

9. *Gittin* 45a.
10. The Gemara, *Bava Batra* 90b, simply states that hoarding is forbidden, without mentioning the type of community involved. However, the Rambam – apparently on the basis of an analogy with other laws cited in the same context – introduced the qualifications mentioned by the *Havvot Ya'ir*; see *Hilkhot Mekhira* 14:5. See also Rashbam, *Bava Batra* 90b, s.v. *otzrei*.
11. 8a. The Gemara relates that a fine equaling the value of a crown was levied upon the Jewish community of Tiberias. Some residents wanted to flee in order to avoid payment and R. Yehuda HaNasi did not stand in their way.
12. I find no intimation of such a position in the section cited. Indeed, if anything, the Rama's note upon 163:2 would appear to suggest the reverse, at least with respect to paying ordinary taxes.
13. I.e., and all must pay them jointly, even though they have been levied against only a segment of the community by the government. Once they have been decreed, an individual not only may not but cannot shirk them by leaving the community. Of course, this applies to communal as opposed to personal taxes.
14. It is not fully clear whether it is the status of partnership which is well known – in which case we have a logical or textual lacuna here – or, as appears more likely, the fact that no objection can be raised. In any event, however, no distinction is explained. Presumably, the *Havvot Ya'ir* is assuming the distinction cited by the Rama: all are jointly responsible for properly and legally imposed taxes, but an unjust fine imposed on the basis of some libel – with which the Halakha has unfortunately had many encounters – is regarded as a calamity afflicting anyone affected by it but imposing no legal responsibility upon other members of the community. In such a

Furthermore, even with respect to one person's causing damage to another through [overt] action, he cannot be restrained unless the damage results immediately or unless he sets up a means which will then itself directly damage his fellow;[15] see *Shulhan Arukh,* [HM] 155:32, and the *Sema* thereon. See also the concluding note upon 388:2 and the *Sema* thereon which cite the [view of the] *Nimmukei Yosef*[16] that if a person is already suffering damage, he may not remove its source [if][17] damage will thereby result to his fellow. For this reason when the town of Worms was held by the French and they wished to destroy two or three houses which formed part of the city's wall in order to make it an open city, I ruled that if the governor had already decreed upon a particular house, it is forbidden to attempt to influence him [to change his decision], as this would result in loss to another. However, these refer solely to clear and definite losses, in which case no distinction is made between [damage to] an individual and a public, except with reference to reimbursement and the prior removal of the source of the damage. None of this applies in our case, however.

Due to our many sins,[18] I am unable to embellish my remarks by reference to the Talmud and earlier authorities as I do not have any book whatsoever in my possession.

---

case – of which the incident in Tiberias is presumed to have been an instance (see *Be'urei HaGra,* HM 163:94) – the Rama states that even those initially subject to the fine who then manage to avoid it, cannot be sued by the rest of the community which then has to shoulder a heavier burden. The *Havvot Ya'ir* goes a step further in holding that the fugitives are not only exempt *post facto* but that it is permissible for them to flee in the first place.

15. These are among the criteria most prominently mentioned by *Rishonim* and later scholars who grappled with the question of defining the limits of liability for damage, especially in relation to the concept of causation. The *locus classicus* of this discussion is the Ramban's monograph on *dina degarmi,* appended to his commentary on *Bava Batra.*
16. *Bava Batra* 8a, in commenting upon R. Alfasi, 5a.
17. The Hebrew equivalent, *im,* does not appear in the text, but this is obviously an error of oversight.
18. A fairly stock phrase, often used as the equivalent of "unfortunately." In some instances it is merely a cliché, but very often it carries something of the force of the theological conception of history in which it is rooted.

שו"ת חוות יאיר סימן ריג

שאלה על הראשון אשר נסתפקת אם הרשות ביד לוי לילך להשתדל בעד נפשו לדור שם שנתיים ימים או ימנע מחשש פן ימטא מזה היזק רבים (פי' כי הרבה יהודים מתגוררים שם גם השררה מקפדת מאד וכמה פעמים הוכרז בבה"כ ע"פ ציווי שלהם שיעקרו משם בעונש וקנס לכן זה המשתדל הוא מעורר ומזכיר הדבר) לכאורה היה נראה דאסור מק"ו שהרי על יחידים הדרים בכפרים מוטל לעקור דירתם אם יש חשש היזק רבים כמ"ש במרדכי הביאו רמ"א בהג"ה בח"מ סי' קנ"ה סעיף כ"ב וא"כ כ"ש לעשות דבר בהשתדלות לצורך עצמו ויש בזה היזק רבים. אבל אחר העיון אין משם ראיה כלל מכמה טעמים.

הא' הוא מצד הנדון הזה כי י"ל שלא נקרא היזק רבים רק באסיפת קהל ועיר ובני המדינה יחד שנתחברו ובכה"ג גורן ואילן סמוך לעיר כבגמ' ובני מדינה שבמרדכי הנ"ל מש"כ אלו לקוטים הבאים מכפרים ועיירות נפרדים ויושבי' לפי שעה בק"ק כיחידים דמי. הב' את"ל דשם רבים אית להו מ"מ ודאי התם בהגה' מרדכי מיירי שאין להם לבני כפרים היזק ידוע וברור ואם יש להם היזק אפשר להם לתבוע מבני המדינה של השר היזקם דמסתמא יש להם פרנסים ומנהיגים באופן שעכ"פ אפשר לניזקי' לתבוע היזקם והכי מוכח ומבואר שם בעצמו ומצד מקור הדין שהוא קוצץ ונותנים דמיו. מש"כ בנדון זה אם ימנע מלהשתדל וע"י כך יגיע להיזק רב ממי יתבע כי ב"ב המתגוררים הם ליקוטים ואין להם חיבור כלל בשום דבר.

הג' הוא חילוק ברור ומוכח כי דווקא גבי אילן וגורן דברור וידוע ההיזק וכן בהג"ה מרדכי שגזר השר שבלי ספק יגזור אומר ויקם כדבר מלך שלטון. מש"כ שיהא אסור לכל יחיד להשתדל ולפקח בטובת עצמו מחשש שע"י זה יגיע נזק ליחיד או לרבים הוא דבר נגד השכל ולא יעלה על לב וכי נאסור על עשיר מלתת דורון שנה חדשה לשר מחשש פן יאנף על שאר עשירים שבקהל.

וראיתי הלכה ונזכרתי מעשה שיחיד מהקציני' העמיד בדין פקיד שר אחד בגליל מגלילות מדינות פפאלץ לפני המשפט הגדול שבק"ק היידלבורג. וע"י זה פחדו ויראו וחיל אחז לכלל יהודים שבמדינה הנ"ל ובפרט יהודי' הדרים באותו פקידות של השר כי בידו להתעולל עלילות

עליהם בכל עת ובכל שעה ודברו עם הקצין בבקשה גדולה ובדמעות שליש שיראה לפשר עמו כי כבר גיזם השר לנקום בב״י ונתרצו למלאות קצת היזקו אבל לומר לו שיפסיד חובו מצד הדין למנוע מהם ההיזק אפילו חלילה יש חשש גירוש לא יוכלו לזכות נגד הקצין וכך הוגד להם מפי גדולים בתורה.

וראיה מהא דק״ל בגמ׳ בגיטין דאין פודין את השבוים יתר על כדי דמיהם והטעם דלא לגררי ולייתו וכדק״ל בי״ד סי׳ רנ״ב ומ״מ ק״ל דיכול אדם לפדות עצמו בכל ממון שירצה. וכן הא דק״ל אין מבריחין את השבוים מחשש הכבדת עול האחרים ומ״מ פשוט דכל יחיד שיכול לברוח בורח ואין לו לחוש על אחרים וכן לא אסרו לאצור פירות אע״פ שבלי ספק יש היזק לרבים ע״י יוקר השער אלא דווקא בא״י או בעיר שרובה ישראלים ובדברים שיש בהם חיי נפש והוא בש״ע ח״מ סי׳ רל״א. והכי מוכח מדמי כלילא פ״ק דב״ב דא״ל ערוקו אע״פ שהיה היזק לנשארים. וכ״כ בהג״ה ש״ע סי׳ קס״ג. ואין להקשות משם ס״ו דלענין מסים הוי כשותפין כידוע להמעיין ואפילו בהיזק יחיד ליחיד במעשיו לא מעכב אא״כ שיבא ההיזק מיד או שעושה זה דבר שהדבר בעצמו מזיק לחבירו ועי׳ בש״ע סי׳ קנ״ה סל״ב ובסמ״ע וע״ע סי׳ שפ״ח ס״ב סוף הג״ה. ושם בסמ״ע בשם נ״י אם כבר בא לו נזק אסור לסלקו אם ע״י כך יבא היזק לחבירו ולכן פסקתי כאשר היתה קק״ו ביד הצרפתים ובקשו להפיל ב׳ ג׳ בתים שהם בחומה לעשותה עיר פרוצה שאם כבר גזר השר על בית פלוני אסור להשתדל כי ע״י זה יגיע נזק לחבירו מ״מ כל אלו בהיזק ודאי וברור ובזה אין חילוק בין יחיד לרבים רק לענין נותן דמים וקדימת סילוק ההיזק מה שכל זה לא שייך בנדון דידן.

ובעו״ה אין בידי לעטר דבריי בעיטור סופרים ש״ס ופוסקים קדמונים כי אין ברשותי שום ספר.

ANALYSIS

I. Introduction

A. Categories of Self-Interest

At the heart of half the world's literature – and almost all its wars – lies the pursuit of self-interest. Not just the struggle for property in the narrow sense – the delineation of *meum* and *tuum* – nor the naked quest for raw power, but aggrandizement broadly conceived as the quest for the realization of personal ambitions generally and worldly aims specifically – this has been much of the human story. And what constitutes so great a part of conduct must loom correspondingly large in ethical theory. So long as we are, if ever, in Locke's or Adam Smith's "state of nature," self-interest is not the most crucial of moral issues. In a developed social context, however – within which one individual normally advances at the direct or indirect expense of another – it poses an array of formidable problems.

These problems fall into two general areas. One concerns the extent to which one individual may impinge upon the property or person of another; the second the extent to which he must give of his own property or self to aid another. Between them – straddling both and yet clearly distinct from either – lies a third area: competition for a presently unowned common. The two primary areas raise different specific issues. The first revolves around interaction and conflict. Its major questions are: How aggressive may one be in pursuing his own interest? How much must he restrain himself when his pursuit impinges upon his neighbor? Or, alternatively, what are the proper responses to insult or injury? The second demands the definition of priorities. Its central questions turn upon duties rather than rights. To what extent may an individual, while inflicting no harm upon others, simply ignore them? In choosing a career, in expending energy and resources, how much weight should he assign his own and others' interests respectively?

It is not only their specific concerns, however, that distinguish these two areas. Their respective frames of reference are totally different. In effect, the central issue in one is what I may; in the other, how much I must. Focusing upon self-interest and altruism, respectively, the first deals with the nether range, the second with the upper range of the moral scale. To go a step further, the first area has a legal rather than a moral cast. Insofar as virtue enters the picture at all, it is, to use Shaftesbury's phrase, that of a "tiger strongly chain'd."[1] The second area, however – itself ranging from grudging performance of duty to self-effacing saintliness – is decidedly ethical.

This very fact lends additional significance to discussion of the total complex of self-interest and altruism within the halakhic framework. One of the central problems of halakhic thought is the relation between the legal and the ethical – a relation frequently misunderstood by adversary and adherent alike. Regarding Halakha myopically, they often interpret it in excessively monochromatic terms. Failure to appreciate its complexity and range leads to the erroneous assumption that because Halakha demands nothing less than the law, itself generally pervaded by ethico-religious content, it also demands nothing more – an assumption which lies at the root of much Christian misconstruction of Judaism. Analysis of an area in which various halakhic dimensions, both minimal and maximal, are manifest, could help dispel misunderstanding and shed some light on the interaction between law and ethics within Jewish tradition.

B. Delimitation of the Discussion

As a moral phenomenon, the problem of self-interest and altruism obviously impinges upon a wide range of issues – from charity to war, from social planning to economic competition, from vocational choice to idiosyncratic architecture. Its discussion is further complicated by several factors. One is purely quantitative. With respect to both levels, how much weight should be assigned to mere numbers? It seems fairly obvious that self-interest should be differently regarded when it opposes the public rather than a private interest. And yet, one may entertain serious reservations about engaging in the numbers game of Bentham's

1. Anthony Ashley Cooper, Earl of Shaftesbury, "An Inquiry Concerning Virtue and Merit," in *Characteristicks of Men, Manners, Opinions, Times* (London, 1737), vol. 2, p. 32.

"felicific calculus." Even when refined by Mill's qualitative differentiation of pleasures or reduced to arithmetic by Edgeworth's three-dimensional units – "Utility, then, has *three* dimensions; a mass of utility, 'lot of pleasure' is greater than another when it has more *intensity-time-number* units"[2] – it still seems like a crude basis for ethical decision.

The second factor revolves around the definition of the "self" – not in metaphysical or psychological terms but simply as the unit of socio-economic relations. So long as we deal with a solitary individual, this of course poses no problem; with respect to any social group, however, it presents some crucial questions. At one plane, we are led to consider the thesis of Niebuhr's *Moral Man and Immoral Society* – that a community is justified in guarding its interests more zealously and more selfishly than an individual. At another, we encounter the oft-discussed dilemma of the corporation – its directors charged with promoting the interests of their stockholding constituents and yet presumably also invested with a responsibility toward the community at large.[3] Within a narrower but more intense context, a similar problem confronts the head of every household. And of course, all three situations are further complicated by the difficulty, if not impossibility, of disentangling personal from collective interest, selfish gain from fiduciary trust. What is good for General Motors is trebly good for its directors; and the inevitably mixed motivation which prompts their actions adds a significant dimension to their moral quandary.

Exhaustive analysis of such a formidable array of issues clearly lies beyond the scope of a middle-distance essay. I shall therefore largely confine myself to discussion of direct interpersonal action. And yet, even where its definitive treatment is not feasible, as a frame of reference such a panoply of problems provides both valuable perspective and suggestive analogies. As a context – to a point, even a matrix – of a particular detailed analysis, it can remind us of broader ramifications and tangential implications, of the field within which our specific focus is only a point.

2. Joan Robinson, *Economic Philosophy* (Chicago, 1962), 67.
3. This refers to real gifts to the community, not just efforts to improve the corporation's public image.

II. Impinging on Another's Person or Property

A. Valid Competing Interests: Harhakat Shekhenim

To begin with our first area, the halakhic limits of self-assertion, their basic lines are quite obvious: murder, kidnapping, assault, damage, robbery, embezzlement, slander – in a word, the unprovoked destruction, mutilation, or seizure, however defined, of property, reputation, or person. Precisely for this reason, however, this proscription sheds little light upon the character of the halakhic ethic.[4] Less patent injunctions – against, for example, taunts, profiteering, taking of interest, seductive advertising, or delay in payment of wages – are considerably more instructive; but these, too, fail to reflect in detail the nuances of the Halakha's attitude toward self-aggrandizement. For this, we might best refer to more questionable cases, with respect to which one could, at the very least, pose as an *advocatus diaboli*. At the practical level, ethical problems generally involve conflict of goods, and it is by its tendency to emphasize one good or the other that the character of a moral system is most clearly revealed. We should therefore particularly look at confrontations of valid competing interests; and, within such contexts, attempt to gauge what priority the Halakha has assigned to the rights and responsibilities of the respective parties.

Perhaps the most prominent is the sphere of *harhakat shekhenim* – literally, "neighborly distancing." No modern urban dweller needs any account of the trials attendant upon living at close range with others. As regards noise, although not sanitation, he is worse off than his medieval or classical counterpart. The problem was already sufficiently acute during the talmudic era, however; and the Rabbis devoted a full chapter of a major tractate, *Bava Batra*, to the delineation of equitable guidelines for neighborly conduct.

In principle, the concept of *harhakat shekhenim* may very well be of *deoraita* origin. One of the last *Geonim*, Rabbenu Hananel, evidently saw the need for such restraints as grounded upon a talmudic interpretation of a biblical verse. The Gemara cites the verse containing Moses' charge to future judges – "Hear [the causes] between your

---

4. I am referring to the general prohibition in principle; the prohibition's details would shed light, but that would take us too far afield.

brothers and judge righteously, between a man and his brother and his sojourner" (*Devarim* 1:16) – with a brief comment: "Even between the lower and upper parts of a house ... even between a stove and an oven" (*Sanhedrin* 7b). Rashi[5] takes both comments to refer to the division of an estate. The judge is being admonished to familiarize himself with the values of the objects mentioned so that he can effect equitable distribution, with rebates to make up for any differential. Rabbenu Hananel, however – while he possibly advances a parallel interpretation of the first comment – explains the second to mean, "And likewise he [i.e., the judge] must know thoroughly what is the [required] distance of the oven from the wall or from the plastering which is beneath the oven" – a reference to two of the regulations discussed by the Mishna in *Bava Batra*.

On this view, *harhakat shekhenim* is specifically mentioned in the Torah as a distinct category. Even if this interpretation be rejected, however, one may still regard the principle as being of biblical origin – not as a category in its own right but as subsumed under a more general concept. Two such possibilities – strikingly differentiated by their respectively positive and negative characters – were suggested by the twelfth-century *Rishon,* Rav Meir Abulafya. With reference to the Gemara's discussion of threshing that causes fallout of grain over a populated area, he notes that although it may engender no liability, it is nevertheless forbidden "because it is forbidden to cause anything that will bring damage upon people, either due to 'You shall not place a stumbling block before the blind' (*Vayikra* 19:14) or due to 'You shall love your neighbor as yourself' (*Vayikra* 19:18)."[6]

Admittedly, this statement specifically refers to situations in which genuine damage – as measured by the halakhic standard of torts – is inflicted only indirectly. It is therefore conceivable that it would not apply to other situations – many of them covered by ordinances subsumed under *harhakat shekhenim* – in which the aggressor effects no real damage but rather discomfort and disruption. However, it is at least equally tenable that the commandments cited by Rav Meir – especially the positive demand for love – apply to the second group as well.

5. S.v. *bein ish* and s.v. *bein gero*.
6. *Yad Rama, Bava Batra,* chap. 2, no. 107.

A third general ground was advanced by the Rosh. In a responsum,[7] he explains that the various ordinances mentioned in the Gemara were instituted "because 'her ways are the ways of pleasantness and all her paths are peace'[8] and the Torah insisted that a person should do nothing within his [domain] which causes damage to his fellow." Finally, one may venture to propose a fourth text: "And thy brother shall live with thee."[9] Drawing upon its context – the earlier part of the verse reads, "Do not take of him interest or increase; and thou shalt fear thy God" – the Gemara applies the injunction to the return of interest: "Return it to him [i.e., the debtor], that he may live with you."[10] However, this application need not be regarded as exhausting the verse's meaning; and broader ramifications are readily apparent. The Ramban, for instance, construed it as a positive commandment to save human life.[11] Rav Yehoshua Falk, the sixteenth-century author of one of the classical commentaries upon *Hoshen Mishpat,* evidently extended it much further.[12] He takes the Rambam's equation of those who hoard staple foodstuffs or raise their price level with usurers to be more than a symbolic or rhetorical statement. It does not simply mean that both ultimately achieve the same effect of depriving the poor or that, morally speaking, both are equally reprehensible. It means, quite literally, that the hoarder, like the usurer, violates the specific commandment, "And thy brother shall live with thee." In effect, this interpretation assumes that the verse contains a sweeping obligation not only to preserve my brother's life but to secure it, and not only to secure his existence proper but something of its quality as well; and that any action which seriously subverts that quality constitutes a violation of this commandment. It hardly seems far-fetched to subsume *harhakat shekhenim* under this rubric.

7. *Klal* 108, *siman* 10.
8. *Mishlei* 3:17. This principle, though citing a verse from *Mishlei,* impacts on *deoraita* laws as well; see *Yevamot* 87b.
9. *Vayikra* 25:36.
10. *Bava Kamma* 112a.
11. Commentary to *Vayikra* 25:36; in this context, the Ramban cites the opinion of Ben Petura, which we shall discuss later.
12. *Sema* 231:43.

While the principle may be of *deoraita* force – and even this has not gone unchallenged[13] – the details of *harhakat shekhenim* are certainly of rabbinic origin. At most, this halakhic area should be regarded as one of those in which the Torah has formulated a general statement and has then authorized the Rabbis to legislate specific ordinances[14] – ordinances which, once enacted, have the normative force of biblical rather than purely rabbinic laws. The details, such as they are found in the Talmud, are essentially the handiwork of its authors. Reflecting *Hazal's* consciously articulated social and ethical perspective, they become, for our purposes, all the more instructive.

B. Contemporary Application and Discerning Halakha's Values

An exposition of the primary halakhot relevant to the area of *harhakat shekhenim* would revolve around two foci: 1) definition of the key factors – precedence, normalcy and context of a given practice, frequency and intensity of respective inconvenience – to be considered in evaluating a neighborly aggression; and 2) delineation of the major positions concerning the weight and emphasis to be assigned the various factors. It would also have to address itself to a third task – translation of the cases cited by the Gemara and the *Rishonim* into roughly comparable contemporary equivalents.[15] A purely theoretical or historical analysis can perhaps evade this challenge; but for any attempt to relate Halakha to the modern world it is central.

It is, however, a difficult if not impossible undertaking. The recreation of any aspect of the past is fraught with difficulty. Yet, depending upon the richness of their material and the vividness of their imagination, historians and historical novelists have often executed it with striking

13. See *Kiryat Sefer, Hilkhot Shekhenim,* ch. 9.
14. Cf. *Hagiga* 18a regarding Hol HaMoed; Me'iri, *Eiruvin* 14b, regarding the measure of large objects exempt from ritual impurity; Me'iri, *Bava Metzia* 50a, regarding *onaa;* Me'iri, *Kiddushin* 11b, regarding the amount of a monetary claim necessary to require an oath; Ramban, *Vayikra* 23:24, regarding performing weekday activities on Shabbat.
15. This would necessitate converting *shiurim* cited in *Hazal* into their modern psychological equivalents. An additional challenge is posed by the elusive nature of modern technology (cf. the problem of *koho*).

success. In our case, however, the difficulty is compounded – partly, by the fact that we are dealing with a remote era; and primarily, because we must not merely reproduce a setting but recapture an attitude. Moreover, the attitude in question is not the articulated or even implicit *esprit de l'âge* sought by the historian of ideas. *Harhakat shekhenim* concerns, rather, innumerable minor and almost instinctive reactions, visceral responses to irritations which may seem petty to an outsider but which can break up a marriage or send a roommate crawling up the walls. These are matters of subtle nuances and they relate moreover to a highly volatile context. Not every neighbor reminds us, like Frost's, of "an old-stone savage armed"; but living at close quarters almost inevitably makes tempers taut. The evaluation of stimuli and responses thus becomes extremely difficult even with reference to the contemporary scene. In dealing with the distant past, the difficulty is almost insuperable. Who can span the centuries to gauge the impact of a redolent tannery, the irritation caused by noisy urchins, or the resentment bred by restriction upon the use of a backyard?

Nevertheless, forgoing precision, we can discern the Halakha's emphasis quite clearly. In doubtful situations, it sides with, if I may use some loaded terms, the aggrieved rather than the aggressor, with his sleeping neighbor rather than with the aspiring pianist. Confronted with the prospect of too little or too much restriction, it prefers to risk the latter. Even a cursory glance at some of the major relevant mishnayot reveals this bias.

This emphasis should surprise no one. For one thing, it consorts with the Halakha's reliance upon law and its readiness to regulate conduct. These, in turn, reflect a proclivity to restraint and a pervasive appeal to responsibility. Finally, such an emphasis is rooted in a more general attitude toward the exercise of economic rights, and particularly property rights. Broadly speaking, the Halakha stands with the twentieth against the nineteenth century. It stresses equality no less than liberty. It places human rights ahead of property rights. As it rejects *laissez faire* in the factory and the marketplace, so it dismisses the proposition that every man's home is his castle. In the interests of communal well-being, it has been ready to curb not only eccentricity – which both Matthew Arnold and Henry Adams regarded as the bane of Victorian society – but economic individualism. Zoning ordinances and pollution control come to it quite naturally. Such ordinances need not be sacrosanct. They may be regarded from the perspective of superior needs and values. The noise generated by a school is treated differently from that caused by a commercial enterprise – although the decibel counts may be identical. Generally speaking, however, the Halakha has not hesitated to restrict the use of property in order to protect either the physical or psychological well-being of one's neighbors.

As with the restriction of certain modes of competition, the effect of such halakhic ordinances would no doubt be to dampen somewhat the brashness, the exuberance, perhaps even the vitality of a society. They would serve to curb its expansive drive and dull its incisive thrust. But there are compensatory gains: increased stability, social harmony, and, above all, peace of mind. One senses the Rabbis generally felt these were well worth the price. They would have preferred Vermont to Texas.[16] In effect, the halakhic approach surrenders something of the quantitative aspect of life, particularly within the economic and technological sphere, in an attempt to preserve and enhance its quality. Moreover, this attempt is not merely an exercise in social engineering. It has individual ethical ramifications. Its *modus operandi* entails inculcation of sensitivity to others and not just inhibition of personal mobility. It brakes appetite as it constricts movement.

The sacrifice of vigor to serenity derives from a pre-industrial era. It would be a mistake, however, to regard it as either historically conditional or currently dated. The modern halakhist in quest of tranquility is not indulging in Ruskinian, much less in Gauguinesque, nostalgia; the Halakha is generally too realistic to leave much room for primitivism or Arcadianism. He is simply responding to deeply Jewish values – concern for integral human existence, respect for the reflective as well as the productive process, the quest for permanence and not just the ephemeral, the assertion, if you will, of spirit over matter, of personality over environment; and he is acting upon the Torah's evident conviction – reflected

16. The texture of urban life is captured in poems like Carl Sandburg's "Chicago," Hart Crane's "To Brooklyn Bridge," and Walt Whitman's "Crossing Brooklyn Ferry."

most clearly in the commandment to observe the Sabbath – that possibly preserving life's meaning takes precedence over maintaining its tempo.

Deceleration does not entail rejection of the urban complex. It does, however, include an attempt to control it. The form and context of control may be significantly different for the modern megalopolis than they were for the Babylonian hamlet. However, the overriding aims and the operative principles are the same. They relate to a need – now so clearly felt quite apart from Halakha – for maintaining an atmosphere of calm and quietude, suffused with an awareness of responsibility to other residents and reasonably free from perpetual sensual and psychological assault; and they reflect a readiness to sacrifice some degree of centrifugal drive in order to attain it. If he could dismiss its pantheistic overtones, the halakhist could find his attitude summarized in the concluding stanzas of Arnold's "Lines Written in Kensington Gardens":

> Calm Soul of all things! Make it mine
> To feel, amid the city's jar,
> That there abides a peace of thine,
> Man did not make, and cannot mar.
>
> The will to neither strive nor cry,
> The power to feel with others give!
> Calm, calm me more! nor let me die
> Before I have begun to live.

III. Economic Competition

A. Competition over Unowned Property: Ani Hamehapekh Beharara

We have so far been primarily concerned with constructing a floor – defining the limits below which the self-seeking aggressor may not sink by assaulting the property or person of his neighbor. Before ascending to the higher reaches of the moral scale – altruistic giving of the self to others – we might pause now to consider an intermediate category: self-assertive behavior vis-à-vis, to use Melville's term, "loose fish," free-floating objects or opportunities that are up for grabs. The central issue here is that of economic competition. Devotees of classical – and, to a lesser extent, contemporary – capitalism have regarded it as positively salvific. Typically enough, however, the Rabbis, considering it a mixed blessing, have generally regarded it less benignly. While details of the definitive halakhic position are a matter of dispute, recognition of the need for a measure – by modern standards, a severe measure – of restraint is not. It is noteworthy that the popular and even semi-technical appellation for illegal competition is *hassagat gevul,* a term which in its strict halakhic sense refers to the theft of land via the shifting of boundary lines. Perhaps, in this vein, it might be fairer to say that while the Rabbis accepted, in principle, unimpeded competition for "free" opportunities, their conceptions of what constitutes a loose or a fast fish were drastically different from the prevalent modern view. Their definitions of established preserves are, by present standards, quite broad; and much of what the Halakha has regarded as off-bounds for competing interlopers would, by most current legal and even ethical criteria, be considered perfectly fair game. However, there can be little question as to the demand for restraint, whatever its basis.

The Halakha's reservations are reflected in two related areas – one seemingly trivial, the other patently far-reaching. The first is the halakha – rooted in an incident cited by the Gemara in *Kiddushin* – known as the law of *ani hamehapekh baharara,* "the poor man turning over a cookie."[17] The Gemara relates that

> R. Giddal was negotiating for a certain [piece of] land. R. Abba went and bought it, [whereupon] R. Giddal went and complained about him to R. Zera who, [in turn,] went and complained to R. Yitzhak Nappaha. "Wait until he comes up to us for the festival," he said to him. When he came up, he [i.e., R. Yitzhak] met him [i.e., R. Abba]. "If a poor man is prospecting[18] for a cookie," he asked him, "and another comes and takes it away from him – what then?" "He is called a *rasha,* a scoundrel," he replied. "Then why

17. Ed. Note: "Cookie" here means a loaf.
18. Lit. turning over.

> did you, Master, act thus?" "I did not know [i.e., that R. Giddal had been negotiating for it]," he rejoined.[19]

As is obvious from the context, the cookie is purely symbolic and the halakha has wide-ranging applications. Both its scope and its basis require elucidation, however. The definition of "prospecting" or "turning" – the degree of initial effort necessary to establish a prior claim – poses one difficulty. *Rishonim*[20] specifically raised it with reference to a mishna in *Pe'ah*: "If [a poor man] took some of the *pe'ah*[21] and threw [something] over the rest, he has none of it.[22] If he fell upon it or spread his cloak over it, [others] dispossess him from it."[23] The subject of the last phrase is ambiguous. The Rambam[24] took it as referring to a halakhic authority – presumably a *beit din* – which, by way of penalizing the finder for excessive greed, confiscates even that to which he had already legally taken proper title.[25] On this view, the mishna has no bearing upon our present problem.[26] Most *Rishonim*, however, assumed that the phrase refers to other paupers who may take what the first does not yet own because his attempted acquisition was invalid. However, inasmuch as the mishna appears to have no qualms about either the legitimacy or the propriety of the second pauper's action, they were confronted by an obvious question. While the first claimant has not acquired absolute title, he has certainly been "poking around" the produce. How then do we permit a second to take it without chastising him as a scoundrel?[27]

---

19. *Kiddushin* 59a.
20. *Bava Metzia* 10a.
21. *Pe'ah* is the uncut produce left in the corner of a field for the poor – ed.
22. According to the Rambam, this means that he cannot take even that which he has already collected; according to the Rash of Sens, it means that he cannot take the rest.
23. *Pe'ah* 4:3.
24. *Hilkhot Mattenot Aniyyim* 2:18; cf. *Melekhet Shlomo, Pe'ah* 4:3.
25. Thus, it is not that others have permission to "dispossess him from it"; rather, the court is mandated to dispossess him from it.
26. In any case this mishna does not pose a problem for the Rambam, for he does not codify the case of *ani hamehapekh baharara*.
27. The *Rishonim* likewise raise this question in connection with the mishna on *Bava Metzia* 10a.

Several answers were suggested, all of them circumscribing the scope of the law of *ani hamehapekh*. One was that it applied only when "he [i.e., the first claimant] had exerted himself and invested effort as this poor man who pressed a householder who [then] promised him a cookie from his dough."[28] A second was that when two people "are walking together, [just] because one has preceded and seized we do not regard him as a *mehapekh baharara*."[29] While this view, unlike the first, does not appear to assume a high degree of effort and involvement, it does contend that the first claimant's moral and legal rights are rooted in his having taken independent initiative. They are groundless when he has undertaken no quest for an object but fortuitously stumbles upon it while walking with another and barely beats him to it. The Ramban went a step further, arguing that the halakha did not apply here "because all are prospecting for [available] frontiers (*peot*) like himself and he is not alone in searching for it."[30] Active independent initiative is not sufficient. It must be exclusive initiative, as it is the head start in terms of effort which is crucial.

The ambiguities latent in these distinctions and the difficulty in applying them need hardly be belabored. There is no absolute yardstick for measuring significant as opposed to casual effort or for determining, in all cases, the point of its inception. The principle remains intact, however – no one may snatch prospective gain from someone else who has established prior involvement – and its application would presumably require some relative, and perhaps even contextual, judgments.

Rabbenu Tam offered a very different qualification – comparatively both clear and radical. He limited the prohibition of snatching from the prospector to situations in which the second claimant can, after forgoing the opportunity, find its reasonable equivalent elsewhere. It would thus apply to most purchases – the context of its initial formulation in *Kiddushin* was that of a land sale – but not, as in the mishna

28. *Shitta Mekubbetzet, Bava Metzia* 10a, s.v. *vekatuv beTosafot Hitzoniyyot.*

29. Ibid., in the name of Rabbenu Meir ben Avigdor.

30. *Bava Batra* 54b, s.v. *nikhsei haKuti.*

in *Pe'ah*, to acquisition of trover[31] or common goods for which no comparable alternative was readily available. This distinction is itself open to several formulations, the primary crux being the definition of a satisfactory alternative. One version might view the general nature of the acquisition – whether an exchange or getting something for nothing – as decisive. Thus, the Ramban states that, according to Rabbenu Tam, the prohibition of snatching applies to a sale "even if he [i.e., the first party] was purchasing at a discount, for as long as it is a sale, there is no room for distinguishing."[32] On this view, it is conceivable that even if no alternative customer or employer is in prospect at all, that the halakha may still apply. This possibility is clearly rejected by the *Or Zarua*,[33] who presents Rabbenu Tam's position as being "that wherever he can find employment elsewhere we restrain him [i.e., from taking a job for which someone else has been negotiating] and he is called a scoundrel." Moreover, R. Yosef Colon challenges even the Ramban's more limited point, contending that the degree of loss should be irrelevant, and that a price discount was, in effect, a partial gift.[34] This version would clearly call for a less formal and more pragmatic conception of Rabbenu Tam's position; and it would consequently require at least some tentative formulation of what the pragmatic criteria might be. A number of responsa grapple with this issue, their points of departure usually being: 1) the *Mordekhai*'s statement that the need for a specific location obviates the halakha;[35] and 2) R. Yosef Colon's above-mentioned qualification that price differentials or similar factors render a sale like a gift only when they are so unusual or substantial that they could be neither duplicated nor approximated even by dint of significant effort. If, however, it is merely a question of saving the time, energy, or aggravation of shopping around, preempting a purchase from a prior party is strictly forbidden. Clearly, however, absolute guidelines are not feasible and the question remains, in a very real sense, perpetually open.

---

31. Ed. note: In this essay, "trover" refers to found or unowned items, or to the acquisition of them.
32. Ramban, *Bava Batra* 54b.
33. Vol. 3, *Piskei Bava Metzia*, #27. Compare *Tosafot*, *Kiddushin* 59a, s.v. *ani*.
34. *Responsa Maharik*, #132.
35. *Mordekhai*, *Bava Batra*, #551.

Whatever its details, the overall implications of Rabbenu Tam's position are clear. By restricting the halakha of *ani hamehapekh* to cases in which its adherent generally suffers little loss, he emasculates much of its legal force and ethical content. What, on Rashi's view, constitutes a fairly drastic curb upon self-assertion is, for Rabbenu Tam, a rather mild demand for a relatively minor sacrifice. The radical nature of his position also requires, however, a reexamination of the basis of the halakha. *A priori*, several possibilities are open. Perhaps the simplest is that seizure of an object with which someone else is already involved constitutes a form of robbery (*gezel*). Although the first claimant has made no valid acquisitive act, the Rabbis have decreed that the object be deemed his[36] – at least for the purpose of proscribing someone else's appropriation. For other purposes, the object may still be regarded as unclaimed. I consider it certain, for instance, that if the first person should lose interest and go his way, no formal divestiture would be required to sever his "ownership." It also appears likely that he could not sell the object. Nevertheless, as regards the preemption of others' possession, it is considered owned.

On this view, the halakha of *ani hamehapekh* has not, legally speaking, dealt with self-assertion vis-à-vis "free" property. It has rather relaxed its standard of acquisition and thus enclosed much which, by ordinarily more rigorous halakhic criteria, would still be considered ownerless. Conceptually, it proscribes poaching upon present preserves rather than encroaching upon future prospects. Such an interpretation would be particularly consonant with the view that the violator does not merely suffer obloquy but must compensate his victim.[37] It is difficult, however, to reconcile this view with Rabbenu Tam's distinction. If involvement confers ownership, it presumably does so regardless of the cost to future competitors. This argument is admittedly not ironclad. It is conceivable that the halakha was initially formulated only with reference to a given area and is virtually nonexistent with respect to another. Where it applies, however, it actually confers ownership. This was evidently the position of R. Yosef Colon, who accepted Rabbenu Tam's distinction and yet held

36. On the question of whether this halakha is of biblical or rabbinic authority, see *Pithei Teshuva*, HM 237:2, and *Sedei Hemed* (*Klalim, Maarekhet Reish, klal* 47).

37. Cited in the Ramban (*Bava Batra*, op. cit.) in the name of Rabbenu Tam.

that the first claimant could actually sell his acquisition – "The Rabbis have made it as if he had acquired it with this prospecting, [and] since the basis is acquisition, he can also sell it."[38] Nevertheless, it seems likelier that the scope of the halakha should indicate its basis. Rabbenu Tam's distinction leads us, then, to seek an alternate interpretation.

As such an alternative, we may consider the possibility that, even at the *derabbanan* level, seizure of the object is not a form of robbery; that, moreover, it cannot be subsumed under any rigorously defined halakhic category. Its prohibition is rather rooted in the general concept of "And thou shalt do the right and the good"[39] – the obligation to act justly and humanely *lifnim mishurat hadin*, regardless of whether or not the strict letter of the law imposes a particular demand. It is thus more a point of equity than of law. To be sure, equity is itself part of the total halakhic demand and by no means a purely voluntary matter. In light of its more flexible character, however, it is more amenable to qualification and *ad hoc* modification than formal *din*, narrowly defined. A distinction such as Rabbenu Tam's poses no difficulty whatsoever.

At least two *Rishonim* did evidently see Rabbenu Tam's position in this light. The *Mordekhai* writes that the halakha applies "only when he has purchased something at its normal price, as this is somewhat similar to the law regarding the borderer, based on 'And thou shalt do the right and the good,' as he [i.e., the second party] will be able to purchase elsewhere. However, with regard to a common object (*hefker*) or if he [i.e., the first party] is pressing [its owner] to give it to him for nothing and someone else comes and acquires it, he is not called a scoundrel, as it is stated, 'The law of the borderer does not apply to gifts.'"[40] The Ran, similarly, cites as support for Rabbenu Tam the fact that a borderer has no option with respect to gifts – "Since we see that in such a case 'And thou shalt do the right and the good' does not apply."[41] Somewhat paradoxically, then, Rabbenu Tam, who drastically restricted the halakha of *ani hamehapekh*, regarded it as a matter of equity; while other *Rishonim*,

38. *Responsa Maharik*, op. cit.

39. *Devarim* 6:18.

40. *Mordekhai, Kiddushin*, 524, citing *Bava Metzia* 108b.

41. Ran on the Rif, *Kiddushin* ch. 3, 24a in Alfasi.

who gave it greater latitude, may – we have no conclusive evidence one way or the other – very well have subsumed it under a rigorous category of law. We should not be fazed by the fact that Rabbenu Tam is reported to have subscribed to the view that the interloper must compensate the prospector. Since equity is hardly a neutral matter, obligations grounded in it may assume aspects of law proper; and the Halakha has recognized the use of sanctions to enforce it. In our case, payment may be considered as punitive damages rather than restitution. The requirement for compensation and the assumption that no robbery has been committed need not therefore be regarded as contradictory.

We might consider yet a third possibility. A number of authorities have noted the fact that the Gemara singled out a poor person as the victim; and they suggested that perhaps it applied only in such a situation. Such a restriction could be applied, however, to one of two cases: exchange or trover. If it is confined to the former, we may ascribe it simply to the fact that a pauper suffers if deprived of a purchase or sale – it is part of the tragedy of poverty that even money doesn't go quite so far – but others are just slightly inconvenienced. As the Ran noted, "The rich person either has bread available at home or can get it from his neighbors."[42] This distinction would shed no light, then, on the basis of the halakha.[43] It's just that the effect – and therefore the venality – of the seizure varies with its victim. Indeed, if the rich should also be significantly deprived – as with the sale of land, for which an equivalent is not always available – the Ran states the prohibition would cover him as well.

This explanation would be fatuous, however, if the victim's identity were relevant to trover as well. In this case, rich or poor are both clearly victimized. Any distinction must therefore derive from a wholly different conception of the nature of this halakha – namely, the assumption that it is grounded upon neither the injunction against robbery nor the demand for equity but upon the obligation to charity and *hesed*. This position should not be confused with Rabbenu Tam's. If the analogy with the borderer's law is any indication, equity, in this case, while

42. Ran, ibid.

43. It does, however, cohere better with Rabbenu Tam's view than with the opposing view.

combining juridical and ethical elements, nevertheless operates within a restricted framework. Within a context of conflict, it is more a call to fairness than to kindness. As such, it fuses negative and positive elements. Its appeal for "the right and the good" focuses upon the former as upon the latter, and its demand for right is itself as much for restraint from injustice as for active justice. It is precisely for this reason that failure to heed the appeal may require compensation. Charity is thoroughly positive, however. While its performance is obligatory – and may at times be exacted – falling short of its demands constitutes failure rather than violation. It is grounded upon others' needs rather than, narrowly speaking, their rights. I am asked to give my fellow of mine rather than merely let him retain his. Within this context, distinction between rich and poor becomes thoroughly tenable.

On this view, the predatory "other," while inviting censure, would presumably incur no obligation to effect reparation. It is conceivable, as suggested in a sixteenth-century *teshuva*, that *beit din* may, *ante facto*, restrain the predator from seizing the object.[44] It is not prone to taking villainy lightly. But charity would probably provide insufficient grounds for reversing a *fait accompli*. It should be kept in mind, however, that, as regards *ani hamehapekh*, the principles of charity and equity are not mutually exclusive bases. The former has wider scope, the latter stronger sanctions, so that the halakha may differ in character in different areas. Thus, in cases of exchange – to which both principles are relevant – it would apply regardless of whether the initial claimant were rich or poor and it might entail restitution. In cases of trover – in which the sacrifice involved may be too great to be exacted by equity – it may be confined to the poor and would require no financial reparation.

Both principles, however, clearly distinguish this halakha from an analogue often discussed in connection with it. The latter is cited in a mishna in *Gittin* as one of a number of ordinances instituted by the Rabbis "in the interests of peace": "If a poor man is gleaning at the top of an olive tree, [taking] that which [falls] beneath him is, in the interests of peace, [reckoned] as robbery. R. Yose says: It constitutes actual

44. *Responsa* Maharshal, #36.

robbery."[45] Various suggestions have been advanced to differentiate between the respective cases. The Rashba emphasized the fact that, in the latter, the poor man "had worked and expended effort upon them to knock them down and to glean them" – more so, that is, than the *ani hamehapekh*;[46] the Rosh accepted this point, evidently not so much as a self-sufficient distinction in its own right but because the greater exertion had produced greater anticipation;[47] the Ritva likewise cited both factors but added that the gleaner had labored in the normal and presumably maximal manner.[48] Whatever the technical difference between the factual situations, the conceptual distinction between the applicable laws should be clear. With respect to the mishna in *Gittin*, whatever may have been the Rabbis' motivation in legislating the ordinance, its substance is pure property law rather than charity or equity. There is, of course, an important disagreement here between R. Yose and his anonymous disputant, "the Rabbis." R. Yose regards the fruit as fully owned by the gleaner; the Rabbis only treat it *as if* it were his property for the purpose of proscribing its seizure. As the Gemara explains, the difference is that, on their view, if the injunction is violated and the object seized, the victim cannot recover it by legal recourse.[49] However, even the Rabbis employ, albeit only with respect to *ante facto* prohibition, rigorous categories of property and theft rather than the moral imperatives of equity or charity which govern the halakha of *ani hamehapekh*.

B. Creating a Commercial Rivalry: Yored Leumnut Havero

The problem of self-interest vis-à-vis common opportunities bears one aspect with regard to *ani hamehapekh*. It assumes quite another with respect to economic competition generally – the creation of a commercial or professional establishment to rival an entrenched predecessor. Needless to say, the stakes are here generally much higher. On the one hand, intrusion may not merely preempt an acquisition or prevent a

45. *Gittin* 59b.
46. *Kiddushin* 59a.
47. *Kiddushin* 3:2.
48. *Kiddushin* 59a.
49. *Kiddushin* 61a.

deal but destroy a livelihood. Yet on the other hand, restraint may entail comparable self-deprivation.

The nature and degree of priority presents a further difference. In one case, the first claimant has drawn a bead on a fairly definite target: a specific object or contract lies within his grasp. In the other, however, he has a generally more tenuous hold upon a broader and less clearly defined area. What he claims is not so much an object or an opportunity as a group – prospective patients, clients, or customers of a given community. This is a rather large claim – and one which no member of a Western-style capitalist society is likely to countenance. Despite some ambivalence, he may react against snatching a deal from an agent who has laid the groundwork for it or filing a patent based on a competitor's work. Anything which smacks of monopoly is pure anathema, however; and any claim staked on its basis is wholly out of court.

For the Halakha, however, such claims at least pose a problem – although the extent to which they may be recognized is a matter of dispute. The *locus classicus* of their discussion is a passage in the second chapter of *Bava Batra*:[50]

> R. Huna said: If a resident of an alley sets up a handmill and another resident of the alley wants to set up one next to him, the first has the right to stop him, because he can say to him, "You are interfering with my livelihood."... On this point there is a difference of opinion among *Tanna'im*, as appears from the following *baraita*: "The residents of an alley can prevent one another from bringing in a tailor or a tanner or a teacher or any other craftsman, but one cannot prevent another [from setting up in opposition]." Rabban Shimon b. Gamliel, however, says that one may prevent another.
>
> R. Huna b. R. Yehoshua said: It is quite clear to me that the resident of one town can prevent the resident of another town [from setting up in opposition in his town], but not, however, if he pays taxes to that town – and that the resident of an alley cannot prevent another resident of the same alley [from setting up

50. 21b.

in opposition in his alley]. R. Huna b. R. Yehoshua then raised the question: Can the resident of one alley prevent the resident of another [from competing with him]? – This must stand over.[51]

IV. Positive Ethical Conduct: Giving of Oneself to Another

A. The Limits of Self-Sacrifice: Hayekha Kodmin

The laws regarding *ani hamehapekh* and economic competition straddle somewhat the two main provinces of our inquiry – the negatively oriented restraint of self-interest and the positively motivated pursuit of altruism. We have now to consider the second area proper – what actions the Halakha has specifically demanded and which direction it has generally encouraged at the level of positive ethical conduct. At this point, an apologist – especially one using professed Christian ethics as a subconscious standard of comparison – might be tempted to try to present the positive aspect of halakhic morality as a paradigm of idealism. Given such a heavy accent upon responsibility in the lower and middle reaches of the moral scale, would it not seem likely that, in its upper regions, we should be summoned to saintly self-sacrifice?

Yet – and this is by no means atypical – any such expectation is not truly satisfied by the Halakha. On the contrary, even by some popular standards – at least by those that were popular until recently – many of its demands are quite moderate; and it certainly does not recommend pure altruism. It recognizes, in fact – to a point, as a matter of principle – an element of selfishness. This element is certainly not the whole story. It is, however, one pole; and any exposition of the upper range of halakhic ethics must take into account the philosophic and practical limits imposed by it. For us, it may serve as a point of departure as well.

Within a context of total confrontation, this element found expression in the course of a celebrated controversy between R. Akiva and Ben Petura:

51. Ed. note: The rest of the discussion on competition is absent from the manuscript.

> If two [people] are traveling on the road and one of them has a pitcher of water in hand; if both drink, they will die, and if one of them drinks, he will reach civilization – Ben Petura taught, "Better that both should drink and die, rather than that one should witness the death of his fellow." Until R. Akiva came [along] and taught, "'And thy brother shall live with thee' – your life takes precedence over that of your fellow."[52]

The awesome rigor of Ben Petura's position evidently derives from the conviction that I may not save my own life at the expense of another's.[53] On this view, possession of the water becomes irrelevant. After all, were my own life not in danger, denying the water to my starving fellow would constitute murder;[54] and while my own danger precludes the crime in our case,[55] nevertheless this view asserts that I have no right to save my skin at the cost of someone else's. Reciprocally applied, this principle leads to a paradoxical result – "Better that both should drink and die rather than that one should witness the death of his fellow." From a pragmatic point of view, such a solution is no doubt thoroughly ridiculous. From an ethical perspective, however, even opponents may regard it as a heroic albeit futile sacrifice – none the less heroic for being so terribly tragic.

Of two alternatives to such noble futility, R. Akiva opted for the less heroic – that is, keeping the water rather than relinquishing it entirely to one's fellow. On this view, possession of the water becomes crucial. This is not because the need for survival cannot justify theft.[56] Of course it does; and, in any event, here it is physical control which is relevant and not legal ownership. It is rather because, under these circumstances, possession defines a status quo in which one individual has

---

52. *Bava Metzia* 62a, citing *Vayikra* 25:36. Compare *Torat Kohanim, Behar,* 5.
53. See *Hiddushei Rabbenu Hayim Halevi, Hilkhot Yesodei HaTorah* 5:1; of course, this is not so in the case of a pursuer (*rodef*).
54. *Sanhedrin* 77a and Rambam, *Hilkhot Rotze'ah* 3:10; even though such a person is not put to death by a court, he is subject to execution by heaven.
55. According to R. Hayyim Brisker's understanding, even according to Ben Petura the denial of water would not constitute murder.
56. *Bava Kamma* 60b.

the wherewithal for life and the other does not. Accidental though it may be, the "have-not" is halakhically enjoined from changing the situation – seizure of the water would very likely constitute murder[57] – and the "have" fully justified in maintaining it.

R. Akiva's dictum – subsequently adopted as definitive Halakha – no doubt simply endorses a course human nature would ordinarily dictate in any event. Yet it would be a mistake to regard it as a mere concession to frailty. The Rabbis acknowledged that the Torah occasionally made such concessions, but I doubt that our case is among them. For one thing, moral realism – awareness of what can normally be required of the ordinary person – is not to be confused with pure pragmatism. Refraining from demanding the almost superhuman is very different from tolerating the essentially subhuman. Moreover, the positive, almost emphatic, tone of R. Akiva's statement clearly suggests that he is formulating a principle rather than capitulating to necessity. The point is quite simply that he saw no reason why one *should* sacrifice his life to save another's. The same halakhic reasoning which required the Jew to accept martyrdom rather than commit murder – because "why do you suppose your blood is redder, perhaps your fellow's blood is redder"[58] – must, if reversed, obviate any imperative to seek martyrdom in order to save someone else.

Indeed, some have even questioned whether one *may* make such a sacrifice. The question may leave us almost incredulous. As regards motivation, after all, the gap between saving myself or my fellow is immense. The modern reader, his ethical sensibility nurtured by Kantian subjectivism, finds it well-nigh impossible to equate the supreme idealism of self-sacrifice with instinctive opting for self-preservation; and, with respect to *post facto* judgment of the moral character of the respective agents, any such equation is thoroughly ridiculous. The normative problem of

57. *Shitta Mekubbetzet, Bava Metzia* 62a, s.v. *shnayim*. I do not enter into the distinction between murder and manslaughter.

58. *Sanhedrin* 74b. *Hiddushei Rabbenu Hayim Halevi, Hilkhot Yesodei HaTorah* 5:1, offers two ways to understand this dictum: since the two lives at stake are equivalent, no action should be taken; or since the two lives are equivalent, the factor of *pikuah nefesh* does not overcome the countervailing prohibition (in this case, murder), whether the prohibition is violated via action or inaction.

ante facto decision – with reference to a moment at which both lives are yet suspended over the razor's edge – may be viewed from a much more objective perspective, however. Inasmuch as life is a divine endowment but not a personal possession, an individual has no autonomous authority to abandon it – even in a noble cause. Taken with utter seriousness, Plato's image of the soldier at his post suggests that, as regards existence itself, I am no more master of myself than of my neighbor.[59] The Rambam classified suicide under murder.[60] The possibility that its possessor not only may but should drink the water should therefore not be ruled out entirely. Jewish tradition knows no Alcestis.[61]

Even if this view be rejected, however, there is no reason for going to the other extreme and regarding R. Akiva's principle as a mere concession. Whatever we may assume about other crises, when life itself is at stake the primacy of self-interest is thoroughly legitimate. It should be emphasized, moreover, that from R. Akiva's perspective, reliance upon his principle is no compromise with necessity. Under the gun, self-interest is wholly untainted. Transcending the need for personal survival reflects superb heroism; but adherence to "your life takes precedence" entails no tinge of guilt.[62]

In a considerably milder form, the primacy of self governs another situation – response to attack. In one sense, any moral dilemma here is far weaker than R. Akiva's, inasmuch as the conflict pits right against wrong rather than involving two competing rights. On the other hand, it goes beyond it, inasmuch as the issue involves active violence against another person rather than simply ignoring his needs. The principle that "your life takes precedence" – in this case, no doubt accepted by Ben Petura as well – prevails, however. The Halakha has had no qualms whatsoever about violent, even deadly, self-defense. Never an adherent of root-and-branch pacifism, it has sanctioned full resistance to attack upon property and person.

---

59. *Phaedo* 61b–62c.
60. *Hilkhot Rotze'ah* 2:2.
61. Cf. Arthur Miller, *Incident at Vichy*.
62. That is, it may give no twinge of conscience but that felt by mere survival; even in the absence of moral guilt, one might still feel survivor's guilt.

To be sure, this sanction is limited. The reaction must be commensurate with the danger. If one's life is endangered – and if one can save it in no other way – one may kill an attacker. Furthermore, if property is being seized, its owner may resist the thief although the latter may then, in turn, be provoked to attempt murder and thus give the intended victim license to kill him. But only the specter of death justifies resort to the ultimate.[63] The protection of property provides no such pretext. "Shooting the looters" – so long as they are purely looters – is simple murder.

Whatever the limits of self-defense, however, it is essential that the nature of both the principle and its moral climate be properly understood. The Halakha knows no resistance to self-defense and no reluctance in applying it. There are no lingering reservations about it. I recall no glorification of anyone who shunned the principle, and would be surprised to encounter it; but, in any event, no shadow at all is cast over whoever resorts to it. The attitude satirized in Voltaire's epigram – "*Cet animal est très méchant; quand on l'attaque, il se défend*" (This animal is very vicious; when one attacks it, it defends itself) – is wholly alien to Halakha.

In confrontations of priority, then – those which impinge upon others through the preemption of a potentially common opportunity rather than through direct impact – the Halakha has permitted the priority of self-interest. This concept's boldest – and, inevitably, most tragic – application is R. Akiva's; but it does not stand alone. The principle has been used, for instance, to explain Rabbenu Tam's view[64] that *ani hamehapekh* does not apply to free acquisition. More significantly, we encounter it in a second gemara dealing with a situation virtually identical with R. Akiva's – except that it concerns property rather than person. With reference to the recovery of lost objects, the Mishna states that if one is confronted by "his own lost article and that of his father" – and, *a fortiori*, that of a stranger – "his own takes precedence." "Whence do we derive this?" the gemara asks. "R. Yehuda said in the name of Rav:

63. *Sanhedrin* 72a; Raavad, *Hilkhot Geneva* 9:8; regarding a case of doubt, see Rashi and other commentators on *Pesahim* 2b. While the general halakhic principles are clear, problems, of course, attend their detailed application.

64. Ramban, *Bava Batra* 54b.

The verse says, 'Save that there shall be no pauper among you'[65] – yours takes precedence over every other person's."[66] The verse is here taken not only in a predictive sense, as a promise, but in a normative sense as well, entailing a right and, to a point, a duty. In this vein, it issues in a variant of R. Akiva's principle – *hayekha kodmin*, "your life takes precedence."

When the choice is, then, of a specific either/or character, the license of *hayekha kodmin* applies to the preservation of property as well as person. Overall, however, once the issue is no longer preservation of person, the scope of self-interest is reduced markedly. For the Halakha does, of course, have a major altruistic thrust. It has prescribed numerous actions and directions for action – mandating some and prescribing others – geared to aiding others, thus diverting resources, energies, and, above all, commitment, from the pursuit of selfish concerns.

Thus, while *hayekha kodmin* relates, as noted, to the preservation of either property or person, its respective applications differ significantly. One difference concerns scope. As regards life, the principle – provided, of course, that the question is one of priority rather than aggression – is essentially unqualified. With respect to property, however, another factor obtrudes itself. In R. Akiva's case, the competing interests may be regarded as equal. While in actuarial terms stakes differ even here – a youngster has more to lose than his elders – there is nevertheless clearly a sense in which life, whatever its expectancy, cannot be quantified.[67] As regards the clash of other interests, however, comparison seems both possible and advisable. Common charity, if not common sense, would suggest that, when my own interest is minuscule and my neighbor's substantial, I should attend to his even to the detriment of mine. The possibility of recognizing this criterion was discussed by the Rabbis – but with reference to communities rather than individuals. In that context, it forms the subject of a controversy – cited in several parallel and slightly variant texts – between R. Yose and an anonymous opponent:

65. *Devarim* 15:4.
66. *Bava Metzia* 33a.
67. Even if life could be quantified, perhaps existence itself is too much to demand normatively for others.

> The townspeople's well – [if it is a question of] their lives and the lives of others, their lives take precedence over the lives of others; their livestock and others', theirs take precedence over others'; their laundering and others', theirs take precedence over others'. [If the question is one of] their laundering and the lives of others, others' lives take precedence over their laundering. R. Yose says: Their laundering takes precedence over the others' lives.[68]

None of the primary sources resolves the issue nor, to my knowledge, do any early *posekim* even cite the controversy. To the trained ear, however, the flow of the Gemara's discussion in *Nedarim* does seem to suggest that R. Yose's was regarded as a minority, perhaps even a singular position, in which case it would ordinarily be rejected. If this be true, the distinction I had suggested earlier would naturally be buttressed. Even if his view should prevail, however, it might be contended that it specifically applies to the situation under discussion, i.e., communities in conflict, but has no bearing upon individuals confronted by the identical dilemma. Public policy lies somewhere between selfish and altruistic activity. Decisions concerning it have greater moral justification for self-interest than do equivalent private choices. With respect to the latter, therefore, it is not inconceivable that even R. Yose might acknowledge the relevance of comparative loss.

Whatever R. Yose's own position, acceptance of the comparative factor as a relevant element appears to be clearly implied in another text dealing with the return of lost objects.[69] Among those exempt from this duty, the Gemara lists a person "whose task" – and therefore the loss to be sustained by its neglect – "is more valuable than [the lost item] of his fellow." The implication seems plain: if the reverse is true, the obligation obtains.[70] More explicit note of this factor was taken by the Rambam

68. *Nedarim* 80b; compare the Tosefta at the end of *Bava Metzia* (11:33–37). Clearly, the invocation of "their lives" in this passage refers not to actual life, but rather to convenience, as noted in *Iggerot Moshe*, YD 1, #145. Compare the use of the term "life" in *Bava Batra* 90b ("*hayei nefesh*") and elsewhere.

69. *Bava Metzia* 30a.

70. However, see Ramban and Ritva, *Bava Metzia* 30b, and *Shitta Mekubbetzet, Bava Metzia* 31b. Rambam does not mention this in his *Mishneh Torah*.

in his *Perush HaMishnayot*. Commenting upon the Mishna's statement that one's *aveda* takes precedence over others', he explains:

> The basis in the Torah[71] [for the fact] that a person may give himself precedence over his fellow is the Merciful One's statement, "Save that there shall be no pauper among you." [This is] as if it had said, "You are obligated to remove an ill from another only when an ill *like that which you removed from him* will not befall you [as a result]. For if the case should be that, if you should give a pauper 'sufficient unto his need,' you will become poor *like him*, you are not obligated to give to him."[72] And this is what [our Rabbis] o.b.m. [meant when they] said, "Yours takes precedence over every other person's."[73]

Especially in view of the source cited – the mitzva of charity – one may venture a step further. Any comparison of respective stakes should be relative rather than absolute. Evaluation should not stop with monetary appraisal but should attempt to gauge the relative importance of an object in the lives of both parties. Judgment itself may very well be objective. It need not be left to the individuals involved. The criteria to be employed, however, should include a subjective factor. In the case of charity, one is exempt only from total reversal of economic roles – not, obviously, from all sacrifice. Analogously, *hayekha kodmin* should only be invoked with an eye to the comparative costs – not only economic but human.

The varied scope of self-interest vis-à-vis property and person is, to a point, technical – grounded, to be sure, upon moral considerations, but nevertheless largely an adjustment governing the legal limits of the concept in one area. There are, however, more basic differences pertaining to the Halakha's attitude toward the principle proper. Inasmuch as

71. The Hebrew translation of the Rambam's commentary (originally written in Arabic) has here "*veharemez*," but this means more than hint; see Ramban's commentary to Rambam's *Sefer HaMitzvot*, *shoresh* 3.
72. In other words, he is not obligated to provide the pauper "sufficient to his need"; but he is not completely exempt from helping the pauper financially, since even a poor person is obligated to give *tzedaka*.
73. Rambam, *Perush HaMishnayot*, *Bava Metzia* 2:11. My italics.

R. Akiva's case concerns an ultimate moment of truth, it is not readily analogous to milder dilemmas.[74] Obviously, for instance, with anything but actual survival at stake, any question as to whether I *may* give my neighbor priority is wholly out of court. The only issue is whether and to what extent I must. *Hayekha kodmin* may here be an option but surely no obligation.

B. From the Permissible to the Ideal

Beyond this, however, even the right of *hayekha kodmin* is variously regarded, depending upon the sphere of its invocation. Whereas its application to survival is wholly unquestioned, we encounter ambivalence about its relevance to economic issues. Thus, after resorting to *hayekha kodmin* to explain the Mishna's statement that my own trover takes precedence over others', the Gemara continues: "R. Yehuda said in the name of Rav: Whoever observes thus [i.e., always invokes the priority of self-interest] with respect to himself, will eventually end up thus [i.e., in poverty]."[75] The statement is no mere imprecation. It has a normative thrust as well. As Rashi explained:[76] "Although the [Torah's] text has not imposed this upon him, a person should go beyond the line of the law and should not insist (*ledakdek*), 'Mine comes first,' unless there is demonstrable loss. If he always insists [upon his rights], he divests himself of the obligations of *gemilut hasadim* (the bestowal of kindness) and charity. Finally, he will [himself] require public assistance." At the level of *lifnim mishurat hadin* ("beyond the line of the law") – itself a halakhic category and, in its own way, often fully normative – equity demands a more altruistic approach. While a finder enjoys the legal prerogative of giving his own loss priority, he does not always have the moral right to invoke it. He must make a contextual ethical judgment regarding the respective stakes and, evidently – unless his own stake is significantly

74. Perhaps that is why the gemara in *Bava Metzia* 33a, which concerns returning lost property, did not quote the verse, "And thy brother shall live with thee," but rather the verse, "Save that there shall be no pauper among you," in deriving that "yours takes precedence over every other person's."
75. *Bava Metzia* 33a.
76. Ad loc., s.v. *kol hamekayem*.

greater – he must generally protect his neighbor's.[77] And this, too, is an aspect of normative Halakha.[78]

This is by no means radical altruism. One is not *always* enjoined to give others priority. It clearly indicates, however, that with respect to economic issues, the Halakha – beyond its minimal narrowly legal level – has not always accepted the priority of self-interest, after all. Nor is this a solitary example. For instance, *Tosafot* suggest that, *lifnim mishurat hadin,* the law concerning *ani hamehapekh* would apply to free acquisition even according to Rabbenu Tam.[79] Or again, the Ramban – followed by many other *Rishonim* – advanced a similar position with respect to *harhakat shekhenim*. While he accepts R. Yose's view that only the actions definable as the user's "own arrows" – i.e., direct aggressive impact – are absolutely forbidden, he contends this applies only to a binding legal prohibition. As regards *lifnim mishurat hadin,* the Rabbis' opposing view – that even many indirect effects constitute a violation – is certainly correct.[80] Such examples no doubt raise fundamental questions about the relation between law and ethics and the existence of contrasting positions within Halakha – questions whose proper analysis lies beyond the scope of this essay. Be this as it may, however, they indicate how differently *hayekha kodmin* might be regarded with respect to conflicts concerning property rather than life.

These instances are clearly pregnant with normative content. They exemplify a level of *lifnim mishurat hadin* which differs from *din* proper in the nature and degree of its imperative, but which nevertheless clearly conveys a demand. They speak in terms of duty; and whoever violates the prescribed counsel, while not guilty of an infraction in the narrowest sense of the word, nevertheless would clearly be considered derelict. Recall Rashi's formulation: *Yesh le'adam likanes lifnim mishurat hadin,*

---

77. From Rashi's wording one may perhaps conclude that the issue is that one should not *regularly* insist upon giving his own interest precedence. It is also possible to understand that the problem with this attitude arises when one gives his own interest precedence even where his neighbor's stake is greater. See the Gra, HM 264:2. But this is not the plain sense of the Gemara.
78. See the essay later in this volume on *lifnim mishurat hadin.*
79. Tosafot, *Bava Batra* 21b, s.v. *marhikin.*
80. Ramban, *Bava Batra* 22b, s.v. *leima.*

"A person *should* go beyond the line of the law" – hence, if he does not, the prediction of dire foreboding. However, *lifnim mishurat hadin* is operative at many levels. It does not constitute a plane but a continuum. Its range runs the gamut from a solid morality to exalted sainthood. As we move toward its upper reaches, its "ought" subtly shifts from obligation to ideal. At this level, we speak more in terms of ultimate direction than of immediate demand. It serves as a polestar toward which the Jew should strive but which he is not ordinarily required or expected to attain. Here, achievement is glorious but failure merits no condemnation.

Analysis of the problem of self-interest requires its examination at this level as well. By the very nature of the question, one must at this point deal with a broader range of material. A number of specific laws remain central, but for primary guidance we must look to overarching philosophic or aggadic statements expressing attitudes or values which inform Torah-halakhic Judaism as a whole. Nevertheless, I trust that their relation to Halakha proper will be manifest.

As we move from the permissible through the imperative and the desirable and on toward the ideal, we find, not surprisingly, that the altruistic element looms increasingly larger. The Mishna lists *gemilut hasadim* among those commandments for whose performance no fixed quantity has been designated[81] – meaning, as the Yerushalmi noted, that they have neither minimal nor maximal levels.[82] Anyone content with the bare discharge of duty can salve his conscience with the slightest of efforts. Every additional act constitutes a further mitzva performance, however, and realization of the commandment's full potential will obviously require all-out effort. A mitzva grounded upon the dual mandate of imitating divine action and realizing human love must be literally boundless. Between those extremes lies a broad spectrum of moral action and stance; and again, correspondingly, varying degrees of imperative pressure to attain this or that level. It is difficult, certainly in broad theoretical terms, to determine precisely the extent of *gemilut hasadim* which might justifiably be normally expected – although that is, in a sense, what this essay is all about. Roughly speaking, I suspect it

81. *Pe'ah* 1:1.
82. Yerushalmi, ad loc.

is a good deal higher than most of us assume. At this point, however, I simply note that the ideal knows no limits.

A second mishna provides an even more radical statement:

> There are four types of men. Whoever says, "Mine is mine and yours is yours" – this is an average quality, but others consider it a Sodom-like quality; "Mine is yours and yours is mine" – is an ignoramus (*am haaretz*); "Mine is yours and yours is yours" – is pious (*hasid*); "Mine is mine and yours is mine" – is a villain (*rasha*).[83]

The idealization of the third stance – to the Rabbis, *hasid* is one of the highest encomiums, *hasidut* standing only below inspired revelation in Rabbi Pinhas ben Yair's celebrated ladder of spiritual ascent – evidently commends utter selflessness with respect to property as an ultimate goal. The mishna clearly does not advocate the headlong abolition of property as a social institution. Its second comment makes this perfectly explicit – nor, in view of the central role of property within Halakha, are we at all surprised. Note that the *hasid* grows toward higher community not because he begins with nothing but precisely because he begins with something to give. There is, indeed, a communism beneath property and a communism above it – the former a confused failure to realize property's potential for the development of personality, and the latter evolving from it and transcending it. The ideal toward which the *hasid* strives is genuine selflessness – which, incidentally, he attains all the more because he expects no reciprocity. His is a personal quest for magnanimity and saintliness rather than a revolutionary crusade. The mishna's typology indicates that this ideal was not regarded as a practicable alternative for the masses (indeed, if everyone pursued this course, it would become impossible) but as a counsel of perfection for an elite. The important point, for our purposes, is that selflessness was indeed regarded as an ideal.

---

83. *Avot* 5:10; some explain this mishna as referring to *tzedaka*, but surely it also has broader scope.

The mishna deals, of course, with property. Other texts strike a similar note with regard to the conduct of interpersonal relations; and they speak, strikingly enough, not of altruism alone but of abnegation. This element is not confined to visionary or hortatory statements. To a far greater extent than is often realized, it is bedrock Halakha. Two *deoraita* prohibitions concerning reprisal illustrate this point graphically:

> What is "revenge" and what is "bearing a grudge"?
>
> If one said to his fellow: "Lend me your sickle," and he replied: "No," and tomorrow the second comes [to the first] and says: "Lend me your axe!" and he replies: "I will not lend it to you, just as you would not lend me your sickle" – that is revenge.
>
> And what is bearing a grudge? If one says to his fellow: "Lend me your axe," he replies: "No," and on the morrow the second asks: "Lend me your garment," and he answers: "Here it is. I am not like you who would not lend me [what I asked for]" – that is bearing a grudge.[84]

The same note is struck in a passage from Rav's prayer – subsequently appended to the standard *Shemoneh Esrei* and thus pronounced thrice daily – "And may my soul be as dust unto all."[85] It was expressed even more forcefully, however, in several talmudic texts, largely aggadic in character and yet laced with normative overtones. One series of such citations expresses this attitude in almost radical terms:

> R. Yohanan said in the name of R. Elazar b. R. Shimon: Wherever you find the words of R. Elazar b. R. Yose the Galilean in an aggada make your ear like a funnel. [For he said: It is written,] "It was not because you were greater than any people that the Lord set His love upon you and chose you" (*Devarim* 7:7). The Holy One, blessed be He, said to Israel: I love you because even when I bestow greatness upon you, you humble yourselves before Me. I bestowed greatness upon Abraham, yet he said to Me, "I am

---

84. *Yoma* 23a.
85. *Berakhot* 17a.

> but dust and ashes" (*Bereshit* 18:27); upon Moses and Aaron, yet they said: "And we are nothing" (*Shemot* 16:7); upon David, yet he said: "But I am a worm and no man" (*Tehillim* 22:7). But with the heathens it is not so. I bestowed greatness upon Nimrod, and he said: "Come, let us build us a city" (*Bereshit* 11:4); upon Pharaoh, and he said: "Who is the Lord?" (*Shemot* 5:2); upon Sennacherib, and he said: "Who are they among all the gods of the countries?" (*II Melakhim* 18:35); upon Nebuchadnezzar, and he said: "I will ascend above the heights of the clouds" (*Yeshayahu* 14:14); upon Hiram king of Tyre, and he said: "I sit in the seat of God, in the heart of the seas" (*Yehezkel* 28:2).
>
> Rava, others say R. Yohanan, said: More significant is that which is said of Moses and Aaron than that which is said of Abraham. Of Abraham it is said: "I am but dust and ashes," whereas of Moses and Aaron it is said: "And we are nothing."
>
> Rava, others say R. Yohanan, also said: The world exists only on account of [the merit of] Moses and Aaron; for it is written here: "And we are nothing," and it is written there [of the world]: "He hangeth the earth upon nothing" (*Iyyov* 26:7).
>
> R. Ilaa said: The world exists only on account of [the merit of] him who restrains himself in strife, for it is written: "He hangeth the earth upon *belima*" [which can mean "nothing" or "restraint"].
>
> R. Abbahu said: On account of [the merit of] him who abases himself, for it is written: "And underneath are the everlasting arms" (*Devarim* 33:27).[86]

The first few statements neither demand nor necessarily recommend total abnegation. They simply extol its practitioners without passing definitive judgment upon their program. Even those who reject a self-effacing ethic as socially and psychologically debilitating might nevertheless admire the moral fortitude of its adherents. The statement of R. Ilaa goes somewhat further, however. It presents passive response to verbal provocation as a positive ideal – perhaps not one the Jew need

86. *Hullin* 89a.

conscientiously pursue but toward which he might at least vaguely strive, and which he should perceive as noble and perhaps even glorious.

A similar tone pervades several other passages. One ascribes supreme silence to God Himself. While imaginatively portraying the Romans' defiant desecration of the Temple's *sanctum sanctorum,* it interjects tersely:

> Abba Hanan said: "Who is a mighty one like unto Thee, O God?" (*Tehillim* 89:9) – Who is like Thee, mighty in self-restraint, that Thou didst hear the blaspheming and insults of that wicked man and keep silent?
>
> In the school of R. Yishmael it was taught: "Who is like Thee among the gods [*elim*]?" (*Shemot* 15:11) – Who is like Thee among the mute ones [*illemim*]?[87]

Probably the best-known is an oft-quoted passage which – particularly in the context within which it is cited by the Rambam – straddles the line between Aggada and Halakha:

> Concerning those who are insulted but do not insult others [in response], who hear themselves reproached without replying, who [perform good] work out of love of the Lord and rejoice in their sufferings, Scripture says: "But they that love Him be as the sun when he goeth forth in his might" (*Shofetim* 5:31).[88]

Even in this form, as a brief encomium, the Gemara[89] at one point assumes that the passage has a normative force. In the Rambam this becomes even clearer, as the citation is incorporated into a typological portrait of the *talmid hakham*'s ideal ethical personality:

> The scholar conducts his business affairs honestly and in good faith. His nay is nay; his yea, yea. In his accounts, he is strict [in

87. *Gittin* 56b.
88. *Yoma* 23a.
89. Ibid.

> meeting his obligations]. At the same time, when buying, he is liberal and does not drive a hard bargain. He pays promptly for his purchases. He declines to act as a surety or trustee; nor will he accept a power of attorney. In commercial matters, he acknowledges liability even where the law would not hold him liable; his principle being to keep his word and not change it. If others have been adjudged liable to him, he is considerate, and even forgives them the amount due. He grants benevolent (interest-free) loans and does favors. He will not encroach on another man's business, and throughout his life will not vex a human being. In short, he belongs to the class of those who are persecuted but do not persecute, who are reviled but do not revile. A man who acts thus is commended in the Scriptural text, "And He said to me: You are My servant Israel, in whom I glory" (*Yeshayahu* 49:3).[90]

The thrust of these passages – grounded partly in an altruistic ethic and partly in otherworldliness – is fairly clear. To an extent, they are perhaps countervailed by other elements. There are passages which commend a more aggressive stance. Indeed, one makes the startling assertion that "R. Yohanan further said in the name of R. Shimon b. Yehotzadak: Any scholar, who does not avenge himself and retain anger like a serpent, is no [real] scholar."[91] On balance, however, I think it is clear that the Halakha has leaned toward accommodation and concession rather than self-assertion or even counterpunching. Its stance is no doubt more muscular than the professed Christian ethic. At one level, it does not celebrate poverty or encourage wholesale giving of one's worldly goods to others.[92] At another,

90. *Hilkhot De'ot* 5:13.
91. *Yoma* 22b–23a; see also Me'iri's explanation ad loc. Yet on the whole, Halakha stresses concession, which fits in with the halakhic stress upon responsibility and seeing things from others' perspective. The problem of relating "Your life takes precedence" to the halakhic stress upon concession is part of the broader problem of *lifnim mishurat hadin* and therefore not for this essay; but see the essay on *lifnim mishurat hadin* later in this volume.
92. This general tendency must be reconciled with assertions to the contrary, such as the above-mentioned mishna, "'Mine is yours and yours is yours' – is pious (*hasid*)" (*Avot* 5:10).

it recognizes a lower threshold of suffering as legitimate moral grounds for responding to provocative aggression. It advises "taking" much less. The point is, however, that it does commend taking a good deal. What Mill, no less than Nietzsche, condemned as the "feminine" element of Christian ethics, has deep Jewish roots. Surely, the Rabbis' attitude is much closer to turning the other cheek than to the self-assertive aggressiveness – and the almost frenetic activism frequently accompanying it – which is so often the hallmark of modern individualism.

Such a bias is thoroughly consonant with the Halakha's general approach to social relations. The key to that approach lies in the centrality of responsibility rather than rights as the dominant category. It may be amply illustrated by two laws, derived from the Gemara although cited here from the Rambam:

> Just as the employer is enjoined not to deprive the poor worker of his hire or withhold it from him when it is due, so is the worker enjoined not to deprive the employer of the benefit of his work by idling away his time, a little here and a little there, thus wasting the whole day deceitfully. Indeed, the worker must be very punctual in the matter of time, seeing that the Sages were so solicitous in this matter that they exempted the worker from saying the fourth benediction of grace.
>
> The worker must work with all his power, seeing that the just Jacob said, "And you know that with all my power I have served your father" (*Bereshit* 31:6), and that he received his reward therefore in this world, too, as it is said, "And the man increased exceedingly" (ibid. 30:43).[93]

> One is forbidden to appear before his debtor, nay even to pass before him, even though he does not make demand upon him – and, needless to say, if he does make demand upon him – lest he frighten or shame him.
>
> Just as the creditor is forbidden to demand payment, so is the debtor forbidden to withhold from the creditor the money

93. *Hilkhot Sekhirut* 13:7.

that is in his hands and to say to him, "Go forth and come back again," provided he has the means of paying. For it is written, "Say not to your neighbor, 'Go, and come again'" (*Mishlei* 3:28).

The debtor is also forbidden to borrow money and spend it unnecessarily or dissipate it, so that the creditor will not find anything from which to collect, even if the creditor be very rich. He who does this is classified as a wicked man. For it is written, "The wicked borrow, but pay not" (*Tehillim* 37:21). And the Sages have enjoined us: "Your fellow's property shall be as dear to you as your own" (*Avot* 2:12).[94]

Analogous statements apply this approach to other roles, and the principle of reciprocal responsibility underlying them governs undefined personal relations as well. Almost by definition, such a position requires seeing things from the other fellow's perspective – and it calls for acting upon that vision. It thus provides a basis for the Halakha's emphasis upon giving – in the sense of both contribution and concession.

The danger inherent in such an approach – that the unscrupulous, interpreting conscience as weakness, will exploit its adherents – is obvious; and the Rabbis were hardly oblivious to it. In a broad sense, their awareness is reflected in their rejection of total pacifism as optimal public policy. Within a more modest context, it was explicitly formulated in the area of interpersonal relations. Speaking of the obligation to help others load or unload merchandise, the Mishna states that if its owner "went aside and sat [down] and said, 'Since it is [incumbent] upon you as a mitzva, if you want to unload – go unload,' he [i.e., the bystander] is exempt, for it is stated, '[If thou see the ass of him that hateth thee lying under its burden, thou shalt forbear to pass by him; thou shalt surely release it] with him' (*Shemot* 23:5)."[95] Inasmuch as the mishna deals with a specific mitzva, its statement might conceivably be confined to that mitzva alone.[96] Thus, some have contended, on textual grounds, that

94. *Hilkhot Malveh VeLoveh* 1:3.
95. *Bava Metzia* 32a.
96. This opinion is cited by the Me'iri (*Kiddushin* 8b, s.v. *haya kelev*) in the name of *yesh omerim*, "there are those who say."

the phrase "with him" qualifies only the context within which it occurs. On logical grounds, one might argue that the obligation to unload is not grounded upon the desire for promoting the owner's material welfare but upon the need for preventing or relieving personal distress – the Rambam specifically focuses upon the possibility of panic – and no such need exists when he is malingering. And yet, it seems at least equally plausible that the principle formulated in the mishna has far broader ramifications at either the formal or the attitudinal level. Thus, both the Me'iri and the Rosh[97] state that one is under no obligation to spend money to save others if they have money of their own but refuse to spend it.[98] With reference to public charity, we encounter a similar view in the Gemara's discussion of a person "who has means but does not wish to live off them (*lehitparnes*),"[99] preferring to become a communal charge or even, as Rashi noted, to lacerate himself in hunger. R. Yehuda holds that we supply his needs during his lifetime but then collect the amount from his estate after his death. R. Shimon rejoins that, provided that there is no prospect of terminal starvation (the Gemara does not mention the qualification but it is halakhically self-evident), we simply ignore him. This difference is no doubt significant, but clearly neither is ready to abandon the public treasury to every extortionist who would play upon communal conscience.[100]

These provisions reflect the Rabbis' awareness of the danger of exploitation. Nevertheless, they do not alter the Halakha's basic orientation. The positive emphasis upon giving – pressed to varying degrees of different levels – remains. The safeguards are just that. They restrict but do not reverse the Jew's primary obligation. To glance momentarily at a current controversy, it is entirely possible that the provision regarding a person "who has means" may include the employable as well as property-owners. Yet I have no doubt but that the pervasive spirit of *hilkhot tzedaka* would require a most lenient construction of this qualification.

97. Me'iri, ibid.; Rosh, *Sanhedrin* 8:2.
98. Of course, one is obligated to save another at the moment of need, but then can demand reimbursement afterward.
99. *Ketubbot* 67b.
100. Ed. note: For more on this topic, see "The Responsibilities of the Recipient of Charity" later in this volume.

If a community must choose between severe guidelines which would preclude cheating but possibly deny some deserving poor as well, and a lax policy which might result in some fraud, I think the Halakha would unquestionably mandate the latter. When capacity for employment is uncertain, the needy would certainly receive the benefit of any doubt. The giver's primary focus remains the fulfillment of his own duty. How responsibly the recipient is acting is an important but very secondary consideration.

Such an emphasis may seem inconsistent with the principle of *hayekha kodmin*. There is no antinomy, however; dialectical tension, perhaps, but no ultimate contradiction. Resolution of the apparent conflict rests, in part, upon recognition of multiple halakhic levels; upon allowance for comparing respective stakes; and, finally, even when I stand to lose as much as my neighbor, upon what that loss might be. I believe it can be fairly stated that the scope and intensity of the Halakha's call for sacrifice varies inversely with the importance of the issue. If the problem is survival, it is virtually nonexistent; if mere vanity, it is both sharp and persistent; if somewhere between these – say, a question of livelihood rather than life – it may impose no demands and yet posit an ideal.

This proportion may be based upon at least two factors. One is the limit upon the burden which can be assigned – at the imperative level, certainly – to the ordinary Jew. The emphasis upon restraint, which encourages acquiescing in humiliation or mandates *harhakat shekhenim*, becomes more difficult to maintain when higher stakes present a more excruciating ethical dilemma. Restricting a mustard patch or toning down a radio may be inconvenient – may even inhibit progress – but they portend no calamity. In highly critical situations, however, the counsel of moderation may be too exacting to demand. Pulling in one's horns means one thing when it requires absorbing an insult or installing a fence; quite another when it jeopardizes a livelihood or life itself. When concession is less demanding, it can be more readily required. The justification for self-serving action clearly increases in proportion to the stakes.

The second factor is a strain of otherworldliness. Some things are simply not worth a struggle – and the person who recognizes this will rather give than fight. With respect to matters of dubious objective significance, I ought to give others precedence because, among other reasons, while they may attach great importance to them, I ought to know better; and if I don't, the demand for giving proper will, quite apart from conferring benefit upon others and developing my own character, advance my axiological education as well. In the long run, of course, others, too, should be developing a different perspective; but my immediate concern – again, the focus upon responsibility – is my own moral well-being and the others' temporal welfare. I am therefore led, somewhat paradoxically, to denigrate the importance of an issue with respect to myself and yet to recognize its value to my fellow.

This otherworldly strain is clearly struck in the Rambam's exposition of the Torah's prohibitions of reprisal:

> He who takes revenge violates a prohibition, as it is said, "You shall not take vengeance" (*Vayikra* 19:18). And although he is not punished with flogging, still such conduct indicates an exceedingly bad disposition. One should rather practice forbearance in all secular matters. For the intelligent realize that these are matters of vanity and vacuity and not worth taking vengeance for.[101]

It should be emphasized, however, that, insofar as it is based upon this second factor, while such an attitude may lead to concession in practice, it does not, conceptually, constitute genuine altruism. Consequently, it poses a problem when the issue, while unrelated to actual survival, nevertheless concerns something which, by every human standard, must be considered truly important. The maintenance of a livelihood provides one example, the stakes being purely financial but hardly to be dismissed as "matters of vanity and vacuity." An even more acute problem is presented by situations – danger of exile, captivity, or serious injury might be prime examples – in which, while life itself is not threatened, the issue affects neither convenience nor money but the fabric and quality of personal existence. How significant a factor can otherworldliness be in such cases?

101. *Hilkhot De'ot* 7:7.

The Talmud does not discuss such situations explicitly. *Rishonim* did, however, and the tone and substance of their remarks convey an emphasis quite different from that prevailing in *harhakat shekhenim*. They focus more upon the right of self-seeking than upon the need for self-sacrifice. With respect to earning a living, the *Tur* quotes Rav Saadya to the effect that "a person is obligated to give his own livelihood precedence over any other person's"[102] – evidently assuming that self-interest was here not only a right but a duty. This seems rather startling and it is perhaps no accident that the Rama's citation of the remark was toned down to read, "one's own livelihood precedes any other person's."[103] Even this formulation, however, inasmuch as it urges no heroic attempt to transcend its permissive counsel, evidently accepts this application of *hayekha kodmin* without reservations.

As to cases of non-economic privation, their treatment may be inferred from the discussion concerning *pidyon shevuyim*, the ransoming of captives. The Mishna states that "captives should not be redeemed for more than their value, to prevent abuses."[104] The Gemara suggests two reasons for this precept. One is simply that exorbitant demands may be too onerous for a community with limited resources. The second is "that the activities [of the raiding captors] may be stimulated." Most

102. *Tur*, YD 251. The term "livelihood" (*parnasa*) may refer to one's needs, as it is used in reference to the husband's obligation to provide for his wife's needs, or the father's obligation to provide for his daughters' needs after his death. In any case, "livelihood" means all of one's needs, and not a specific item.

103. *Shulhan Arukh*, YD 251:3. The *Tur* and the Rama added that one is not obligated to give *tzedaka* until one has provided for his own *parnasa*. Yet this is perplexing in light of the ruling in *Gittin* 7b, cited by the *Shulhan Arukh* (YD 248:1), that even a pauper supported by charity must himself give charity. In addressing this problem, the Shakh (YD 248:1) opined that the pauper must give charity only when his own *parnasa* has been provided for. However, the *Nahalat Tzvi* (ibid.) cogently questioned this conclusion, offering a different resolution: even a pauper must give some small amount of *tzedaka*, while one whose livelihood is secure must give the poor "sufficient to their lack" (*Devarim* 15:8). In other words, there are two obligating factors: (a) the need to share my property with others – and here the focus is subjective; (b) the need to provide the needs of others – and here the focus is objective and result-oriented. A pauper has the first obligating factor but not the second. See also *Iggerot Moshe*, YD I:145.

104. *Gittin* 4:6, 45a.

Rishonim assumed that the Mishna refers solely to cases in which the captives' lives are not actually in danger. Indeed, otherwise the Gemara's first explanation becomes puzzling; *pikuah nefesh* should presumably override purely monetary considerations. Furthermore, they tended to accept the Gemara's second explanation as the more prevalent; i.e., they regarded the payment of exorbitant ransom as actually forbidden as a potential threat to the community rather than as a burden with which it could not be saddled but which relatives or friends could assume on their own. Nevertheless, a number of authorities clearly assumed that the captive himself was not prohibited from paying any sum necessary to secure his release. Among the arguments presented for permitting and probably requiring a husband to ransom his wife at any cost, perhaps the most prominent is that "one's wife is like his own self." This of course presumes that the prisoner proper is exempt from the Mishna's prohibition. It also implies, in turn, that a serious threat to the quality of personal existence provides license for indirectly subjecting others to the same danger.

On this view, a prisoner would very likely be similarly exempt from a companion prohibition cited in the same mishna: "Captives should not be helped to escape, to prevent abuses. Rabban Shimon b. Gamliel says [that the reason is] to prevent the ill-treatment of fellow captives." It should be obvious, however, that the basis of this exemption – the assumption that, short of direct aggressive action, a person may risk severely disrupting the lives of others when the fabric of his own hangs in the balance – cannot be readily and mechanically extrapolated. For one thing, the aggression permitted in these cases is not only indirect but uncertain. Even within unstable Hellenistic or medieval societies – far more accustomed to kidnappings or captivity than our own – marauders' reactions to the lure of ransom or the defiance of flight must have been highly problematic. This uncertainty – or rather, the fact that one's present release is assured and the capture of others only a threatening prospect – is clearly a crucial factor. Its relevance should require little elaboration, but an analogy may prove useful. As we have seen, an individual is not required to sacrifice his life in order to save someone else's. Nevertheless, a number of *Rishonim* state – some indeed quote the Yerushalmi as having said so explicitly – that where

I must face possible danger in order to save someone else from certain death, I am obligated to do so.[105] Conversely, it is entirely possible that a prisoner – or anyone in a comparable situation – may save himself at the cost of endangering others only when their danger is uncertain.

And then there is the question of gauging degrees of risk. This question evidently lies at the heart of the dispute concerning stimulation of prisoners' flight. R. Shimon b. Gamliel apparently assumed that only the highly probable threat of immediate reprisal against remaining prisoners should deter efforts to abet escape. Animated by a more cautious spirit, the anonymous "Rabbis" regarded the prospect of future raids and captures as sufficient ground for abstaining from encouraging flight. As the majority view, the Rabbis' position has prevailed, but a similar problem exists with respect to the license granted the prisoner proper, as well as in innumerable comparable situations. With life itself at stake, R. Akiva's principle permits saving one's own skin no matter how dire and how certain the consequences to another. Short of that, however, we are in an area in which the intensity, the duration, and the probability of suffering by oneself or by others must be weighed as elements in an interrelated complex. Such factors cannot be measured, however, according to the computations of some felicific calculus, and within such a context, the most Halakha can do is point a direction and suggest an emphasis. As regards these, I believe it can be fairly stated that the Halakha has permitted – although not necessarily encouraged – the priority of self-interest. Against a background of awareness of this halakhic attitude, the final judgment must be a matter of conscience.

In specific dilemmas of either/or priority, the judgment of conscience is exercised within a narrow context. Obviously, however, cases such as these, while they loom large in casuistic discourse – and hence both reflect and refine basic principles – comprise the bulk of neither moral theory nor ethical existence. As I hope much of the preceding discussion has made clear, the problem of self-interest has a far broader focus. It entails a total orientation – the formulation of overall personal

105. *Kesef Mishneh* (*Hilkhot Rotze'ah* 1:14) in the name of *Haggahot Maimoniyot*. See also the note by R. Hayyim Heller in his edition of *Sefer HaMitzvot*, negative commandment 297.

and public policy. The attempt to formulate it with an eye to both areas is complicated, however, by Mandeville's celebrated paradox, briefly stated in the subtitle of his *The Fable of the Bees: or, Private Vices, Public Benefits* and extensively discussed in the body of the work. Mandeville argues that, while loudly decried, the persistent pursuit of self-interest actually confers great social benefit. It is the prospect of personal profit which motivates the businessman or the politician to act aggressively and imaginatively – to the ultimate benefit of the whole community. In the absence of such a stimulus, individual effort invariably droops and progress grinds to a halt. Hence, from a long-range point of view, the pursuit of self-interest – which the prevalent Christian ethic deplores as narrow and selfish – actually represents the most enlightened and altruistic course. Personal "immorality" serves the public interest better than supposed virtue. Inducing lassitude and producing a more lethargic economy, excessive altruism proves ultimately detrimental to its presumed beneficiaries. An altruistic society may distribute victuals more justly; but there is less to go around.

Among his eighteenth-century contemporaries, Mandeville's thesis evoked a storm of righteous indignation. Yet, given its psychological assumptions, it is far from specious; and as to the assumptions, subsequent events have lent more credence to Mandeville's position than to the more optimistic appraisals of Shaftesbury and Hutcheson. Precisely because it contains a significant element of truth, however, Mandeville's thesis is, for the moralist, profoundly disturbing. The economist may be content to draw the logical inference that, *mirabile dictu*, personal and public interest coincide: the demands of selfishness and of altruism are one; and at this level, Mandeville exerted considerable influence upon both Adam Smith and nineteenth-century utilitarianism. The moralist, however – concerned with personality as well as production and with outlook as well as output – cannot be content. For one thing, the presumed coincidence is a large-scale projection. In specific instances, the pursuit of self-interest may cause considerable public hardship. At best, therefore, we must – as with technological unemployment – balance long-term gain against interim loss. Primarily, however, inasmuch as the prospect of profit rather than the moment of duty is posited as the basic motive of action – this is, after all, the linchpin of the whole argument – the moral character of its agent suffers, even if the economy does indeed subsequently prosper.[106] The danger is doubly great insofar as the very marvel of the coincidence serves as a moral anodyne. It would be a fine ethical sensitivity indeed which would not be somewhat dulled by the comforting knowledge that profit and virtue are fortuitously identical. The prospect of subjective moral decline must therefore be weighed against that of objective material growth.

Keynes qualified this thesis on economic grounds, acknowledging that it was only true of periods of underemployment but lacked universal validity. Even if this argument be correct, however – and I am hardly competent to judge – the moral problem persists. Periods of underemployment are by no means rare; and even when this condition does not pervade a whole economy, its equivalent may easily govern significant segments of a society. From a rigorous Kantian perspective, the problem can have only one solution. Retardation of economic development is a small price to pay for virtue. Indeed, on the public no less than the private plane, renunciation may very well define virtue.[107]

---

106. Of course, this would not be the case if one identified the good and right with results; see Richard Brandt, *Ethical Theory* (Englewood Cliffs, NJ, 1959).

107. Ed. note: The continuation of this discussion is missing. In addition, this essay – unlike the previous two – lacks a conclusion tying it back to the responsum (*Havvot Ya'ir* #213).

The Varieties of Halakhic Law: The Concept of *Lifnim Mishurat Hadin*

I. Introduction

Of Judaism, few things can be said with so much certitude as that it rests upon law. Nevertheless, both the nature of that law and its relation to the tradition as a whole are frequently misconstrued. While differently motivated, adversaries and adherents alike often tend to overstate the extent to which its legal aspect, *narrowly defined,* can be identified with the totality of Torah. Impelled by hostile theological and psychological premises and somewhat misled by sheer ignorance, critics from Paul through Luther to Buber have seen normative Judaism as nothing but mechanistic legalism – to be contrasted with liberating spirit, with vital grace, or with dialogic encounter. On the other hand, advocates concerned with upholding the moral character of Jewish law – again, narrowly defined – are occasionally driven to the apologetic excess of denying the possibility of an ethical dimension beyond it. Thus, Professor Kahana declares "that in Jewish civil law there is no separation of law and morals and that there is no distinction between what the law *is* and what the law *ought* to be."[1] Such statements are no doubt intended to underscore a basic fact – the essential difference in ethical character between contemporary secular law and religiously oriented Jewish law. In this sense, they emphasize the sweeping scope Judaism has accorded law – with its full normative force – rather than rely fully upon the constricted power of supralegal morality. Nevertheless, as bald formulations, they should not stand unchallenged; and, with reference to popular practice, it should be honestly recognized that the attitude expressed in them can give rise, albeit through a measure of distortion, to the very legalism charged by opponents – the notion that whatever the law does not specifically require can make no demands upon the Jew.

The Rabbis knew of such a notion – and they rejected it categorically. "R. Yohanan said," the Gemara in *Bava Metzia* tells us, "'Jerusalem was but destroyed because they [i.e., its inhabitants] judged [in accordance with] Torah law within it.' Well, should they rather have followed the law of the Magians?! Say, rather, because they based their judgments solely upon Torah law and did not act *lifnim mishurat hadin* [i.e., beyond the line of the law]."[2] The Ramban was even more outspoken. In a celebrated passage, he explains that the general command, "Ye shall be holy," was issued because the scope of the Torah's injunctions concerning personal conduct notwithstanding, a lustful sybarite could observe all of their details and yet remain a "scoundrel with the Torah's license." The same holds true, he continues, with regard to social ethics. "And this is the Torah's mode: to detail and [then] to generalize in a similar vein. For after the admonition [about] the details of civil law and all interpersonal dealings – 'Thou shalt not steal,' 'Thou shalt not rob,' 'Ye shall not exploit,' and the rest of [such] injunctions – it says generally, 'and

1. K. Kahana, *The Case for Jewish Civil Law in the Jewish State* (London, 1960), 28n; his italics.
2. *Bava Metzia* 30b. The term *din* in the text here may refer either to litigation initiated through insistence upon one's rights or, more generally, to the letter of Torah law.

thou shalt do the right and the good,' as it includes under this positive command justice and equalization and all [action undertaken] *lifnim mishurat hadin* in order to oblige one's fellows."[3]

While rejecting narrow legalism, however, the Rabbis did not pour out the baby with the bath water. Invested with neither antinomian impulses nor transcendental authority, they did not reject the concept of a comprehensive code. Instead, they sought to complement it by fleshing out the idea of a body of principles and values which, while lacking the definitive and detailed character of positive law, should nevertheless, in a more contextual way, guide and inspire conduct. They would thus take their place alongside law proper as a normative element within the total halakhic system.

The term most commonly employed to signify this idea – it occurs in both of the passages I have cited – is, "beyond the line of the law." This essay will attempt to analyze the term and the concept, to discuss its major specific applications within the halakhic tradition, and to deal, however briefly, with some of its broader philosophic implications.

II. Distinctions Among Mitzvot

The most prevalent misconception regarding Halakha concerns its presumed monochromatic character. Among the uninformed, it is widely regarded as a catalogue of do's and don'ts, all pretty much qualitatively equal. Some things are required, others forbidden, and everything else is neutral – but there is no significant variation within any of these areas. The facts, however, belie this thesis completely. The relevant evidence makes it patently clear that qualitative distinction is an integral aspect of the Halakha's normative structure. There is, of course, a sense in which all commandments are equal. Insofar as they are all expressions of God's will, they all stand on the same footing. The performance of

3. *Vayikra* 19:1. The concept of a general norm blanketing an area within which a number of specific injunctions had been formulated was also specifically applied by the Ramban to Sabbath observance. See his comments here and *Vayikra* 23:24. The verses cited by the Ramban are from *Devarim* 5:17, *Vayikra* 19:13, *Vayikra* 25:17, and *Devarim* 6:18, respectively.

every positive mitzva constitutes a response to a divine call. Conversely, the willful violation of any prohibition is an act of rebellion. Its inherent turpitude aside, it constitutes a gesture of disobedience – the degree of revolt depending, as the Halakha has amply recognized, upon the spirit in which the act is conceived and executed, but, so long as it is willful, always present in some measure. The catalogue of sins Milton[4] descried in the first human transgression is, in a sense, present in all. Beyond this basic common status, however, there is also another sense in which the Halakha has differentiated among its constituent elements. The very mishna which urges, "Be as careful with respect to a lesser as with respect to a graver mitzva,"[5] recognizes, after all, that the two are not identical.

Distinctions are made among both negative and positive commandments. As regards prohibitions, differing penalties for their violation are of course suggestive. But lest we ascribe this difference to some extraneous factor – the role of punishment as deterrent, for instance – the Mishna[6] makes it clear that it reflects the quality of respective sins. By postulating that sins for which the Torah has imposed severe penalties require greater atonement, it clearly indicates that it is indeed their gravity which exacts a stronger punishment. Moreover, qualitative distinctions are recognized even when penalties are equal or nonexistent. Thus, false swearing in vain is described as one of the graver sins although, as

4. See *De Doctrina Christiana*, in *The Complete Works of John Milton* (New York, 1934), XV, 181; I, xi. From this perspective, any sin may merit the most severe of punishments. One recalls Plutarch's statement that Draco, "being once asked why he made death the punishment of most offences, replied, 'Small ones deserve that, and I have no higher for the greater crimes'" ("Life of Solon," in *Plutarch's Lives*, trans. John Dryden [New York, n.d.], 107). From a Jewish point of view, such a position is unthinkable with respect to crime but is, at one level, tenable with regard to sin. This point is reflected in the celebrated statement of the Yerushalmi (*Makkot* 2:6) that the response of "prophecy" to the question, "A sinner: what shall be his punishment?" was Yehezkel's unqualified statement, "The sinning soul shall die" (*Yehezkel* 18:20). It is only tenable, however, as a theoretical and theological formulation – not, of course, as a legal ordinance. The Yerushalmi's conclusion – that God's response was "Let him repent and be forgiven" – underscores this distinction.
5. *Avot* 2:1.
6. See *Yoma* 85b. The same point is suggested by the Rambam's view that only the violation of injunctions for which punishment has been prescribed classifies the violator as a *rasha*, disqualifying him as a witness. See *Hilkhot Eidut* 10:1–2.

regards punishment, it is no different from any other negative biblical injunction.[7] In a similar, albeit more moral vein, the Rabbis[8] acknowledge a difference between sexual promiscuity and, say, trading in fruits of the Sabbatical year.

These distinctions concern, at a *deoraita* level, the very essence of various injunctions. Others, somewhat less basic, pertain to their application. Situations which are proscribed *ante facto* but tolerated as a *fait accompli*; "This is the halakha but we do not instruct thus";[9] rights which one can exercise as "we listen to him but it is not fitting to do thus because of [the breach of] civility"[10] – all are familiar to students of Halakha and all reflect a measure of subtlety governing the application of prohibitions. To a degree, they attest, in a broader sense, to the Rambam's statement that "the idea of the forbidden and the permissible

7. See *Shevuot* 39a. The Gemara relates the gravity of this injunction ("Thou shalt not bear the Name of the Lord your God vainly") to the fact that the verse in which it is formulated concludes with the admonition that its punishment is beyond total remission – "For the Lord will not absolve him who shall bear His name vainly" (*Shemot* 20:7). In this connection, a distinction grounded in an observation once made by Rav Joseph B. Soleveitchik is highly relevant. The identical word *lashav* appears in the same verse twice. Onkelos, however, translates it – both here and in *Devarim* 5:11 – first, *lemagana*, "needlessly," and then, *leshikra*, "falsely." The explanation lies in the fact that the injunction of swearing *lashav* – that which is formulated in the first half of the verse – includes affirming both the obviously true and the obviously false; see Yerushalmi, *Shevuot* 3:8, and Rambam, *Hilkhot Shevuot* 1:5. Onkelos evidently assumed, however, that the unique gravity of the injunction – which is based on the second half of the verse – applies only to swearing falsely.
8. See *Yoma* 86b. The distinction is part of a parable and is put into the mouth of a violator. Its validity does appear to be accepted by the Gemara, however.
9. *Bava Kamma* 30b, *Beitza* 28b, and *Eiruvin* 7a. This concept does not constitute a quality of esoteric and exoteric Halakha but rather reflects ambivalent hesitation with respect to certain individual halakhot. See, however, *Shabbat* 38a and commentaries on the Alfasi, ad loc.
10. Rambam, *Hilkhot Ishut* 14:17. The term rendered here as "civility" is *derekh eretz* in the original. In current usage, it generally denotes social virtues – politeness, propriety, and the like. Initially, however, it was charged with considerable moral significance. Cf. the similar changes of terms such as "manners," "courtesy," "gentleman" – or, for that matter, "civility." See also references cited in Boaz Cohen, *Law and Tradition in Judaism* (New York, 1959), 183n., to which should be added N. S. Greenspan, *Mishpat Am HaAretz* (Jerusalem, 1946), ch. 1.

is not identical with the idea of the repugnant and the odious and the desirable and the cherished and that which it is fitting to do in the way of modesty and the ultimate in chastity."[11] The range and complexity of halakhic gradations are best seen, however, with reference to positive obligation; and it is to this, as the primary focus of this essay, that we now turn.

Nothing need here be said about mitzvot – the law concerning divorce is an obvious example – which demand nothing but command *about* something. These are in no sense normative. They simply prescribe a legal procedure for attaining what is, at best, a purely neutral end, and their performance bears no religious character whatsoever. Gradations may be noted, however, even among genuinely normative mitzvot. "There are positive commandments," the Rambam states, "which a person is obligated to seek and to pursue until he performs it [sic], such as *tefillin, sukka, lulav,* and *shofar*; and these are described [as] obligation, because a person is obligated to do [them] under all circumstances. There is also a [type of] mitzva which is not a [categorized] obligation but resembles an option, such as *mezuza* or *maakeh*. For a person is not obligated to reside in a house requiring a *mezuza* in order that he should install a *mezuza*. Rather, if he wants to live in a tent or a ship all his life, he can stay there. Likewise, he is not obligated to build a house in order to install a *maakeh*."[12] Moreover, distinctions exist within the latter group proper. The examples cited by the Rambam, for instance, result in a mitzva performance once a person fulfills them after entering circumstances which render them obligatory. It is nowhere suggested, however, that any special merit attaches to buying a house which should make them mandatory. With respect to *tzizit*, however – on the face of it, identical with *mezuza* and *maakeh* – reaching out for the obligating situation is clearly encouraged. To cite the Rambam again: "Although a person is not obligated to purchase a garment and to wear it so that he should [have to] put *tzizit* on it, [nevertheless] it is not fitting for a pious person to exempt himself from this mitzva. Rather, one should

11. *Perush HaMishnayot, Sanhedrin* 7:4.
12. *Hilkhot Berakhot* 11:2. Cf. the list of unconditional positive commandments which the Rambam appended to the section on *mitzvot aseh* in his *Sefer HaMitzvot*.

always seek to be clothed in a garment requiring *tzizit* so that he should fulfill this mitzva. One should always be scrupulous with respect to the mitzva of *tzizit* as Scripture has equated it with and linked to it all of the mitzvot, as has been said, 'And ye shall see it and ye shall remember all of the Lord's commandments.'"[13] As the Rosh[14] noted, *tzizit* is not an isolated example, and he finds a source for the Rambam's statement in an aggadic comment: "R. Simlai taught: Why did Moses, our master, thirst to enter *Eretz Yisrael*? Did he, then, need to eat of its fruit? Or did he need to be sated by its bounty? Rather, Moses said thus: 'Israel has been commanded many mitzvot which can only be fulfilled in *Eretz Yisrael*. Let me enter the land so that they should all be fulfilled by me.'"[15] From this perspective, we are dealing here with the need for an active rather than passive or even reluctant involvement with mitzvot, and the total harnessing of personality in the service of God. It should be noted again, however, that the exhortation does not apply – certainly does not apply equally – to all mitzvot. The tithing of produce constitutes a positive normative performance. And yet, so long as there is no recourse to evasive loopholes – that is of course another question and a practice roundly criticized by the Rabbis[16] – we are nowhere urged to produce or consume foods which would require tithing.[17]

---

13. *Hilkhot Tzitzit* 3:11–12. The verse cited is from *Bemidbar* 15:29. The term *adam hasid*, rendered here as "a pious person," usually refers to a very high spiritual station. Hence, the Rambam's statement may not have very strong and immediate imperative force with respect to the average Jew. The principle of the distinction between *tzizit* and *mezuza* stands, however. It may also be noted that the Rosh specifically speaks in broader terms: "It is proper for every *yerei shamayim* [i.e., God-fearing person] …."
14. See *Tosafei HaRosh, Nidda* 61a–b, s.v. *aval*. He does not refer to the Rambam but advances a similar position, generalized by the citation of R. Simlai's statement. See also *Menahot* 41a.
15. *Sota* 14a. The Rosh, however, cites *Bereshit Rabba* as his source. I have been unable to locate the passage.
16. *Berakhot* 35b; cf. *Menahot* 67a and Rashi, s.v. *gezera*.
17. Once one has produced such foods, however, some authorities hold he should – perhaps even must – tithe even if he does not plan to consume them. See *Taz*, YD 1:17, and Rav Akiva Eiger's comment, ad loc.

Halakhic differentiation goes a step further, however. It is not only horizontal but vertical: it distinguishes between levels of obligation and performance of the same mitzva as well as between different mitzvot. As regards subjective factors such as motivation, this is of course obvious. One need hardly be a Kantian to recognize that the inherent value and content of an action or, at the very least, to cite Mill's distinction,[18] the worth of its agent, is very much a function of the purity of will which impels them. In halakhic terms, this recognition is most forcefully expressed in the concept of *lishmah,* that one embrace Torah or a mitzva "for its own sake" – a mode of thought and action which, in normative terms, is subsumed under the command to love God. "The substance of this love," the Ramban comments, "has been explained by our Rabbis, the most explicit of their statements being that which is stated in the *Sifre*: Lest you shall say, 'I will study Torah in order that I should be called a scholar, in order that I should sit in the academy, in order that I should live long, or in order that I should merit the World to Come,' [therefore,] the verse teaches, 'to love etc.'"[19] Characteristically, however, vertical differentiation with Halakha concerns objective factors as well – the "what" as well as the "why" of behavior. ("How," of course, straddles both subjective and objective elements.) Quite apart from inevitable differences of individual fulfillment, the Halakha itself posits varied qualitative and quantitative scope for the performance of specific mitzvot – and, by extension, for moral and religious existence as a whole. In doing so, it employs several categories. Standard terms such as *mitzva min hamuvhar,* "a choice mitzva,"[20] or *hiddur mitzva,* "the embellishment of a mitzva,"[21] are suggestive by way of exemplification. The most prominent, however – being both most fundamental and most comprehensive – is *lifnim mishurat hadin*; and it is to its definition and analysis that we now turn.

---

18. See John Stuart Mill, "*Utilitarianism*," in *Utilitarianism, Liberty, and Representative Government* (London, 1910), 17. Cf. D. M. Mackinnon, *A Study in Ethical Theory* (New York, 1962), chs. 2–3.
19. *Devarim* 6:5. The *Sifre* is found in *Ekev,* 42, as a comment upon the verse cited here from *Devarim* 11:13. Cf. also Rambam, *Hilkhot Teshuva* 10:1–5.
20. *Nazir* 23a.
21. *Bava Kamma* 9b.

III. Defining *Din*

Quite obviously, *lifnim mishurat hadin* can only be defined with reference to that which it extends and transcends – namely, *din* proper. The general import of the term is clear: law, order, rationality. It would be worthwhile, however, to discriminate among specific cognate meanings. One may discern at least ten distinct senses: 1) a specific law; 2) a legal system; 3) law or justice as an ideal universal, especially as a divine attribute; 4) a specific legal case, usually one involving litigation; 5) the process of trying a case; 6) a legal right or status; 7) a legal sentence; 8) a punishment; 9) a correct logical inference, particularly *a fortiori* deduction; 10) a behavioral or customary norm.[22] Not all of these, of course, impinge upon our problem. Neither should it be assumed, however, that only the first two are relevant. *Rishonim,* at least, sometimes speak of *lifnim mishurat hadin* with reference to a non-legal context, evidently with *din* as behavioral norm in mind. Thus, the *Nimmukei Yosef* speaks of disqualifying a witness from testifying about a situation regarding which one of the litigants has treated him with unusual leniency, as "there is ground for fearing that since he is embarrassed on account of this person who is treating him *lifnim mishurat hadin,* he will help him."[23]

Likewise, the third sense is equally relevant. Quite strikingly, the Rabbis speak of *lifnim mishurat hadin* with reference to God Himself. In a passage pregnant with theological implications, the Gemara states that in dealing with man on the basis of Torah – or, as the passage figuratively portrays it, when engaged in the study of Torah – God adheres to a scrupulous standard of justice. In dealing with man within context of law – or, in figurative terms, while engaged in judging man – God may, quite paradoxically, deviate from it somewhat. The reason given is that with regard to "Torah, concerning which [the term] 'truth' is written, as it is written, 'Acquire truth and do not sell it,' the Holy One, blessed be He, does not act *lifnim mishurat hadin*; [with regard to] judgment, concerning which [the term] 'truth' is not written, the Holy One, blessed be

22. See Rav Chaim Josua Kasowski, *Otzar Leshon HaTalmud* (Jerusalem, 1961), s.v. *din,* especially IX, 129–31 and 149–53.

23. *Bava Batra* 29a (14b in Alfasi).

He, acts *lifnim mishurat hadin*."[24] The passage should not be understood as referring to pure grace – a concept whose significance within Judaism is, incidentally, often greatly underestimated. That would presumably operate apart from judgment entirely, and would lie not so much beyond the line of law as above and independent of it. The process described by the Gemara is rather closer to the tempering or "sweetening" of judgments which is so prominent in kabbalistic thought. Be this as it may, the statement clearly speaks of action beyond an ideal law, rather than beyond a positive – even divinely positive – law.

The same point is made in a far more famous passage often cited in numerous other connections. After making the startling assertion that, in a sense, we may regard God as praying, the Gemara cites Rav's view concerning the substance of divine prayer. It is: "May there issue from before Me the will that My mercies should suppress My wrath, that they should override My standards, and that I should deal with My children through the quality of mercy and enter with them *lifnim mishurat hadin*."[25] Here again, the point of reference is ideal rather than statutory justice; and, in this case, the context of implicit contrast between the two primary divine attributes of justice and mercy – a contrast so prominent in aggadic and kabbalistic thought and reflected in many areas of Halakha as well – is noteworthy.

Nevertheless, it is as positive law, be it a specific norm or an entire legal system, that *din* most relates to – and therefore helps define – *lifnim mishurat hadin*; and it is with this sense of the latter term that we shall henceforth be primarily concerned. Even at this place, the term may support various meanings. The Ritva[26] employs it, for instance, to describe a rabbinic provision for dividing an estate in an unorthodox mode. In this sense, it retains a distinctly legislative ring. Ordinarily, however, it denotes personal behavior which extends beyond the specifically and absolutely required.

As such, the problem of the relations of *din* and *lifnim mishurat hadin* bears a resemblance to that of law and morals. Not Antigone's

---

24. *Avoda Zara* 4b. The verse cited is from *Mishlei* 23:23.
25. *Berakhot* 7a.
26. *Hiddushei HaRitva, Kiddushin* 42a.

problem, which immediately springs to mind in contemporary consciousness. Rather, the question of the contiguity, overlapping, or divergence of the two which, as trenchantly expounded in an early book of Roscoe Pound,[27] constituted one of the central concerns of nineteenth-century jurisprudence. To a point, the analogy is both valid and suggestive. As should become obvious presently, a number of key issues are common to both areas. At bottom, however, the analogy breaks down simply because *din* and law – as the latter is usually defined in jurisprudential discourse, i.e., as a body of rules ordained by society and enforced by its organs – are incommensurate terms. With reference to law, Vinogradoff's judgment is widely shared: "Law is clearly distinguishable from morality. The object of law is the submission of the individual to the will of organized society, while the tendency of morality is to subject the individual to the dictates of his own conscience."[28] It is, however, quite inapplicable to *din*, which encompasses much – one need go no further than basic precepts prohibiting covetousness or demanding neighborly love – that, being neither action nor actionable, no jurist would classify as law. Moreover, even those inclined to reject Vinogradoff's judgment generally accept his basic conception of what law is. They simply disagree over how broadly it should be applied. Modern disputants in the age-old controversy over legal regulation of private morals – Mill and Stephen in the nineteenth century, H. L. A. Hart and P. Devlin in the twentieth – debate the scope of governmental involvement in personal behavior. They are usually at one, however, in assuming the sociopolitical character of law and the fact that it is geared to enforcement.[29]

With reference to Halakha, however, such an account of *din* is thoroughly inaccurate. While enforcement is central to some areas, there are significant tracts to which it is unrelated. This is not only because, in

27. *Law and Morals* (Chapel Hill, N. C., 1924).

28. Paul Vinogradoff, *Common Sense in Law* (London, 1914), 25.

29. Indeed, the basis of Devlin's defense of regulation is precisely the social and political, rather than purely moral, consequences of immoral conduct. See his *The Enforcement of Morals* (Oxford, 1965), ch. 1. Jacob Ross's article, "Morality and the Law," *Tradition*, X (1968): 5–16, attempts to relate the Hart-Devlin controversy to Jewish thought, but is misled by failing to distinguish sufficiently between *din* and "law."

some cases, it is, for all practical purposes, a virtual impossibility.[30] Who can ordinarily check whether one has tithed his produce or inserted the proper scrolls in his *tefillin*? Beyond this, however, there are laws which are simply not subject to enforcement. The Gemara's citation of R. Yehoshua's statement illustrates this graphically: "[There are] four things whose doer is absolved as regards human law but is liable (*hayyav*) as regards heavenly law."[31] The term *hayyav* could mean either subject to punishment or obligated to make restitution. The former is clearly indicated by the Tosefta's variant of the same citation: "Four [persons] are exempt from payment according to the law but Heaven does not pardon them until they pay."[32] However, the latter may very well be implied as well. Thus, the Me'iri explains: "Everyone of whom we have written here that he is liable as regards heavenly law, this means that he is obligated with respect to restitution. For, concerning prohibition, even that with respect to which he is exempt as regards heavenly law, a prohibition nevertheless obtains."[33] On either reading – they are not, of course, mutually exclusive – it should be emphasized that the absence of direct enforcement notwithstanding, we are here dealing with *din* proper and not with purely pietistic devotion. Thus, Rabbenu Meshullam, author of the twelfth-century Provencal commentary, *Sefer HaHashlama*,[34] held that, in these cases, the perpetrator would be regarded as a *rasha* (villain) and disqualified from serving as a witness until he had paid – a view with which the Me'iri[35] concurred. Furthermore, many *posekim* have held that if the aggrieved party were to seize commensurate property of the violator, he would be recognized as its lawful owner[36] – clearly indicating, again, that we are here dealing with genuine, and yet unenforceable, *din* rather than pietism.

---

30. See *Bava Metzia* 61b.
31. *Bava Kamma* 55b.
32. *Shevuot* 3:2; likewise, Yerushalmi, *Bava Kamma* 6:1.
33. *Beit HaBehira, Bava Kamma* 56a; p. 169.
34. *Bava Kamma* 6:1. On this view, a measure of enforcement does, in one sense, apply to these cases. Strictly speaking, however, the disqualification is not a direct sanction but an incidental consequence.
35. Ibid.
36. See commentaries upon *Hoshen Mishpat* 28:1.

Hence, insofar as the term "law" can be applied to *din*, it must be understood as including not only enforceable civil and criminal statutes, but aspects of the moral law as well. Of course, not all aspects of *din* are, narrowly speaking, equally moral. Some laws are – in an immediate, though not, perhaps, in an ultimate sense – amoral, dealing with non-rational rituals or injunctions. Others, of a permissive or procedural character, may even, to a point, flout morality. I do not mean this in Kierkegaard's sense of the religious suspension of the ethical. It is doubtful that this is a significant Jewish category. They flout morality in the much more pedestrian sense that, by way of reluctant compromise with human frailty, the Torah has sometimes permitted personal or collective practices which admittedly fall short of the highest moral standards. At times, as the Gemara put it, "The Torah has but spoken vis-à-vis the evil inclination."[37] On the other hand, in some areas, the moral standard is so high as to be almost insuperable. The demands imposed by the mitzva of parental respect are so rigorous that R. Yohanan could be led to exclaim that, with respect to one factor, "Fortunate is he who has never seen them"[38] – "because," as Rashi explains, "it is impossible to realize their honor sufficiently and he [i.e., the child] is punished therefore."[39] Differences between halakhic areas notwithstanding, however, it is clear

37. *Kiddushin* 21b.

38. Ibid. 31b.

39. S.v. *ashrei*. The punishment referred to is eventual divine retribution and not human sanction. It should be added that the remark should be understood in a limited sense – with respect to this factor regarded in isolation. It would be ludicrous to regard it as a summary assessment of filial relations generally. These occupy a central role within the Torah-halakhic *Weltanschauung* as a major positive force in both the development of personality and in spiritual education. The tendency to abstract an element from a complex situation and to focus upon it in isolation in order to highlight its significance recurs rather frequently in *Hazal*. One should be wary of mistaking such dicta for evaluations of the total situations from whose context an element may have been drawn. In this respect, their mode of expression is often closer to the late classical and medieval method of presenting qualities (or even characters as their exemplars) from one perspective at a time – Griselda, as Douglas Bush once noted, was a marvelous wife but a terrible mother – than to the modern insistence upon "round" characterization (to use E. M. Forster's term) and panoramic problematic. This is partly a question of style and partly a question of substance; but more the proper subject of a monograph than of a footnote.

that, taken as a whole, *din,* in its normative aspect, imposes an ethical dimension; that, governing private as well as interpersonal existence, it is concerned with the totality of moral being rather than being maximally confined, as is modern Western law generally, to social relations; that, imposing definitive obligations which lie beyond enforcement, it often bears a conscientious rather than a judicial aspect; that, in short, it includes much which, in terms of general modern usage, would be regarded as moral rather than legal.

Consequently, while the analogy to general law need not be rejected entirely, neither can we simply equate the relation of *din* to *lifnim mishurat hadin* with that of law to morals. *Din* constitutes an amalgam of legal, moral, and ritual statutes. Its relation to *lifnim mishurat hadin* should not, therefore, be defined with reference to general areas of application. It must rather be clarified in terms of the level at which they respectively relate to the same area.

IV. Distinguishing Between *Din* and *Lifnim Mishurat Hadin*

From this perspective, the primary distinction no doubt concerns the element of obligation. As popularly understood, the distinction is very simple: *din* is obligatory and *lifnim mishurat hadin* is not. The latter is widely regarded as an optional although not a neutral sphere – a kind of laborer's overtime or schoolboyish extra credit exercise translated, at a higher level, into pietistic virtue. Where *din* commands, *lifnim mishurat hadin* only beckons. All the more power to whoever responds; but there is nothing imperious or imperative about the call. Virtually by definition, we are here concerned with commendable volunteer effort – purely self-imposed and the very antithesis of obligation.

Properly understood, there is some truth to this contrast. Yet, baldly stated, it is thoroughly untenable – both theoretically erroneous and practically dangerous. For one thing, it does not do justice to the complexity of *din*. While *din* does ordinarily require or proscribe a particular action or emotion, its character, as has been noted, is by no means monochromatic. Primarily, however, so stark a contrast does violence to the concept of *lifnim mishurat hadin*. Insofar as it wholly extracts the sense of obligation from this area, it is ultimately false; and inasmuch as it operates with a simplistic conception of a complex phenomenon, it is rather misleading.

A glance at the three primary sources of *lifnim mishurat hadin* clearly establishes the fact that obligation is not wholly foreign to it. The first is adduced in a *baraita* found in the *Mekhilta* and twice cited, with minor variations, by the Gemara. Commenting upon a verse in which the Torah quotes – and implicitly accepts – Yitro's counsel to Moses,[40] the *Mekhilta* anatomizes and elaborates upon it:

> "And thou shalt instruct them the path" – this is the study of Torah; "and the action that they shall take" – this is good action. [These are] the words of R. Yehoshua.
>
> R. Eliezer of Modiin says: "And thou shalt instruct them" – teach them life's course;[41] "the path" – this is visiting the sick; "they shall walk" – this is burying the dead; "therein" – this is engaging in lovingkindness;[42] "and the action" – this is the line of *din*; "that they shall take" – this is *lifnim mishurat hadin*.[43]

Its inclusion within this catalogue clearly suggests that *lifnim mishurat hadin* is hardly a purely neutral or even an optional matter. This view is reinforced by the context within which the second source is presented – a story told by the Gemara of a specific incident of supralegal conduct. Some porters who were working for Rabba b. R. Huna broke a barrel

---

40. *Shemot* 18:20.

41. Literally, "the house of life." In *Bava Kamma* 100a, Rashi, s.v. *beit*, interprets this as "the study of Torah"; in *Bava Metzia* 30b, s.v. *zeh*, as "a trade by which to earn a living."

42. Of course, some of the activities mentioned previously come under this category of *gemilut hasadim*. It is, however, much more general and covers a myriad of other practical and emotional elements. See *Sukka* 49b and Rambam, *Hilkhot Evel* 14:1.

43. *Mekhilta DeRabbi Yishmael*, *Yitro*, sec. 2; *Mekhilta DeRabbi Shimon ben Yohai*, ed. J. N. Epstein and E. Z. Melamed (Jerusalem, 1955), 133. The verse cited is from *Shemot* 18:20. The citations in the Gemara are in *Bava Kamma* 99b–100a and *Bava Metzia* 30b. The Gemara only quotes R. Elazar's position, but this is not to suggest – as assumed by Rav Menahem Krakowski, *Avodat HaMelekh* (Vilna, 1931), *De'ot*, 1:5 – that for R. Yehoshua, *lifnim mishurat hadin* is optional. Obviously, the other matters cited by R. Elazar are not. The question is one of interpreting the verse.

of wine they were handling. Inasmuch as they had, as Rashi[44] explains, evidently been somewhat negligent, the strict letter of the law would have held them liable for the damage; and, since they had not performed their assigned task, allowed them no pay.[45] By way of guaranteeing their payment of the damage, Rabba held onto their garments – which had apparently been left in his possession – as surety; whereupon:

> They came and told Rav, [who, in turn,] told him, "Return their garments to them."
>
> "Is this the *din*?" he asked.
>
> "Yes," he answered – "'That thou mayest walk in the way of good men.'"
>
> He, then, returned their garments, whereupon they said to him, "We are poor, we have labored all day, and [now] we are hungry and left with nothing."
>
> [So] he said to him, "Go and pay their wages."
>
> "Is this the *din*?" he asked.
>
> "Yes," he answered – "'and keep the path of the righteous.'"[46]

While the term *lifnim mishurat hadin* is not specifically employed here, it is, broadly speaking, clearly the relevant category; and Rashi[47] did not hesitate to apply it. On this assumption, the fact that it was employed as the basis for deciding a case offers further evidence that an element of obligation may inhere in conduct *lifnim mishurat hadin*.

The third source, finally, is explicitly formulated – indeed, repeated – by the Torah proper: "And thou shalt do the right and the good in the eyes of the Lord, your God."[48] Within Halakha, this verse

44. *Bava Metzia* 83a, s.v. *shekulai*. If no negligence had been involved, they would not have been liable; see ibid. 82b–83a and *Bava Kamma* 99b.
45. If there was no gross negligence, the right to compensation may depend on whether they had been hired by the job or on the basis of time. Presumably, in this case, it was the former.
46. *Bava Metzia* 83a. The verse cited, in two sections, is from *Mishlei* 2:20.
47. Ibid., s.v. *bederekh*.
48. *Devarim* 6:18. Cf. ibid. 12:28, where the sequence is reversed; and see also ibid. 12:25, 13:19, 21:9, and *Shemot* 15:26.

has found varied applications. The Gemara cites it as the textual and conceptual basis for two supralegal practices which are virtually given legal status by the Rabbis: 1) that when land is being put up for sale, an abutter always has the first option to purchase it;[49] 2) that a debtor whose property was assigned to a creditor in payment of a debt may recover it at any time by producing the money he had owed.[50] The Raavad uses it to pass sweeping judgment upon a whole halakhic area, that of *yibbum* (levirate marriage) and *halitza* (loosing of the shoe).[51] Addressing himself to the question of which is preferable,[52] he argues for the latter – but for a singularly unusual reason. Citing Bar Kappara's statement, "Let one always stay away from three [things] and cleave to three"[53] – *halitza* being one of the latter group – he argues that it does not, as is generally assumed, define the legal order of precedence. It offers, instead, moral counsel, and actually represents the views of those who contend that, legally speaking, *yibbum* takes precedence: "Since he says, 'he should cleave' and 'he should stay away' [and does not use more imperative language], he is not speaking of the course of *din* but by way of 'the right and the good,' and even according to the first mishna [which had stated that *yibbum* takes precedence]."[54]

---

49. See *Bava Metzia* 108a.
50. See ibid. 35a.
51. A procedure, alternative to *yibbum*, through which the prospective *levir* would proclaim that he does not wish to marry his deceased brother's wife. In the course of the proceedings, she would remove his shoe; hence, the term *halitza*. See *Devarim* 25:7–10.
52. See *Bekhorot* 13a and *Yevamot* 39b.
53. *Yevamot* 109a.
54. *Hassagot* on Alfasi, *Ketubbot* 64a. The Raavad goes on to speak of *yibbum*, generally, as being a *mitzva meruheket be'eineihem*, i.e., one upon which the Rabbis looked askance, so that, morally speaking, all of them agreed that *halitza* was preferable. This presumably means that the view that *yibbum* takes precedence only states that the *levir* has the legal right to prefer it, not that he ought to do so. On the face of it, this position seems to be in direct contradiction to the account in the Torah and the procedure of *halitza* proper, from both of which it is self-evident that the *levir* is criticized for not entering upon *yibbum*. It must be assumed that the Raavad's remarks are confined to cases in which the widow is reluctant to go through with *yibbum*. If she is anxious for it, then this view – excepting, that is, Abba Shaul's position that *yibbum* is now to be shunned because the *levir* is often motivated by

Whatever the specific application, however, the import of the principle is clear. It was most fully articulated by the Ramban. After suggesting a more strictly literal rendering of "the right and the good" as the collective body of specific mitzvot, he presents an alternative:

> And our Rabbis[55] have a fine interpretation of this. They said: "This refers to compromise and *lifnim mishurat hadin*."[56] The intent of this is that, initially,[57] He said that you should observe His laws and statutes which He has commanded you. Now He says that with respect to what He has not commanded you, likewise, take heed to do the good and the right in His eyes, for He loves the good and the right. And this is a great matter. For it is impossible to mention in the Torah all of a person's actions toward his neighbors and acquaintances, all his commercial activity, and all the institutions of society and states. So after He had mentioned many of them such as [in stating], "Thou shalt not go about as a tale-bearer," "Thou shalt not take vengeance nor bear any grudge," "Thou shalt not stand idly by the blood of thy neighbor," "Thou shalt not curse the deaf," "Thou shalt rise up before age,"[58] and the like, He resumes to say generally that one should do the good and the right in all matters, to the point that there are included in this compromise, *lifnim mishurat hadin*, and [matters] similar to that which they [i.e., the Rabbis] mentioned concerning the law of the abutter – even that which they said, "whose youth had been unblemished"[59] or "he converses with

---

sexual passion rather than the desire to perform the mitzva and help preserve the family of his deceased brother – would regard *yibbum* as preferable. See also the Ramban's critique in *Sefer HaZekhut*, ad loc.

55. In his edition of the Ramban's commentary – *Perush HaRamban Al HaTorah* (Jerusalem, 1960), II, 376n. – C. B. Chavel notes that no extant source of this comment is known.

56. Rashi, *Devarim* 6:18, comments, "This is compromise *lifnim mishurat hadin*," omitting the conjunction. This reading – he is presumably quoting the same source the Ramban cites – narrows the scope of the remark considerably.

57. I.e., in the preceding verse, *Devarim* 6:17.

58. The verses cited are from *Vayikra* 19:16, 18, 16, 14, and 32, respectively.

59. *Taanit* 16a.

> people with gentleness,"[60] so that he is regarded as perfect and right in all matters.[61]

The substance and tone of the passage speak for themselves. And they clearly leave little question about the imperative character of *lifnim mishurat hadin.*

The difference from *din* does not concern, then, the very existence of obligation. It revolves, rather, around its rigor. This, in turn, involves two major distinctions, corresponding to two senses of "rigor." In one sense, the issue is the quality and degree of obligation. Generally speaking, of course – and this *is* virtually by definition – the imperative force of *din* exceeds that of *lifnim mishurat hadin.* While the element of duty is common to both, one ordinarily says "you must," the other, "you should" – hardly an inconsequential difference. The extent of this difference may vary considerably, however. The imperative thrust of *din* is reasonably constant. That of *lifnim mishurat hadin* is not. Its variety may be traced back to the very definition of the area. It is, in a very real sense, negatively defined. With respect, at least, to the objective actions required by it, *din* can be readily described as a specific moral station. *Lifnim mishurat hadin,* however, is simply something above this. It is, therefore, not one station but many; and inasmuch as it has a floor but no ceiling, their number can be almost unlimited. Hence, it is better regarded as a spectrum rather than a designated level. The characteristically specific and frequently absolute injunctions of *din* constitute a minimal mandatory bedrock of religious existence. It is not minimal in the sense of being barely adequate for civilized and humane life. Insofar as it incorporates so many rigorous, almost ideal, demands, one cannot say of *din* in the same vein as Lord Devlin has said of general law that "the law is concerned with the minimum and not the maximum .... We all recognize the gap between the moral law and the law of the land."[62] Nevertheless, relative to the Torah's ultimate ideal, *din* does represent the lowest rung on the ladder; and if this minimal level is, by ordinary

60. *Yoma* 86a.
61. *Devarim* 6:18.
62. *The Enforcement of Morals* (Oxford, 1965), 19.

standards, quite high, the principle underlying Lord Devlin's comment is still fully applicable. *Din* "is concerned with the minimum and not the maximum." It defines, therefore, a designated level. Beyond it, there stretches a scale ranging from the slightest increment upon *din* to the highest reaches of moral and spiritual existence.

The implications for the question of comparative obligation are fairly obvious. The imperative element in *din* is reasonably static; that of *lifnim mishurat hadin* varies considerably. It varies in inverse proportion to the spiritual elevation. The more demanding a course of action, the less forcefully it can be demanded. The more pedestrian a supralegal act, the greater the duty to perform it, realization being less of an achievement than omission is a fault. The further we ascend, on the other hand, the more persistence becomes truly noble but failure unstigmatic, increasingly to be regarded as a shortcoming rather than malfeasance – and the call to persevere ever less insistent. But it is never wholly silent.

A useful analogue is provided by Professor Fuller's discussion of "two moralities," those of aspiration and duty, respectively. The one "is the morality of the Good Life, of excellence, of the fullest realization of human powers"[63] – in short (although Fuller does not use the term), of *arête*. The other is concerned with the imperative need for fundamental goods. "Where the morality of aspiration starts at the top of human achievement, the morality of duty starts at the bottom. It lays down the basic rules without which an ordered society is impossible, or without which an ordered society directed toward certain specific goals must fail of its mark."[64] Adapting a figure from Adam Smith, Fuller suggests that "the morality of duty 'may be compared to the rules of grammar'; the morality of aspiration 'to the rules which critics lay down for the attainment of what is sublime and elegant in composition.'"[65] The one sets its sights lower and exerts the pressure of demands. The other aims higher and simply posits "the challenge of excellence."

For my purposes, Fuller's discussion is obviously quite relevant; and it is brought closer to home by his suggestion that the respective

63. Lon L. Fuller, *The Morality of Law* (New Haven, 1964), 5.
64. Ibid., 5–6.
65. Ibid., 6.

moralities are archetypally Hellenic and Judaic. "The morality of aspiration is most plainly exemplified in Greek philosophy.... Generally with the Greeks, instead of ideas of right and wrong, of moral claim and moral duty, we have rather the conception of proper and fitting conduct, conduct such as beseems a human being functioning at his best."[66] The morality of duty, by contrast, "is the morality of the Old Testament and the Ten Commandments. It speaks in terms of 'thou shalt not,' and, less frequently, 'thou shalt.'"[67] Taken as historical judgments, these generalizations are open to serious question. Certainly, if one looks to Greek culture as a whole – to Sophocles as well as Socrates, to the *Eumenides* as well as the *Eudemian Ethics* – "ideas of right and wrong, of moral claim and moral duty" do exert a powerful pull; and, as evidenced by Stoicism particularly, Fuller's assertion is by no means definitive even as regards the philosophers. Moreover, the implication that "the morality of aspiration" is alien or, at least, peripheral to the Bible and hence to Judaism as a whole, is unfounded (as I hope this essay will make clear).

Historical judgments aside, however, I am more concerned with the substance of Fuller's argument, particularly with his premises. *Prima facie*, the two moralities clearly parallel *din* and *lifnim mishurat hadin*. Beyond this, as I have already suggested and shall argue presently, they may correspond to different areas of *lifnim mishurat hadin* proper. To this extent, Fuller's description of the respective characters of the two moralities is most helpful. I must part company with him, however, over the question of their relations. Fuller does not quite regard them as antithetical. He acknowledges, indeed, that "in a morality of aspiration there may be overtones of a notion approaching that of duty." He goes on to submit, however, that "these overtones are usually muted, as they are in Plato and Aristotle,"[68] and underlying the whole discussion is the assumption that while a single individual or culture may operate with both moralities, applying them to different areas, there is not fruitful interaction between the two. He argues, in fact, that there *ought* to be no interaction. "If the morality of duty reaches upward beyond its

66. Ibid., 5.
67. Ibid., 6.
68. Ibid., 5.

proper sphere the iron hand of imposed obligation may stifle experiment, inspiration, and spontaneity."[69]

This is a dichotomy which the Halakha must reject. For the Jew, aspiration is itself a duty. The quest for excellence is not just humanistic striving for self-realization but a moral and religious obligation. The concept of "the challenge of excellence" and a sense of the ideal man are of fundamental importance in Judaism. They do not, as is sometimes imagined, enter via the back door of Wisdom literature or the Hellenic streak Shadal and his school have presumed to see in the Rambam. They are present, *ab initio,* in God's command to Abraham, "Walk before Me, and be perfect (*tamim*)."[70] The perfection involved is not, of course, identical with the Greek ideal. The Hebrew *tamim*[71] includes elements of simplicity, perhaps even naiveté, absent from *arête* or the even more manly *virtu.* Be this as it may, however, the verse does issue a call to excellence – and it issues it as a command. This is, likewise, the burden of other overarching commandments – "Be ye holy," "Sanctify yourselves and be holy, for I am the Lord, your God," "And thou shalt walk in His ways," or "And thou shalt do the right and the good."[72] Even when he is not responding to a specific directive, the Jew says with the psalmist, "I

69. Ibid., 27–28.
70. *Bereshit* 17:1.
71. The relevance of this text to my argument depends on interpreting the word *tamim* along the general lines of the Sforno's comment: "And attain the maximal perfection achievable by mankind, [i.e.,] understanding and knowing Me through the knowledge of My ways and in resembling Me as far as possible." This sense of general personal excellence is conveyed by the Septuagint's *amemptos* and the Vulgate's *perfectus*. It is also clearly assumed – although partially applied, with reference to circumcision, to physical as well as spiritual perfection – by the various comments made in *Nedarim* 31b–32a, one of which Rashi cites here in paraphrase. However, Ibn Ezra and the Ramban – and, although less forcefully, Rashi himself – interpret the term in a much narrower sense: having unquestioning faith in and placing total reliance upon God. The first sense is closer to the root and most common meaning in *Humash* – "physically unblemished," but the second is more consonant with the context of a very similar passage in *Devarim* 18:13; see also the Ramban's comment there. In any event, my argument does not stand or fall with the relevance of this text.
72. *Vayikra* 19:1 and 20:7, *Devarim* 28:9 and 6:18, respectively.

have set the Lord as always before me";[73] and he strives for excellence in relation to a commanding presence. He exists, in the words of the greatest of "Hebraic" Gentile poets, "As ever in my great task-Master's eye";[74] and this normative awareness impels his total spiritual being, making the drive toward perfection itself a matter of duty.

This is not to dismiss the validity or the value of Fuller's distinction. The two moralities do differ in essential respects. The degree of obligation attendant upon them varies. Their specific demands vary. Their psychological contexts vary. No Wordsworthian is likely to confuse the mood of the *Ode to Duty* with that of *The Prelude*. The point is, however, that there is no need to divorce the two. While acknowledging that their specific implementation and orientation differs, the halakhist – as, from a different perspective, the Kantian – sees the one as, at bottom, motivated by the other.

V. The Rambam's Approach

In developing this exposition, Professor Fuller perceptively suggests that "as we consider the whole range of moral issues, we may conveniently imagine a kind of scale or yardstick which begins at the bottom with the most obvious demands of social living and extends upward to the highest reaches of human aspiration. Somewhere along this scale there is an invisible pointer that marks the dividing line where the pressure of duty leaves off and the challenge of excellence begins. The whole field of moral argument is dominated by a great undeclared war over the location of this pointer."[75] I have earlier suggested that it does not – or rather, does not always – coincide with the border between din and *lifnim mishurat hadin*, but rather frequently lies within the sphere of the latter. This assertion needs to be examined, however, with reference to basic halakhic texts.

The Ramban, in his treatment of the "right and the good" as well as in his exposition of "ye shall be holy," clearly assumed this. In neither

73. *Tehillim* 16:8.
74. Milton, "Sonnet: How Soon Hath Time...."
75. Fuller, *The Morality of Law*, 9–10.

discussion does he regard *lifnim mishurat hadin* as simply *middat hasidut*, a superior degree of pious virtue. In the one, he delineates a whole spectrum of activities, clearly suggesting that some are as inherently worthwhile or reprehensible as certain aspects of *din*, except that the Torah simply could not set down everything in exhaustive detail.[76] In the other, he implies that by eschewing *lifnim mishurat hadin* completely, one may become a "scoundrel with the Torah's license."

It would appear, however, that the Rambam took a radically different approach. He defined the concept in relation to the ideal of the "golden mean":

> Every person whose dispositions are all median and mean is called wise. And whoever is particularly scrupulous with respect to himself and deviates a bit from the median disposition, in one direction or the other, is called a *hasid*.[77] For instance, whoever avoids haughtiness to the utmost extent and becomes exceedingly meek, is called a *hasid*; and this is a quality of saintliness (*middat hasidut*). If he only avoids it as far as the mean, he is called wise,

76. The Ramban, of course, speaks only of the inherent character of these activities. With respect to those who have been commanded, the very fact that an action has been proscribed or required may now affect its worth.
77. I know of no English term which could render this term adequately. The attribute of *hasidut* can be fairly accurately translated as "saintliness," though perhaps more in the Jamesian than in the popular sense of total selflessness and/or otherworldliness. As a *nomen agentis*, however, "saint" is too ethereal. It has, moreover, hagiolatrous associations which make many a Jew see red. "Pietist" is perhaps more accurate inasmuch as it catches the scrupulosity which, as opposed to some of the antinomian impulses of early modern Hasidism, is central to the term in *Hazal*. In contemporary usage, it is, however, quite cold. It sounds more like a denominational affiliation than a personal characterization.

    It might be noted, finally, that while the term *hasidut* always has favorable overtones – it is sometimes even described as the highest spiritual stratum short of prophecy; see *Avoda Zara* 20b – *hasid* occasionally has negative connotations. It sometimes suggests an over-scrupulous concern, marked by a trace of priggishness and partially rooted in ignorance, for meticulous observance even when special circumstances make it halakhically unwarranted. See *Shabbat* 63a and 121b and *Sota* 21b. Generally, however, it has very positive meaning; see Kasowski, *Otzar Leshon HaTalmud*, XIV, 650–51.

> and this is a quality of wisdom. Likewise, with regard to other dispositions. The early *hasidim*[78] would turn their dispositions away from the exact mean toward the extremes. They would turn one disposition toward the last bound [i.e., excess] and another toward the first [i.e., restraint]; and this is *lifnim mishurat hadin.*[79]

The Rambam here is clearly dealing with a rare and rarefied spiritual quality. *Lifnim mishurat hadin* is explicitly identified with *middat hasidut* and regarded as a stratum of supreme moral existence, a lofty pinnacle attained by only a select few. No tinge of duty is attendant upon it; and whatever the merits of those who meet its challenge, certainly no shadow whatsoever is cast upon those who eschew it and adhere to *din* alone. This is made crystal clear by the remarks with which the passage continues:

> We are commanded to walk in these median paths and they are the good and right paths, as it is said, "And thou shalt walk in His ways."[80] Thus have [the Rabbis] taught in explanation of this mitzva: "As He is called gracious, so you be gracious; as He is called merciful, so you be merciful; as He is called holy, so you be holy."[81] And in this manner, the prophets have described the Almighty by all those attributes, "long-suffering, abounding in kindness, righteous and upright, perfect, mighty and powerful," and the like, in order to teach that these are good and right ways and a person is obligated to train himself in them and to imitate [the ways of God] to the best of his ability.... And inasmuch as the attributes by which the Creator is called constitute the median path in which we are obligated to walk, this path is

78. A term used in the Gemara – see especially *Berakhot* 32b and *Nedarim* 10b – for an especially elite group (even among the *hasidim*) marked by unusual and almost legendary piety. Here it does not seem to refer to any specific group but generally to individual predecessors, presumably among *Hazal,* who had worked hard at developing character.
79. *Hilkhot De'ot* 1:4–5.
80. *Devarim* 28:9.
81. *Shabbat* 133b and *Sifre, Ekev,* 49 (on *Devarim* 11:22, but without the equation regarding holiness).

> called "the path of God." It is that which our patriarch Abraham taught his children, as it is said, "For I have minded him because he will command [his children and his household after him, that they may keep the way of God, doing charity and justice];"[82] and whosoever walks in this path brings happiness and blessing upon himself, as it is said, "In order that God may bring upon Abraham that which He had spoken concerning him."[83]

Obviously, there is here no chasm between *din* and "the right and the good" which action *lifnim mishurat hadin* must transcend.

Indeed, in an earlier parallel passage, the Rambam went even further. In the passage I have quoted from *Mishneh Torah*, *lifnim mishurat hadin* is devoid of the pressure of duty; but, where pursued, it does seem to be invested with an inherent positive character. The impression conveyed by a similar discussion in *Shemona Perakim*, the preface to the commentary on *Avot*, is that even this is highly uncertain. In a chapter which is tellingly titled, "Of the Cures of the Soul's Diseases," the Rambam opens with an account of the mean as ideal and proceeds to describe the steps to be taken if one falls short of it. First, he argues that where one has strayed in one direction, genuine balance cannot be attained by aiming at the moderation which is ultimately desired. The corrective must include a radical swing toward the other extreme, so that the pendulum will eventually arrive at dead center. In the same vein he suggests – as had Aristotle[84] in a similar context – that inasmuch as natural inclination usually produces either deficiency or excess, rather than aim at the mean proper *ab initio*, it is better to deviate a bit counter to the natural list so that one is thus assured that the combination of conscience and inclination will keep him pretty much on target. "And for this reason," he continues, "the *hasidim* would not maintain the position of their souls in precise equilibrium, but they would, rather, turn

82. *Bereshit* 18:19.

83. *Hilkhot De'ot* 1:5–7. The last verse cited is the second half of the preceding.

84. *Nicomachean Ethics*, II, 9; 1109a–b. One should avoid, however, any facile overall equation of the Rambam's position with Aristotle's. The Rambam's focus is *imitatio actorum Dei* rather than the pursuit of *eudaimonia*.

slightly toward excess or deficiency by way of prevention and safeguard. I mean, for instance, that they would deviate slightly from temperance toward abstinence from sensual pleasure; from fortitude toward risking danger; from generosity toward its excess; from humility toward meekness; and so on, with respect to other qualities. This is what they intended when they spoke of *lifnim mishurat hadin*."[85] Here it would appear that the ultimate ideal – even for the *hasidim* – is the mean. *Lifnim mishurat hadin* is simply a stratagem to assure its attainment. In *Mishneh Torah*, the Rambam reversed himself. There, I think it is clear that *middat hasidut* is radically different from the Ramban's. It belongs wholly to the "morality of aspiration."

As regards the semantic definition of *lifnim mishurat hadin*, the difference is fundamental. As such, it has important implications for the interpretation of passages in which the term appears; and we shall have occasion to note some of these subsequently. As regards, however, attitudes toward ethical conduct, it is, in large measure, illusory. If we think in terms of the conventional definition of the term – supererogatory conduct going beyond what the specific letter of the law explicitly requires – the Rambam would find himself in very substantial agreement with the Ramban. For the Rambam's definition is presented in conjunction with what might be described as a radical expansion of *din* proper. Much, perhaps most, of what the Ramban included under "the right and the good" and which he, and popular usage after him, identified with *lifnim mishurat hadin*, is, for the Rambam, subsumed under the rubric of an absolutely obligatory mitzva: *Vehalakhta biderakhav*, "And thou shalt walk in His ways." The pursuit of equity, the implementation of social justice, the dispensation of kindness, the generation of love, the preservation of dignity – all are integral aspects of *imitatio actorum Dei*. The details have not all been explicitly recorded; and in this respect, this mitzva differs somewhat from what is conventionally regarded as *din*. The overarching goals have, however, been clearly defined. The Rambam specifically singles out three – kindness, charity, and justice, ideals to whose exposition he was to return in the semi-devotional conclusion of

85. Ch. 4.

the *Moreh Nevukhim.*[86] And there is nothing optional about their pursuit. It is a matter of highest duty. No doubt, here too we might think in terms of a moral scale and "two moralities." But again, the aspiration itself is imbued with duty.

The Rambam therefore had no need to apply the term *lifnim mishurat hadin* to supralegal conduct, narrowly conceived. He applied it, instead, to the extraordinary cultivation of supernal virtue. Moreover, he speaks of it not so much in relation to laws as with respect to personal traits. Its ethical context is more psychological than legal. The line that is being crossed defines a virtue rather than a right or an obligation. The result is a rather unusual definition of the term; but we should make no mistake about the practical issues. As regards ultimate guidelines for supererogatory conduct, there is no reason to assume any major divergence from the position later formulated by the Ramban. Both postulate a number of broadly defined ethical ideals whose realization is incumbent upon the Jew – the one deriving the obligation from "And thou shalt walk in His ways," the other from "And thou shalt do the right and the good in the eyes of the Lord." This difference between a theological and a moral focus is itself perhaps significant.[87] It should not be mistaken, however, for what it is not. There is no basis for assuming major disagreement over the character and scope of actual conduct in this area of Halakha.

VI. Five Talmudic Cases of *Lifnim Mishurat Hadin*

The Rambam's conception of *lifnim mishurat hadin* – oriented to virtues rather than to laws, elitist and perhaps even wholly voluntary – is quite singular. True, other *Rishonim* recognized *hasidut* as an integral aspect of *lifnim mishurat hadin*. Thus, Rabbenu Yona, in a passage which may very well echo the Rambam, touches on both the elitist element and on the relation to virtues. Commenting on the Mishna's statement, "Nor can

86. III, 53.

87. Of course, insofar as it deals with that which is right and good "in the eyes of the Lord," the Ramban's source also has a theological focus. Nevertheless, a difference in emphasis clearly exists.

the *am haaretz*[88] be a *hasid*," he explains that this is because *hasidut* "is a quality which requires purity of heart and wholesomeness of soul and he [i.e., the *am haaretz*] does not possess the wisdom to turn him from the median line toward the yonder end [in order] to act *lifnim mishurat hadin*."[89] They did not, however, define the essence and scope of *lifnim mishurat hadin* in terms of *middat hasidut* alone. Their treatments are not generally of a systematic character, as the Gemara nowhere presents a thorough analysis of the concept. It cites, instead, a number of specific applications; and *Rishonim*'s views must generally be gleaned from comments upon these. A brief survey of these cases leads, I believe, to two conclusions. First, as compared to the Rambam's definition, the concept of *lifnim mishurat hadin* is generally given greater latitude, relating to laws as well as virtues and allowing for elements of duty and aspiration both. Second, as regards the degree of obligation attendant upon particular cases – the location of Fuller's invisible pointer – there are, not unexpectedly, differences of attitude and emphasis.

The Gemara ascribes *lifnim mishurat hadin* to five isolated incidents. One concerns a sale involving R. Papa. He had purchased land from a seller who had expected to use the proceeds to buy some oxen. He was subsequently unable to do so, whereupon R. Papa returned the property.[90] While the incident may shed some light on the mode of *lifnim mishurat hadin*, *Rishonim* ignored it; and with obvious reason. This interpretation of R. Papa's action was advanced in the Gemara's discussion at a point at which it was assumed that cancellation of the sale was not required by *din* proper. Inasmuch as the Gemara subsequently reverses itself, concluding that the seller has a legal right to invalidate the transaction, its previous explanation is superseded.[91]

88. In current usage, this term usually refers to an ignorant person, especially one ignorant of traditional texts. In *Hazal*, however, it often refers to either the religiously unobservant or to persons generally lacking in culture and civility. See Greenspan, *Mishpat Am HaAretz*, ch. 1.

89. *Avot* 2:5.

90. See *Ketubbot* 97a.

91. The incident may yet be relevant, however, if one assumes – as did *Tosafot* (ibid., s.v. *zavin*), the Rambam (*Hilkhot Mekhira* 11:8), and many other *Rishonim* – that the sale can be invalidated only if the seller mentioned his motivation at the time of

A second incident, again involving R. Papa, is concerned with an aspect of *zimmun* – the halakha that when three or more people eat together, they should participate in a collective *Birkat HaMazon* (grace after meals) at its conclusion. After citing a *baraita* to the effect that "if three ate together, one interrupts [his meal] for the sake of two [who have finished eating and want to recite *Birkat HaMazon*], but two do not interrupt [their meals] for the sake of one," the Gemara asks: "But did not R. Papa, along with another [person], interrupt for his son, Abba Mar?" The answer given is that "R. Papa had acted *lifnim mishurat hadin*"[92] – in order, as Rashi[93] explains, to give his son status.

Amongst *Rishonim*, we encounter three distinct approaches to this text. Rav Moshe of Coucy, author of the *Sefer Mitzvot Gadol*,[94] generalizes from the incident, evidently regarding it as something which can be normatively set down as that which everyone should do, although one is not obligated to do so. "Although," he writes, "according to *din*, two do not [i.e., according to the Gemara, two are not expected to interrupt their meals for the sake of one], nevertheless, *lifnim mishurat hadin*, they [should] interrupt their meals and join with him in *zimmun* until [the end of the blessing of] *hazan*, as R. Papa, and another with him, did for someone."[95] Several other *Rishonim* glance at R. Papa's action, but do not suggest that one should emulate him, only that one may. Thus, the Me'iri

the sale, although he did not make it conditional. Rashi (ibid., s.v. *zavin*) assumed, however, that no such mention is necessary, so long as the motivation is publicly clear.

92. *Berakhot* 45b. My discussion here assumes Rashi's interpretation of the text – namely, that the issue is interruption of one's meal so that the other(s) may recite *Birkat HaMazon*. For a possible alternative, see *Kesef Mishneh, Hilkhot Berakhot* 7:6. Even in Rashi's view, however, the person who interrupts may resume his meal after participating in one blessing while the other(s) recite(s) the rest.

93. S.v. *lifnim*.

94. A thirteenth-century halakhic compendium, a product of the Franco-German school and incorporating many *tosafot*. This work is somewhat neglected today but was a staple of halakhic study until the eighteenth century and it exerted an enormous influence upon the early commentaries upon the *Shulhan Arukh*.

95. *Mitzvot Aseh*, 27. I have translated the term *posekim* as "should interrupt." Grammatically, it is an indicative form, but, depending upon the context, very often has a measure of imperative force.

states that "if they wish to give up their honor and to interrupt for him, they may do so."[96] "We had only said," the *Shitta Mekubbetzet* explains, "that two are not obligated to interrupt for one, but if they want, they can do it, and they fulfill the duty of *zimmun*."[97] This group was evidently troubled by the possibility that the two *could* not interrupt in order to accommodate their fellow and then continue eating. Perhaps *zimmun* is only valid if a majority of the three-man complement actually goes on to recite the whole of *Birkat HaMazon* at the time.[98] Hence, they felt compelled to state that this may be done. As to the merit of doing it, they are wholly silent, however.

A third group – instructively, consisting of *posekim* as well as commentators – ignores the incident completely. Apart from talmudic commentaries, which are of course frequently selective, it is omitted by a number of the generally more comprehensive *posekim*. The Rif, Rambam,[99] *Shibbolei HaLeket*,[100] *Orhot Hayim*,[101] or, for that matter, the *Shulhan Arukh*[102] and its commentaries, all cite the basic halakha but make no reference to the element of *lifnim mishurat hadin*. Their silence is best explained on the assumption that, unlike the *Semag*, they did not regard R. Papa's action as a universal paradigm which could be set down in normative or even strongly hortatory terms. Possibly, this is because there may have been some special factors involved. More likely, however, it is because the degree of forbearance involved simply lies beyond the pale of obligation and, even at the level of *lifnim mishurat hadin*, is not to be set down as a general demand. It belongs to the realm of aspiration rather than of duty.

---

96. *Beit HaBehira*, *Berakhot* 45b.
97. *Berakhot* 45b.
98. We do encounter applications of the concept of majority to *zimmun* elsewhere. See *Berakhot* 48a and commentaries, ad loc.
99. *Hilkhot Berakhot* 7:6.
100. Sec. 150.
101. *Birkat HaMazon*, 32.
102. OH 200:1. In this connection, it should be noted that the Rosh, *Berakhot* 7:7, cites a controversy between Rashi and Rabbenu Yona as to whether the obligation of the solitary eater to interrupt is a matter of propriety and courtesy or is a matter of strict law. This might have some implications for the nature of *lifnim mishurat hadin* here; see *Bah*, OH 200.

With respect to this question, it may be suggested that some distinction should be made, depending upon the situation. Rashi explains that R. Papa acted in order to accord some status to his son. Understandably, this may not be regarded as a matter of general duty. Thus, the Raavya writes that "two do not interrupt for one, and if they wish to honor him, they may interrupt"[103] – treating the honor as a largely voluntary matter. However, if the question is not purely honorific but, say, the third one is anxious to leave – for the moment, he is locked in, as he is obligated to participate in *zimmun* but cannot proceed until they join him – the need to treat others with kindness would certainly inject an element of obligation. If the interruption would not inconvenience them, the two are, as shall become clear later, absolutely bound to stop. Even if it would inconvenience them in slight measure, however, one senses that *lifnim mishurat hadin* here should be regarded as a matter of duty.

This case involves the interaction of ritual obligation, on the one hand, and of the niceties of courtesy – itself, in a sense, a halakhic category – on the other. A third incident is rooted in the complexities of commercial life. The halakha is that if an amateur is consulted about a question and offers an incorrect opinion, he is liable for whatever financial losses result from his error. Inasmuch as he lacked the proper qualifications, he had no business proffering advice in the first place, and is therefore held responsible for its consequences. However, a professional who unwittingly offers wrong advice is not liable. His mistake is simply ascribed to the possibility of error extant in every fallible human judgment – one which whoever consults him must inevitably accept. Nevertheless, the Gemara recounts that R. Hiyya, although professionally qualified to judge coins, reimbursed a person who had shown him currency which he certified but which turned out to be counterfeit; and it explains that he had acted *lifnim mishurat hadin.*[104]

Here, again, we find different approaches. The Rif and the Rosh[105] cite the incident without comment – suggesting by this kind of silence that some trace of duty exists here, the text being not merely narrative

---

103. Sec. 124.
104. See *Bava Kamma* 99b.
105. *Bava Kamma,* 9:16.

but in some sense normative. The Rambam,[106] however – again, not surprisingly – omits it, as do the *Tur* and the *Shulhan Arukh*.[107] The Me'iri infers from it but in a somewhat qualified way: "Nevertheless, it is fitting (*ra'uy*) for scholars (*talmidei hakhamim*) and men of [right] action (*anshei maaseh*) to pay for any loss which results from their statement and to deal with other people *lifnim mishurat hadin*."[108] Somewhat in the same vein, the Maharshal quotes the incident and comments: "And this is a *middat hasidut*."[109] The elitist element is wholly absent, however, from Rabbenu Hananel's formulation: "And although this is the halakha [i.e., that a professional is not liable], if he saw a coin and erred and it turned out to be counterfeit, he should exchange it, *lifnim mishurat hadin*."[110] This unqualified statement clearly seems to express an element of general duty.

Two more cases, finally, concern two cognate mitzvot – that of retrieving and returning lost property and that of helping someone load goods on and unload goods from an animal. One deals with the halakha, formulated with regard to both of these – that "an elder for whom it would not be in accordance with his dignity" to perform the mitzva is exempt. Nevertheless, the Gemara states that, although he fell in this category, R. Yishmael b. R. Yose helped unload goods from an animal; and it explains that he did so *lifnim mishurat hadin*.[111] In this instance, virtually all *posekim*[112] take note of the incident; but again, the degree

106. See *Hilkhot Sekhirut* 10:5.

107. See *Hoshen Mishpat* 306:6.

108. *Beit HaBehira, Bava Kamma* 99b.

109. *Yam Shel Shlomo, Bava Kamma*, 9:24.

110. Quoted in *Or Zarua*, sec. 407.

111. See *Bava Metzia* 30a–b. While the incident deals with unloading, it obviously has equal implications for returning lost property; and it is primarily in that connection that *posekim* discussed it.

112. The sole significant exception is the *Tur*, HM 263, who omits it. The *Beit Yosef* there notes that his omission is probably due to the fact that he accepted the view of his father, the Rosh, that, inasmuch as the Torah has exempted him, an elder perhaps has no right to degrade his person. If he wishes to act *lifnim mishurat hadin*, he should rather give the loser the value of the object as a gift. Subsequently, however – with respect to loading and unloading, in *Hoshen Mishpat* 272 – the *Tur* quotes both his father's and the Rambam's opposing views. This may be due to the fact that

of obligation they attach to it differs. The *Or Zarua* injects a fairly strong imperative note: "And if he [i.e., the finder] is a conscientious person, although it is below his dignity, and although he has not yet started handling it, he is obligated (*mihayev*) to [retrieve it] because of 'that they shall do' – this is *lifnim mishurat hadin*."[113] The Me'iri's formulation is somewhat milder: "Although we have relaxed the whip so that any one for whom it is beneath his dignity is not bound to return [an *aveda*] or to help unload or load, nevertheless it is fitting (*ra'uy*) for every person to treat himself with levity in these matters and to enter into the perfection of virtues *lifnim mishurat hadin*."[114] Still milder is the statement of a fourteenth-century contemporary, a student of the Rashba: "Although we have stated that an elder for whom it is not in accordance with his dignity is not obligated, according to *din*, to retrieve [an *aveda*], whoever gives up his honor and acts *lifnim mishurat hadin* and returns [it] even when this is below his dignity – may blessings come upon him."[115]

In light of what we have observed previously, the Rambam's formulation is of particular interest: "He who walks in the path of the good and the right and acts *lifnim mishurat hadin* [should(?)] return(s) an *aveda* everywhere, although it is not in accordance with his dignity."[116] This statement is strikingly similar to a parallel passage dealing with the mitzva of coming to the aid of someone who is loading or unloading his goods. There, the Rambam states: "And if he was a *hasid* and [one

there, apart from the owner's monetary loss, problems of the animal's comfort and perhaps even the owner's safety also exist. Hence, the Rambam's position is stronger. It might be added that the *Shulhan Arukh* – HM 263:3 and 272:3 – accepts the Rambam's view but that, in both cases, the Rama cites the Rosh's alternative view in a gloss. It should also be noted, finally, that the criterion of degradation is, in large measure, relative. It depends upon what one would be willing to do to save one's own property, and would obviously be much different in a democratic society and in an aristocratic one.

113. Sec. 84.

114. *Beit HaBehira, Bava Metzia* 30b.

115. *Piskei Talmid HaRashba*, in *Shittat HaKadmonim, Bava Metzia*, ed. M. Y. Blau (New York, 1967), 86.

116. *Hilkhot Gezela* 11:17. It is noteworthy that here and ibid., 11:7, the Rambam associates the "right and the good" with *lifnim mishurat hadin*. In *Hilkhot De'ot* 1:5, he uses these adjectives to describe the ideal mean.

who] acts *lifnim mishurat hadin*, even if he was the greatest leader, and he saw his fellow's animal sagging beneath its load of hay or reeds and the like, he unloads and loads with him."[117] I think the passages are open to two interpretations, depending on whether the key verbs – *mahzir* or *porek veto'en* – are understood in descriptive or prescriptive terms. The Rambam may simply be stating that this is the way a person of superior virtue acts, thus implicitly praising the action by pointing out the model but without actually demanding or even exhorting. Alternatively, he may be saying that those who have attained this lofty station actually should – perhaps even must – act in this manner. The underlying principle here may be the concept that responsibility is a function of spiritual attainment. The more accomplished the individual, in a moral and religious sense, the greater his obligations. Thus, while the area of its specific application may vary, the pressure of duty – in normative, although not necessarily in psychological, terms – never evaporates. The standard to which a person is held accountable simply rises. "You only have I known of all the families of the earth; therefore I will visit upon you all your iniquities."[118] Or, as the Rabbis put it, "The Holy One, blessed be He, is scrupulous to the point of hair's breadth [in dealing] with those close to Him."[119] Hence, what is relatively optional for the ordinary man may become a matter of duty for his moral superior.

The difference between these two interpretations is significant. On either reading, however, the Rambam's formulations are poles removed from the *Or Zarua*'s or the Me'iri's. They are, however, consonant with the Rambam's general conception of *lifnim mishurat hadin*. They are essentially concerned with select rather than mass behavior. Indeed, it is entirely possible that the Rambam only commends such action, implicitly or explicitly, as part of a total effort to rise to greater spiritual heights. As an isolated effort inconsistent with one's overall mien, it might actually be discouraged as a mark of vain self-righteousness. In addition, while the passages deal immediately with the

117. *Hilkhot Rotze'ah* 13:4. The "greatest leader" refers to either a king or the head of the Sanhedrin.

118. *Amos* 3:2.

119. *Bava Kamma* 50a.

heightened performance of specific mitzvot, they are couched in terms which, even according to the second interpretation, simultaneously focus upon the development of attributes and the chiseling of a spiritual *gestalt*.

The last case, finally, also concerns *hashavat aveda*, returning a lost item. "Shmuel's father," the Gemara recounts, "found some donkeys in the wilderness and returned them to their owner, after twelve months, *lifnim mishurat hadin*."[120] Rashi[121] – evidently assuming that by the time a year has elapsed the owner has presumably abandoned hope, thus relieving the finder of the obligation to retrieve it – explains the object was found after twelve months. *Tosafot*[122] reject this premise and, therefore, are driven to relate this incident to another halakha. The *din* is that any *aveda*, e.g., an animal, which both produces and consumes, and whose owner has not yet appeared, must be kept for a year, at the end of which the finder may sell it and hold the proceeds for the owner.[123] Shmuel's father, however, undertook to bother with the donkeys beyond the required time.

On either reading, this incident goes beyond the preceding, in that it deals with a situation in which *din* grants a general rather than a personal dispensation. As such, it serves readily as a basis for extending *lifnim mishurat hadin* to other exemptions. One such extrapolation was made by the Gemara itself, which alludes to the incident in stating that *lifnim mishurat hadin* extends to the return of an *aveda* whose owner had probably abandoned hope because it had been lost in a town whose residents were mostly Gentile and, therefore, unlikely to return lost objects.[124] The Rama[125] went a step further, applying the concept to objects which

---

120. *Bava Metzia* 24b.
121. *Bava Metzia* 24b, s.v. *batar*.
122. S.v. *levatar*.
123. See *Bava Metzia* 28b.
124. Ibid. 24b.
125. HM 259:2. The Rama infers this from a question cited in the *Mordekhai*, 257, as to why *lifnim mishurat hadin* had not been invoked "there," which we take to refer to a case of a sunken ship mentioned just a bit earlier by the *Mordekhai*. It seems far more likely, however, that it refers to a case of an object lost in a Gentile town, which the Gemara (24b) declares to be beyond recovery through the owner's vigorous protest, since it is as if he were protesting his continued ownership of a sunken ship. The question is clearly why the Gemara (24b) cites two discussions

were "lost to him (i.e., the owner) and to every man" – i.e., not simply mislaid, but momentarily beyond human control, e.g., by being swept out to sea, in which case they are, of course, regarded as more fully lost.

In *hashavat aveda,*[126] we again encounter a spectrum of views concerning the degree of possible duty attendant upon *lifnim mishurat hadin.* Some closely parallel positions taken by the same *Rishonim* with respect to our previous case. Thus, the Rambam writes that "he who wishes to go in the path of good and the right and (who) acts *lifnim mishurat hadin*"[127] – again focusing upon the spiritual *gestalt* of the total personality – returns, or perhaps should return, an *aveda,* even if he found it after its owner had given up on it. The Me'iri and the anonymous disciple of the Rashba speak in terms of exhortation tinged with a call to duty. The one, after explaining that once the owner has abandoned hope his subsequent protests are ignored, states that "nevertheless, the mode of *hasidut* would be to return it; and a person should always act *lifnim mishurat hadin,* [as] our Rabbis have interpreted, 'And thou shalt teach them, etc....'"[128] The other, echoing a second source for *lifnim mishurat hadin,* states that such an *aveda* should be returned because "it is fitting (*ra'uy*) for a person to strive for *hasidut* and to go

about such objects, invoking *lifnim mishurat hadin* in the one but ignoring it in the other. Moreover, a parallel citation of the same question in *Haggahot Maimoniyot, Hilkhot Gezela* 11:3, omits the word "there."

126. For the purpose of this discussion, I have lumped together the various cases cited in the preceding paragraphs and treated them as one: the return of forlorn objects. On logical grounds, one could perhaps distinguish between them. The last case, particularly, could be distinguished from the others, as most *Rishonim* – with the major exceptions of the Rambam (*Hilkhot Gezela* 11:10) and possibly Rashi (*Bava Kamma* 66a, s.v. *motzei*) – assume the owner's hope or despair is irrelevant. This would take us too far afield, however.

127. *Hilkhot Gezela* 11:7. One should note, however, that the Rambam here speaks of an aspirant to walking in the path of the good and the right, whereas in our previous case, he spoke of one already habituated to it. This reduces the elitist element markedly, and subtly introduces a greater measure of duty here.

128. *Beit HaBehira, Bava Metzia* 24a, s.v. *hamatzil.* This statement deals with objects lost in Gentile towns. With regard to objects found after a year's lapse, his tone is a bit firmer: "Nevertheless, as an act of kindness (*gemilut hesed*) he is obligated to return" (24b, s.v. *kevar*). The net import is not significantly different, however.

in the path of the good."[129] The *Tur* speaks in a still milder vein, sounding no direct call, but simply declaring that "although, according to the *din*, one is not obligated to return [an *aveda*] in a place in which most of the people are Gentiles, nevertheless it is good and right to return [it] *lifnim mishurat hadin*."[130]

It is noteworthy, moreover, that here the Gemara itself sheds some light on our problem. It relates that as R. Yehuda was walking through a certain market with Shmuel, he turned and asked what would be the halakhic status of, say, a wallet found there. Shmuel replied that it would belong to the finder, presumably because the Jewish owner, knowing that the population was predominantly Gentile, could be assumed to have despaired of its return. R. Yehuda thereupon asked what would happen if the owner were to appear to present identifying information, to which Shmuel replied that the finder would have to return it. Confronted with the apparent contradiction, he answered that this return takes place at the level of *lifnim mishurat hadin*. The discussion is then concluded with the incident involving the donkeys being cited as an analogue.[131]

In light of Shmuel's elucidation, his initial response to R. Yehuda's second question appears rather striking. *Hayyav lehahzir*, "he is obligated to return" – particularly when stated without qualification – has a sharp imperative ring. The sense of duty the phrase conveys is, perhaps, stronger than anything we have encountered with respect to *lifnim mishurat hadin*. Its thrust did not go unnoticed. Indeed, the Ritva suggests that R. Yehuda was misled by it. He is troubled, as had been the Rashba, by the fact that R. Yehuda had apparently repeated his initial question. If "finders keepers," he is, presumably, not bound to return the *aveda*; so why the second question? The Ritva answers that R. Yehuda had taken the first answer as definitive with respect to *din*; but his second question, then, was whether the finder need do anything at all – i.e., "whether he is obligated to return *lifnim mishurat hadin*." However, whereas his question had been open-ended, the tenor of Shmuel's reply was so firm

129. P. 73.

130. HM 259.

131. See *Bava Metzia* 24b.

that R. Yehuda understood it in terms of *din*, whereupon he confronted Shmuel with the apparent contradiction.[132]

What the Ritva regarded as a momentary misunderstanding may also have more lasting consequences. For one thing, the intent of R. Yehuda's second question, as interpreted by the Ritva, is revealing. It indicates that he thought readily in terms of a category of obligation *lifnim mishurat hadin*. Beyond this, in the Gemara itself, the fact remains that Shmuel's final explanation does not expunge the force of his initial response. The phrase *hayyav lehahzir* had been used with respect to *lifnim mishurat hadin*. A number of *Rishonim* – perhaps significantly, again, of *hakhmei Ashkenaz* – evidently made considerable capital of the phrase. They go so far as to assert that *lifnim mishurat hadin* is here not only obligatory, but compulsory. Its performance is strictly enforceable by a *beit din*.

The course of this startling contention is a bit obscure. It is set forth by some of the later *baalei haTosafot*, the thirteenth-century authors and compilers of the *Mordekhai* and the *Haggahot Maimoniyot*, but ascribed by them to their predecessors – specifically, to two of the giants of the Ashkenazic tradition, the twelfth-century Rav Eliezer ben Natan, known as the Raavan, and his grandson, Rav Eliezer ben Yo'el, known as the Raavya. The published text of the Raavan's own compendium does not convey so rigorous an impression. Referring to what had evidently been an actual case in which "Reuven lost his pouch in the marketplace and Shimon found it, [this occurring] in a place frequented by the public," he first quotes the Gemara's statement that the owner has no legal recourse. Nevertheless, he continues, "This is the *din*, but a person ought to act *lifnim mishurat hadin* and return [the object]," and he quotes as proof-texts our gemara, the *Mekhilta*'s source for *lifnim mishurat hadin*, and R. Yohanan's statement concerning its importance. "Therefore," he concludes, "it is incumbent upon Shimon by law (*dina hu al Shimon*) to act *lifnim mishurat hadin* and to return his pouch to

132. See *Hiddushei HaRitva HaHadashim*: *Bava Metzia*, ed. A. Halpern (London, 1962), 57. The question had initially been raised by the Rashba, who suggested a possible textual emendation but then left the matter in a quandary; see *Hiddushei HaRashba*, *Bava Metzia* 24b, s.v. *matza*.

Reuven."[133] This is strong language; but standing alone, it does appear to fall short of enforcement. However, the Raavya, whose works on this area of Halakha are no longer extant, evidently had been very clear on this point. The *Haggahot Maimoniyot*[134] quotes him as sanctioning enforcement explicitly, and both that work and *Mordekhai*[135] cite in the Raavya's name a detailed textual question grounded on this premise. It is, therefore, possible that they interpreted the Raavan's passage in light of the Raavya's view, or that they had some other oral or written evidence to support ascription of that view to the Raavan. Be this as it may, this conception of *hayyav lehahzir* is the most radical instance we have encountered of the existence of duty within *lifnim mishurat hadin*.

It is, however, more than this. There is no reason whatsoever to regard this instance as exceptional rather than exemplary. Obviously, it serves to expand the bounds of the whole category. In the famous words of R. Yishmael, "It does not come to teach about itself [alone] but about the whole principle."[136] The clear inference is that whole tracts of *lifnim mishurat hadin* are subject to enforcement. The Raavya did not cavil at this conclusion. Indeed, while he discusses the point in relation to this gemara, he appears to have accepted the concept independently. He quotes other sources to back up his interpretation: one, the incident involving Rabba b. R. Huna and the porters, to support the notion of enforcement specifically; a second, the gemara concerning the destruction of Jerusalem, by way of buttressing the importance of *lifnim mishurat hadin* generally;[137] and a third, a discussion concerning the payment of a debt one is not sure he has incurred,[138] to provide an analogue for the use of so strong a term as *hayyav* with respect to it. The evidence provided by these texts is, perhaps, open to question. The first may be regarded as a special case of a master imposing supererogatory obligation upon

133. *Sefer Raavan*, ed. S. Z. Ehrenreich (reprinted New York, 1958), II, 177b–178a. The case sounds authentic, but the names are fictitious. The Raavan invariably uses these names even when he supplies details of a clearly contemporary incident.

134. *Hilkhot Gezela* 11:3.

135. Sec. 257.

136. "Preface" to *Sifra*.

137. See, respectively, supra, pp. 231–232 and p. 218.

138. See *Bava Kamma* 118a.

his disciple, but not as a general procedure. The second speaks of the imperative need for *lifnim mishurat hadin* and of divine punishment for its neglect, but says nothing of judicial enforcement. The third may not be a case of *lifnim mishurat hadin* at all.[139] Nevertheless, the fact that the Raavya wove all of them into his argument indicates that he regarded the element of *hiyyuv* in *lifnim mishurat hadin* to be universal.

This inference was drawn by the Rama. Speaking of judicial compromise, the *peshara* which, as we have seen,[140] an anonymous rabbinic source had identified with *lifnim mishurat hadin*, he cites conflicting views as to whether it can be imposed: "*Beit din* cannot coerce [the litigants] to go *lifnim mishurat hadin*, even though it seems to them that this would be fitting (*ra'uy*); but some disagree."[141] The latter are, of course, the Raavya and his school. However, the radical nature – I speak of course, in halakhic rather than political terms – of this position has somewhat hindered its general acceptance. True, Rav Yo'el Sirkes – for whom these questions were far from academic; he lived at the turn of the seventeenth century, when the autonomy of the Polish Jewish community, and the power of *beit din* within it, were at their zenith – endorses it enthusiastically. In his famous commentary on the *Tur, Bayit Hadash* (*Bah*), he argues in favor of it, contending that even *Rishonim* who rejected it, such as the Rosh and his disciple Rabbenu Yeruham, only did so on a qualified basis and would accept it in many cases. Moreover, he attests to the fact that enforcement was actually being implemented: "And this is the practice in every *beit din* in Jewry to compel the affluent with respect to matters which are proper and equitable, even though this may not accord with *din*."[142] Others were more reluctant, however, sometimes

139. The language employed there is, "He is obligated to pay by way of fulfilling his duty vis-à-vis Heaven." Although weaker than an analogous phrase, "He is liable according to the laws of Heaven" – here the "debtor" would certainly not be disqualified as a witness nor could the "creditor" keep his property if he had seized it – it is stronger than that generally accompanying *lifnim mishurat hadin* and may very well denote a different concept. The Ramban, at one point, specifically speaks of an action as being "*lifnim mishurat hadin* and beyond the line of fulfilling duty vis-à-vis Heaven" (*Milhamot Hashem, Bava Kamma* 114a; 41a in Alfasi).

140. See supra, p. 234.

141. HM 12:2.

142. HM 12.

going to the point of modifying the position proper. Thus, Rav Yonatan Eybeschutz[143] contended that the compulsion of which the *Mordekhai* had spoken must be understood as verbal pressure rather than actual coercion. The eighteenth- to nineteenth-century author of the *Ketzot HaHoshen,*[144] a classic commentary upon *Hoshen Mishpat,* acknowledged that the question had been one of coercion proper but argued that the Raavya's view applied only to the case of *hashavat aveda* at issue where, he presumes, a specific rabbinic ordinance to that effect had been instituted. Ordinarily, however, everyone would reject compulsion. This interpretation of the Raavya constitutes a "minority of one"; and, as we have seen, it is hardly borne out by the substance and flow of his remarks. Nevertheless, it is a useful reminder of the radical character of his position and the natural resistance engendered by it.

A measure of support for the Raavya may, however, be found in a brief comment by Rashi and Rabbenu Gershom upon a gemara in *Bava Batra.*[145] Near the end of a discussion about exclusive franchises and the rights of their owners to bar competitors, the gemara states that as regards the sale of cosmetics or jewelry, these rights are modified. Inasmuch as it was deemed important to provide women with an assured and varied supply of these, the owner of a local franchise can prevent only the establishment of a rival resident outlet. He cannot bar traveling salesmen. Going beyond this, the gemara states that if the prospective competitor is a rabbinic scholar, he can even set himself up permanently, "as Rava permitted R. Yoshiya and R. Ovadya to establish [themselves] contrary to the Halakha; Rashi explains: "'contrary to the Halakha' – but rather *lifnim mishurat hadin.*"[146] Rabbenu Gershom[147] gives the phrase "contrary to the Halakha" a slightly different emphasis, explaining that it was inserted so that Rava's action should not be mistaken for a universal precedent; but he, too, speaks of his having acted *lifnim mishurat hadin.* Rav Yosef Karo found this thoroughly incomprehensible. "Who

143. See *Urim VeTummim,* 12:4. See also *Pithei Teshuva,* 12:6.

144. 259:3; cf. 356:6.

145. *Bava Batra* 22a.

146. Ibid., s.v. *delo.*

147. Ibid., s.v. *delo.* It might be noted that this commentary is published under Rabbenu Gershom's name, but its authorship is a matter of dispute.

authorized Rava to act *lifnim mishurat hadin* so as to prejudice the interests of the townspeople without consent?"[148] The case obviously raises a number of complex and varied issues. As regards our immediate concern, however, it indicates that Rashi and Rabbenu Gershom recognized the possibility of compulsory *lifnim mishurat hadin*.

It should be emphasized, however, that the Raavya would not countenance coercion with respect to all action *lifnim mishurat hadin*. As we have seen, this constitutes a spectrum rather than a plane, ranging from acts strongly demanded by duty to others almost purely inspired by aspiration. Inasmuch as the pressure of duty declines as we ascend the moral scale, it is self-evident that the prospect of compulsion would decline and eventually disappear correspondingly. In comparing cases cited in the Gemara, therefore, one cannot readily argue from one to the other. One can prove, as did the Raavya, that the principle of compulsion exists by citing any case in which it is applied. This would only mean, however, that sanctions are *possible* in all cases. It would not follow that they should actually be applied, as this would depend upon the wavelength of the act upon the moral spectrum. No generalization can be proven, therefore, by the absence of sanctions in any given case. Hence, it seems to me that a question posed by the Gaon of Vilna[149] should present no difficulty for the Raavya. Citing the gemara concerning an expert who had unwittingly offered incorrect advice,[150] the Gaon notes that R. Hiyya was singled out as one who had taken an apparently unusual and voluntary step of repaying his client. The tenor of the discussion, as well as the Gemara's silence concerning any sanctions, suggest that ordinarily the issue is pretty much in the hands of the expert – contrary, the Gaon argues, to the Raavya's position. However, once we recognize the diversity of *lifnim mishurat hadin*, the Gemara presents no real problem. The Raavya will simply argue that the cases are not comparable. Moreover, the text would bear this out clearly. The discussion in *Bava Kamma* regarding the expert who offered incorrect advice contains no phrase with imperative force even remotely comparable to *hayyav lehahzir*.

148. *Beit Yosef*, HM 156.

149. See his notes to *Hoshen Misphat* 12:8.

150. *Bava Kamma* 99b.

The Raavya's position raises an obvious problem: In what respect do the enforceable aspects of *lifnim mishurat hadin* differ from *din* proper? It is a question to be considered presently; and, as we shall see, the Raavya himself provided a major clue to its solution. For the moment, however, I might simply point out the implications of that position. Like the phenomenon of *lifnim mishurat hadin* itself, these extend far beyond the isolated instances mentioned in the Gemara. If we keep in mind, particularly, the cognate terms of "the right and the good" or "the way of the good and the paths of the righteous,"[151] it becomes clear that we are here dealing with the scope and *modus operandi* of basic universal categories. Those to whom the temper of Halakha is alien and its methods obscure may find it difficult to envision that detailed discussion of pausing for some blessings or of returning a couple of donkeys should be relevant for the resolution of fundamental moral problems. Yet, the minutiae of the former contain momentous implications for the latter. Basic principles are common to both. Light shed upon the character of *lifnim mishurat hadin* by these incidents has important bearing upon the application of that concept to, say, so significant an issue as self-interest vs. altruism in ethics. From this perspective, the controversy between the Raavya and his opponents is portentous, indeed.

VII. Formal *Din* and Contextual *Lifnim Mishurat Hadin*

The implications of this general distinction between *din* and *lifnim mishurat hadin* should be fully realized. Of the Raavya's case, it can perhaps be said – I am not quite sure – that "the right" remains objectively defined as the return of the *aveda* but that some people are exempt from pursuing it. Or, to put it differently, we may say that "the right" becomes a matter of duty for some and of aspiration for others. As I have already suggested, however, I think we should extend the concept of *lifnim mishurat hadin* to other cases in which the definition

151. I have restricted the immediately preceding discussion to cases in which the term *lifnim mishurat hadin* was specifically used by the Gemara or, in one instance, by *Rishonim*. The areas to which these cognate categories are applied will be analyzed subsequently.

of "the right" is itself a function of context. So long as we deal with authoritative commands – mandated by divine revelation or rabbinic tradition – or their corollaries, duty is defined in terms of response to an imperative call. It does not, of course, exhaust itself in mere obeisance. Obviously, it must be equally related to the attainment of those purposes, so far as they can be intuited, to whose fulfillment the command was directed. Moreover, obedience may itself take greatly varied form at diverse spiritual levels. However, response to command does constitute an integral and indispensable aspect of duty. It serves, therefore, as a limiting factor, positing a specific formal element as a minimal point of departure.

The formal aspect is the hallmark of *din*. In the area of *lifnim mishurat hadin*, however, no specific commands exist. Action is still ideally motivated by response to a divine call, but the call is teleologically rather than formally oriented. It looks to the attainment of broad values rather than the performance of particular acts. Hence, even the rules which the Halakha has posited in this area do not assume the character of commands – not even of rabbinic commands. They are rather advisory guidelines defining what, in a given set of circumstances, is likely to be the optimal course of action. As such, they may play an important role in providing authoritative counsel for those frequently lacking the knowledge and/or sensitivity to walk unaided. In this capacity, rules may function as convenient generalizations delineating duty; but they do not determine it. Duty is determined by judgment in the light of the immediate situation, with no absolute fealty owed the rule.

It is, of course, still conceivable that an individual Jew may be under some obligation to consult spiritual authority and to heed its voice. While sloppy thinking often confuses them, the two questions – which criteria should be used to judge a problem and who is to do the judging – are wholly distinct. There is nothing inconsistent in the position that some issues should be resolved on the basis of contextual insight rather than formal principles, but that the insight should devolve from the conscience of a spiritual mentor rather than from that of the individual most directly involved. However, in that case, fealty is granted the mentor rather than the rule; and he, in turn is free to apply, modify, or reject it, without rebuffing those who formulated it. In the absence of definitive commands, the determination of the right and the good in the sphere of *lifnim mishurat hadin* becomes perforce a function of context.

Returning now to the question raised above, the Raavya's position poses an obvious problem: If certain aspects of *lifnim mishurat hadin* are enforceable, what, then, is the difference between them and *din* proper? Distinction between the two areas in general is not, of course, in question. The Raavya would certainly grant that the upper range of *lifnim mishurat hadin* is beyond compulsion. No matter where one draws the line of enforcement, there must, virtually *a priori*, remain degrees of moral and religious achievement which transcend it. With respect to those aspects which are, however, so much of the "morality of duty" that they are enforceable, the question remains: Ought these not rather be assigned to *din* proper? In what sense, if any, are they distinct from it?

The answer revolves, again, around the rigor of obligation – but around a different sense of the term. I suggested earlier that the primary distinction between *din* and *lifnim mishurat hadin* lies in the fact that the obligations imposed by them were not equally rigorous; and we have heretofore been concerned with one facet of this distinction – the degree and force of obligation. In this connection, it has been noted that the imperative thrust of one area exceeds that of the other, and some attempt has been made to define and measure this gap with respect to the specific cases cited by the Gemara. There is, however, a second sense in which *lifnim mishurat hadin* is less rigorous than *din*: namely, its flexible and situational character.

Immediately following the discussion between R. Yehuda and Shmuel regarding the retrieval of an *aveda* found after its owner had despaired of it, the Gemara cites a similar exchange between Rava and R. Nahman, virtually identical with the first except for its conclusion.[152] Where Shmuel's second reply had been that the finder is obligated to return the object, *lifnim mishurat hadin,* R. Nahman reiterates that the finder may keep it; and in response to Rava's retort that the owner is presently objecting vehemently, he simply answers that "he is regarded as one who is protesting with regard to his fallen house or sunken ship" – i.e., his claims are null and void. The apparent contradiction poses

152. *Bava Metzia* 24b.

a problem of sorts for all *Rishonim*. For the Raavya, however, it presents a peculiar difficulty. On the more prevalent view, the omission of the element of *lifnim mishurat hadin* may be explained away on the ground that it is supererogatory, and R. Nahman was merely defining for Rava the applicable law to be implemented should an actual case arise. On the Raavya's view, however, any finder would actually be compelled to return the *aveda*. Ought not R. Nahman, then, to have taken the level of *lifnim mishurat hadin* into account as well?

The Raavya raises this question, *en passant*; and he suggests that, in this case, "perhaps the finder was poor and the owner of the *aveda* well-to-do." This is a rather startling distinction. Powerful as is the obligation upon the affluent to help the relatively disadvantaged, it is a general responsibility to a group and enforceable only through a third party, the community and its *beit din*. While many *posekim* regard charity as a legal and collectible debt rather than a mere act of grace, an individual pauper certainly has no right – except with regard to certain agriculture tithes – to seize his more affluent neighbor's property. No comparable distinction would be countenanced with respect to any *aveda* found before despair. While the degree and form of obligation may differ, no radical distinction is made between rich and poor. There are no separate Torahs for different classes. A pauper who has borrowed money or caused damage is as liable as a tycoon – although, to be sure, actual collection must proceed humanely and stop short of necessities. The same holds true with respect to positive commandments.[153] Even the mitzva of giving charity is fully incumbent upon the poor.[154] We have here, then, a striking instance of the contextual nature of *lifnim mishurat hadin*, which distinguishes it from *din* even according to the Raavya.

---

153. "Even the poorest Jew," the Mishna states, "should have no less than four cups [at the *seder*]" (*Pesahim* 10:1); and the *Mordekhai*, strikingly enough, was troubled as to why there was need to state such a self-evident point: "Of what is he [i.e., the *Tanna* of the mishna] enlightening us? Obviously, inasmuch as one is obligated concerning four cups, what does it matter if he is rich or poor?" (*Mordekhai, Tosefet MeArvei Pesahim*).

154. *Gittin* 7b: "And even a pauper being supported by charity is obligated to give charity"; Rambam, *Hilkhot Mattenot Aniyyim* 7:5.

The flexible character of *lifnim mishurat hadin* stands most fully revealed in an area in which, paradoxically, it is at its most rigorous. As we have seen, the Gemara has little in the way of full-blown discussion of the category as a whole or of any specific instances. Nor, in the light of its essentially *ad hoc* character, is this particularly surprising. There is, however, a group of cases, subsumed by the Gemara under "And thou shalt do the right and the good" and explicitly identified by the Ramban with *lifnim mishurat hadin*, which do receive extensive detailed analysis. These are cases in which a halakha, initially grounded in *lifnim mishurat hadin*, acquires, evidently through rabbinic legislation, the virtual status of *din* proper. The Gemara has two such instances: one, *dina debar metzra*, the right of an abutter to first option to purchase any land being put up for sale by his neighbor;[155] the second, *shuma hadra le'olam*, the law that a debtor whose property has been requisitioned in collection of a debt may recover it at any time by producing the money he had owed.[156] Several *Rishonim* added a third: *ani hamehapekh baharara*, literally, the law concerning "a poor man who was turning over a cookie" prior to acquiring it, but signifying more generally the prohibition against interloping to take objects or opportunities for whose prospective acquisition someone else had already laid the groundwork.[157] The force of law is evident in all these cases. With respect to the first, the Gemara goes so far as to say that should the owner sell to someone else, the abutter can compel the purchaser to resell it to him; moreover, that, should the value of the land have risen in the interim, he need only pay him what he had paid the original owner rather than the present market price. Indeed, some *Rishonim* explain that, should the abutter choose to exercise his option, we do not describe his acquisition as a resale at all. Rather, the purchaser is then fictively regarded as having bought the property as an agent of the abutter instead of on his own behalf; and it is precisely for this reason that the price differential becomes irrelevant. In the second case, likewise, the virtually legal force of the Halakha is clear. The debtor can institute full-dress proceedings to compel the return of his

155. *Bava Metzia* 108b.

156. Ibid. 16b.

157. *Kiddshin* 59a. Ed. note: See pp. 180–189 above.

property. Some *Rishonim* even suggested that he does not so much buy it back as cancel the original requisition. Hence, some contended that no new formal acquisitive act would be necessary; others, that any fruits which had grown in the interim would belong to the debtor; still others, that if the creditor made any improvements in the field he would only be compensated on the scale of a stranger who had proceeded, on his own, to improve someone else's property, but not for their full present value. Finally, with respect to *ani hamehapekh,* Rabbenu Tam held that if the interloper did seize someone else's potential property, the original prospector can sue and compel him to give it up.

The force of law is, then, very much in evidence here. Yet, a nagging question persists. Having been integrated, as it were, into *din,* are these laws now wholly indistinguishable from others? Or do they still differ by virtue of their distinctive source? Is their origin in "the right and the good" merely a matter of historical and ideological genesis or an integral aspect of their permanent character and structure?

The question was raised by *Rishonim*; and it was the subject of disagreement amongst them. It arose first in connection with a somewhat enigmatic incident cited by the Gemara in *Bava Batra.*[158] Property abutting that of the famous Babylonian *Amora* Ravina was purchased by someone named Runya – probably the same person described elsewhere as Ravina's gardener. Ravina sought to invoke his prerogative as an abutter, whereupon another *Amora,* R. Safra b. R. Yeva, restrained him by citing a popular proverb concerning payment for tanning or poverty and wealth in relation to tanners. The exact meaning of the proverb as well as its symbolic application are obscure; and *Rishonim* offered at least half a dozen divergent interpretations. Most, however, assumed its general import to be an affirmation of the rights or needs of the relatively underprivileged; and, from this perspective, they drew from the discussion an inference crucially relevant to our question: that *dina debar metzra* does not apply if the purchaser is poor and the abutter relatively affluent. Thus, Rabbenu Gershom explains: "He told him a parable, to wit: The phenomenon of the abutter [and his right] is but because of 'And thou shalt do the right and the good.' Inasmuch

158. 5a.

as this Runya is poor, he can't get along without a field and if he won't buy now he will lose his money and will have no means of livelihood. Consequently, you won't be able to evict him, as there is no greater [fulfillment of] 'And thou shalt do the right and the good' than this – that you should let him purchase it." This is, likewise, the substantive conclusion which emerges from two of the possible interpretations cited by Rashi. Among Sephardic commentaries, the same note is struck – albeit with an additional moral theme of the ethical implications of the leveling power of death – by Rashi's younger contemporary, Rav Yosef ibn Migash: "He told him, that since you have another field next to this one, why do you still want to buy this one and to vacate this poor man from this purchase concerning which he had labored for himself? This property that you are accumulating – will you, then, have anything of it after death but the four cubits of the grave within which you are buried, just like the pauper who has nothing?" This application of *memento mori,* so familiar to readers of *Hamlet,* lends a more persuasive and perhaps less definitive ring to the discussion; but I believe the practical conclusion would be the same. *Dina debar metzra* does not apply if the purchaser is poor and the abutter is not.

Rabbenu Tam, however, rejected this approach completely. His assault upon it is frontal: *Ein merahamim bedin,* "We do not exercise mercy in law."[159] The phrase is a quotation from a mishna in which R. Tarfon states that if a person died and left a variety of claimants – creditors, heirs, and his wife – to assets held by others, these should be given to the "most faltering of them"; whereby R. Akiva retorts – and his view was subsequently accepted as definitive – with the statement cited by Rabbenu Tam.[160] In a broader sense, R. Akiva's position relates to the biblical precept, "Neither shalt thou favor a poor man in his cause"[161] – the embodiment of the principle that litigation, *per se,* is not the arena of pity; that, if law is to be both inherently meaningful and to command communal respect, it must be genuinely even-handed; and that, attractive as the short-cut often seems, judicial distortion is not the proper means of

159. *Bava Batra* 5a, s.v. *arbaa.*
160. Mishna *Ketubbot* 9:2.
161. *Shemot* 23:3.

redressing social wrongs. The point is that this rigor – call it, if you will, rigidity – is the hallmark of the disposition of *din*. It has, however, no bearing upon *lifnim mishurat hadin* – neither upon the moral responsibility of the individual litigant nor upon the decision of the judge; for in this instance the judgment is itself contextual. Rabbenu Tam's question, as his language explicitly indicates, is predicated upon the assumption that we are here dealing with *din* proper or its equivalent. His controversy with Rashi turns, therefore, upon the extent to which laws growing out of "the right and the good" but subsequently established as rabbinic ordinances retain something of their original character.

The question is obviously not confined to the specific instance of a poor purchaser. Rashi, for instance, cites a third interpretation according to which *dina debar metzra* is inapplicable whenever the purchaser has nearly (although not actually) adjacent fields, so that he, too, could effect some economics by consolidating certain expenses. The broader implications of Rashi's interpretation were especially noted in a striking passage in the *Or Zarua*, in which his position is both applied and more articulately formulated: "Even according to those who apply *dina debar metzra* to houses [in a case in which] Reuven wants to sell his house to Shimon and Levi is Reuven's abutter and wishes to prevent Shimon from buying, if Levi has a residential house and Shimon doesn't, he cannot prevent Shimon from buying. For the *dina debar metzra* was only instituted in cases in which both the purchaser and the abutter have residences, or neither has. However, if the abutter has a residential house and the purchaser doesn't, how can we tell the purchaser that he should let the abutter buy to excess because of 'the right and the good' and himself should be tossed about hither and yon? The Torah has said, 'Her ways are the ways of pleasantness and all her paths are peace'; and it is neither the way of pleasantness nor the path of peace that one should be tossed about and the other buy to excess."[162] After citing Rashi's interpretation of Ravina's incident as evidence, he goes on to discuss Rabbenu Tam's objection. R. Akiva had justifiably objected to the intrusion of the element of mercy upon the domain of strict litigation. "Here, however, the very character of the law of abutment is such: The Rabbis did not impose

162. *Or Zarua, Piskei Bava Metzia* 359.

upon him [i.e., the purchaser] an obligation to wander and be tossed about from house to house so as to extend kindness toward another who will buy a house for profit. The Torah has, after all said, 'Your life takes precedence over that of your fellow.'"[163]

The *Or Zarua*'s conception of *dina debar metzra*, contextual in character and axiological in focus, was even more definitively formulated by one of the later *Rishonim*, the mid-fourteenth-century author of a major treatise on the Rambam, *Maggid Mishneh*. The Rambam concludes *Hilkhot Shekhenim* with the statement – based upon the Rif's interpretation of a gemara in *Bava Metzia*[164] – that, even when no abutter is involved, some prospective purchasers may be given priority over others. Thus, a relative or a neighbor, albeit not actually an abutter, has priority over strangers; or, if both a neighbor, albeit not an actual abutter, and a relative want to buy the same property, "the neighbor takes precedence as this, too, is included in the good and the right."[165] However, the Rambam adds, this right is weaker than the usual *dina debar metzra* and only exists *ante facto*: "If one went ahead and bought, he takes title and his fellow who ought to have received precedence cannot remove him since neither of them is an abutter. For the Rabbis only commanded regarding this [matter] by way of *hasidut*; and it is a virtuous soul which acts thus."[166] Whereupon the *Maggid Mishneh* comments:

> The point of *dina debar metzra* is that our perfect Torah has laid down [general] principles concerning the development of man's character and his conduct in the world; as, in stating "Ye shall be holy,"[167] meaning, as they [i.e., the Rabbis] said, "Sanctify yourself with respect to that which is permitted you,"[168] that one should not be swept away by the pursuit of lust. Likewise, it said, "And thou shalt do the right and the good," meaning that one's interpersonal conduct should be good and just. With regard to all

163. Ibid.
164. 108a.
165. *Hilkhot Shekhenim* 14:5.
166. Ibid.
167. *Vayikra* 19:2.
168. *Yevamot* 20a.

> this, it would not have been proper to give detailed instructions. For the Torah's commands apply at all times, in every period, and under all circumstances, whereas man's characteristics and behavior vary, depending upon the time and the individual. The Rabbis [therefore] set down some relevant details subsumed under these principles, some of which they made [the equivalent of] absolute *din* and others [only] *ante facto* and by way of *hasidut*, all [however] ordained by them. And it is with reference to this that they said,[169] "The words of consorts [i.e., the Rabbis] are more beloved than the wine of Torah, as stated, 'For thy love is better than wine.'"

Needless to say, the *Maggid Mishneh* is not espousing an exclusively relativistic or situational ethic. No conscientious halakhist could countenance such a position. He is, however, defining the character of *dina debar metzra*, specifically, and of "the right and the good," generally; and beyond this, he is noting that, from a certain perspective, the greater flexibility and latitude attendant upon rabbinic injunctions formulated within this area gives them an edge, as it were, over the Torah's absolutely rigorous *din*.

VIII. Two Types of *Lifnim Mishurat Hadin*

Distinguishing it from *din* proper, the relative pliancy of *lifnim mishurat hadin* serves to define it negatively. Obviously, however, the term remains almost meaningless in the absence of a complementary positive definition. Two aspects, in particular, require analysis: mode and *telos*. Broadly speaking, of course, *lifnim mishurat hadin* refers to supererogatory conduct directed toward the realization of spiritual goals. But both the goals and the means of attaining them need to be spelled out more specifically.

To begin with the latter, a moment's reflection suggests a clear distinction. While *lifnim mishurat hadin* generally entails transcending minimal halakhic demands, this can be done in two ways. In an area with reference to which the Halakha has formulated specific standards,

169. *Avoda Zara* 35a; the verse is from *Shir HaShirim* 1:2.

one can move to surpass them, qualitatively or quantitatively. This mode may itself take one of several forms: 1) refusal to avail oneself of personal exemption from a mitzva; 2) disregard of technicalities when they exclude from a law situations which, morally and substantively, belong within its pale; 3) extending the scope of a mitzva by applying it to circumstances clearly beyond its legal construction but nevertheless sufficiently similar to relate to its specific *telos*. The last is, of course, the most radical. It entails genuinely breaking lush ground, acting in accordance with the spirit of the law in the sense of striving to realize its axiological purpose rather than of simply fulfilling its evident legal intent. Yet even this course is narrowly based, in that it is oriented to a very particular law. Its pursuit entails the extension of clearly defined obligation; perhaps, even formally speaking, the fulfillment, albeit voluntary, of a specific commandment. In this sense, *lifnim mishurat hadin* constitutes the penumbra of mitzvot.

An alternative mode goes beyond *din* by transcending its totality.[170] It does not operate through formally designated laws but above or, if you will, between them. It addresses itself to areas regarding which the Torah, at the level of clearly defined action, has remained totally silent. The focus is therefore not so much individual halakhot as Halakha as whole – although, let us remember again, the process of supererogation is itself part of the ultimate halakhic complex.

The distinction between the two modes of *lifnim mishurat hadin* bears no necessary relation to some theoretical moral scale. The second mode may find the Jew raising his ethical and religious level not only by extending the bounds of Halakha but also by filling in its gaps. Narrowly defined, halakhic ethics are strikingly uneven – almost incredibly demanding in some areas, singularly neutral in others. The standard of honor due to parents is so high that, as noted above, R. Yohanan was led to exclaim, "Fortunate is he who has never seen them [i.e, his parents],"[171]

---

170. Ed. note: To clarify, the first mode of *lifnim mishurat hadin* – namely, surpassing clearly formulated standards – is exemplified by the five talmudic examples examined in section VI of this essay. The second mode – namely, filling in the gaps – is exemplified by the principles of *kofin al middat Sedom* (to be discussed) and *latzet yedei shamayim* (not discussed).

171. *Kiddushin* 31b.

as only a person who has never met his parents can escape censure for laxity in attaining this standard. Respect for the property or personal reputation of others is so strongly emphasized that Rav could observe that most violate laws concerning the one and all those concerning the other,[172] while R. Safra was so wary of injunctions against backbiting that he incisively cautioned: "A person ought never discuss his fellow's virtues, for from his virtues he'll soon get around to his faults."[173] Yet gluttony and indolence – two of the medieval world's "seven deadly sins" and both certainly contrary to the overall thrust of Halakha – are nowhere explicitly prohibited as such. Numerous mitzvot are oriented toward curbing both; but, as the Ramban noted, the inevitable gaps permit the sensualist to indulge to gross excess as "a scoundrel with the Torah's license."[174] Nor is the unevenness solely due to legalistic exploitation of loopholes. It is equally the result of outright halakhic omissions. The Rabbis tell us that sometimes "the Torah has but spoken vis-à-vis the evil inclination," licensing certain dubious practices so as to deter the immoral from still greater evils. We ought not to be surprised, therefore, if it sometimes kept its peace for the same reason. But the compromises remain just that; and, at the level of *lifnim mishurat hadin,* we are called upon to transcend them.

In this sense, *lifnim mishurat hadin* does not consist of codicils and footnotes. Rather than simply expanding individual mitzvot, it fleshes out the total corpus of Torah by mandating actions which advance some of its ultimate goals but which have nowhere been singled out as the subject of a specific halakha. These may range from the upper to the nether ends of the ethical scale. What distinguishes this mode from the preceding is not so much its moral altitude as independence of any particular formal *din.*

A clear instance of the second mode is furnished by the law of *kofin al middat Sedom,* "we coerce over a trait of Sodom."[175] As defined

172. *Bava Batra* 165a.

173. Ibid. 164b.

174. Commentary to *Vayikra* 19:2.

175. *Ketubbot* 103a. Ed. note: For an analysis of this concept, see the chapter "*Kofin Al Middat Sedom*: Compulsory Altruism?" below.

by most *Rishonim*, this refers to an inordinate privatism that leaves one preoccupied with personal concerns to the neglect of the concerns of others; a degree of selfishness so intense that it denies the other at no gain to oneself. There need be no actual spite. Simple indifference may suffice. Nor is *middat Sedom*, despite the severity of the term, confined to what popular morality might regard as nastiness or mindless apathy. One view in the Mishna – the definitive view, according to most *Rishonim* – subsumed under it the attitude that "mine is mine and yours is yours."[176] Coercion over it may, consequently, have revolutionary implications. Their potential may be gauged by the fact that a number of *posekim* explicitly state that a court may compel a person to let someone else live on his land gratis if the property would otherwise lie idle, being neither used by its owner nor put up for rent. Whatever the details, however, *middat Sedom* broadly denotes obsession with one's private property and the consequent erection of excessive legal and psychological barriers between man and man. As such, it was not only condemned but rendered actionable.

To the best of my knowledge, *Hazal* nowhere explicitly formulate the basis of this halakha. It seems likely, however, that it is subsumed under *lifnim mishurat hadin*; and if this be so, we have here a striking instance of its second mode – extension to lacunae rather than expansion of specific mitzvot. Admittedly, many of us do not instinctively associate the two concepts. However, this is simply another manifestation of our failure to appreciate the full character and sweep of *lifnim mishurat hadin*. So long as it is regarded as purely the sphere of supererogatory extra-credit conduct, it can hardly include rejection of actions so reprehensible as to warrant the epithet *middat Sedom*. Once we recognize its true scope – that it ranges from basic obligatory canons to supreme idealism – we should have little difficulty with the association.[177]

---

176. *Avot* 5:10.

177. The Maharal, at any rate, had none – precisely because he emphasized the centrality and force of *lifnim mishurat hadin*. This emphasis was clearly expressed in the course of his discussion of *gemilut hasadim* (*Netivot Olam*, "*Netiv Gemilut Hasadim*," ch. 5). "The antithesis of this trait," he writes, "is [a person] who does not want to do any good toward another, standing upon the *din* and refusing to act *lifnim mishurat hadin*." This virtual equation of *hesed* and *lifnim mishurat hadin* then becomes the

It may be further objected, however, that even if *kofin al middat Sedom* be grounded in *lifnim mishurat hadin*, it exemplifies no second mode of its operation. Rather, the renunciation of *middat Sedom* is simply one aspect of the mitzva of *gemilut hasadim*. Hence, the objection would continue, we are dealing once more with the expansion of a particular mitzva rather than with presumed virgin territory. In reply, I would simply state that the premise of this argument is entirely correct, but the inference from it is not. As we shall see, and as the Maharal clearly implies,[178] not only the renunciation of *middat Sedom* but much – if not all – of *lifnim mishurat hadin* can be subsumed under *gemilut hasadim*. Yet the distinction I have suggested is in no way invalidated. Inasmuch as *gemilut hasadim* is amorphous both quantitatively[179] and formally, one may properly speak of fleshing it out, or of interstices between aspects which *have* been pinpointed, by the Torah or by the Rabbis, as specific and definitive duties.

In speaking of the unevenness of halakhic ethics, I do not of course mean to suggest that matters of significant moral import can be regarded as halakhically neutral. I simply note – and here I am only paraphrasing the Ramban – that while some duties have been designated as the objects of formal and detailed laws, others remain anonymous elements comprehended under general principles. *Gemilut hasadim*

---

basis for an explanation of the Gemara's comment regarding the destruction of Jerusalem. This was not, the Maharal explains, retributive punishment. It was a natural consequence, for a wholly legalistic community simply cannot exist. Supralegal conduct is the cement of human society. Its absence results in disintegration: "Standing upon *din* entails ruin." Likewise, excessive commitment to law invites disaster on a broader scale, for, by correspondence, it both recognizes and enthrones natural law as cosmic sovereign, thus rejecting the providential grace of miracles that deviate from it. Finally, rejection of *lifnim mishurat hadin* is defined as the hallmark of Sodom, whose evil, although it issued in corruption, nevertheless was grounded in total fealty to legal nicety: "For this was their nature, to concede nothing, as the Rabbis said, 'Mine is mine and yours is yours: this is the trait of Sodom.' And they have everywhere said, *kofin al middat Sodom.*" The identification of *lifnim mishurat hadin* as the source of such coercion is here fairly explicit; and the conjunction of its denial with the biblical apotheosis of malice reflects the importance that the Maharal attached to supralegal conduct.

178. See the previous footnote.

179. The Mishna (*Pe'ah* 1:1) lists it among mitzvot lacking any prescribed limit.

constitutes one such principle, "the right and the good" another. The realization of either requires doing much which no specific *din* has formulated. Hence, while, due to their overlap, *lifnim mishurat hadin* does clearly impinge upon *gemilut hasadim*, its relation to the latter is qualitatively distinct from its relation to more formally detailed norms. In the case of *hashavat aveda*, for instance, since the core *din* is clearly formulated, anything beyond it is readily identifiable as its contiguous embellishment. With respect to *gemilut hasadim*, however, *lifnim mishurat hadin* exists in a dual capacity. At one level, it represents here, too, the supererogatory aspects of the mitzva. At a second, it denotes other aspects which define its basic fabric, which, their anonymity notwithstanding, are therefore very much part of the Jew's minimal obligation. In this sense, it fills in gaps between specific ethical norms – many themselves broadly subsumed under *gemilut hasadim*. *Lifnim mishurat hadin* thus fleshes out the Halakha's "morality of duty."

Kofin al middat Sedom probably constitutes the best example of the second mode of *lifnim mishurat hadin*. It does not stand alone, however. Equally relevant, if less striking, instances are provided by obligations subsumed under *latzet yedei shamayim* (to fulfill their obligation to Heaven). The concept appears in several places, most commonly with reference to doubtful situations. If, for instance,[180] A claims he has lent B $100 and B doesn't remember, the alleged debt is not collectible; but nevertheless, *latzet yedei shamayim*, it should be paid.

Ed. note: At this point, the manuscript ends. Sections I–VI of this essay were edited by the author and appear as a typescript with endnotes; these sections were followed in the typescript by the author's outline for the remainder of the essay (see below). Subsequently, the author appended sections VII and VIII in handwriting. These correspond, respectively, to item 1 and item 2 (including the first half of item 3) in the outline. The rest of the essay was never completed.

180. *Bava Kamma* 118a; Rambam, *Hilkhot To'en VeNitan* 1:9.

OUTLINE OF THE REMAINDER OF THE ESSAY

1. *Lifnim mishurat hadin* less rigorous in a second sense: flexible and situational.
   - A. Normative and contextual elements within halakhic ethics, with some comparison with current debate within both Christian and secular circles.
   - B. Analysis of areas, e.g., *dina debar metzra* in which *lifnim mishurat hadin* has become virtually incorporated into law, becoming both fully obligatory and enforceable.
2. Distinguishing between two types of *lifnim mishurat hadin*:
   - A. Going beyond a particular *din*, where the Halakha has laid down a specific standard.
   - B. Going beyond the totality of *din*, by acting in situations which the Halakha has essentially ignored but which nevertheless have clear ethical import.
3. Discuss *kofin al midat Sedom* in relation to 2.B. Compare with *latzet yedei shamayim*.
4. Analyze meaning and content of *hayashar vehatov*:
   - A. Generally; cf. modern discussions by G. E. Moore, W. D. Ross, et al.
   - B. *Be'einei Hashem*, specifically. Theological problem of *Euthyphro*: relation of "the good" to God's will.
5. In light of 4.B, relate *ve'asita hayashar vehatov* to *vehalakhta biderakhav*.
6. Discuss general role of voluntary, as opposed to programmed, aspect of Halakha.
   - A. List and analyze voluntary areas, e.g., *korban nedava*.
   - B. In what sense, if at all, does *lifnim mishurat hadin* apply to *bein adam laMakom*?
     1. "Anyone who is exempt from something and nevertheless does it is called a *hedyot*."
     2. "Greater is one who is commanded and performs than one who is not commanded and performs."

Kofin Al Middat Sedom: Compulsory Altruism?

I. Introduction

Throughout the generations, the city of Sodom has symbolized ultimate evil and destruction. This is the way Sodom is presented in the words of the Prophets, and in later periods the description of its nature and fate has been further broadened. This general meaning has become crystallized in the expression "*middat Sedom*," behavior characteristic of Sodom: a shocking and frightening trait. In the framework of Halakha, however, this term acquires a narrower connotation, as is the tendency of legal definitions. On the other hand, the term has been expanded from a concept that relates exclusively to the wicked of the world to a factor that is connected to the life of every individual. This essay will deal with the definition of the term in its halakhic formulation, and primarily with the

Translated by David Strauss. This essay originally appeared in Hebrew as "*Leveirur 'Kofin Al Middat Sedom*,'" in *Hagut Ivrit BeAmerica* I (1972), 362–382, and the English translation first appeared in *Alei Etzion* 16 (2009), pp. 31–70.

clarification of a specific law connected to it: "*Kofin al middat Sedom,*" "We compel one who acts in the manner of Sodom" (or, more loosely, "We compel one not to act in the manner of Sodom").

At the outset we will briefly present the talmudic sources that explicitly deal with *kofin al middat Sedom*. This idea is mentioned in five places. In two of them, the Gemara brings it as the foundation of some unclear dispute: the one, a dispute among *Tanna'im* whether a court record known as a *shtar beirurin* can be written separately for each litigant, or whether they must share one copy;[1] the second, a dispute among *Amora'im* whether a person may prevent his neighbor from opening a window facing into his courtyard, even if the window is higher than four cubits, so that there is no concern about *hezzek re'iyya* (damage caused by exposure to the public).[2] In both cases the Gemara concludes that "all agree that we compel one who acts in the manner of Sodom," but there is disagreement about whether these cases fall into the category of *middat Sedom.*

In two other places, the concept is mentioned almost incidentally in connection with specific laws. In one place, it relates to issues of merging domains on Shabbat to allow carrying between them. In this case, in the interests of the greatest good for the greatest number of people, the residents of a courtyard situated between two alleyways are forced "to utilize the less frequently used alleyway, for in such a case, *kofin al middat Sedom.*"[3] In the second place, which is closer to the matter at hand – civil law – the Gemara relates the case of one who leases his mill to another, and they agree that the lessee pays by providing the service of grinding the lessor's grain for free. If the lessor purchases another mill and then asks that in the future the lessee pay for his lease in cash, what is the law? Following a short discussion, the Gemara concludes that the lessee can refuse – but with one limitation: "This, however, applies only in a case where [the lessee] has no [other orders for] grinding at his mill." Rashi

1. See *Bava Batra* 167b–168a. As for the meaning of *shtarei beirurin,* the Gemara (ad loc.) records two understandings: documents that record the arguments of the two litigants or documents that refer to the selection of the arbiters.
2. See ibid. 59a.
3. *Eiruvin* 49a.

explains: "Therefore he can say: 'Inasmuch as I am sitting idle, I would rather mill for you and not pay in cash.'" The Gemara concludes: "But if he has [sufficient orders for] grinding at his mill, in such a case, *kofin oto al middat Sedom*."[4]

A concentrated discussion of the topic is found in a passage dealing with the division of joint property, where this compulsion is the subject of a dispute among *Amora'im*. Three cases are discussed in that passage,[5] but all three branch out from one general problem: when a person possesses a field of his own adjacent to jointly owned property, can he demand the portion of that property that borders on his own field? In explaining the details of the passage, however, the *Rishonim* pave diverse paths; we shall attempt below to understand the various positions.[6]

II. "Mine Is Mine, and Yours Is Yours"

As descriptions of isolated cases or laws, these sources give the appearance of being unimportant tidbits. They do, however, reflect a common foundation that has ramifications for many remotely connected matters; and from this perspective they have an entirely different nature. The fundamental axis is not so much the matter of the compulsion, but rather

---

4. *Ketubbot* 103a; see footnote 74 below about the phrasing in this passage.
5. See *Bava Batra* 12b–13a. The summary presented here follows Rashi. According to Rabbenu Tam, the passage must be understood differently; see below.
6. This brief review refers only to those sources where the principle of *kofin al middat Sedom* is explicitly mentioned. Several other halakhot based on this principle are found both in the Mishna and in the Gemara. In addition to the sources that we will discuss below, we may add the mishna in *Demai* 7:8, according to the Rambam's commentary ad loc.; this source is already cited by the *Or Same'ah, Hilkhot Shekhenim* 12:1. This, however, is only true according to the Rambam's commentary as found in the regular editions, which, according to Rav Kafah, constitutes an early version of the work. In the third version, which Rav Kafah published – *Mishna Im Perush Rabbenu Moshe ben Maimon: Seder Zera'im* (Jerusalem, 5723), 155 – the Rambam interprets the mishna as referring to a matter of ritual law rather than civil law. The same ruling is found in *Hilkhot Maaser* 15:14. There is also the law governing two people holding fast to a document, *Bava Metzia* 7a, according to one understanding cited in *Hiddushei HaRamban*, ad loc.; and the law that we split the money instead of the *tallit*, *Bava Metzia* 8a, according to *Hiddushei HaRitva*, ad loc. See also *Yad Rama, Bava Batra*, ch. 3, no. 290; and *Piskei HaRosh, Bava Metzia*, 9:9.

the definition of *middat Sedom* in and of itself. In the aforementioned passages, we do not find an explicit definition; to the best of my knowledge, there is also no other talmudic source that describes this trait in abstract and universal terms. The content of the concept itself, however, as it follows from the aforementioned sources, is, generally speaking, sufficiently clear: the practice of evil against, and even the denial of good toward, one's fellow, that does not stem from excessive egotism – this already would be an improvement, though it constitutes a problem of its own – but from indifference to his situation. Borrowing a formulation that the Rabbis used in other areas, we might say that *middat Sedom* is doing evil in a spirit of defiance (*lehakhis*), rather than to satisfy one's appetite (*lete'avon*), in accordance with those who maintain that "one who does not care" falls into the category of *lehakhis*.[7] This concept and this reality have very broad significance.

Leading *Rishonim* stress this aspect and some reformulate it with the expression found in a famous passage (*Bava Kamma* 20b): "*Zeh neheneh vezeh lo haser*," "This one benefits, and this one suffers no loss."[8] (The same gemara also discusses the parallel case of "*Zeh neheneh vezeh haser*," "This one benefits, and this one suffers a loss.") Indeed, if we need a precise and comprehensive definition, we will discover that it is the subject of controversy – and not just one controversy, but multiple controversies. The first is found in the only mishna that explicitly mentions *middat Sedom* among its classification of human attributes: "He who says 'Mine is mine, and yours is yours' is an average character; some say (*yesh omerim*) that this is *middat Sedom*."[9] This, of course, is not a formal definition, but merely a judgment and assessment of a particular detail. Clearly, however, this judgment sheds light on the parameters of the trait in general. We must still, however, consider three interwoven

7. See Rama, YD 2:5; *Be'urei HaGra*, ad loc., 16.
8. See, for example, Rashi, *Eiruvin* 49a, s.v. *middat*; Rashbam, *Bava Batra* 59a, s.v. *middat*, and commentary attributed to Rabbenu Gershom, and *Hiddushei HaRashba*, ad loc.; Rambam, *Hilkhot Shekhenim* 7:5; *Yad Rama, Bava Batra*, ch. 10, no. 81; *Or Zarua*, III, no. 24.
9. *Avot* 5:10. Interestingly, the harsh expression *middat Sedom* is not used by the Sages to describe the highest level of evil, as the level of *rasha* (wicked) mentioned there is even worse. Compare *Avot DeRabbi Natan*, ed. Schechter, version 1, ch. 40.

questions: 1) What is the mishna dealing with? 2) On what point do the *Tanna'im* disagree? 3) How does this mishna relate to the issue of *kofin al middat Sedom*?

When we examine the explanations offered by the *Rishonim*, we see that they adopt various approaches. On the one hand, Rabbenu Yona emphasizes that the mishna is dealing with a spiritual quality, rather than an action or its absence. The mishna is not referring to one who refrains from giving charity, for such a person is

> a totally wicked man.... Rather, here we are dealing with a person who gives charity out of the fear of God, though by nature, he is miserly. Therefore, since he supports the poor and needy, what should one care about his nature? The quality itself is average. However, the *yesh omerim* hold that it is *middat Sedom*, and that its root is exceedingly evil, since by nature he is miserly.[10]

According to this, the mishna discusses the degree of importance that must be attached to objective and subjective factors as the determining factors of ethics – though from a halakhic perspective, one must consider both of them, that is, the source of the action and its result. Following this approach, it is necessary to distinguish between the *middat Sedom* discussed in the Mishna and that which is mentioned in the Gemara in connection with compulsion. Despite the importance of the heart's intentions in Halakha in general and in connection with the mitzva of giving charity in particular,[11] the courts will clearly not compel "one

10. Commentary of Rabbenu Yona, ad loc.
11. See *Devarim* 15:10: "You shall surely give him, and your heart shall not be grieved when you give to him." According to the Ramban, this warning constitutes a separate negative precept: "We may not be angry when we give charity to the poor, and we may not give it to them with ill-will" (Additions to Rambam's *Sefer HaMitzvot*, negative commandment 17; see also Ramban's *Derasha* on *Kohelet*, in *Kitvei HaRamban*, ed. C. D. Chavel [Jerusalem, 5723], vol. 1, p. 205). The problem of subjectivity and objectivity as determinants of character in the realms of ethics and action assumes a central role in Judaism and also occupies the minds of non-Jewish thinkers, particularly from the time of Kant and the Utilitarianism school. This, however, is not the forum to discuss the matter at length.

who gives charity out of the fear of God, but by nature is miserly," to do so out of joy.[12]

This distinction follows also from a comment of R. Shimon ben Tzemah, the Tashbetz – though in an entirely different form. First, according to him, "This mishna does not deal with the trait of charity; it is in the other mishna (5:13) where we learn that there are four types of charitable donors. This mishna speaks of the acts of kindness that well-to-do householders perform for each other." Second, in accordance with his general position that "there is no disagreement in this tractate (*Avot*)," the Tashbetz suggests that there is no fundamental disagreement between the two positions, as the second position is not dealing with real *middat Sedom*: "...the first *Tanna* maintains that a person of average character is permitted to maintain that character"; and thus, "the [second] *Tanna* comes only to add that this character involves evil that is close to *middat Sedom*.... He who never provides his fellow with benefaction, if this quality grows in him, will come to withhold benefaction from another person even in that which causes him no loss.... This is *middat Sedom*.... About this quality, the Sages said: '*Kofin al middat Sedom*.'"[13] He seems to understand that the definition of the trait is, in the sense of the talmudic passages, *zeh neheneh vezeh lo haser*. However, the case of "one who says 'Mine is mine, and yours is yours'" is not included in this definition, for here he would suffer a loss if he would give to others. The mishna is dealing exclusively with a sort of protective measure – a decree regarding a case of *zeh neheneh vezeh haser* because of the slippery slope to withholding benefit even when *zeh neheneh vezeh lo haser*.

12. It is, however, possible that the two sources discuss the same trait, but at different levels. In the one case, it merely distorts the person's will, without constraining his actions when he submits to his Maker's commandments. In the other case, it even impacts on his actions. However, almost certainly this very domination over his actions indicates a fundamental distinction in the nature and strength of *middat Sedom* and is not merely the result of the strengthening of other inclinations. Furthermore, when dealing with the giving of charity, it is difficult to invoke the concept of *zeh neheneh vezeh lo haser*. In the end, the giver always suffers a loss. Thus, according to Rabbenu Yona, we are forced to distinguish between the subject of the mishna and the talmudic passages.
13. *Magen Avot* (New York; photo offset, 5706), ch. 5, no. 10.

As opposed to Rabbenu Yona and the Tashbetz, several *Rishonim* are inclined to identify the *middat Sedom* mentioned in the Mishna with the subject of the talmudic passages. This identification is explicitly suggested by Rabbenu Bahya ben Asher. In the course of his explanation of the former, Rabbenu Bahya refers also to the latter: "Therefore, our Rabbis, of blessed memory, saw fit and ruled that we compel one who exhibits the trait of Sodom; *zeh neheneh vezeh lo haser* – this is *middat Sedom.*"[14] This identification also follows from the words of Rashi. In his commentary to the passage in *Eiruvin*, Rashi explains: "*Middat Sedom* – that even when he suffers no loss, he does not benefit his fellow"; in his next comment, he adds: "*Middat Sedom* – 'Mine is mine.'"[15] Thus, we see a three-fold connection – between the mishna in *Avot*, the talmudic passage dealing with the principle of *zeh neheneh vezeh lo haser*, and the law of *kofin al middat Sedom.*

It would seem to follow then that the *Tanna'im* disagree about the principle of *zeh neheneh vezeh lo haser*. Some *Rishonim*, however, appear to be unprepared to accept this conclusion; therefore, they are forced to explain that there is no disagreement whatsoever in the mishna. In one form, we find this in the commentary of Rabbenu Bahya: "The first *Tanna* calls this 'average character' only because he is innocent of theft and doesn't covet his fellow's property; but if others do not derive benefit from his property, it is certainly an evil trait in his soul, and this is *middat Sedom.*"[16] The Me'iri indeed sees the two designations as contradictory, but he argues that they do not relate to the same circumstance. The *yesh omerim* are dealing with an actual case of *zeh neheneh vezeh lo haser*, "but [in] the first case, were he to benefit [his fellow], he or his property would suffer a slight loss, even though the other person would make his own property available in similar circumstances. Such withholding, since there is a loss, is not *middat Sedom*, for he does not want to cause a loss to others or to be caused a loss by others."[17]

14. Commentary of Rabbenu Bahya to *Avot* (Jerusalem, n.d.), 5:10.
15. *Eiruvin* 49a; see the commentary attributed to Rabbenu Gershom, *Bava Batra* 12b and 59a.
16. Commentary to *Avot*, 5:10.
17. *Beit HaBehira* on Tractate *Avot* (Jerusalem, 5704), 5:12.

If, however, we assume, as do other *Rishonim*, and as is implied by the plain sense of the mishna, that it reflects a real difference of opinion, then it turns out that the law of *zeh neheneh vezeh lo haser* is the subject of controversy. From a purely interpretive perspective, it is possible to understand that the first *Tanna* denies the very concept. From a moral perspective, however, this explanation is exceedingly difficult. Is it possible that one of the *Tanna'im* – and one whose position is presented anonymously – would make peace with a person withholding something that causes him no damage but could benefit another? Is there a hardening of the heart greater than the refusal to extend help to another person, in a case where the helper would not suffer any loss, neither to his person nor to his property? By what moral standard can insensitivity of this sort, and even worse than this, be referred to as "average character"?

Anyone who is sensitive to the values of the Sages and connected to their ways of thinking is forced, then, to adopt a different approach. Indeed, when we carefully examine the wording of the mishna, we see that a distinction can be made – even according to Rashi and Rabbenu Gershom – between the mishna and the talmudic passages. Withholding benefit from one's fellow without accruing any advantage to oneself is possible in two ways. The first is embodied in a specific and particular case, in which the determining facts are clear: a person moves to a new apartment and throws the extra set of keys to his old apartment into the sewer, rather than passing them on to the next tenant; a person has tickets to a series of cultural events and, while he cannot take full advantage of them, refuses to give the unused tickets to another person. In such cases, we unquestionably are dealing with *middat Sedom*.

The mishna, however, is not dealing with this type of *zeh neheneh vezeh lo haser*. Rather, the mishna is dealing with a personality trait, or to put it differently, a way of life. The withholding of benefit from one's fellow does not take place in a narrow framework where the injustice is blatant. It is rooted in one's general conduct and approach – and especially in an exaggerated emphasis on privacy and a distorted idea of ownership. A person who shuts himself in his four cubits, who denies, and perhaps even loathes, sharing and partnership; who agrees to open his hand to the unfortunate, but not to extend it to his neighbor; who knows and recognizes that his position reduces his own pleasure and the pleasure of his fellow, but is ready, for the sake of his personal independence, to place the burden on the two of them – it is about such a person that the *Tanna'im* disagree. The result of such an approach – and almost certainly its proponent fully understands this truth – is a quantitative, and perhaps even qualitative reduction in the enjoyment derived by society as a whole from the totality of its assets. In this point, the *Rishonim* saw a connection between our mishna and the passage dealing with *kofin al middat Sedom*, but the means of this reduction are entirely different.

In the mishna, the emphasis is not on direct refusal but on missing an opportunity. Withholding benefit from one's fellow stems from a loathing of exchanging favors and productive sharing, and not from a specific hardening of the heart. Therefore, here, regarding excessive privacy that causes a reduction of benefit to one's fellow, without achieving any benefit for one's own person – there is room for a dispute among *Tanna'im*. Despite the saddening results, the first *Tanna* sees this quality – narrow-minded but not malicious, rooted in egocentricity, but not evil – as average character. By contrast, the *yesh omerim* maintain that in the end we are dealing with indifference toward one's fellow, even where the person himself loses nothing.[18]

If one would wish to claim that the position of "Mine is mine" is rooted purely in the yearning for additional privacy – "Your guarantor needs a guarantor," as the proverb goes (*Gittin* 28b) – who can assure us that this yearning itself does not involve *middat Sedom*?[19] The fact

---

18. The gist of this approach to the mishna is found in the commentary of one of the Rambam's disciples, Rabbenu Avraham of Ferisol, though he apparently understands that there is no disagreement in the mishna: "There is a reason for the two designations. The one who calls it 'average character' does well, for it is midway between two opposites: he does not want to overburden his fellow, or that others should overburden him. However, the one who called it '*middat Sedom*' is also right, for the people of Sodom were wicked sinners, and it is known that they hated each other and despised charity and acts of kindness, so as not to help one another" (*Commentary of Rabbenu Avraham Ferisol on Avot* [Jerusalem, 5724], 5:10).
19. Halakha attaches great importance to the right of privacy, as is proven by the laws governing neighbors, especially *hezzek re'iyya*. We are dealing here with an entirely different kind of privacy: not the appreciation of quiet and the possibility of seclusion – an appreciation that is rooted in the feelings of human dignity and sanctity – but rather the desire for absolute control over a particular unit. A person's

that the position of "Mine is mine" fills a subjective longing does not clear up the doubt as to whether this is defined as a situation involving loss on the part of the giver – for we must not see the negation of every longing as a loss. In defining "loss," the arbitrariness of a person's heart is not the only determining factor. We must consider also the moral-ideal perspective to decide what disappointment should rightfully be regarded as a "loss." Even if the withholding of good from one's fellow is rooted in the desire to maintain a certain emotional identity, without any intention to cause harm, is it not possible that this approach itself involves *middat Sedom*?

The basis for this distinction is the unmediated nature of the injustice – is it clear and specific, or is it only the general, and sometimes even indirect, result of an overall way of life? However, we may also suggest a second distinction connected to the definition of "loss." This may be understood through a brief review of the talmudic passages cited above. Three of them suggest, as fact or as a possibility, that there exists a dispute regarding compulsion. In two – which deal with the merging of domains and the leasing of the mill – the rule of *kofin al middat Sedom* is stated definitively. How is this disagreement between the *sugyot* to be understood?

The answer seems to be rooted in a difference between the cases. In the last two cases, the one who benefits does not actually use the other person's property. The *Eiruvin* passage discusses attributing the courtyard, on the theoretical level, to one alleyway or the other. In the *Ketubbot* passage, the one who benefits encroaches upon the other person, demanding money instead of the service of milling, but even there he does not actually enter his domain. The relationship of ownership of an article as an article – not in the exclusively legal sense, but in the sense of a personal and emotional connection – does not exist with respect to money. Money is meant to be spent; its value is symbolic and not intrinsic. A person has nothing in money – unless he is a miser or

---

exaggerated emphasis of this idea stems from his excessive aspiration for ownership and lordship.

a coin collector – other than its purchasing power.[20] Therefore, as long as the owner of the mill does not suffer a monetary loss, he does not suffer *any* loss.

In the three other cases, on the other hand, the benefit involves the use of the other person's property. Thus, it involves taking control of that property and the person himself. It might be argued that such a situation can be regarded as a case where *zeh neheneh vezeh haser:* there is no monetary loss, but an emotional loss is certainly present. Thus, there is room for disagreement. In one form, and in connection with compulsion, we encounter this phenomenon in three of the talmudic passages. In another form, and in connection with the definition of *middat Sedom* itself, we see it in the mishna. The *Tanna'im* do not disagree whether *zeh neheneh vezeh lo haser* is *middat Sedom*. They do, however, disagree whether the negation of "Mine is mine" is a loss.

As for the relationship between the three passages and the mishna, this too does not constitute a problem. The emotional loss that stems from the constriction of absolute domination lends itself to gradation. It is possible – and we cannot prove this one way or the other – that it is not as severe in the three talmudic passages as in the mishna. Joint possession of a *shtar beirurin,* for example, is one level. A neighbor's use of his fellow's property is a different level. Therefore, even if we define the *middat Sedom* in both cases as "Mine is mine, and yours is yours," there is no need to identify the talmudic passages with the mishna, or to assume that they can be reconciled only with the position of the *yesh omerim*.

III. The Definition of "This One Suffers No Loss"

Thus far we have seen three types of *middat Sedom*: 1) failure to give charity or perform acts of *hesed*; 2) an overall lifestyle that places inordinate emphasis on privacy, and thus reduces the benefit that one person derives

20. Therefore, the law is that while one partner cannot divide jointly owned property without the other's consent, "money is as if it is divided" (*Bava Metzia* 69a), and he may take his share on his own. See also *Bava Metzia* 31b, *Bava Batra* 106b, and the *Rishonim* in both places, especially *Hiddushei HaRi Migash, Bava Batra* 106b.

from another and the development of society as a whole; 3) a clear and specific case of one person refusing to confer benefit upon another person even when that benefit would not cost the first person anything. The last type of *middat Sedom* divides into two: a) a case where the second party, who would derive benefit, would use the first party's property; b) a case where the second party would benefit, but without taking hold of the first party's property. In order to complete the definition of this quality, however, we must reexamine the last of the aforementioned talmudic passages – the one that deals with the division of jointly owned property. Let us first present the passage (*Bava Batra* 12b) in full:

> A certain man bought a field adjacent to the estate of his father. When they came to divide the latter's estate, he said: "Give me my share next to my own field." Rabba said: "In such a case, *kofin al middat Sedom.*" R. Yosef strongly objected to this, on the grounds that the brothers can say to him: "We value this field like those [prime fields] of Bar Maryon."[21] The law follows R. Yosef.
>
> If there are two fields with two channels [running by them, and when the owner dies, one of his sons requests the field adjacent to his own], Rabba said: "In such a case, *kofin al middat Sedom.*" R. Yosef strongly objected to this, on the grounds that sometimes one channel may continue running while the other dries up. The law follows R. Yosef.

21. I have presented here the printed version: "*maalinan leih illuya.*" There are several variant readings, most of which are insignificant, with the exception of one important difference. Regarding R. Yosef's first comment, Rashi reads: "*Maalinan leih illu'ei,*" and comments: "for us it is high quality" (*illu'ei* = for us). The *Behag* reads "*maalinan lah alakh,*" and similarly the reading of the Rashba and the Rosh is "*maalinan lakh,*" and the reading of Rabbenu Yona and *Tosafot* (cited by the Ramban in the name of Rashi) is "*maalinan leih.*" According to these readings, we can understand "we value this for him" or "we value this for you," even without offering a reason, following the position of Rabbenu Tam below. A third reading, "*maalinan leih alluya,*" seems to correspond to the position of the Ri Migash – see his *Hiddushim*, ad loc., s.v. *tartei* – that the other heirs cannot object unless they are prepared to assess the value of the abutting field at higher than its ordinary assessment (in the case of *iddit*, prime land). However, see *Yad Rama*, ch. 1, sec. 159, and *Dikdukei Soferim* here.

> If, however, there are two fields adjoining one channel [and they are therefore of equal value], R. Yosef said, "In such a case, *kofin al middat Sedom*." Abbaye objected to this strongly, on the grounds that the one can say: "I want you to have more tenant farmers" [i.e., one brother can object that he wants the other brother to possess two non-adjacent fields, so that the large number of tenant farmers on the two fields will protect his own field in the middle]. The law, however, follows R. Yosef; the increase in the number of tenant farmers is not a matter of consequence.

The issues in dispute in the three controversies cited here are, generally speaking, quite clear. It is also clear that Rabba, R. Yosef, and Abbaye all accept the principle that *kofin al middat Sedom*; they disagree only about its precise parameters. As for the particulars (and primarily with respect to the first dispute), the *Rishonim* disagree. Their explanations of the passage – both the assumptions in light of which they approach it, as well as the conclusions that they derive from it – teach us fundamental principles regarding the matter at hand.

The first dispute – whether we compel the other heirs to give their brother who owns the adjacent field his portion of the estate from the property abutting his field – immediately raises a difficulty, as the Ritva comments:

> It may be asked: What case are we discussing? If the portions are absolutely equal, regarding land of the highest quality and land of intermediate quality, Rabba said well that it is *middat Sedom*; and if they are not equal, R. Yosef said well, even when the abutting portion that he requests is land of the poorest quality, for there are those who prefer a large parcel of land of the poorest quality over a small parcel of land of the highest quality.[22]

We find that earlier *Rishonim*, each in his own way, accept one of these two possibilities. The Ri Migash[23] understands the passage as referring

22. *Hiddushei HaRitva, Bava Batra*, ed. M. Y. Blau (New York, 5714), 12b.
23. See *Hiddushei HaRi Migash, Bava Batra* 12b.

to a case where the fields are not equal, and therefore he rules – as does, in his wake, the Rambam[24] – that when the fields are of equal quality, we do indeed compel the brothers. This is true despite the fact that the Gemara rules explicitly in accordance with the position of R. Yosef. If we accept this approach, the parameters of *middat Sedom* expand greatly, according to Rabba. Though by right the brothers may have just claims regarding the quality of the fields they are to receive, they must ignore these claims for the good of the brother who owns the neighboring field, and we compel them to do so. Even though their situation is impaired, though we are not dealing with a financial loss in the bookkeeping sense, Rabba still views the case as one of *zeh neheneh vezeh lo haser.* "For since he gave them the additional value in that portion over the other portions, why should they care?"[25] It is on this point – and on this point alone – that R. Yosef disagrees, and the law is decided in his favor.

Rashi also notes the confusion in our passage. He understands that in a case of real equality, R. Yosef would deny the argument of "we value this field like those of Bar Maryon." Regarding the case of inequality, however, Rashi followed an entirely different path: "It stands to reason that R. Yosef is talking about a case of a *sedeh baal,* about which they can say that sometimes it receives greater blessing than the other fields."[26] In other words, when the fields are really equal, and this situation is expected to continue in the future, all agree that we compel the other heirs to give the brother who owns the neighboring field his share of the estate adjacent to his field. So, too, R. Yosef agrees about the case of "two fields adjoining one channel." Perforce, then, the disagreement revolves around the definition of "equality": What is the law governing articles that currently are equal in value, but are liable, whether by nature or habit, and not only as a result of extraordinary circumstances, to change in value in the future? It is for this reason that Rabbenu Yo'el and the Maharam of Rothenburg[27] rely on Rashi when they say that in

24. *Hilkhot Shekhenim* 12:1; see there.
25. *Hiddushei HaRi Migash,* ad loc.
26. S.v. *ameru;* a *sedeh baal* is a field sufficiently watered by rain and requiring no artificial irrigation.
27. See *Mordekhai,* sec. 507.

the case of houses, which are less likely to change in value, we do indeed compel the others.

In contrast to the approaches of the Ri Migash and Rashi, Rabbenu Tam interpreted the passage as referring to a case where the fields are truly equal in value. According to him, the argument that "we value this field like those of Bar Maryon" requires no justification. It constitutes clear and absolute refusal: "We will only give you the right that we have in the field in exchange for a high price, like the sons of Maryon who were wealthy and would only sell their property in exchange for a high price."[28] Already the Ritva noted that according to this understanding, it is the position of R. Yosef that requires explanation; and the *Rishonim* offer two ways of understanding R. Yosef's position.

First, we can view the division of the estate as a sort of transfer of ownership, regarding which there is no room for compulsion. "Where do we find," asks Rabbenu Yona in the context of a later passage, "that a person can take property belonging to his fellow, and exchange it for his own without his fellow's consent, on the grounds that *zeh neheneh vezeh lo haser*? Furthermore, in the first chapter we also say: 'We value this field like those of Bar Maryon.'"[29] "In this case, there is no *middat Sedom*," writes the Rosh in explanation of Rabbenu Tam, "for we have a right in this lottery [to determine who gets what portion], so that if it falls to us in the lottery between the two fields, it is our right not to exchange it if not at a high price. Now, too, there is no *middat Sedom* if we do not give up our portion for you."[30]

The Ritva suggests an entirely different explanation: "Some say that they disagree even when the portions are equal, for when they are unequal, R. Yosef said well. Here R. Yosef's argument is that this is [a case of] *zeh neheneh vezeh haser*. For the brothers can say to him that if that portion falls to us in the lottery, it is worth more to us than the other portions, because you will buy it from us at a high price. Since we will

28. *Bava Batra* 12b, s.v. *maalinan*.
29. Cited in *Shitta Mekubbetzet, Bava Batra* 99b, in the context of the Rashba's explanation of the passage. See also *Hiddushei HaRan* and *Hiddushei HaRashba*, ad loc.; they explain it without making any reference to *kofin al middat Sedom*. See also *Shut Beit Efrayim*, HM, no. 49.
30. *Bava Batra* 1:46.

benefit if we divide it in accordance with Torah law, you have no right to cancel the lottery."[31] According to this approach, the reason for not applying *kofin* is not that a person cannot be compelled to perform a transaction, but that the necessary conditions for such compulsion are not met here. While at the initial stage there existed a situation of *zeh neheneh vezeh lo haser*, since the brother with the neighboring property is ready to pay money to receive the portion adjacent to his property, his brother would suffer a loss if he gave it to him for free.

There is a fundamental difference between these two understandings. According to the first explanation, Rabba and R. Yosef agree that *middat Sedom* is present in the argument that "we value this field like those of Bar Maryon." Their disagreement – whether we relate it to the scope of the compulsion or connect it to the nature of the division of an estate – is limited to the issue of compulsion. On the other hand, according to the Ritva, since the brothers are regarded as suffering a loss, the argument that "we value this field like those of Bar Maryon" is not regarded as an example of *middat Sedom*. Here, however, his explanation encounters a severe difficulty, which is already noted by the Rosh in one of his responsa. According to R. Yosef,

> In every case of *zeh neheneh vezeh lo haser* in which we compel one who exhibits *middat Sedom*, why do we compel him? Surely he suffers the loss of the money that the other person would give him for his benefit, were we not to compel him to do it for free! Rather, certainly, since he has no loss other than the money which he could force the other person to give him for his benefit, this is *middat Sedom*.[32]

The entire law of *kofin al middat Sedom* is based on the assumption that the forfeiture of money that the benefiting party would have been willing to pay for his benefit is not regarded as a loss. If we define the owner's loss in light of the mutual relations with the party receiving the benefit, we just about wipe out this type of compulsion.

31. *Hiddushei HaRitva, Bava Batra* 12b.
32. *Teshuvot HaRosh,* 97:2.

According to Rabbenu Tam, we are forced to distinguish between two situations of *zeh lo haser. Kofin al middat Sedom* applies in the case where the benefiting party does not derive benefit that could be the object of negotiation (such as rental, sale, or the like) were the problem of the value of that benefit to arise. In such cases – which are discussed in the other passages – refusal to confer benefit involves injustice, monetary claims, and exploitation, as there is no transaction for which payment could be demanded. If, however, negotiations are conducted, and the problem that presents itself is the assessment of the benefit, the owner can assess it in accordance with what the party receiving the benefit would be willing to pay for it, and not according to what others, who do not share his special interests, would be willing to offer. According to the Rosh, the value is established in relation to the general social framework;[33] and if the owners do not suffer a loss, we compel them to provide the benefiting party the addition that exists only for him but not for others, or the benefit that would accrue to them in his absence. According to Rabbenu Tam, even Rabba agrees to this. According to R. Yosef, however, the owner is permitted to take into account the unique situation and will of the benefiting party when defining the value. This does not involve robbery or exploitation, but a simple assessment of value.[34]

33. It should be noted that the Rashba (*Bava Batra* 12b) accepts the position of Rabbenu Tam, but with a certain addition. He emphasizes that since there is a person who owns the adjacent field and is willing to pay more for it, the field goes up in value even with respect to other potential buyers, because they take into account the possibility of selling the property at a price higher than that which they paid.
34. It may be asked of Rabbenu Tam: Why is selling at the price of Bar Maryon not considered a violation of the prohibition of *onaa* (overcharging)? See especially *Bava Metzia* 58b, the dispute between R. Yehuda and the Sages there. Regarding the division of the property itself, there is no question, because it may not be included at all in the laws of *onaa*. See *Gittin* 48a and *Tosafot*, s.v. *I*, who assume that according to the position that brothers who divide up their father's estate are regarded as heirs, there is no *onaa* in the division. See, however, Me'iri, *Kiddushin*, 42b, s.v. *haahin*. The Rosh implies that according to Rabbenu Tam, even sale at a higher price is possible. Perhaps he relies on the fact that real estate is excluded from the laws of *onaa* (*Bava Metzia* 56b), and he maintains, in opposition to the Ramban (commentary to *Vayikra* 25:15), that there is also no prohibition. Alternatively, perhaps he maintains that for the purpose of assessment we ignore the prohibition. See also *Ketubbot* 109b.

In this passage,[35] then, we see four fundamental concepts of "loss":

1. a quantitative bookkeeping loss (Rabba, according to the Rambam);
2. diminished quality of the property (R. Yosef, according to the Rambam; all opinions, according to most of the *Rishonim*);
3. concern about a change of value in the future (Rabba, according to Rashi); and
4. loss of the unique additional value to the party deriving the benefit (R. Yosef, according to Rabbinu Tam).

It follows, of course, that we have also raised thereby the number of definitions of *middat Sedom*.

However, the most radical definition of *middat Sedom* appears, according to some *Rishonim*, in a framework that makes no mention whatsoever of *middat Sedom*: the passage in *Bava Kamma* that deals directly and explicitly with the principle of *zeh neheneh vezeh lo haser*. That passage does not discuss personality traits or prohibitions, but rather obligations. If a person, who would otherwise rent living quarters, lives without the owner's knowledge in a house that is not up for rent – must he pay him rent? The final decision is that he is exempt,[36]

35. I have limited myself to the first dispute in the passage. Important details follow from the other two disputes, but they are not fundamental to the discussion.

36. The passage in *Bava Kamma* 20b–21a brings two reasons for exemption: 1) the absence of a reason to obligate payment – "What did he do to him? What loss or damage did he cause him?"; 2) "The gate is struck with destruction" (*Yeshayahu* 24:12) – in other words, the squatter in fact benefits the owner, because owing to his presence, the house is not empty and forsaken. According to the second reason, it is possible to conclude that the exemption applies only to houses, but in general, when *zeh neheneh vezeh lo haser*, the one who derives benefit must pay. This is explicitly proposed in *Bava Kamma* 97a. Some *Rishonim* recoil from such a conclusion, ruling that he is exempt in all cases, even reconciling the end of the passage in various ways. See especially *Hiddushei HaRashba*, s.v. *amar* (though below, p. 97a, s.v. *amar*, he implies otherwise), and Rosh, *Bava Kamma* 2:6. The Rambam also omits the second reason, and in his wake also Rav Yosef Karo in the *Shulhan Arukh*; see *Hilkhot Gezela* 3:9, and HM 363:6, and *Be'urei HaGra*, ad loc., no. 16.

but this ruling relates only to the situation after the fact (*bediavad*). Nevertheless, the question still remains whether a person is permitted to squat in another person's house despite the owner's objections, or may the owner prevent him from so doing?[37] *Tosafot* (ad loc.) assume as obvious that "even according to the one who says in the first chapter of *Bava Kamma* that *kofin al middat Sedom* and that we give him the portion that is adjacent to his property... he can prevent him from the outset from living in his house."[38] However, the Tosafists disagree on the matter. The *Or Zarua* cites two opinions:

> Some say that we compel the owner to allow the other person to live there. Since it is not up for rent, in such a case, *kofin al middat Sedom*, as we say in *Bava Batra* regarding the case of the two fields with a single channel....
>
> Others say that it is different there, because even had he taken the field abutting the field that the other one bought, he would not have gained anything, because they are equal. Even had he wanted to profit, he would have been unable to do so; in such a case, therefore, *kofin al middat Sedom*. However, here, had the owner wanted to rent it out to someone else, he would have profited; now that he does not rent it out, we do not compel him [to let the squatter reside there for free].[39]

We see, then, that according to one opinion, preventing a person from living in a house that is not up for rent is included in *middat Sedom*, and that

37. Logically speaking, it is possible to distinguish at the first stage between the squatter's permission and the owner's right: it is possible that the squatter is not permitted to live there, but the owner does not have the right to evict him; but I have not found any *Rishonim* who suggest this distinction. See, however, in *Bava Metzia* 117b, the view of R. Yehuda according to R. Yohanan, "A person is forbidden to derive benefit from another's property," according to *Tosafot*, s.v. *bishlosha*, who understand that by strict law he is exempt, but nevertheless forbidden. See also below.
38. *Tosafot*, *Bava Kamma* 20b, s.v. *ha*.
39. *Or Zarua*, III, nos. 122–123. See also *Haggahot Maimoniyyot*, *Hilkhot Gezela* 3:4, and *Mordekhai*, *Bava Kamma*, 16, who note that the two opinions are brought by the Raavya, who does not decide between them.

as long as the house is standing empty, anybody can harness the power of the court to allow him to live there, even against the owner's wishes.

Furthermore, to a certain degree, it is possible that this is not a sole dissident opinion, and that perhaps even *Tosafot* might agree in part. Their position lends itself to two understandings. The one – and this is in accordance with the suggestion made earlier regarding the mishna in *Avot* – says that preventing others from using one's property does not constitute *middat Sedom*. While with respect to an obligation of payment, "loss" requires a real monetary loss, in the moral dimension we must consider several other types of loss as well. This being the case, the owner must not be condemned as exhibiting *middat Sedom*, unless all these losses are absent, psychological no less than monetary. This formulation follows almost explicitly from the words of Rav Aharon HaLevi (the Raa):

> Even though in general we maintain that in a case of *zeh neheneh vezeh lo haser*, the rule of *kofin al middat Sedom* is enforced, that applies to land belonging to the two of them where he is not using the other person's property at all, but he can compel him by law not to do it.... But to use the other person's property – they never said this, for otherwise there is no person who will not compel his fellow against his will.[40]

The *Or Zarua*'s wording, however – "Here, had the owner wanted to rent it out to someone else, he would have profited; now that he does not rent it out, we do not compel him" – implies an entirely different understanding. This explanation is based on the assumption that it is in the hands of the owner – who has both the ability and the authority – to turn the house into one that is "up for rent," in such a manner that he himself would then be regarded as suffering a loss. Therefore, even if the state of the house remains the same, we still cannot compel the owner, because he is not bound by an absolute obligation to allow someone else to live there for free.

40. Brought in *Nimmukei Yosef, Bava Kamma* 20a [in Alfasi 8b].

According to this, it is plainly evident that the distinction between *lekhathilla* (*ab initio*) and *bediavad* relates only to the possibility of compulsion. As for the definition of *middat Sedom* in and of itself, as long as there is no real change in the status of the house, preventing another person from living there from the outset is also included in this category. As long as the house is not up for rent, and the owner is not suffering a loss, the injustice exists. Thus, it is possible that even *Tosafot* cast upon us a difficult moral obligation, for even they may agree that anyone who prevents another person from living in his house when he does not need it and the house is not up for rent is guilty of *middat Sedom*.[41]

This position is of special importance, because as it would appear, the Rama accepts it as normative law. In his gloss on Rav Yosef Karo's ruling that "one who lives in another person's courtyard without his knowledge… is not obligated to pay him rent," the Rama comments:

> This is only if he has already lived there, but he cannot compel him from the outset to allow him to live there, even though *kofin al middat Sedom* when *zeh neheneh vezeh lo haser*. For this applies only in a case where had the owner wished to derive benefit, he would have been unable to do so. But in a case where the owner would have been able to derive benefit and rent out his courtyard, only he does not want to, we do not compel him to do it for free.[42]

The meaning is clear: if a person cannot rent out his property or derive any benefit from it, another person can use it *lekhathilla*, even against the owner's wishes.[43]

---

41. This appears to contradict the last explanation proposed above to the controversy among the *Tanna'im* in the mishna in *Avot*; it seems understandable only according to the explanation of the Raa. In truth, however, it can be maintained according to all opinions. It is possible that the words of the *Rishonim* on this passage are stated only according to the position of the *yesh omerim*, that "mine is mine, and yours is yours" is *middat Sedom*. According to the first *Tanna*, there might be a difference between *zeh neheneh vezeh lo haser* in general and the use of another's property in particular.
42. HM 363:6.
43. This conclusion put off the *Noda BiYehuda* (2nd ed., HM, 24), who says: "This is like one who wishes to live in another person's courtyard, even if it is not up for rent. Is

It seems, then, that the allowance to use another person's property continues to broaden. It is possible, however, that the scope of the Rama's ruling must be narrowed in light of a famous law that appears to contradict it: one who borrows an article without the owner's knowledge is regarded as a thief.[44] Several possible resolutions of the contradiction may be proposed.

1. The scope of the *Or Zarua*'s ruling need not be constricted. The law regarding one who borrows without the owner's knowledge applies only when the owner could have derived benefit from the property or rented it out at the same time that the other person had been using it. If the owner could not have benefited from his property, then the borrower took nothing from him and cannot be called a thief. On the contrary, the owner is bound by an obligation to allow the other person to use it; and even if the latter used it without permission, it is as if he took that which was due him, so that it is not thievery.[45]
2. The allowance to use the other person's property stems from the principle of *kofin al middat Sedom*. Therefore, it applies only by way of compulsion – namely, through the court. There is no room here for executing judgment independent of the court;

---

it possible to imagine that he can force the other person to allow him to live in his courtyard for free?" Yet the words of the Rama are almost explicit. Indeed, almost immediately thereafter the *Noda BiYehuda* cites his position, noting that he thinks that it is stated only according to the Rambam – who maintains that the argument "We value this field like those of Bar Maryon" applies only in a case where the fields are equal – but not according to those who disagree with him.

44. See *Bava Batra* 88a and *Bava Metzia* 41a and 43b.
45. This is most reasonable according to the Raavad, who understands that the law that borrowing without the owner's consent makes one a thief is not by strict law, but a penalty. See *Hiddushei HaRaavad Al Bava Kamma*, ed. Atlas, 2nd ed. (Jerusalem, 5723), 97b: "He is like one who borrows without the owner's knowledge. Even though we treat him like a thief regarding death resulting from the animal's labor and all cases of unusual accidents (*ones*), nevertheless, he is not excluded from the category of borrower, and even for depreciation that involves a change, we assess the broken pieces like a borrower, for we do not penalize him to such a great extent."

anyone who uses his fellow's property without permission is regarded as a thief.

3. The Gemara does not say that borrowing "without the owner's knowledge" involves a violation of the *prohibition* of stealing. The talmudic passages all discuss the manner of restoration and the obligations that devolve upon one who borrows without permission if the article is broken or lost. Thus, the term "thief" may be imprecise, and is only used by extension in the sense of maximal responsibility. According to the position that a borrower without permission is a "borrower," he enjoys the exemptions granted to a borrower – when the owner is with him or in a case where the animal dies of its labor – and according to the position that he is a thief, he is obligated in all cases. In fact, if he does not cause the owner any loss, there is no violation of the prohibition of stealing.[46]
4. The Ramban argues that the law that states that one who borrows without the owner's permission is a thief applies only when "the use that he makes of it involves damage to the owner's property, and even though it does not suffer a loss through his use, it is possible that when he moves it, it will break or suffer other damage." On the other hand, concerning "something that cannot suffer damage when moved, there is nobody who says that one who borrows without the owner's knowledge is a thief, for he has done nothing."[47] Even those who disagree with the Ramban[48]

46. The Rambam, however, understands that he violates the prohibition of theft, for he calls him a "wicked man." See *Teshuvot HaRambam*, ed. J. Blau (Jerusalem, 1960), II, no. 615. However, the possibility that a borrower without the knowledge of the owner should be liable for *ones* and for the animal's dying of its labor, even if he does not violate the prohibition of theft, is proposed by the *Mahaneh Efrayim*. See what he says (*Hilkhot Gezela*, no. 17) regarding one who borrows another person's horse in order to rescue his own money. While he is permitted to do so according to those who rule in accordance with R. Yishmael b. R. Yehuda b. Beteira (see *Bava Kamma* 81b), nevertheless he is liable for *ones* like a thief, against the view of the *Terumat HaDeshen*, no. 316.
47. Thus it is cited in the name of the Ramban in *Hiddushei HaRitva HaHadashim, Bava Metzia* (ed. A. Halperin, [London, 5722]) 41a, and in *Shitta Mekubbetzet, Bava Metzia* 41a.
48. See *Mahaneh Efrayim, Hilkhot Gezela*, no. 20.

> would presumably agree that a distinction can be made between movables, which are at risk of being stolen even when they are not liable to suffer breakage, and real estate. The *Or Zarua* and the Rama deal with a courtyard or a house. By contrast, the talmudic passages deal with movables, for there are no liabilities of borrowing or theft with respect to landed property,[49] and regarding movables the fear of theft or breakage remains in place. Therefore, we do not compel him for exhibiting *middat Sedom*, as the usage is liable to cause the owner a loss – and perhaps even the worry itself is regarded as a loss.[50]

If we accept this last proposal, the importance of the Rama's ruling on the practical level diminishes. It must be emphasized, however, that even in that case the principle does not change: ownership does not authorize a person to prevent another person from using his property for no reason. The effort to prevent such usage, which is rooted in the strong desire to emphasize the exclusivity of "private property," may be seen as *middat Sedom*.

---

49. See *Bava Metzia* 56a. The Mishna does not mention a borrower, but most *Rishonim* assumed that he is included as well. See, for example, Rambam, *Hilkhot Sekhirut* 2:1, and *Tosafot*, *Shevuot* 42b, s.v. *shomer*, and *Hiddushei HaRashba*, ad loc., s.v. *matnitin*. But see also *Or Zarua*, III, no. 125, who says that "real estate is not excluded from the law of a borrower the way it is excluded from the laws governing an unpaid or paid bailee."
50. See also Ramban, *Milhamot Hashem*, *Bava Metzia* 41a (23b in Alfasi): "It seems to me that one who borrows an article without the owner's knowledge is neither a borrower nor a thief unless he has the intention to borrow it and moves it from its place for his own needs...but a shepherd who sets his stick or bag down on something has no intention of borrowing it and does not remove it at all from the owner's possession." If we emphasize the idea of removing the article from the owner's possession, there is additional reason to distinguish between movables and real estate. Below, however, the Ramban himself implies that this removal in and of itself is not the critical factor; rather, in certain situations its absence testifies that the user had had no intention of borrowing and that he did not take the article for himself or change it from the use assigned to it by the owner.

IV. The Nature of Compulsion

Thus far our survey of the principle of *kofin al middat Sedom* has focused on the definition of the trait of *middat Sedom*. We shall now begin to analyze the compulsion itself. As we have already seen, the parameters of the two are not identical. There can be *middat Sedom* that does not lead to compulsion – whether because it does not express itself in a particular act, but in a general and amorphous way of life; or because it has only taken root as a personality trait, but has not yet found practical expression; or because of secondary factors, e.g., the possibility of changing the situation under discussion ("Had the owner wanted to rent it out to someone else, he would have profited"), or because of a more or less arbitrary claim ("Sometimes one channel may continue running while the other dries up"). The details of these conditions in and of themselves allow for discussion and definition. When does the severity of the trait or the degree of its realization lead to the law of compulsion? How subjective can a claim be and still be acceptable? Where do we draw the line between a direct and specific action, on the one hand, and general behavior or an indirect action, on the other? Questions of this sort do not lend themselves to clear-cut answers, and perforce any answer will be slightly vague and even ambiguous, and subject to differences of opinion. Even if we do not inquire into such details, we must still clarify the parameters of compulsion and its relationship to *middat Sedom*.

In order to answer this question, we must first determine the foundation of the law that *kofin al middat Sedom* – both regarding the condemnation of the trait itself and regarding the compulsion. The first point does not present a difficult problem. In the extreme form of the trait, namely, a real case of *lehakhis*, there may be a violation of the prohibition of hating one's fellow, and in many cases, also verbal oppression (*onaat devarim*).[51] As for its more moderate form, namely, indifference to one's fellow man, the loathing of the trait stems from the obligation to

51. The sin of hating one's fellow would seem to apply in every case of "*lehakhis*," but the sin of verbal oppression applies only if one relates directly to the party seeking benefit and provokes him.

practice acts of lovingkindness – and therefore, as asserted by the Ritzba,[52] it applies by Torah law. The description of Sodom in the book of *Yehezkel* mentions only the neglect of giving charity: "Behold this was the iniquity of your sister Sodom: she and her daughters had pride, surfeit of bread, and abundance of idleness, but she did not strengthen the hand of the poor and needy."[53] The Sages, however, understand that it includes also the neglect of performing acts of lovingkindness. Moreover, the Gemara in *Sanhedrin* emphasizes precisely this point: "[The people of Sodom] said: 'Since there comes forth bread out of [our] earth, and it has the dust of gold, why should we suffer wayfarers, who come to us only to deplete our wealth? Come, let us abolish the practice of traveling in our land.'"[54] The obligation to condemn this trait stems then from the two general sources of the mitzva to perform acts of lovingkindness – "You shall walk in His ways" (*Devarim* 28:9), on the one hand, and "You shall love your neighbor as yourself" (*Vayikra* 19:18), on the other.[55] Its source is also found in another general verse, "You shall do what is right and what is good" (*Devarim* 6:18), this being the source for moral conduct that goes beyond the letter of the law[56] – which should be understood as a full-fledged obligation, not just an act of special piety.

---

52. See *Bava Batra* 12b, *Tosafot*, s.v. *kegon*. By Torah law, acts of lovingkindness have only a general character, but no specific expression (by rabbinic law, the mitzva is assigned clearly defined actions; see Rambam, *Hilkhot Evel* 14:1). This general character is helping one's fellow in need. The definition of "in need," however, is relative, and therefore it comes to include the wealthy. In the realm of *middat Sedom*, anyone who "derives benefit" is regarded as one in need in relation to one who "suffers no loss." This being the case, the condemnation of the trait is included in the positive precept of performing acts of lovingkindness.
53. *Yehezkel* 16:49.
54. *Sanhedrin* 109a. The distinction between charity and acts of lovingkindness is explained in *Sukka* 49b; see there.
55. The Gemara in *Sota* 14a and the *baraita* in *Sifre, Ekev*, 49, base the obligation of performing acts of lovingkindness on the first source. The Rambam (*Hilkhot Evel* 14:1), however, cites the second source. The interweaving of the two motifs is an important principle in Jewish ethics, but this is not the forum to discuss the matter at great length.
56. See especially the Ramban's commentary to *Vayikra* 19:2 and *Devarim* 6:18. [Ed. note: Regarding the nature and definition of the concept of "*lifnim mishurat hadin*," "beyond the letter of the law," see the previous chapter in this volume, as well as

When, however, we come to examine the basis for compulsion, both its objective and its rationale, we encounter confusion. Is the foundation for coercion moral or practical? Two questions arise that are parallel and independent, but to a certain degree also intertwined. What obligates the compulsion, and in what circumstances is it enforced? Specifically, is the compulsion rooted in the moral obligation of the owners, so that it is executed as a response to their negligence? Or perhaps the possibility of providing for the needs of others suffices in order to coerce the owners? Put differently, what is the determining factor: the mitzva of the person who is "*lo haser*" or the giving to the person who seeks to be "*neheneh*"?

The clarification of these issues has important halakhic ramifications. For example, does the principle of *kofin al middat Sedom* apply to a minor? If the moral factor is decisive, then it cannot apply to a minor; for example, we do not collect a debt from minor heirs (even if we know that their father did not repay his debt during his lifetime), because "repaying a debt is a mitzva, and minors are not obligated to perform mitzvot."[57] Similarly, "[Legal guardians] cannot undertake on [the orphans'] behalf to give charity or to redeem captives."[58] If, however, the other person's need is the critical factor, there is no room to distinguish between adult and minor. Regarding what is stated in the Mishna, "[A resident of a city] may be compelled to contribute to the building of a wall, folding doors, and a crossbar," the Gemara adds: "R. Yehuda said: All must contribute to the building of doors in the town gates, even orphans."[59]

I am unable, based on the words of *Hazal* and the *Rishonim*, to offer clear answers to these questions. It is, possible, however, to point to various sources which, in my opinion, touch on the aforementioned

---

Rabbi Lichtenstein's article, "Does Jewish Tradition Recognize an Ethic Independent of Halakha?" in Marvin Fox, ed., *Modern Jewish Ethics* (Columbus, 1975), 62–88.

57. *Bava Batra* 174a. Compare Rambam, *Hilkhot Malveh VeLoveh* 26:10: "A minor who borrows is obligated to repay when he reaches maturity" – but not beforehand.
58. *Gittin* 52a; while the passage implies that were there a fixed amount of charity to give, the minor would be forced to contribute, that is not because of a basic obligation, but because of the law of *hinnukh*, educating minors.
59. *Bava Batra* 7b and 8a.

issues. One such source is the disagreement between Rabba and R. Yosef regarding the division of an estate, according to the understanding of Rashi, which we already mentioned above. Their disagreement revolves around the refusal of one heir to allow his brother to take his portion from that part of the estate that adjoins land that he already owns – in a situation where one of the portions is liable to go up in value in the future, though it is not known now which portion will appreciate. It seems to me that in light of the present knowledge, which does not justify preferring one portion over the other, the brother who does not own the adjoining property should be classified as one who suffers no loss; and his refusal to give his brother the portion that is adjacent to his own property should constitute, from a subjective perspective, outright *middat Sedom*. Therefore, if refinement of the soul suffices to impose compulsion, Rabba is correct. If, however, the obligation of compulsion stems from the obligation to aid another person, there is room to say that the obligation to help him is limited to a case where there is not a trace of loss to the owner, so that the benefit to the other party derives, as it were, from ownerless property. However, if, objectively speaking, the compulsion is liable to cause the owner a loss, despite the fact that from his perspective we are dealing with purely arbitrary stubbornness which constitutes *middat Sedom* in the full sense of the word, he cannot be compelled. Since we rule here in accordance with R. Yosef, we must conclude, according to Rashi, that the moral factor alone does not suffice to obligate compulsion.

According to Rashi, it is Rabba who emphasizes the subjective element regarding compulsion. According to the Rambam, on the other hand, it seems just the opposite. According to him, the Gemara deals with parcels of land of different quality, one tract of the best quality and the other tract of the poorest quality; all this notwithstanding, Rabba maintains that since there is no real loss in the bookkeeping sense, we compel the brother to relinquish. In such a case, it is clearly impossible to view the one brother as a terribly cruel person who arbitrarily wishes to deny benefit to his brother who owns the adjoining property. He puts forward a reasonable claim, and if we compel him, it must be that this is not to refine his character, but to bestow benefit upon the other. As for the position of R. Yosef, he too might agree with this understanding of compulsion, but he maintains that the difference in quality between the fields constitutes a real loss, "for how is it possible that Rabba should call this *middat Sedom,* when this is the *midda* of the Torah, which says that damages are collected from land of the best quality, and debts are collected from land of the poorest quality?"[60] According to him, we are not at all dealing here with a case of *zeh neheneh vezeh lo haser.*

According to one of the *Rishonim,* it is possible to connect our question to the controversy between Rabban Shimon b. Gamliel and the Sages regarding the writing of two *shtarei beirurin.* The Gemara explains the position of Rabban Shimon b. Gamliel: "Because one can say to the other, 'I do not like your rights to be beside my rights, for you appear to me as a lurking lion'";[61] but the Gemara does not explain the view of the Sages. The *Rishonim* adopt several approaches. The *Yad Rama*[62] understands that they simply see Rabban Shimon b. Gamliel's concern as farfetched and without value. The Rashba,[63] however, writes that even the Sages recognize the validity of the concern, but they are inclined to reject it because of the monetary loss suffered by the other party. This being the case, it is difficult to assume that we compel here in order to uproot the compelled party's wickedness. Indeed, if we were asked to decide the case based on the subjective state of the compelled party, we would be unable to compel, because the level of Sodom's evil – refusal to help another person even when it involves no loss whatsoever – does not find expression here. We are forced to say that, according to the Rashba, we compel because, objectively speaking, it is possible to cause one person to benefit without causing another person to suffer a loss. The practical factor suffices to impose compulsion. Of course, even if we accept this assumption, there is still room to question his position. It is possible to see the very fear – which according to the Rashba does not fall into the category of excessive paranoia – as a loss; whenever there is any degree of loss, the argument of the *Ketzot HaHoshen* is certainly reasonable: "Whenever there is even a small loss, even if it is

60. Rashba, *Bava Batra* 12b, as an objection against the view of the Ri Migash.

61. *Bava Batra* 168a.

62. *Bava Batra,* ch. 10, no. 81.

63. *Hiddushei HaRashba,* ad loc. See also *Shut HaRashba,* I, 889.

very minute, it is no longer regarded as *middat Sedom*."[64] In any event, it seems certain that according to the Rashba, the practical factor suffices to employ compulsion.

Moreover, if we go back for a moment to the passage of Rabba and R. Yosef, it seems that according to the Rashba the benefit derived by the other party is the only decisive factor. In the course of his explanation,[65] the Rashba agrees with those who maintain that we only compel according to Rabba if the ownership of the adjoining property preceded the division of the estate. This seems to be difficult, as pointed out by Rabbenu Yona in his *Aliyyot*: "There is no basis for this, for inasmuch as Rabba's rationale is not based on the strict law, but rather on the rule that *kofin al middat Sedom,* why is [allowing him to obtain the adjoining field in] one case considered doing 'the right and the good' more than the other?"[66] We are forced to say that the Rashba does not see the moral education of the owner as sufficient reason for *kofin,* for from this perspective the wickedness of the brother is equal in the two cases, and there is no difference between them. However, if the benefit derived by the other party is the decisive factor, it is perhaps possible to view the compulsion as a sort of right belonging to the brother who owns the adjoining property; and this exists only when he actually owns the adjoining property. If at the beginning of the division of the estate, this right had not been established, there is no room for compulsion.

Finally, I think that this uncertainty is echoed in a disagreement among the *Rishonim* regarding preventing squatting *lekhathilla,* in a case where the squatter would otherwise rent living quarters and the house is not up for rent. If the reason that we do not compel in such a case is that the person seeking the benefit is trying to take control of his fellow's property, and this in itself turns the owner into one who suffers a loss, then this disagreement has no connection to our question. But if the reason is that the owner can turn his house into one that is up

64. 154, no. 1; as opposed to the view of the *Even HaAzel, Hilkhot Shekhenim* 12:1. The obligation to perform acts of *hesed* applies, of course, even in a case of minor financial loss, but its absence should not be seen as an instance of *middat Sedom* in a case of *zeh neheneh vezeh lo haser*.

65. See *Hiddushei HaRashba, Bava Batra* 12b.

66. *Aliyyot DeRabbenu Yona,* ed. R. M. Hirschler (Jerusalem, 5726), *Bava Batra* 12b.

for rent, then the question may be raised: As long as there has been no change, and he has not yet put the house on the rental market, does his refusal not stem from *middat Sedom*? Must we be concerned about what might happen? If the wickedness in and of itself obligates compulsion, this argument is certainly correct. And perhaps this is the way to understand the view of those who maintain that in such a case we do compel the owner. If, however, the subjective injustice does not suffice, and we compel only in order to allow the other person to derive benefit from "ownerless property," then it can surely be suggested that whenever it is within the owner's authority to change the character of his property, we do not allow others to derive benefit from it. The fact that he has not yet changed the status of his house does not at all impair his control over it.

These proofs relate to the factors that activate *kofin al middat Sedom*. But we must still present a different question: What is the nature and objective of this compulsion? However we define the conditions that obligate compulsion, what is its teleological nature? Again we are faced with two possibilities: 1) the moral improvement of the party who refuses to allow his fellow to benefit from his property; 2) helping that other party to derive benefit. From one perspective, *kofin* is directed inward and constitutes an educational effort to uproot the wickedness in the compelled party's soul; from another perspective, its aim is outward, and it constitutes a means to achieve a pragmatic goal. Here, the emphasis is on the refinement of a person's soul; there, on the benefit to his fellow.[67] The nature of the compulsion also varies according to the definition. According to the first understanding, the compulsion is against the person. On the practical level, the court might deal with his

67. Here too the root of the confusion is whether the foundation of the compulsion is moral or practical; however, despite the fact that our answers regarding the two of them are likely, from a psychological perspective, to draw from mutual influence, this question should not be identified with the previous one. Logically, one must not confuse the rationale for the definition; even though in the legislative process, the essence of an enactment is usually fashioned in light of the objective of its initiators, there is no real equivalency. It is possible, for example, that the reason for *kofin* is to help the party seeking benefit, but the only way to do that is via the moral and educational route.

property, similar to the position of the Ramban[68] regarding compulsion in the case of repayment of a debt. Essentially, however, the coercion relates to the owner of the property: we compel the owner to waive that which belongs to him. According to the second understanding, however, the compulsion relates directly to the property. Those who compel – generally, the court – take control of the property, claiming the rights of the one who seeks benefit, without any connection to the owner. So, too, the role of the court as enforcer varies – here as teacher of justice and moral guide, there as ruler of the people, responsible for their welfare.

Here, too, this is not a merely theoretical discussion. There is a clear and simple practical ramification, perhaps of wider scope than those connected to the previous question. Does compulsion apply to a person who continues in his stubborn ways? If the objective is moral refinement, there is no room for further compulsion; but if we are concerned about benefit, there is certainly room. From here we see that there is a possibility for the sinner to profit, for if the goal of the compulsion is the compelled party's moral improvement, we are dealing here with a crooked person who cannot be straightened. In this framework, the question is not whether it is appropriate to compel, but whether it is possible to compel. If, in the depths of his heart, a person refuses to heed the instruction of the Sages, and their efforts only harden him in his rebellion, then surely their rebuke is included in the category of "words that are not [going to be] heeded," regarding which there is a mitzva not to voice them (*Yevamot* 65b).

Needless to say, this question has great practical ramifications. Halakha recognizes compulsion – but employs it with a heavy heart and in the absence of alternatives. Halakha's goal is elevation of the spirit, and not a bringing low of the body; a repair of the vessels, and not their breaking. Its means, at the initial stage, are education and guidance – *tokhaha*, "rebuke," in the sense of instruction, rather than punishment. "The Merciful seeks the heart."[69] As stated above, however, despite its ideal aspirations, Halakha does not recoil from compulsion. Coercive measures

68. See *Hiddushei HaRamban, Bava Batra* 175b, and see also *Ketzot HaHoshen*, 39, no. 1 (end).
69. *Sanhedrin* 106b.

are sometimes employed in order to prevent some objective evil; and sometimes they are even seen as a means to educate the coerced party himself. The efficiency of employing coercion as an educational tool, however, is dependent upon the character and emotional makeup of the individual. Not everybody responds in the same way.

A person who generally recognizes the authority of the coercer and his values, and who accepts his commands even though he is not always scrupulous about following them, is likely to derive educational benefit from compulsion. In its wake he will not only repair the concrete injustice, but also repent, and thereby he will strengthen his inner acceptance of obligation in the future. Modern man, however, who is raised on an individualistic outlook and a liberal tradition, is generally inclined to react negatively to coercion. Even if he values the coercer's goal and is perhaps prepared to realize it over time, the very fact of coercion stirs up fierce bitterness within him.[70] Instead of the Ritva's question, "How is it possible to think that we would not compel one who exhibits the trait of Sodom?"[71] the modern Jew is liable to ask just the reverse. This is not out of insensitivity to evil, in society or in his soul, but out of insistence on his own dignity. Thus the question stands: To what extent should compulsion be employed against one who exhibits *middat Sedom*, when the expected response to compulsion is negative?

The wording employed by the Rosh in a responsum implies that the goal of compulsion is indeed educational: "We compel him to distance himself from evil traits and to perform acts of lovingkindness for his fellow in a situation where he suffers no loss."[72] However, apart from this source, I have found no other sources, or even well-founded indirect proofs, in the words of our Sages, that would allow me to provide a clear answer. Perhaps we can adduce proof from the fact that we do not find regarding *middat Sedom* a halakha similar to that found regarding charity – "We confiscate his property in his presence and take what is

70. Elsewhere, I have dealt with this issue at greater length. See my article, "Religion and State: The Case for Interaction," *Judaism* XV (1966): 399–403, and the sources cited therein (reprinted in *Leaves of Faith: The World of Jewish Living* [Jersey City, 2004], 1–32).

71. *Hiddushei HaRitva, Bava Batra* 59a.

72. *Teshuvot HaRosh*, 97, 2.

appropriate for him to give"[73] – that is, that the coercive measures can be employed only in the owner's presence. Perhaps we can also draw inferences from the fact that the literal Hebrew wording is "*kofin al middat Sedom*," "we compel for the trait of Sodom,"[74] with no direct object, rather than "*kofin oto*," "we compel him."

Standing on their own, however, these precise readings cannot decide the matter. My intention is to raise the question, and not to settle the issue; to present it as a vibrant question, which many have struggled with in the past, and not to resolve all the problems in its regard. Nevertheless, allow me to add two points. First, there is no contradiction between the two approaches. It is certainly possible that the achievement of either goal justifies compulsion; and it is possible that in certain conditions it is the one factor that is critical and in other circumstances it is the other factor. It is also possible that compulsion is only an option when there is a combination of both the educational and the practical factors. We are not necessarily required to choose between the two.

Secondly, in certain cases we encounter a compulsion that is more authoritative than anything that we have seen thus far. The various modes of compulsion described above all require certain actions on the part of the coercing party – whether against the owner or against his property. In other cases, however, the right of the other party exists on its own, and it stems from a new definition that restricts the concept of ownership itself. When the court gets involved, its role is legislative, rather than juridical. Its action is based on the principle that "property declared ownerless by the court is ownerless" (*Yevamot* 89b) and its means is a general ordinance, rather than taking control of a particular individual.

This concept is rooted in a talmudic passage at the end of chapter *Hezkat HaBattim*, dealing with two neighbors, one of whom wishes to extend a projection over the airspace of his fellow's courtyard: "[Regarding] a projection [which projects not less than] a handbreadth, there is

---

73. Rambam, *Hilkhot Mattenot Aniyyim* 7:10; following *Ketubbot* 49b, and see there.
74. This is the reading in all the passages except for *Ketubbot* 103a; there, too, see *Shitta Mekubbetzet*, in the name of Rashi and *Tosefot Rid*, omitting the word "*oto*." According to *Dikdukei Soferim*, *Bava Batra* 12b, all the manuscripts read "*kofin*," except for MS Hamburg which reads "*kofin oto*." So too in *Dikdukei Soferim*, *Eiruvin* 49a, we find a reading of "*kofin ota*," in the name of the Saloniki edition.

a *hazzaka* (presumption of right), and the owner of the courtyard can prevent it [from being made in the first place]. If it is less than a handbreadth, there is no *hazzaka* for it, and he cannot prevent it [from being made]."[75] In its discussion regarding the second clause, the Gemara records a disagreement between R. Huna and R. Yehuda concerning the question of whether it is only the owner of the roof who cannot prevent the owner of the courtyard from using the projection, or whether even the owner of the courtyard cannot prevent the owner of the roof from using it.[76] The Gemara explains that the *Amora'im* disagree whether or not the owner of the courtyard can raise the claim of *hezzek re'iyya*, because the owner of the roof will gaze into his courtyard when he places things on the projection.

In light of our generally accepted notions, a simple question arises: Why must we examine the validity and justice of the claim raised by the owner of the courtyard? Surely the airspace of his courtyard belongs to him – about that there is no disagreement; surely this is so, because he is able to acquire objects by virtue of their having entered his airspace! Does he not then have the legal right to prevent other people from using it? Do not his desires – even if they are totally arbitrary – constitute a barrier to use that must be respected? On the other hand, however: Who has given the owner of the courtyard the right to use the projection? Even if we grant him the right to force his neighbor to remove it, surely as long as it is standing, for whatever reason, the owner of the courtyard should not be able to prevent his neighbor from using it!

This question, with all of its ramifications, has no answer; it can, however, be resolved if we undermine its fundamental assumption, which is mistaken: in the framework of Halakha, ownership does not have such extensive scope, for the reason already alluded to by the Rashbam. We do not accept the argument put forward by the owner of the roof, "For he cannot object and say, 'Do not use the projection,' for what loss is caused to the owner of the roof?"[77] This point is clarified by

75. *Bava Batra* 59a.
76. Ibid. 59b.
77. S.v. *bevaal.*

the Rashbam's comment on the first clause, which accepts the objection of the owner of the courtyard:

> That is to say, if someone comes from the outset to extend a projection not less than a handbreadth over his neighbor's courtyard, the owner of the courtyard can prevent him from filling the airspace of his courtyard. We do not say, *Zeh neheneh vezeh lo haser,* for surely there is a loss, as the Gemara says regarding a projection less than a handbreadth: since the owner of the roof uses the projection, he looks into the courtyard, and there is *hezzek re'iyya.*[78]

The inference is clear: were it not for the damage caused by exposure, there would be no room for objection, for *zeh neheneh vezeh lo haser.* Here is the foundation of the law. In this passage, however, there is no mention of anything like *kofin al middat Sedom,* for there is no need for a particular coercive measure. Here the ownership is not sufficient to allow the owner to act in the manner of Sodom.

V. The Right to Private Property

It is difficult to determine how far-reaching our halakha is. However, two points must be emphasized. First, this level of coercion does exist; second, the limitation set on ownership constitutes an important motif in the whole issue of *kofin al middat Sedom,* and not only in the stage reflected in the passage in *Hezkat HaBattim.* Even when halakha makes use of coercive measures, the result is also a diminution of proprietary rights. The fact that this diminution takes place only by way of a particular legal procedure does not negate the content and validity of the concept. The scope of the restriction is the subject of controversy – between the two opinions cited in the *Or Zarua,* between Rashi and Rabbenu Tam, and others. However, there is no disagreement about the principle. The extent to which this reaches may be seen in a law inferred by the Rambam – and agreed to by several other *Rishonim* – from an incident related at the beginning of *Bava Batra*:

78. S.v. *veyakhol.*

> If someone has windows down below in his wall, and his neighbor wishes to build in front of them, and he says to him, "I will make other windows for you in this same wall above these," he can prevent him from so doing, saying, "When you make the windows, you will damage the wall and make it unstable." Even if he says, "I will take down the entire wall, build you a new one, make windows up above and rent a house for you to live in until I finish the building," he can prevent him, saying, "I do not want to trouble myself with moving from place to place." Therefore, if there is no trouble whatsoever, and he does not have to move, he cannot prevent him, and we compel him to allow his neighbor to close the window below and open a window above, for this is *middat Sedom*. Similarly, regarding any instance in which *zeh neheneh vezeh lo haser*, we compel him.[79]

From the Rambam's formulation, we are liable to conclude that if the owner suffers no loss, his property is given over to his neighbor for demolition and reconstruction. In my opinion, such a conclusion is excessively far-reaching. It is more reasonable to assume that the owner of the wall can prevent his neighbor from touching his property, but he forgoes the right of a neighbor to demand a certain distance on the part of a neighbor who comes to build in front of his window. Even in this watered-down form, in this compulsion – and the Rambam sets it up as typical – there is a constriction of the arbitrary control that we ordinarily associate with ownership.

The spirit of this halakha is illustrated once again in the words of one of the leading *Aharonim*. Commenting on the words of the Rama, "[Regarding] a wall separating between [the properties of] Reuven and Shimon, and the wall belongs to one of them, he can demolish it if he wishes, and his neighbor cannot prevent him [from so doing],"[80] the *Netivot HaMishpat* writes: "It seems that this applies when he has some need to demolish the old wall, e.g., the original wall was built entirely on

79. *Hilkhot Shekhenim* 7:8. The Rambam derives this law from a passage in *Bava Batra* 7a; see *Yad Rama*, ad loc., ch. 1, no. 67.

80. HM 154:13.

his property, or the like. However, if there is no such need, we compel him [not to exhibit] *middat Sedom,* and he receives [from his neighbor] half the value [of the wall]."[81]

The simple truth may be told: *kofin al middat Sedom* absolutely contradicts the prevailing notion that a person is the supreme ruler over his property, that his assets are "like clay in the hands of the potter" (*Yirmiyahu* 18:6), and that as long as he does not cause others direct damage, he can do with his property as he pleases.[82] Halakha is animated by a different spirit. It likewise stands in opposition (though from a totally different perspective) to the philosophical formulation of this individualistic position – the position of Hegel and his followers – which sees in the idea of ownership an extension and realization of the free self, and therefore denies any limitation on proprietary rights whatsoever as a restriction on the person himself.

It is true that the relationship between the person and his ownership is not foreign to Halakha. The Sages recognized the human feeling that "a person prefers one *kav* of his own to nine *kabbim* of another"[83] and even conceded its value; but the source of their outlook is different. In Hegel's thought, this idea is filled with metaphysical content, which turns ownership into a right that is more or less absolute, which can only be set aside by the needs of the state as a whole. What is critical here is not the benefit derived from the property but the status of ownership in and of itself. "If the emphasis is placed on my needs," writes Hegel, "then ownership of property is an appropriate means of filling them. But the true view is that from the perspective of liberty, ownership is the first realization of liberty, and is thus an essential goal in and of itself."[84]

---

81. *Mishpat HaUrim,* HM 154, no. 13. He receives only half of its value, because he must participate in the expense of building a wall in order to prevent *hezzek re'iyya.*
82. According to this viewpoint, the right to act in the manner of *middat Sedom* is the very definition of ownership. See Arthur T. Hadley, *The Conflict Between Liberty and Equality* (Cambridge, Mass., 1925), 49–50. Compare also Huntington Cairns, *Law and the Social Sciences* (London, 1935), 57–60.
83. *Bava Metzia* 38a.
84. G. W. F. Hegel, *Grundlinien der Philosophie des Rechts,* ed. G. Lasson, 2nd ed. (Leipzig, 1927), par. 45. See also Henry Scott Holland, "Property and Personality," in *Property: Its Duties and Rights Historically, Philosophically, and Religiously Regarded,* ed. C. Gore (London, 1913), 175–82.

According to Judaism, however, the value of realizing the person through property constitutes only one aspect of a fundamental social category. It is liable to be set aside in the face of other moral factors – including the welfare of others. As for the value of property in general, the emphasis is indeed placed on the idea of fulfilling man's needs – "It shall be yours to eat" (*Bereshit* 1:29, 9:3). In the framework of Halakha, there is almost no trace of the recoiling from private property found in the writings of a number of Church fathers.[85] The idea has an important, even central place in many realms – from marriage to offerings, from *bikkurim* to *lulav*, and especially in *eiruv tehumin* – not to mention, of course, the realm of monetary laws. Never, however, does Halakha idolize this concept, and other moral demands are liable to bring about its restriction. If Halakha is very far from Proudhon's declaration that "private ownership is theft,"[86] on the other hand, it refuses to agree with the popular adage that "an Englishman's home is his castle."

To a certain degree, this restriction corresponds to the development of social life in our day. The French Revolution's slogan linked the principles of equality, liberty, and fraternity, and raised them together to the same level. The bitter fact is, however, that from the socioeconomic perspective (as opposed to the legal perspective), the principles of equality and liberty tend to contradict each other; and the experience of the last hundred years testifies to the ascent of the former at the cost of the latter. This direction stands out especially in the tendency to limit proprietary rights in order to realize personal rights, and thus the parallel to the spirit of our law. This point, however, should not be overstated, and without a doubt we should not adopt apologetics that come to present *kofin al middat Sedom* as a modern phenomenon.

The truth is that in the restricted realm of *zeh neheneh vezeh lo haser*, this halakha is still far-reaching. First, as we have seen, its objective is not only social goals, but also refinement of the individual; in

85. See Paul Christophe, *Les Devoirs Moraux des Riches: L'usage Chrétien du Droit de Propriété dans L'Ecriture et la Tradition Patristique* (Paris, 1964); E. R. Hardy, "The Way of the Early Church," in *Christianity and Property*, ed. Joseph F. Fletcher (Philadelphia, 1947), 44–71.

86. Pierre J. Proudhon, *Qu'est-ce que la Propriété?* (Paris, 1849), 2.

the words of the Rosh, "We compel him to distance himself from evil traits and to perform acts of *hesed* for his fellow."[87] Second, its scope is wider. Essentially – and perhaps this point is connected to the previous one – modern legislation that restricts the right of ownership generally deals with commerce and industry as impersonal phenomena. *Kofin al middat Sedom* touches on a more delicate point – the actual relations between an individual and his fellow.

Thus far we have dealt with a qualitative restriction. However, the principle regarding *zeh neheneh vezeh lo haser* leads also to the problem of the quantitative restriction. Here we encounter a position adopted by Locke, father of classical liberalism, and fighter for the right of ownership. He professes that ownership applies only to that which the owner can make use of to any advantage before it spoils: "Whatever is beyond this, is more than his share, and belongs to others."[88] Or, as formulated by a later thinker (he, too, a follower of the liberal tradition): We must distinguish between "ownership for the purpose of use" and "ownership for the purpose of control,"[89] adopting one and condemning the other. If a person who has amassed great wealth sets aside a small amount for the poor, would not such an action, with respect to its impact on his life, be considered *zeh neheneh vezeh lo haser*?

Here we touch upon Halakha's attitude to property in general, on the one hand, and the obligation to give charity and perform acts of *hesed*, on the other, and to their interweaving – both in the definition of *middat Sedom* as a moral phenomenon and in the definition of compulsion in its regard.[90] This problem positions us before a wide

87. *Shut HaRosh*, 97:2.

88. John Locke, *Treatise of Civil Government*, V, 31.

89. L. T. Hobhouse, "The Historical Evolution of Property, in Fact and in Idea," in *Property: Its Rights and Duties*, 25–6; cf. R. H. Tawney, *The Acquisitive Society* (New York, 1920), passim. Emphasizing ownership for the purpose of use rather than control has, of course, early roots in classical and medieval thought. See especially Thomas Aquinas, *Summa Theologica* II–II, 66:2; but this is not the forum to discuss the matter at length.

90. The compulsion here, however, is restricted, of course, to the legal framework. The party seeking benefit cannot act independently. In accordance with its general approach to social problems, here, too, Halakha imposes and emphasizes mutual responsibilities, rather than mutual rights. If the obligation regarding charity and

and splendid horizon – the relationship between personal rights and proprietary rights. This topic, however, requires a more comprehensive discussion that is not possible here.

acts of *hesed* that is cast upon the man of means is clear, the obligation of the one in need is no less solid. Even if pragmatically we cannot say that "anyone who steals from his fellow the value of a *peruta* is regarded as having taken his soul from him" (*Bava Kamma* 119a), the prohibition of theft remains in place.

The Responsibilities of the Recipient of Charity

One of the fundamental problems troubling those involved in providing welfare services, whether as individuals or as part of the public system, is the issue of the recipient's participation in and attitude toward the assistance extended to him. There is, of course, no disagreement that it is preferable to involve the recipient in the process of and responsibility for providing for his own needs. In countless cases, however, the recipient appears not to be working as hard as he can, preferring rather to cast the burden upon others. In such circumstances, a piercing question arises: To what degree and by what means should we press for the increased participation of the recipient of aid, and to what extent is it possible to condition the extension of assistance on his readiness to

Translated by David Strauss. This article originally appeared in Hebrew as "*Saod Tisod Immo – Hishtatfut HaMekabbel BiGemilut Hasadim,*" in *Sefer HaZikkaron LeAvraham Spiegelman* (Jerusalem, 1979) and in English translation in Alei Etzion 16 (2009), pp. 7–30.

share the burden? Regarding this point, opinions differ, and Judaism's position on the matter must be clarified.

The search for an answer will initially be directed, of course, to the halakhic sources, but it will be quickly discovered – and this fact in itself demands investigation – that the fundamental sources in which an answer might be found, whether in the writings of *Hazal* or in the works of the *posekim*, are exceedingly meager. There are, indeed, limitations that determine who is fit to receive charity. The Mishna in *Pe'ah* states: "One who has two hundred *zuz* must not take gleanings, forgotten produce, field-corner produce, or poor man's tithe."[1] This standard, which applies to agricultural gifts to the poor, was codified as law with respect to charity as well, and was translated into buying power by several *Rishonim*: "Some [authorities] say that these standards applied only in their [*Hazal*'s] day, but today one may take [charity] as long as one does not have capital from which to support oneself and one's household from the profits thereof; and this is a well-reasoned position."[2] This limitation does not, however, resolve our difficulty. First of all, it is restricted to *tzedaka* (charity) – that is to say, monetary assistance – and does not relate to assistance falling into the category of *gemilut hasadim* (acts of kindness)

---

1. *Pe'ah* 8:8.
2. *Yoreh De'ah* 253:2. The Mishna cites the measure of two hundred *zuz* with respect to agricultural gifts for the poor, but not with respect to charity. Logically, there are grounds to distinguish. Gifts for the poor are in limited supply, and so it is necessary to establish priority regarding eligibility. This is not the case regarding charity, which is not limited, in the sense that one can give twice. The *Rishonim* discuss this point; see *Or Zarua, Hilkhot Tzedaka*, sec. 14. This measure, however, has been codified as law regarding *tzedaka*.

   It should be noted that the measure mentioned here, which is based on the assumption that the needy person will live on his earnings and not eat away at his capital, seems to be exceedingly far-reaching when applied to modern economic reality. A person with an average sized family (4–5 people) in the United States, who receives a 10% return on his investments (a very good rate), would be considered a pauper who is entitled to receive charity, according to this definition, even if he has capital approaching $150,000! [Ed. note: This was written in 1979, and the figure would now have to be increased severalfold.] This seems to be very novel, and the matter must be examined in light of the *Tur*'s comment (YD 253), "It is all in accordance with the time and the place."

that must be extended to "both the poor and the rich."[3] Second, while it provides a test of means that excludes the "rich" from receiving charity, it does not offer any guidelines on how to relate to one who qualifies for charity because he is poor.[4]

More directly related to our issue is a tannaitic dispute that appears to reflect different attitudes toward the matter at hand:

> Our Rabbis taught: "Lend" (*Devarim* 15:8) – This [refers to someone] who has nothing and does not wish to be supported [from charity], to whom we give [money] as a loan, and afterward we give [it] to him as a gift. "Surely lend him" (ibid.) – This [refers to someone] who has [resources of his own] but does not wish to support himself [from them], to whom we give [money] as a gift, and afterward we collect [it] from him after his death. [These are] the words of R. Yehuda.
>
> But the Sages say: [If] he has [resources of his own] but does not wish to support himself [from them], we are not bound to [help] him. How, then, do I explain "Surely lend him"? The Torah spoke in the language of people [and we cannot infer anything from this phrase].[5]

We see that according to R. Yehuda a person who has means that he does not wish to exploit is still defined as a needy person who must be treated and granted aid – and this seems to derive from the mitzva of *tzedaka*, not only from *gemilut hasadim* – though he does not acquire the charity money permanently. His situation is similar to that of a person who is stuck on the road without any money, about whom R. Eliezer ruled that "if a property-holder was traveling from place to place and

3. *Sukka* 49b.
4. It seems to me that regarding other laws – e.g., *arakhin* or a *korban oleh veyored* – a person without any money, but capable of going out to work, should be regarded as a poor person; his liability should be evaluated in terms of his present situation. Our discussion here relates to the realms of charity and *hesed* (lovingkindness), regarding which the determining factor is not the poverty in and of itself, but the distress that is suffered. This point requires further examination.
5. *Ketubbot* 67b.

in need of taking gleanings, forgotten produce, field-corner produce, or poor man's tithe, he may take them, but when he returns home he must repay them."[6] According to the Sages, however, the fact that a person "has resources of his own" in and of itself exempts others from all responsibility to take care of his needs – at least, in the framework of the mitzva of gifts for the poor.

Despite the striking difference in attitude reflected in this dispute, it does not suffice to resolve our question, for we must define the term "someone who has resources of his own." Rashi explains: "[This means] someone who has resources of his own, but does not want to support himself from his own resources, but rather from charity, and he afflicts himself with hunger."[7] Rambam sharpens the point: "A wealthy person who starves himself, and is miserly about his assets, not to eat or drink from them – we do not concern ourselves with him."[8] This formulation was codified as law in the *Shulhan Arukh*.[9] We appear to be dealing with a miser who prefers to save and starve – or to take from charity – rather than use the resources already in his possession. Despite all the criticism that may be leveled against a passive person who takes no steps to help himself, he certainly cannot be compared to a person of means who mortifies himself. Even one who maintains that the latter is responsible for his lot[10] can require the extension of assistance to the former.

A clearer source relates to a mitzva that involves not *tzedaka* but *gemilut hasadim* – *perika* and *te'ina* ("unloading and loading," the positive commandment to help another person unload an animal that has fallen under its load, or to help the master reload the animal that has fallen):

6. *Pe'ah* 5:4.
7. *Ketubbot* 67b, s.v. *yesh lo.*
8. *Hilkhot Mattenot Aniyyim* 7:9.
9. YD 253:10.
10. A similar idea is found in Rambam regarding the restoration of lost property: "If one willfully causes his property to become lost, we do not concern ourselves with him. How so? If one leaves his cow untied in a shed that has no door and goes away... although a spectator may not take the property for himself, he is not obligated to return it. For Scripture states, 'Which he has lost' (*Devarim* 22:3), excluding cases where one willfully causes property to become lost" (*Hilkhot Gezela VaAveda* 11:11). It is, of course, possible to distinguish between one who refrains from earning a living and one who is negligent about his property.

"[If the owner] went and sat down and said: 'Since the commandment is upon you, if it is your wish to unload, unload,' he is exempt, as it is said: 'With him' (*Shemot* 23:5)."[11] This case parallels our question; but the talmudic passage is unclear as to whether this limitation is unique to the mitzva of *perika* and *te'ina*, based on the Scriptural decree "with him," or whether it embodies a principle that is valid regarding the provision of assistance in general.

In his commentary to the Torah, *Keli Yakar*, Rabbi Shlomo Efrayim Luntshitz adopted the second position. The verse reads, "If you see the donkey of him that hates you lying under its burden, and would forbear to unload it (*vehadalta me'azov lo*), you shall surely unload it with him" (*Shemot* 23:5). As opposed to Rashi, *Keli Yakar* understands that the word *vehadalta* grants an allowance *not* to offer assistance:

> Therefore it says "and would forbear to unload it," because the word "*lo*" does not mean "with him," and [therefore we infer that] you are permitted to forbear helping him when he refuses to join you in the task. This is an answer to some of the poor among our people who cast themselves on the community and refuse to do any work, even if they are able to engage in certain work or in some other endeavor that will bring food to the table, and they complain if they are not given whatever they are lacking. For God did not command this, but rather, "You shall surely unload it *with him*," and "You shall surely *help him* to lift them up again" (*Devarim* 22:4). For the needy person must do whatever is in his power to do, and if, despite all his efforts, he fails to earn a living, then every man in Israel is obligated to support and strengthen him, and to provide him with whatever he is lacking, and unload even a hundred times.[12]

As opposed to *Keli Yakar*'s certainty about this issue, we find that one of the *Rishonim*, the Me'iri, was in doubt about the matter. In the course of a discussion regarding a talmudic passage in *Kiddushin*, he mentions

11. *Bava Metzia* 32a.

12. *Keli Yakar, Shemot* 23:5.

the two possibilities raised above, without deciding between them. The Gemara there states that if a man says to a woman, "Be betrothed to me with this loaf of bread," and she tells him to give it to a dog, she is betrothed to him only if the dog is hers, for only then is she regarded as having derived benefit from the dog's eating. In the continuation, the Gemara raises the following question, which it leaves unresolved: "R. Mari asked: What if the dog was pursuing her? [Do we say that] in return for the benefit of saving herself from it she resolves and cedes herself to him; or perhaps she can say to him, 'By Torah law you were indeed bound to save me'?"[13] On this, the Me'iri comments:

> If a dog was pursuing her in order to bite her, the validity of her betrothal is in doubt. For perhaps owing to his saving her, she resolved and ceded herself to him; or perhaps, since he too is bound to act in that manner, for the Torah states, "Neither shall you stand idly by the blood of your neighbor" (*Vayikra* 19:16), she does not resolve to cede herself.
>
> Now this applies when she agrees to return the value of the loaf of bread, for if not, he is not obligated to save her, for one is even forbidden to save himself with another person's money. But there are some who say that while he himself is forbidden to save himself with another person's money when the owner of that money is not there, nevertheless whenever the owner of the money is present, he is obligated to save [the person in distress] even on condition that he will not recover from him what he spends on saving him, and he cannot collect that sum from him in court. This is what [the Sages] said regarding the mitzva of unloading: "[If the owner] went and sat down and said, 'Since the commandment is upon you, if it is your wish to unload, unload,' he is exempt, as it is said: 'With him.'" The reason is that it says "With him," but without that [stipulation] he is obligated.
>
> And if you propose to say that even where it does not state "With him," the same law applies – [I would answer that in the case of unloading an animal one is exempt from helping if the

13. *Kiddushin* 8b.

> owner refuses to participate] because the injured party can help him, and if he refuses to help, others do not have a greater obligation to save his money than he does. Furthermore, there we are only dealing with the rescue of money, but here where we are dealing with the rescue of the person himself, and that person is unable to save himself, [the onlooker] is obligated to rescue him even if it causes him a [financial] loss, and he cannot collect from him what he expended on his rescue.[14]

Me'iri's words are instructive in and of themselves, but in light of the silence of the rest of the *Rishonim* and *posekim*, they do not negate the fact that our problem has not been exhaustively discussed in the primary halakhic sources. This silence has left us room to investigate the matter. Specifically, it has left room for a discussion which is based on the halakhic foundations of *gemilut hasadim*, and which by its very nature will bring under consideration the moral and ethical dimension of the issue.

---

14. *Beit HaBehira*, ad loc., s.v. *haya kelev.* Me'iri mentions two distinctions connected to separate realms: 1) regarding the nature of the recipient's need – rescuing someone as opposed to saving his property; 2) regarding the degree of possible self-help – the ability of the person in need to rescue himself as opposed to the provision of money. The relationship between the two is unclear. Perhaps, according to Me'iri, each factor is a sufficient condition – that is to say, one must rescue his fellow, even if that other person is capable of saving himself; and on the other hand, as long as the person in need cannot help himself, he is not obligated to compensate the rescuer, even if the latter only saves his property. Alternatively, the Me'iri may believe that each factor is a necessary but not sufficient condition, so that there is no obligation to help another unless both factors are present, as in the case in *Kiddushin*. This question, of course, has halakhic and conceptual ramifications. But in any event, Me'iri raises the issue of comparing the mitzvot of *perika* and *te'ina* to other realms of assistance.

    It should be added that Me'iri speaks of an obligation to compensate the rescuer after the fact and not about his obligation to rescue in the first place. But the two are interdependent. If Reuven is obligated to save Shimon, Shimon is not obligated to compensate him, for Reuven was not acting on his behalf, but in God's service, though Shimon was the direct beneficiary. This should be compared to the dispute among the *Rishonim* about whether a physician is permitted to receive compensation for his services; see *Kitvei HaRamban* (ed. R. Chavel), II, 43–45.

It is precisely this dimension which is problematic, for our problem is rooted in a clash of values.

On the one hand, there is the mitzva of *gemilut hasadim*, with all the halakhic and social obligations that it involves, which demand of the benefactor maximal assistance. On the other hand, there is a demand, perhaps no less legitimate, to minimize the aid and to share the burden. This demand has at least three components – one related to the limitations of the benefactor, and two connected to the welfare of the recipient.

First of all, since we are talking about dividing up limited resources, generosity toward one person always comes at the expense of his fellow. This consideration is true about every act of benevolence, but it is especially valid with respect to a public system built on the money and efforts of others upon whom are made coercive demands. While its full political weight is felt in trying times, whether because of real political and economic limitations or against the background of a taxpayers' revolt, it is valid at all times as a moral argument.[15]

Second, unqualified giving, even were it possible in a practical and budgetary sense, is liable to clash with the fundamental objective of any relief plan: the rehabilitation of the recipient to the point that he is capable of standing on his own two feet, emotionally and functionally. If Rambam placed at the top of the scale of charity "a person who assists a poor Jew by providing him with a gift or a loan or by accepting him into a business partnership or by helping him find employment – in a word, by putting him where he can dispense with other people's aid,"[16] then it is clear that the highest goal in helping a person who has already fallen low is the restoration of his independence. It is precisely abundant aid that is liable to block the attainment of this goal, by intensifying the reality and the feeling of dependence to the point of degeneration

15. Logically speaking, there is, of course, room to distinguish between *tzedaka* as a mitzva devolving upon the individual, which applies even with respect to those who fail to help themselves, and the distribution of communal charity funds. A similar distinction was proposed by several *Rishonim* regarding a person's right to receive charity before he sells all of his expensive belongings; see *Ketubbot* 68a, and *Tosafot*, s.v. *kan*; Rif (ad loc.); *Tur*, YD 253.
16. *Hilkhot Mattenot Aniyyim* 10:7.

and even paralysis of the emotional strengths that are necessary for the rehabilitation process.

Lastly, the participation of the recipient is necessary for his moral benefit, no less than for his psychological benefit. One need not adopt the views of Emerson or Carlyle in order to understand that the ability to assume responsibility is a measure not only of a person's emotional health, but also of his spiritual level. Therefore, whenever this ability is impaired by unconditional giving – or by giving to which only minimal conditions are attached – there exists an additional dimension to the clash of values that stands at the center of our problem.

This clash necessitates a dual approach, in the spirit of the words of Napoleon – that a person should pray as if everything depended upon God and fight as if everything depended upon him. When relating to the needy person, one ought to encourage personal effort and stimulate self-confidence. This point has a universal moral foundation, but it draws special strength from the enormous emphasis that Judaism places on free will. The entire halakhic system is based on one central fact – "Free will is bestowed on every human being. If one desires to turn toward the good way and be righteous, he has the power to do so. If one wishes to turn toward the evil way and be wicked, he is at liberty to do so. And thus it is written in the Torah: 'Behold, the man is become as one of us, to know good and evil' (*Bereshit* 3:22) – which means that the human species had become unique in the world, there being no other species like it in the following respect, namely, that man, of himself and by exercise of his own intelligence and reason, knows what is good and what is evil, and there is none who can prevent him from doing that which is good or that which is evil"[17] – and upon the conclusion that may be drawn from it: "Since every human being, as we have explained, has free will, a man should strive to repent, make verbal expression of his sins, and renounce them, so that he may die penitent and thus be worthy of life in the World to Come."[18] What is true about penitence on the spiritual level is true about rehabilitation on the emotional and physical level. Since every man has free will, he must strive to rehabilitate himself and

17. Rambam, *Hilkhot Teshuva* 5:1.
18. Ibid. 7:1.

confront his problems and overcome his difficulties so that he may live and merit life in this world. The Torah asserts that, factually, a person is capable; and therefore, morally, he is obligated. *Pouvoir oblige.* The recognition of free will is a basic component in the Torah's outlook regarding the provision of support in general, and it is especially important in assessing the recipient's contribution to his own rehabilitation. His personal responsibility stands at the center of Judaism's ethics and psychological understanding, and its practical expression in treating the needy is strengthening the feeling and reality of his personal strength.

As for our problem, this emphasis does not exhaust itself in encouragement. It seems to me that it expresses itself in criticism as well. The final mishna in Tractate *Pe'ah* states: "And anyone who is not in need of taking and does take will not die before he will be dependent on others."[19] The mishna does not clarify – nor does the Gemara here or anywhere else – to whom it refers. But it is difficult to assume that it is talking about someone who has two hundred *zuz* (or fifty with which he conducts business), but nevertheless takes charity. Such a person is a real thief. It may be suggested that we are dealing here with a person who does not have two hundred *zuz*, but is capable of earning such a sum. Formally, such a person is entitled to accept gifts for the poor, because he is still defined as a pauper. But since he refuses to develop his abilities, *Hazal* do not spare him their criticism. Indeed, when Rambam codifies the mishna's ruling, he adds a source, but ignores the element of theft: "He who, having no need of alms, obtains alms by deception will, ere he die of old age, fall into a dependency that is real. Such a person comes under the characterization: 'Cursed is the man that trusts in man' (*Yirmiyahu* 17:5)."[20] It is not clear whether the evil lies in his lack of trust in God and his reliance on man – which belongs, of course, to the realm of the relations between man and God – or in the unnecessary exploitation of people through their deception. In any event, we

19. *Pe'ah* 8:9.
20. *Hilkhot Mattenot Aniyyim* 10:19. The Mishna cites the parallel verse, "Blessed is the man who trusts in God" (*Yirmiyahu* 17:7), as the source of its ruling regarding "one who is in need of taking, and does not do so," but it does not explain itself. Radbaz (ad loc.) understands that Rambam inferred "that 'blessed' implies 'cursed.'"

are certainly not dealing here with real thievery, and it is reasonable to assume that the reference is to someone who is capable of sharing the burden, but renounces his responsibility.

When relating to the benefactor, the situation is reversed. His readiness and obligation to extend assistance to another person is in great measure a function of that other person's weakness. The stronger the recipient, the more the inclination to help him dissipates. Here, then, is the essence of our question; and it divides into two. First of all, does there exist, fundamentally, an obligation to offer charity and acts of kindness to a person who is capable of overcoming his difficulties, but for some reason gives up? Second, if indeed such an obligation exists, what factors determine the circumstances in which it applies?

The answer to the first question is connected to the roots of the obligation of *gemilut hasadim*. This mitzva has two different but complementary sources. The first is the foundation of interpersonal mitzvot, the great principle of R. Akiva: "And you shall love your neighbor as yourself" (*Vayikra* 19:18). This fact should be understandable by itself, but in any event, Rambam explained it:

> The following positive commands were ordained by the Rabbis: visiting the sick, comforting the mourners, joining a funeral procession, dowering a bride, escorting departing guests, performing for the dead the last tender offices, acting as a pallbearer, going before the bier, making lamentation [for the dead], digging a grave and burying the body, causing the bride and the bridegroom to rejoice, providing them with all their needs [for the wedding]. These constitute deeds of kindness performed in person and for which no fixed measure is prescribed. Although all these commands are only on rabbinical authority, they are implied in the precept, "And you shall love your neighbor as yourself," that is: what you would have others do to you, do to him who is your brother in the Law and in the performance of the commandments.[21]

---

21. *Hilkhot Evel* 14:1.

The second source is one of the focal aspects of mitzvot between man and God: "You shall walk in His ways" (*Devarim* 28:9). Some of the actions included in Rambam's list under the heading of "loving your neighbor" are characterized by the Gemara in *Sota* as part of the obligation of *imitatio Dei*, imitating God:

> R. Hama b. R. Hanina said: What means the text, "You shall walk after the Lord your God" (*Devarim* 13:5)? Is it possible for a human being to walk after the *Shekhina*; for has it not been said, "For the Lord your God is a devouring fire" (ibid. 4:24)? But [the meaning is] to walk after the attributes of the Holy One, blessed be He. As He clothes the naked, for it is written, "And the Lord God made for Adam and for his wife coats of skin, and clothed them" (*Bereshit* 3:21), so do you also clothe the naked. The Holy One, blessed be He, visited the sick, for it is written, "And the Lord appeared unto him by the oaks of Mamre" (ibid. 18:1), so do you also visit the sick. The Holy One, blessed be He, comforted mourners, for it is written, "And it came to pass after the death of Abraham, that God blessed Isaac his son" (ibid. 25:11), so do you also comfort mourners. The Holy One, blessed be He, buried the dead, for it is written, "And He buried him in the valley" (*Devarim* 34:6), so do you also bury the dead.[22]

On the practical level, the two sources of obligation are generally congruent, but from a theoretical perspective, they are very different; and with respect to our question, it seems to me that a distinction should be drawn between them. Based on "You shall love your neighbor as yourself," it is unreasonable to obligate a person to do for his neighbor that which he would not make the effort to do for himself. The obligation toward his neighbor and his neighbor's right to receive acts of kindness

22. *Sota* 14a. The Gemara here relates to the verse, "You shall walk after the Lord your God" (*Devarim* 13:5), whereas Rambam, who speaks about character traits rather than about actions (*Hilkhot De'ot* 1:6), cites the verse, "You shall walk in His ways" (*Devarim* 28:9). It is necessary to understand the difference between the verses, but this is not the forum to expand upon the matter.

seem to be conditioned on his neighbor's readiness to do his share. However, the obligation to imitate God does not depend upon any other factor, for God's kindness is unconditional. There is indeed a saying that "God helps those who help themselves," which implies that He does not help those who don't help themselves; and whole generations of people who ignored the unfortunate, and even abused them, soothed their consciences with this idea. This, however, is not the Jewish outlook.

Judaism does, of course, recognizes man's obligation to do whatever he can to provide for his own needs, and even forbids reliance on miracles, but it does not condition divine assistance on man's contribution. With all the importance of "earthly stirring" (*itaruta diletata*), "heavenly stirring" (*itaruta dile'eila*) does not depend upon it: "'And I will be gracious to whom I will be gracious' (*Shemot* 33:19) – although he may not deserve it. 'And I will show mercy to whom I will show mercy' (ibid.) – although he may not deserve it."[23] Lovingkindness is provided even to one who is "undeserving" because he is negligent in his efforts to advance himself. The quantitative and qualitative dimensions of God's mercy – "'Abundant in mercy' – to those who need mercy because they have not sufficient merits [to be saved by them]"[24] – include, without a reckoning, even those who are undeserving. If God would do a reckoning, who in fact would be able to stand? The same applies, then, to man's obligation to engage in acts of lovingkindness out of a desire to follow in God's ways. Not with calculated and planned steps, and not out of considerations of reciprocity and mutuality, agreement and parallelism, does man walk in the footsteps of his Creator, but precisely with acts of kindness that breach the dams of balance and reckoning; which are given, as formulated by Rambam, even to "one who has no right at all to claim this from you."[25]

It is possible to suggest another difference between the two sources of obligation, as far as our question is concerned, if we examine the nature of the relationship to the other person. *Gemilut hasadim* that is based on love of one's fellow has an interpersonal foundation. The

---

23. *Berakhot* 7a.
24. Rashi, *Shemot* 34:6.
25. *Moreh Nevukhim*, III, 53.

recipient is considered as a party with standing, as a *gavra* (subject), in the framework of mutual, if not equal, relations. Thus, it is reasonable to condition the obligation of the one party on the conduct of the other. But *gemilut chasadim* that is based on walking in the ways of God is not rooted in a relationship with another person. It constitutes a personal moral and religious challenge in the context of which the other person is merely the field of activity, sort of a *heftza* (object) with which the mitzva is fulfilled – and as it applies even to animals, for "the Holy One, blessed be He, sustains [all creatures,] from the horns of wild oxen to the eggs of vermin"[26] – but not a party with any standing in the matter. Thus it follows that the negligence of the recipient does not negate the obligation of the benefactor. Is a reckoning done with the horns of wild oxen and the eggs of vermin?

According to the aforementioned understanding, there is indeed an obligation to help the needy who do not do their part to help themselves to the best of their ability. But the fact that this duty is based on only one of the two sources of obligation of *gemilut hasadim* dulls its force. While on the one hand, as we have seen, the obligation to imitate God has wider application than the obligation to love one's neighbor, on the other hand, its validity is less clear and obligating. With respect to the nature of the mitzva and its obligation, the love of one's neighbor, as it is applied on the practical level – over and beyond the fulfillment in the heart that it requires – is similar to other mitzvot. In specified circumstances, the actions that are demanded by this duty are as obligatory as wearing *tzitzit* and constructing a railing on one's roof, as blowing a *shofar* and donning *tefillin*. There is no escaping its demands, and it may not be pushed aside because of other spiritual demands, barring cases in which any mitzva would be pushed aside (because of the rule that one who is already engaged in a mitzva is exempt from performing other mitzvot, or the like). For example, one may not neglect *gemilut hasadim* that is connected to the love of one's fellow only in order to study Torah, just as one may not neglect the mitzva of *lulav* for that reason. Moreover, it is possible that such actions are not merely means to achieve an emotional

26. *Shabbat* 107b.

relationship, or even the external expression that reflects that relationship, but rather the practical dimension of the mitzva.

For this reason, the mitzva also divides, if only by rabbinic decree, into various branches, each one being defined as a mitzva in its own right, to the point that Rambam discusses the priority given to each one:

> It seems to me that the duty of comforting mourners takes precedence over the duty of visiting the sick, because comforting mourners is an act of benevolence toward the living and the dead.[27]

As I heard on various occasions from my revered teacher, Maran HaGaon Rabbi Joseph B. Soloveitchik, such a discussion is possible only if we assume that by rabbinic law, the comforting of mourners, the visiting of the sick, and similar obligations each become separate entities and categories. Otherwise, it would be necessary to adopt a contextual approach that would judge each case according to its specific circumstances. It seems to me that it is reasonable to add that the basis for this development is the Torah level of the mitzva that grants *gemilut hasadim* and its specific actions the status of actions and fulfillments of the mitzva of "You shall love your neighbor as yourself."

The nature of benevolence that is based on walking in God's ways is entirely different. This mitzva, in all its aspects and with all its offshoots, outlines a direction and a goal, but it lacks absolute and specific content. The moral action that it demands is part of an overall spiritual effort. Thus, it competes with parallel efforts for a person's attention and for the allocation of his resources – such as expanding Torah study or deepening the fear of Heaven; and circumstances are possible in which a person's priorities will demand that preference be given to other objectives at the cost of *gemilut hasadim*. In this framework, the focus is upon the personality of the benefactor that is fashioned and expressed through his actions, and not the needs of the recipient. To the extent that his spiritual personality can develop more in other ways, the needs of the other person – inasmuch as they are just a means and not the objective – are

27. *Hilkhot Evel* 14:7.

liable to be set aside. Therefore, basing a specific act of *hesed* exclusively on walking in God's ways narrows the dimensions of the obligation.[28]

To this limitation, which is connected to the circumstances of the benefactor, we can add a second limitation that is connected to the situation of the recipient and his capability of rehabilitating himself. It seems to me that it is possible to distinguish between two levels of capability. In one, a person is in distress – there being no halakhic doubt about this fact – but he is capable, through intensive efforts, to contribute to the solution of his problems, and perhaps even to rehabilitate himself. Regarding such a person, there is room to discuss, at the very most, whether or not his refusal to exert himself as required exempts others from doing for him what he is not prepared to do for himself. Beyond a certain point, however – and I openly admit that, practically speaking, I don't know where to draw the line – it is so easy for the needy person to help himself that his situation cannot be called one of distress. When his own salvation is easy to achieve, but for some reason he refuses to help himself, it is difficult to view him as in need. In such a case, the allowance to ignore his problems is not an exemption that stems from his refusal, but an absence of obligation that is rooted in the fact that he simply is not included in the parameters of the mitzva. With regard to the mitzvot of *perika* and *te'ina* or *gemilut hesed*, he is like a rich man with regard to the mitzva of *tzedaka*. A doubt may even be raised whether one who goes out and helps a "needy" person of this sort fulfills these mitzvot. Regarding the obligation, in any event, it is certainly possible to distinguish between these two levels. Regarding the one, the other person is fundamentally obligated to extend assistance, though there might be some practical limitations. Regarding the second, he is entirely out of the picture.

---

28. In light of what has been said here, there is room to discuss whether one who engages in such *hesed* is exempt from performing other mitzvot. Regarding *hesed* based on the love of one's fellow, there is no doubt that the principle that one who is occupied in a mitzva is exempt from other mitzvot is valid, and there is no difference between it and the mitzva of *tzedaka*. Whether there exists a communal obligation of *hesed* based exclusively on the obligation to imitate God must also be examined, for it is possible that this obligation applies only to the individual, but not to the community. This, however, is not the forum to discuss these issues at length.

This point brings us to the practical complications of our problem. Reaching a fundamental decision and establishing operative guidelines are two different things. The conclusion that there is room to include in the mitzva of *gemilut hasadim* the extension of relief to the negligent does not mean that it should be extended – or extended in the same measure – in every case.

Before concluding, we must survey the main factors that must be considered when performing such *hesed*. One, that has already been mentioned, is the needy person's ability to help himself. Even in cases where the indigent person is certainly regarded as being in need – for example, where a person can do much to alleviate his distress, but cannot remove it altogether on his own[29] – it is clear that the needy person's ability to help himself must impact upon the obligation to help him. The more possible the mission, the more restricted the obligation – both because the recipient is less needy and because his responsibility, in the double sense of burden and guilt, is greater. It is, of course, impossible to establish precise criteria for this point. Regarding loading and unloading when the owner stands on the side, the Mishna states: "If [the owner] is old or sick, [the passerby] is obligated."[30] But it does not clarify the level of old age or illness, and certainly there is room here for different approaches. I myself am inclined to a liberal definition, but clearly there is no absolute answer; and the same applies with respect to our general question regarding *gemilut hasadim*. If we are talking about finding a job – and that is the primary practical point in our day – there is yet another vague factor: dependency on others. As opposed to the cases of loading and unloading, here efforts in and of themselves are no guarantee of success. Thus, it is possible to apply the words of the author of the *Me'il Tzedaka*:

29. It may be assumed that the mishna that exempts a person from the obligation of loading and unloading if the person in need does not help out, based on the Scriptural decree "You shall surely unload it with him," relates to a case where the person in need can only help. Were he able to solve the problem entirely on his own, it is possible that even without the verse, the other person would be exempt, for in that case the person being helped would not be defined as being in need.
30. *Bava Metzia* 32a.

> Children, life, and sustenance do not depend on merit, for it is written: "And I will be gracious to whom I will be gracious" (*Shemot* 33:19) – although he may not deserve it. We learn from here that whoever sends out his hand to take, we give him. And there is no proof that if he is healthy, he is fit to work, for his fate does not help him earn a profit, even if he works all day long.[31]

Nevertheless, there is room to distinguish between one who is looking for a job, but fails to find one, and one who sits back doing nothing, if we just adopt the principle – as apparently *Me'il Tzedaka* did – that a person's refusal to take advantage of his own abilities lessens the obligation upon others to act charitably toward him.

On this level, one point requires special emphasis. It may be assumed that the illness mentioned in the mishna – parallel to old age – is a physical illness, the definition of which is relatively simple. The serious difficulty arises with respect to emotional illnesses or hindrances, both because their scientific definition is less precise and because they are subject to sharp ideological controversy. Psychological disability – fear of responsibility, difficulty in adapting oneself to a steady routine, distaste for authority, dependency on the home – can eat away at the ability to work no less than a lame foot. Without a doubt, however, it is less recognized, in both senses of the word.

The degree of recognition depends in no small measure on the idea of free will. This is why the halakhist will be inclined to adopt an ambivalent attitude toward the struggle over welfare budgets across the Western world today, between conservative politicians who are "stingy" and social workers who are "generous." On the one hand, Halakha's excessive valuation of *hesed* and of society's responsibility toward the needy brings him to support the expansion of aid. But on the other hand, the more that this demand is based on the argument that aid must be expanded because psycho-social circumstances fetter the needy and

---

31. Rabbi Eliyahu HaKohen of Izmir, *Me'il Tzedaka*, no. 196. This book, written three hundred years ago, is a treasure trove of almost two thousand essays relating to *tzedaka* and *gemilut hasadim*.

prevent them from joining the work force, it clashes with the emphasis that Judaism places upon free will.

Halakha indeed recognizes psychological causality, and *Hazal* even saw such circumstances as a factor that mitigates or even altogether removes responsibility and guilt. For example, we find suffering as a mitigating circumstance:

> R. Sheshet said in the name of R. Elazar b. Azarya: I could exempt the entire world [Rashi: the Jewish world] from judgment from the day of the destruction of the Temple until the present time, for it is said in Scripture: "Therefore, hear now this, you afflicted and drunken but not of wine" (*Yeshayahu* 51:1).[32]

With regard to circumstances of seduction the Gemara states:

> What is "And Di Zahav" (*Devarim* 1:1)? They said in the school of R. Yannai: Thus spoke Moses before the Holy One, blessed be He: Master of the Universe, the silver and gold (*zahav*) which you showered on Israel until they said, "Enough (*dai*)," that was what led to their making the calf.... R. Hiyya bar Abba said in the name of R. Yohanan: It is like the case of a man who had a son; he bathed him and anointed him and gave him plenty to eat and drink and hung a purse around his neck and set him down at the door of a brothel. How could the boy help sinning?[33]

Generally, however, the heavy emphasis that Halakha places on man's freedom and ability and the fundamental trust that it puts in him stand in absolute opposition to the psychological determinism that is prevalent in wide circles of those who support an "enlightened and liberal" welfare policy. Trusting man and emphasizing his responsibility means believing that he is capable of transformation, if he so desires. Shifting the focus from ability to will narrows the definition of "an old or sick

32. *Eiruvin* 65a.
33. *Berakhot* 32a.

man," and it is also liable to diminish the feelings of obligation and sympathy toward the needy:

> R. Elazar said: Any person who has no knowledge – it is forbidden to have mercy upon him, as it is stated: "For it is a people of no understanding; therefore He that made them will not have compassion upon them, and He that formed them will not be gracious unto them" (*Yeshayahu* 27:11).[34]

From a certain perspective, it is possible to respond in the manner that Rav Chen reported in the name of his father: "How much mercy [has been shown] to one to whom it is forbidden to show mercy."[35] But with all the sympathy over his lack of understanding, the fact that a person is regarded as one with unused abilities certainly tends to diminish the degree to which one fulfills *gemilut hasadim* in his regard.

This point borders on a second important factor: the needy person's motives. A lazy person who sneers at society and expects it to support him certainly cannot be compared to a refined person who prefers to remain within the confines of gentility rather than skin carcasses in the market; and between these two extremes there is a broad spectrum. According to the determinist view, this point is significant only with respect to the treatment: help offered to the "lazy" should be restricted or canceled because it is liable to encourage an antisocial attitude or undermine his ability to function. From a Jewish perspective, however, this distinction is replete with clear moral content, and as such, it has great weight on the operational plane. In certain situations, the needy person's spiritual benefit, irrespective of the benefactor's limitations, demands a cessation of *hesed* that is liable to produce corruption; and this should be given priority. However, it falls upon the benefactor or the welfare agency to ascertain, honestly and sincerely, that this consideration, and not the natural inclination to scrimp, is the driving force behind this withholding of assistance. If indeed the move is dictated not

34. *Sanhedrin* 92a.
35. R. Avraham Chen, *BeMalkhut HaYahadut* (Jerusalem, 5724), II, p. 426.

by budgetary considerations but rather by conscience, the denial of aid might be absolutely justified.

The third factor is the need of the recipient. The graver his situation – and most importantly, the more dangerous it is – the more difficult it becomes to withhold aid, even when it seems appropriate from other perspectives. In the extreme case, where the person in need is in mortal danger, it would be unthinkable to allow him to deteriorate because he is responsible for his troubles. This follows by way of a *kal vahomer* argument. If in the case of a person who wishes to commit suicide, we are obligated to frustrate his design and save him – and this seems to be obvious[36] – then surely in the case of a person who endangers himself in indirect ways, where his "guilt" is less clear, all the more so must we come to his rescue. Without a doubt, even R. Shimon, who maintains that if a person has resources of his own but does not wish to support himself from them, we are not bound to help him, will concede that we may not ignore a person who mortifies himself to the point that his life is placed in jeopardy. Maharam of Rothenburg has already written:

36. The author of the *Minhat Hinnukh*, however, thought otherwise: "It seems that if a person wishes to commit suicide and another person can save him, it is possible that he is not governed by this negative precept [i.e., 'Neither shall you stand idly by the blood of your neighbor' (*Vayikra* 19:16)]. It is unnecessary to say that he is not governed by the positive precept, '"And you shall restore" – to include the loss of his body,' for the positive precept of restoring lost property does not apply to property that was intentionally lost.... But he is not even governed by this negative precept" (mitzva 237; in old editions, this appears in *Kometz Minha*, printed at the end of the *Minhat Hinnukh*). He tries to adduce proof for his position from the fact that the Gemara in *Sanhedrin* 73a does not distinguish between the positive and negative precepts. His position, however, is very astonishing. As for his proof from the Gemara, it seems quite the opposite. Regarding bodily harm, even the positive precept is valid. The exemption regarding intentionally lost property applies to property, whether because of *hefker*, as argued by *Tur* (HM 261; and see Rosh, *Bava Kamma* 2:16, and Shakh, HM 261:3); or because we don't burden others when the owners themselves abandon and waive their property, as argued by the Rambam. Regarding bodily harm, we can certainly not speak of *hefker*, nor of waiver, for a person has no proprietary rights over his life. Therefore, one who threatens suicide must be saved both because of the mitzva of restoring lost property, and because of the prohibition of standing idly by the blood of your neighbor.

> I was asked about a teacher who had entrusted a deposit in the hands of his landlord, and he was arrested on false charges, and he instructed his landlord not to ransom him; I wrote that he must ransom him against his will.... Even if he says, "I do not want you to ransom me," we ransom him with his money against his will.... For we learn from a verse that one who sees his fellow drowning in a river is obligated to save him and exert himself and hire rescuers, and it is obvious that even if he commands, "Do not save me," one must save him and later one can collect one's expenses from him.[37]

The severity of the situation – and *Hazal*[38] viewed the dangers of captivity as exceedingly great – magnifies the obligation to rescue, the responsibility of the person in danger be as it may. While Maharam's conclusion that expenses may be collected from the ransomed captive differs from the position of R. Shimon (which was codified as law regarding the provision of financial support), this difference is clearly attributable to the differing needs in the two cases.

This point is reflected in the words of Me'iri cited earlier. As may be remembered, one of the distinctions that he offered between the talmudic passage in *Kiddushin*, which implies that the obligation of rescue falls entirely on the rescuer, and the Mishna in *Bava Metzia*, from which he infers that it falls also on the rescued party, was the difference between saving a life and saving property. Me'iri does not explain, but it seems to me that at the root of the matter is the assumption that regarding bodily danger there is an absolute obligation that leaves no room for any kind of reckoning. Even the lazy and those who take advantage of others have a right to life. As for property, it is possible to demand, at the very least, the needy person's participation – whether in order not to place too heavy a burden on the benefactor, or in order not to detract from others in need, or in order to teach him a lesson. But as for life, the obligation to

37. *Responsa Maharam ben Barukh*, ed. Prague, no. 39. The gist of the responsum is cited in his name by *Mordekhai, Bava Kamma*, sec. 59.
38. See *Bava Batra* 8b.

rescue stands above all other considerations.[39] From this type of danger,

39. This is more persuasive if we understand that according to Me'iri mortal danger is a sufficient condition to distinguish between the passages in *Bava Metzia* and *Kiddushin.* But even if he understands that it is merely a necessary condition (see above, note 14), and even if we accept the position that he cites at the beginning of the passage, that if the woman does not want to return to the rescuer the value of the bread, "he is not obligated to save her," it seems to me that a distinction should be made between a threat to life and a threat to property. Regarding property, it is possible that there is no obligation whatsoever, even *lekhathilla*. Regarding life, one is certainly obligated to save the person – with or without the possibility of recovering expenses – but according to this opinion, it is possible to recover expenses after the rescue. The continuation of the words of Me'iri, "For he too is forbidden to save himself with another person's money," proves this. For is it conceivable that a person who is faced with two choices, either to die or to cause a financial loss to his fellow, is obligated to sacrifice his life? Surely, *Tosafot* already explained the Gemara's problem (*Bava Kamma* 60b), "What is the law about saving oneself by appropriating another's money?" as follows: "He asks whether he is obligated to pay when he saved himself because of *pikuah nefesh*" (ibid., *Tosafot*, s.v. *mahu*). Rambam also understood the problem as a question regarding payment: "One who saves himself by appropriating another's money must repay it" (*Hilkhot Hovel UMazik* 8:2). It seems to me that there is no other way to understand the Gemara. The Gemara indeed uses the formulation, "A person is forbidden to save himself," but one must not understand that this means that *lekhathilla* he must refrain from saving himself, for damages and theft are not included among the prohibitions that are not set aside for *pikuah nefesh*. Rather, "forbidden" here means that his act has ramifications regarding payment. If the act is outright permissible, it means that the Torah permitted the other person's property to the saved party, as if it had pledged it for this purpose and removed the other person's proprietary rights to it. Thus, there is no room for compensation, for the rescued party did not make use of property belonging to another person, but rather Halakha granted him use of the property from the very outset. If, however, a person is forbidden to save himself by appropriating another's property, the other person's proprietary rights remain in place, and the saved party, when he sets aside this "prohibition" for reasons of *pikuah nefesh*, makes use of money that was not given to him for that purpose, and therefore he is obligated to make compensation. See Me'iri, *Bava Kamma* 114b, who writes that a person is permitted to save himself with another's property having in mind to make restitution, but if he has in mind not to make restitution, he is forbidden to use another's property. Clearly, he means that *lekhathilla* he must have in mind to make restitution, but not – if no possibility of restitution exists – that he should die rather than make use of the property. (Rabbi Yaakov Ettlinger understood, however, that according to Rashi, following his understanding of his position in *Bava Kamma* 60b, a person must indeed sacrifice his life in such a situation; see

while rather extreme, we may infer, in the framework of our discussion, the law governing other situations. The principle underlying the words of the Me'iri is valid regarding assistance in general: the obligation to assist the "lazy" is a function of the danger threatening them.

In the end, of course, these factors, each one independently or taken all together, cannot be translated into precise solutions for the problem of assistance to those who are negligent about helping themselves. While they outline a direction and propose guidelines, the need to deal on both a moral and a practical level with the particular aspects of each individual case and every public framework remains in place. This is rooted in both the complex social reality and the outlook of Halakha. The effort to encourage sensitivity on the one hand, and responsibility on the other, to nurture both a work ethic and an ethic of giving, to hold onto both *tzedek* (justice) and *tzedaka* (charity), reflects Halakha's values. It is in this complex of values that our problem lies, and within it are also found the foundations of its solution. One must, however, strive to reach it, and for the proper motives.

Responsa Binyan Tziyyon, no. 167, and *Responsa Binyan Tziyyon HaHadashot*, no. 173. But his words are very astonishing. This, however, is not the forum to discuss his position.) Thus, the earlier line in Me'iri, "He is not obligated to save her," should also be understood to mean that in actual practice he is obligated to save her, but since he is not obligated financially, then the loaf of bread the rescuer gives her for this purpose is his own, and not hers by virtue of his obligation to God, and thus, there is a transfer of betrothal money.

Source Index

I. BIBLICAL SOURCES

Bereshit/Genesis
1:28 14n17
1:29 315
3:21 51, 330
3:22 327
6:5 40
8:21 40
9:3 315
11:4 104
17:1 238
18:1 330
18:12–13 76
18:19 242
18:21 121
18:25 145
18:27 203–4
25:11 330
30:43 207
31:6 207
Shemot/Exodus
1:2 60
5:2 204
15:11 205
15:26 232n48
16:7 204
18:20 231
20:7 221n7
20:14 156n43
20:23 79
23:3 266
23:5 208, 323
23:7 77
24:7 62
31:16 73
33:8 12
33:19 331, 336
Vayikra/Leviticus
14:36 122n19
15:26 13n6
18:5 72
19:1 238
19:2 268

19:13 218
19:14 175, 234
19:16 234, 324, 339n36
19:18 52, 175, 211, 234, 302, 329
19:32 234
20:7 238
22:32 120n7
23:11 60
25:17 218
25:36 176, 196
25:42 63
Bemidbar/Numbers
5:8 13n6
6:11 55
15:29 223
Devarim/Deuteronomy
1:1 337
1:16 174–75
4:15 122
4:24 52, 330
5:11 221n7, and Onkelos
5:17 218
5:18 156n43
6:5 64
6:17 234
6:18 186, 218–19, 232, 238, 302
7:7 203
11:13 224
11:22 51, 241
12:18 54
12:25 232n48
12:28 232n48
13:5 52, 330
13:9 232n48
14:26 54
15:4 196
15:8 212n103, 321
15:10 281n11
17:11 18n34
17:16 150
17:17 150
18:13 238n71
18:14 115n2
20:19 122
21:9 232n48
22:1 82
22:3 322n10
22:4 323
25:5–9 24n55
25:7–10 233n51
27:7 54
28:9 238, 241, 302, 330
28:14 18n34
33:27 204
34:6 51, 330
Shofetim/Judges
5:31 205
I Melakhim/I Kings
10:29 150
11:4 150
II Melakhim/II Kings
18:35 204
Yeshayahu/Isaiah
14:14 204
24:12 294n36
27:11 338
49:3 206
51:1 337
Yirmiyahu/Jeremiah
10:10 145
17:5 328
17:7 328n20
Yehezkel/Ezekiel
16:49 302
18:20 220n4
28:2 204
Yo'el/Joel
3:5 52

Amos
3:2 251
Mikha/Micah
6:3 51
Tehillim/Psalms
8 41–42
16:8 68, 238–39
19:9 3
22:7 204
37:21 208
89:9 205
90:10 124
119:162 3
Mishlei/Proverbs
2:20 232
3:17 61, 89, 176
3:28 208
13:7 126
21:30 84
23:23 225
Iyyov/Job
11:7 148
26:7 204
Shir HaShirim/Song of Songs
1:2 269
Ruth
3 13n6
4:7 123n25
Kohelet/Ecclesiastes
3:19 40–41, 44

II. RABBINIC SOURCES

A. Mishna

Pe'ah
1:1 52n52, 201, 273n179
4:3 182
5:4 321–22
8:8 320
8:9 328
Demai
7:8 279n6
Shevi'it
10:3–4 143, 144n22
Bikkurim
3:7 21n43
Pesahim
10:1 263n153
Ketubbot
9:2 266
Gittin
4:6 212–213
Eduyot
5:7 98n205
Avot
2:1 220
2:5 244–45
2:9 102
2:12 56, 208
3:14 38
4:21 69
4:22 69
5:10 202, 206n92, 272, 280
6:2 63

B. Talmud Bavli/Babylonian Talmud

Berakhot
7a 226, 331
9a 99
13a 3, 60, 62, 93
13b 78

14a–b 145
17a 203
19b 18, 80n159, 82, 84, 88
19b–20a 75
32a 337
32b 241n78
35b 223
45a 26
45b 246
61b 57, 64

Shabbat
10b 78n151
23b 76
31a 51
38a 221n9
42a 90n184
45a 94n196
63a 240n77
81b 75n137, 80n159
88a 62
94b 75n137, 80n159
95a 107n229
107b 332
118b–119a 54n58
121b 240n77
129a 78n150
130a 13
133b 52n49

Eiruvin
7a 221
13b 97
38b 9n20
41b 80n159
46a 94n196
49a 278
65a 337
104a 107n228

Pesahim
5a 78n150
51b 98n205
68b 54n58
105a 26
109a 54n58

Yoma
22b–23a 206
23a 203, 205
44b 61
67b 147n29
85b 73, 229n
86a 120n7, 234–35
86b 221

Sukka
25b 50n44, 92
26a 107
32a 61n90
49b 50–51, 53n55, 231n42, 302n54, 321

Beitza
2b 96
5b 107
15b 69
16a 57
17a 9n20
18a 108
28b 221
36b 6–9, 14, 20
37a 8

Rosh HaShana
16a–b 151
20a 14

Taanit
16a 234

Moed Katan
23a 105n224

Hagiga
18a 177n14

Yevamot
3b 88n179
14a 98n205

20a 268
39b 233
47a 60
61a 74n135
61b 14n16
62b 54n60
65b 19n35, 76n145, 308
87b 61n90, 176n8
89b 310
90b 81
93a 128n47
93a–b 117n7
109a 233

Ketubbot
11a 63n97
17a 77
47b 136n4
49b 309–10
58b 16n25
60a 90
65b 16
67b 209, 321
68a 326n15
83a–84a 137n7
97a 245
103a 271, 278–79, 310n74
104a 57
109b 293n34

Nedarim
9b 58
10b 241n78
27b 117n4
31b–32a 238n71
80b 197

Nazir
23a 224

Sota
14a 51–52, 140, 302n55, 330
21b 77n240
41b 76n145

Gittin
7b 212n103, 263
10b 164n3
36a–b 138n10
36a–37b 143
45a 162, 166–67, 212
48a 293n34
49b 152n38
52a 303
56b 205
59b 120n4, 188–89

Kiddushin
8b 324
21a 152n38
21b 139, 229
30b 40
31b 27n69, 229, 270
33b 12n3
40a 120n6
41a 19
59a 120n5, 181–82, 264
61a 189
68b 152n38
82a 39

Bava Kamma
9b 224
20b 280
20b–21a 294n36
30b 221
38a 74n135
50a 251
55b 228
56b 119n2
60b 192, 341n39
62a 121n11
81b 299n46
90b 122
91b 55
92a 122, 137
97a 294n36

99b 232n44, 248, 259
99b–100a 231
100a 135n3
112a 176
114a 119n2
116b 138n10
118a 119n2, 256, 274
119a 316n90
Bava Metzia
10a 182
16a 124n30
16b 264
23b–24a 78n149
24b 252, 254, 262
28b 252
30a 197
30a–b 249
30b 218, 231
31b 287n20
32a 208, 323, 335
33a 195–96, 199
35a 233
41a 298
43b 298
48b 117n4
51a 136
56a 300
56b 293n34
58b 293n34
60a 156
61b 123, 227–28
62a 191–92
66a–b 117n4
66b 127–28
68b–69a 142n17
69a 287n20
73b 117n4
82b–83a 232n44
83a 135n3, 231–32
94a 136
104b–105a 142n17
108a 233, 268
108b 186, 264
115a 152n38
117b 295n37
Bava Batra
5a 265
7a 313n79
7b–8a 303
8a 167
8b 340
8b–9a 138n10
9a 153n40, 153n41
12b 164n3, 288–89
12b–13a 279
21b 161, 190–91
22a 258
24b 164n3, 165
59a 278, 310–11
59b 311
88a 298
90b 167n10, 197n68
106a 287n20
126b 136
164b 271
165a 271
167b–168a 278
168a 117, 305
174a 303
Sanhedrin
6b 4
7b 174–75
11a 78n150
21b 150
24b 123n26
24b–25a 117n4
37a 39
38a 39, 45
46a 92n191
59a 74n135

72a 195
73a 339n36
74a–b 72n126
74b 193
77a 192
92a 338
106b 308
109a 302
Makkot
3b 136
23b 63
Shevuot
39a 62–63, 220–21
Avoda Zara
4b 225–26
7a 94
11a 57–58
13a 82n168
20b 240n77
35a 269
Zevahim
100a 76n144
Menahot
37b 80n159
41a 141n16, 223n14
65a 60
67a 223n16
76b 61
Hullin
5a 74n134
49b 101n212
89a 203–4
94a 81
116a 98n205
141a 19n35
Bekhorot
13a 233
Arakhin
16b 53–54
Nidda
6a–b 94n196
9b 94n196, 100n210

C. Talmud Yerushalmi/Jerusalem Talmud

Berakhot
1:1 98n205
3:1 75, 82n168
Pe'ah
1:1 76n145, 102, 201
Kilayim
9:1 75, 85
Bikkurim
3:3 12n3
Shabbat
15:3 54n58
Pesahim
3:7 76
Yoma
1:1 9, 15–16
8:5 72
Rosh HaShana
1:3 145–46
Yevamot
4:12 143
Kiddushin
4:12 55–56
Bava Kamma
6:1 228
Makkot
2:6 220n4
Shevuot
3:8 221n7

D. Prayer

Rosh HaShana 63
Ne'ila 40–41

E. Other

Avot DeRabbi Natan
A–text, 11 54–55
A–text, 28 57
A–text, 31 39
A–text, 40 280n9
B–text, 30 56
Bereshit Rabba
8:1 45
19:5 39
Masekhet Semahot
4:25–26 82n168
Mekhilta DeRabbi Shimon ben Yohai
18:20 231
Mekhilta DeRabbi Yishmael
Masekhta DeAmalek (Yitro) 2 231
Masekhta DeBaHodesh (Yitro) 11 79–80
Midrash Tanhuma
Tzav, 3 86
Shemot Rabba 8:2 41
Sifra
Preface 256
Metzora, ch. 5, letter 12 122
Kedoshim, ch. 4, letter 12 52
Sifre
Naso, 42 76n145
Ekev, 42 224
Ekev, 49 51–52, 241, 302n55
Torat Kohanim
Behar, 5 192n52
Tosefta
Moed, ed. Saul Lieberman (New York, 1962), Beitza 4:4, p. 300 23
Bava Metzia 11:33–37
Shevuot 3:2 228
Vayikra Rabba
9:9 76n145
34:3 56n68
Yalkut Shimoni
Bereshit 57 39

III. MAIMONIDEAN SOURCES

A. Mishneh Torah

Sefer HaMadda
Yesodei HaTorah 5:1–3 72n126
Yesodei HaTorah 5:1 120n7
Yesodei HaTorah 5:4 72
De'ot 1:4–7 240–42
De'ot 1:5 250n116
De'ot 1:6 52n49, 330n22
De'ot 2:6 84
De'ot 5:13 205–6
De'ot 7:7 211
Teshuva 5:1 327
Teshuva 7:1 327
Teshuva 10:1–5 224n19
Sefer Ahava
Tzitzit 3:11 140–41
Tzitzit 3:11–12 222–23
Berakhot 7:6 247
Berakhot 7:6, *Kesef Mishneh* 246n92
Berakhot 11:2 222
Sefer Zemanim
Shabbat 2:1 72
Shabbat 23:14 17n29
Shabbat 30:7–10 54n58
Shabbat 30:15 73

Yom Tov 6:16–20 54n58
Hametz UMatza 1:4 108
Hametz UMatza 3:8, *Kesef Mishneh* 76n144
Hametz UMatza 3: 9 76n144
Taaniyot 1:1–2 54n57
Hanukka 4:14 88–89, 102
Sefer Nashim
Ishut 3:19 19n38
Ishut 10:1 10n21
Ishut 12:1–2 136n4
Ishut 12:6–7 136n5
Ishut 14:17 221
Ishut 15:3 54n60
Ishut 15:16 54n60
Sefer Haflaa
Shevuot 1:15 221n7
Shevuot 5:7 75n141
Nedarim 13:23–24 58n78
Nezirut 10:14 58n78
Sefer Zera'im
Kilayim 10:29 75
Mattenot Aniyyim 2:18 182
Mattenot Aniyyim 7:5 263
Mattenot Aniyyim 7:9 322
Mattenot Aniyyim 7:10 309–10
Mattenot Aniyyim 10:7 326
Mattenot Aniyyim 10:19, and *Radbaz* 328
Maaser 15:14 279n6
Sefer Nezikin
Geneva 9:8, *Hasagot HaRaavad* 195
Gezela VaAveda 1:9–11 156n43
Gezela VaAveda 3:9 294n36
Gezela VaAveda 6:7 125n35
Gezela VaAveda 11:7 250n116, 253
Gezela VaAveda 11:10 253n126
Gezela VaAveda 11:11 322n10
Gezela VaAveda 11:17 250
Hovel UMazik 8:2 341n39
Rotze'ah 1:14, *Kesef Mishneh* 213–14
Rotze'ah 2:2 194n60
Rotze'ah 3:10 192
Rotze'ah 13:4 250–51
Sefer Kinyan
Mekhira 11:8 245n91
Mekhira 11:16, and *Hasagot HaRaavad* 117
Mekhira 14:5 167n10
Mekhira 14:11, and *Maggid Mishneh* 153n41
Mekhira 18:1 84
Mekhira 21:3 125
Shekhenim 7:5 280n8
Shekhenim 7:8 313
Shekhenim 12:1 290
Shekhenim 14:5, and *Maggid Mishneh* 268–69
Sefer Mishpatim
Sekhirut 2:1 300n49
Sekhirut 10:5 249
Sekhirut 13:7 207
Malveh VeLoveh 1:3 207–8
Malveh VeLoveh 4:13 122
Malveh VeLoveh 26:10 303n57
To'en VeNitan 1:9 274
Sefer Shofetim
Sanhedrin 24:10 83
Edut 10:1–2 220n6
Edut 10:4 125n35
Mamrim 2:4 73n131
Evel 3:14 82
Evel 6:5 105n224
Evel 14:1 52, 231n42, 302n52, 302n54, 329

Evel 14:7 333
Melakhim 6:10 122n15

B. Other

Moreh Nevukhim/Guide for the Perplexed
I:1–2 47n36
III:13 39n9, 39n10, 41
III:26 147n31
III:53 243–44, 331

Perush HaMishnayot/Commentary on the Mishnah
Pe'ah 4:3 182n22
Demai 7:8 279n6
Bava Metzia 2:11 198
Sanhedrin 7:4 221–22

Sefer HaMitzvot
Shoresh 1 53n54
Shoresh 2 75n141
negative commandment 297, note by R. Hayyim Heller 214n105
appendix to positive commandments 222n12

Shemonah Perakim
Ch. 4 242–43

Teshuvot/Responsa
715 59
II, 631–33 75n141
II, 615 299n46

IV. MEDIEVAL AND MODERN SOURCES

Avodat HaMelekh (R. Menahem Krakowski)
De'ot 1:5 231n43

Baalei HaNefesh (Kafach Edition)
p. 15 55

Bayit Hadash
Orah Hayim 200 247n102
Hoshen Mishpat 12 257

Beit Efrayim
Responsa, Hoshen Mishpat 49 291n29

Beit Yosef
Hoshen Mishpat 156 258–59
Hoshen Mishpat 207 117n6
Hoshen Mishpat 263 249n112
Orah Hayim 339 25, 107n228

BeMalkhut HaYahadut
II, p. 426 338

Be'urei HaGra
Hoshen Mishpat 12:8 259
Hoshen Mishpat 264:2 200n77
Yoreh De'ah 2:16 280

Binyan Tziyyon
Responsa, 167 341n39
Responsa HaHadashot, 173 341n39

Darkhei Moshe
Even HaEzer 64:4 22

Dikdukei Soferim
Eiruvin 49a 310n74
Bava Batra 12b 288n21, 310n74

Eiger, R. Akiva
Responsa, 85 95n199

Encyclopedia Talmudit
9:260–61 94n197
9:697–713 143n20
10:36–37 106n225
16:417–21 10n22

Even HaAzel
Shekhenim 12:1 306n64

Haggahot Maimoniyot
Ishut 10:14 (letter nun) 18n33
Gezela VaAveda 3:4 295n39
Gezela VaAveda 11:3 252n125, 256
Edut 10:5 126n37
Haggahot Mordekhai
Kiddushin 561–62 160–62, 164
Havvot Ya'ir
Responsa, 42–44 154n42
Responsa, 50 127
Responsa, 163 115–57
Ibn Ezra
Bereshit 17:1 238n71
Iggerot Moshe
Yoreh De'ah, 1:145 197n68, 212n103
Kaftor VaFerah
ch. 5 108n233
Keli Yakar
Shemot 23:5 323
Ketzot HaHoshen
39:1 308
154:1 305–6
259:3 258
356:6 258
Kiryat Sefer
Shekhenim ch. 9 177n13
Madregat HaAdam
third edition, pp. 1–27 49n43
Mahaneh Efrayim
Hilkhot Gezela 17 299n46
Hilkhot Gezela 20 299
Maharal
Derekh Hayim on *Avot*, 3:14 39n8
Kitvei Maharal MiPrague, II, 54 39n8
Kitvei Maharal MiPrague (A. Kariv edition), introduction, I, xxiii–xxxii 39n8
Netivot Olam, "Netiv Gemilut Hasadim," ch. 5 272–73
Maharam of Rothenburg
Responsa, 39 339–40
Maharik
Responsa, 132 184–86
Responsa, 167 91
Maharshal
Responsa, 36 188
Yam Shel Shlomo, Ketubbot 1:2 18n33
Yam Shel Shlomo, Bava Kamma 9:24 249
Me'il Tzedaka
no. 196 335–36
Meiri
Hiddushim, Beitza 5b 108n233
Beit HaBehira, Berakhot 45b 246–47
Beit HaBehira, Eiruvin 14b 177n14
Beit HaBehira, Yoma 23a 206n91
Beit HaBehira, Kiddushin 8b 208n96, 209, 324–25, 340–42
Beit HaBehira, Kiddushin 11b 177n14
Beit HaBehira, Kiddushin 42b 293n34
Beit HaBehira, Bava Kamma 56a 228
Beit HaBehira, Bava Kamma 99b 249
Beit HaBehira, Bava Kamma 114b 341n39
Beit HaBehira, Bava Metzia 24a 253
Beit HaBehira, Bava Metzia 24b 253n128
Beit HaBehira, Bava Metzia 30b 250

Beit HaBehira, Bava Metzia 50a 177n14
Beit HaBehira, Avot 5:10 (5:12 in Jerusalem edition) 283
Melekhet Shlomo
Pe'ah 4:3 182n24
Mesillat Yesharim
ch. 13 56
Minhat Hinnukh
mitzva 237 339n36
Mordekhai
Pesahim 99b 153n263
Pesahim 100b 79
Beitza 697–98 17n28
Kiddushin 524 186
Bava Kamma 16 295n39
Bava Kamma 59 340n37
Bava Metzia 257 252n125, 256
Bava Batra 507 290–91
Bava Batra 551 184
Nahalat Tzvi
Yoreh De'ah 248:1 212n103
Netivot HaMishpat
Hoshen Mishpat 154:13 313–14
Nimmukei Yosef
Bava Kamma 8b 296
Bava Batra 5b 168
Bava Batra 14b 225
Noda BiYehuda
first edition, Yoreh De'ah 48 95n199
first edition, Yoreh De'ah 57 95n199
first edition, Yoreh De'ah 61 95n199
second edition, Hoshen Mishpat 24 297n43
Or Same'ah
Shekhenim 12:1 279n6
Or Zarua
Volume A, Tzedaka, 14 320n2
Volume B, Sukka, 306 100n210
Volume C, Bava Kamma, 122–23 295–96
Volume C, Bava Kamma, 125 300n49
Volume C, Bava Kamma, 407 249
Volume C, Bava Metzia, 27 184
Volume C, Bava Metzia, 84 250
Volume C, Bava Metzia, 359 267–68
Volume C, Bava Metzia, 24 280n8
Volume D, Sanhedrin, 67 100n210
Orhot Hayim
Birkat HaMazon, 32 247
Orhot Hayim (Keter Rosh)
Sec. 14 98n206
Peri Hadash
Yoreh De'ah 116 108n233
Piskei Talmid HaRashba (in *Shittat HaKadmonim)*
Bava Metzia 24b 253–54
Bava Metzia 30b 250
Pithei Teshuva
Hoshen Mishpat 12:6 258n143
Hoshen Mishpat 237:2 185n36
Yoreh De'ah 31:2 100n211
Raavad
Hasagot on the Rif, Ketubbot 27b, and *Sefer HaZekhut* 233
Hiddushim, Bava Kamma 97b 298n45
Raavan
177b–178a (in S. Z. Ehrenreich publication) 255–56
Raavya
Sec. 124 248
Rabbenu Avraham Ferisol
Commentary on Avot, 5:10 285n18
Rabbenu Bahya
Commentary on Avot, 5:10 283
Rabbenu Gershom
Bava Batra 5a 265–66

Bava Batra 9a 153n40
Bava Batra 12b 283n15
Bava Batra 22a 258
Bava Batra 59a 280n8, 283n15
Rabbenu Hananel
Sanhedrin 7b 175
Rabbenu Hayim HaLevi, *Hiddushim*
Yesodei HaTorah 5:1 192n53, 193n58
Rabbenu Yona
Bava Batra 12b 288n21, 291, 306
Avot 2:5 245
Avot 5:10 281
Rama
Responsa, 11 79
Responsa, 125 12–33
Ramban, *Derasha* on *Kohelet*
Kitvei HaRamban (Chavel) vol. 1 p. 205 281n11
Ramban, *Hasagot on Sefer HaMitzvot*
Shoresh 3 198n71
negative commandment 17 281n11
Ramban, *Hiddushim al HaShas*
Shabbat 42a 90n184
Bava Metzia 7a 279n6
Bava Metzia 30b 70n197
Bava Batra 9a 153n39, 153n40, 153n41
Bava Batra 54b 183–84, 195
Bava Batra 175b 308
Kuntres Dina Degarmi 168n15
Ramban, *Milhamot Hashem*
Bava Kamma 41a 119n2, 257n139
Bava Metzia 23b 300n50
Ramban, *Perush HaTorah*
Bereshit 17:1 238n71
Shemot 15:26 51n47
Shemot 20:8 88n179
Shemot 21:1 122n21
Vayikra 13:47 122n19
Vayikra 19:1 218–19
Vayikra 19:2 271, 302n56
Vayikra 19:19 147
Vayikra 23:24 117n14, 219n3
Vayikra 25:15 293n34
Vaykira 25:36 176
Devarim 6:5 224
Devarim 6:18 234–35, 302n56
Devarim 18:13 238n71
Devarim 22:6 147n31
Ramban, *Torat HaAdam*
Preface 69n121
Shaar HaMihush, Inyan HaSakana 73, 325n14
Shaar HaSof, Inyan Mi SheMeto Muttal Lefanav 75n142
Ran
on the Rif, Beitza 20a 23
on the Rif, Kiddushin 24a 186–87
Hiddushim, Bava Batra 9a 153n39, 153n40
Hiddushim, Bava Batra 12b 291n29, 306
Hiddushim, Sanhedrin 2b 122n21
Hiddushim, Shevuot 23b 75n141
Rash of Sens
Pe'ah 4:3 182n22
Rashba
Hiddushim, Kiddushin 59a 189
Hiddushim, Bava Kamma 21a 294n36
Hiddushim, Bava Kamma 97a 294n36
Hiddushim, Bava Batra 9a 153n41
Hiddushim, Bava Batra 12b 288n21, 291n29, 293n33, 305
Hiddushim, Bava Batra 59a 280n8
Hiddushim, Bava Batra 168a 305
Hiddushim, Shevuot 42b 300n49
Responsa, 1:248 108
Responsa, 1:253 94n197, 98n205, 106n225

Responsa, 1:769 138n10
Responsa, 1:889
Responsa, 4:185 138, 138n10, 153n39
Rashbam
Bava Batra 59a 280n8
Bava Batra 59b 311–12
Bava Batra 90b 167n10
Rashi, Commentary on the Talmud
Berakhot 19b 81n162
Berakhot 45b 246
Shabbat 23b 88n181
Shabbat 31a 51n47
Shabbat 81b 82
Eiruvin 49a 280n8, 283
Pesahim 2b 195n63
Pesahim 5a 78n150
Sukka 25a 92n191
Beitza 2b 96
Beitza 36b 7, 14
Ketubbot 57a 99
Ketubbot 67b 322
Ketubbot 97a 245n91
Ketubbot 103a 279
Ketubbot 104a 57
Kiddushin 31b 229
Bava Kamma 66a 253n126
Bava Kamma 100a 231n41
Bava Metzia 24b 252, 255n132
Bava Metzia 30b 231n41
Bava Metzia 33a 199–201
Bava Metzia 60a 156n44
Bava Metzia 66b 128
Bava Metzia 83a 232
Bava Batra 5a 266
Bava Batra 12b 290
Bava Batra 22a 258
Sanhedrin 7b 175
Menahot 67a 223n16
Hullin 5a 74n134
Hullin 94a 81
Rashi, Commentary on the Tanakh
Bereshit 17:1 238n71
Shemot 34:6 331
Vayikra 19:19 147
Devarim, 6:18 234n56
Ri Migash
Bava Batra 5a 266
Bava Batra 12b 288n21, 289–90
Bava Batra 106a 287n20
Rif
Beitza 20a 17n29
Ketubbot 29b 326n15
Bava Metzia 12b–13a 78n149
Ritva
Shabbat 23b 88n181
Eiruvin 13b 97–98
Kiddushin 42a 226
Kiddushin 59a 189
Bava Metzia 8a 279n6
Bava Metzia 24b 254–55
Bava Metzia 30b 197n70
Bava Metzia 41a 299
Bava Batra 9a 153n41
Bava Batra 12b 289, 291–92
Bava Batra 59a 309
Rivash
Responsa, 399 138n10, 153n41
Rosh
Berakhot 7:7 247n102
Kilayim 9:4 85
Beitza 5:2 17n29
Ketubbot 1:3 22
Kiddushin 3:2 189
Bava Kamma 2:6 294n36
Bava Kamma 2:16 339n36
Bava Kamma 9:16 248
Bava Metzia 9:9 279n6
Bava Batra 1:33 153n40, 153n41
Bava Batra 1:46 288n21, 291
Sanhedrin 8:2 209

Tosfei HaRosh, Nidda 61b 140, 223
Teshuvot HaRosh, 27:5 19n36
Teshuvot HaRosh, 97:2 292, 309, 316
Teshuvot HaRosh, 108:10 176
Sedei Hemed
Klalim, Maarekhet Reish, klal 47 185n36
Sefer HaHashlama
Bava Kamma 6:1 228
Sefer HaRoke'ah
pp. 8–11 54n57
Sefer HaYashar
23 19n36
48:10 18n33
Sefer Me'irat Einayim
Hoshen Mishpat 209:2–3 124
Hoshen Mishpat 209: 3 125
Hoshen Mishpat 231:43 176
Hoshen Mishpat 378:1 123
Sefer Mitzvot Gadol
Mitzvot Aseh, 27 246
Mitzvot Lo Taaseh, 75 18, 22
Sefer Mitzvot Katan
174 25
Sforno
Bereshit 17:1 238n71
Shabbat HaArez
Introduction, 41–44 (3rd ed.) 100n210
Shibbolei HaLeket
Sec. 150 247
Shiltei HaGibborim
Shabbat 48a (Alfasi) 100n210
Shitta Mekubbetzet
Berakhot 45b 247
Ketubbot 103a 271, 278–79, 310n74
Bava Metzia 10a 183
Bava Metzia 31a 70n197
Bava Metzia 41a 299
Bava Metzia 62a 193
Bava Batra 9a 153n41
Bava Batra 12b 291
Shulhan Arukh
Even HaEzer 37:8 – and Rama 19n38
Even HaEzer 55:1 10n22
Hoshen Mishpat 2:1 138n10
Hoshen Mishpat 12:2 – Rama 257
Hoshen MIshpat 28:1 228n36
Hoshen Mishpat 60:2 124
Hoshen Mishpat 154:13 – Rama 313
Hoshen Mishpat 155:22 – Rama 164–65
Hoshen Mishpat 155:32 – and Sema 168
Hoshen Mishpat 163:6 – Rama, and *Be'urei HaGra* 94 167
Hoshen Mishpat 203:10 – Rama 126
Hoshen Mishpat 207 117n4
Hoshen Mishpat 207:13 – Rama 123, 126nn37–38, 127
Hoshen Mishpat 207:21 124
Hoshen Mishpat 208 117n3
Hoshen Mishpat 209 117n7
Hoshen Mishpat 209:1–2 124–25
Hoshen Mishpat 209:4 128
Hoshen Mishpat 231:24 167
Hoshen Mishpat 231:28 – and *Pithei Teshuva* 138n10
Hoshen Mishpat 259:2 – Rama 252
Hoshen Mishpat 263:3 – and Rama 249n112
Hoshen Mishpat 272:3 – and Rama 249n112
Hoshen Mishpat 306:6 249
Hoshen Mishpat 348:1 123
Hoshen Mishpat 363:6 – and Rama, *Be'urei HaGra* 16 294n36, 297

Hoshen Mishpat 388:2 – and Sema 168
Orah Hayim 1:1 – Rama 68
Orah Hayim 34:2 98n206
Orah Hayim 200:1 247
Orah Hayim 306:14 73n132
Orah Hayim 317:1 – Rama 90–91
Orah Hayim 328:17 90n183, n185
Orah Hayim 339:3 – and Rama 107n228
Orah Hayim 339:4 – Rama 109
Orah Hayim 619:1 – Rama 111
Yoreh De'ah 2:5 – Rama 280
Yoreh De'ah 36:16 – Rama 95n198
Yoreh De'ah 39:2 – Rama 95n198
Yoreh De'ah 39:13 – Rama 95n198
Yoreh De'ah 69:2 – Rama 95n198
Yoreh De'ah 92:4 – Rama 95n198
Yoreh De'ah 108:1–2– Rama 95n198
Yoreh De'ah 135:1– Rama 95n198
Yoreh De'ah 157:1 61
Yoreh De'ah 240:25 – Rama 91
Yoreh De'ah 248:1 212n103
Yoreh De'ah 251:3 – Rama 212
Yoreh De'ah 252:4 166
Yoreh De'ah 253:2 320
Yoreh De'ah 253:10 322
Yoreh De'ah 303:1 85
Yoreh De'ah 372:1 85
Yoreh De'ah 392:1–2 105n224

Siftei Kohen
Hoshen Mishpat 33:1 75n141
Hoshen Mishpat 261:2 339n36
Yoreh De'ah 157:3 90n183
Yoreh De'ah 242 (concluding discourse) 94n197, 100n210
Yoreh De'ah 248:1 212n103

Tashbetz
Magen Avot, 5:10 282

Terumat HaDeshen
316 299n46

Torat HaOla
I, i 104
II, ii 104
III, xxxviii 104
IV, xxxii 104

Torat Hatat
Introduction 106

Tosafot
Eiruvin 82a 126n37
Pesahim 5a 78n150
Pesahim 39a 61n90
Beitza 30a 9, 20, 107
Beitza 36b 7, 9, 15n22, 22–23
Yevamot 2a 61n90
Ketubbot 17a 77n148
Ketubbot 56a–b 137n8
Ketubbot 60a 91n190
Ketubbot 68a 326n15
Ketubbot 97a 245n91
Ketubbot 104a 57
Gittin 45a 166n8
Gittin 48a 293n34
Gittin 49b 152n38
Gittin 77b 23–24
Kiddushin 41a 19–20
Kiddushin 59a 184n32
Bava Kamma 60b 341n39
Bava Kamma 91b 58n78, 122n13
Bava Metzia 20b 295
Bava Metzia 23b 78n149
Bava Metzia 24b 252
Bava Metzia 117b 295n37
Bava Batra 5a 266
Bava Batra 12b 288n21, 291, 302
Bava Batra 15a 21n43
Bava Batra 21b 200
Sanhedrin 24b 123n26
Shevuot 42b 300n49

Avoda Zara 2a 108n233
Avoda Zara 15a 108n233
Avoda Zara 27b 72n129
Avoda Zara 57b 108n233
Hullin 49b 101n212
Arakhin 2b 141n16
Nidda 6b 100n211
Tosefta KiFshuta (New York, 1962)
Moed 1000–1001 23n52
Tur
Even HaEzer 64 22
Even HaEzer 136 23
Hoshen Mishpat 209 128
Hoshen Misphat 259 254
Hoshen Mishpat 261 339n36
Hoshen Mishpat 263 249n112
Hoshen Mishpat 272 249n112
Hoshen Mishpat 348 123
Orah Hayim 339 17, 22
Yoreh De'ah 251 212
Yoreh De'ah 253 320n2, 326n15
Turei Even
Megilla 3b 82n164
Turei Zahav
Yoreh De'ah 1:17, and R. Akiva Eiger 223n17
Yoreh De'ah 192:6 5n11
Urim VeTummim
Hoshen Mishpat 12:4 258
Yad Rama
Bava Batra 9a 153n40, 153n41
Bava Batra 7a 313n79
Bava Batra 12b 288n21
Bava Batra 26b 175
Bava Batra 60b 279n6
Bava Batra 168a 280n8, 305

General Index

A

Absolutism (moral theory) 71, 134
Altruism 143, 171–72, 191–216
  compulsory altruism – See *Kofin al middat Sedom*
Asceticism 49, 54–61
Ashkenazi, R. Gershon 127

B

Bacharach, R. Ya'ir Hayim (*Havvot Ya'ir*) 113–15, 163
Bahya, Rabbenu 38
Belkin, R. Samuel 34n2

C

Chavel, R. Charles B. 234n55
Christianity 50, 64–66, 70–71, 191, 206–7,215, 315
  See Humanism, Christian Humanism
  Christian view of Judaism 63, 172,217
Cracow 1–2, 109n234
Custom 111n236

E

Economics
  Halakha's approach to economic competition 115–57, 180–91, 200
  Halakha's general approach to economic rights 178–80, 312–17
  harhakat shekhenim 174–79, 200
  importance of competition in a capitalist economy 154–57, 180–81, 214–16
Eliezer of Worms, R. 54n57
Elijah of Vilna, R.
  See Vilna Gaon

F

Falke, R. Yehoshua 123n23
Free will 62–63, 327–28, 336–37

H

Halakha
  adaptation/circumvention 134–44,152–57
  as relating to human freedom/autonomy 42–44, 61–64, 309

compulsion – See *Kofin al middat Sedom*
concern for human welfare 49–59
demanding sacrifice 59–64, 91–92,102–3
deviation via stipulations 136–38, 140
exceptional deviations 6–8, 69–92
mandating social involvement 64–68
pluralistic conception 96–101, 150
teleology (*ta'amei hamitzvot*) 141– 52, 270
Hananel, Rabbenu 75
Hellenism 46, 237–38
Heller, R. Hayyim 214n105
Hen, R. Avraham 78
Hesed 50–54, 96, 103, 187–88, 199, 201, 231n42, 242–43, 272–74, 302, 306n64, 316, 319–42
Source of obligation 329–34
Humanism
Christian humanism 34n2, 44–47, 50
definition 35–37
relation to Torah Judaism 37–47, 49–69, 71–103
Hurwitz, R. Isaiah 113
Hurwitz, R. Yosef Yosel 49

I
Imitatio Dei 51–52, 96, 241–43, 302, 330–34
Isserles, R. Moshe 1–3, 5–11, 12n3, 15n22, 103–12

J
Job (biblical character) 45, 145

K
Kabbala 2, 114
Kagan, R. Yisrael Meir (Hafetz Hayim) 93
Kahana, Kopel 218
Karo, R. Yosef 11
Kasowski, R. Chaim Josua 225n22, 240n77
Kedusha 55, 67–68
Kevod Haberiyyot 8, 74–75, 79–85,87–89, 93, 104–5, 110–11
Kofin al middat Sedom 271–74, 277–317
Kook, R. Avraham Yitzchak 38, 66

L
Lieberman, R. Saul 56–57, 146n27
Lifnim Mishurat Hadin 135, 139n13, 149,186, 199–201, 206n91, 217–19, 224–75,302
Luzzatto, R. Moshe Hayyim 56
Luzzatto, R. Samuel David 238

M
Maharal 38–39, 113

N
Neoplatonism 49
Neriyah, R. M. Z. 138n10
Nowaredok 49

P
Peretz, Rabbenu 15n22
Pesak (process)
difference between different posekim 100–101
in cases of conflict with human need 3–5, 95–96, 98–101, 103, 111–12
Pikuah Nefesh 72–74, 80, 88, 90, 93,193n58, 339–41
Plato 45n29, 101–2, 134, 145, 194, 237

R
Raavad 55
Rambam (Maimonides) 38–39, 47n36, 55, 103, 238; see also source index
Relativism 97, 134, 146, 269

S
Self-defense 194–95
Self-sacrifice 191–94, 212–13
Shachna, R. Shalom 1
Shalom 75–80, 85–89, 104–5
Shapiro, R. David S. 151n37
Shulhan Arukh 1–2
See also Source Index
Siev, R. Asher 2n3, 6n12, 106n225
Silberg, Moshe 108n233, 143n20
Soloveitchik, R. Hayyim 73n132, 88, 93
Soloveitchik, R. Joseph B. 43n26, 59,66–67, 73n132, 92n191, 93n194, 221n7,333
Stoicism 237

T
Twersky, R. Isadore 67
Tzaar 90–92
Tzelem Elokim (the image of God) 38–39, 44, 51–52

V
Vilna Gaon 38n6, 98

W
Wisdom literature 238
Wurzberger, R. Walter S. 67n110

Y
Yitzhak of Corbeil, R. 11

Z
Zevin, R. S. J. 54n57, 93n192

Name Index

A
Abelard, Peter 50
Achilles (character) 35
Adams, Henry 178
Aeschylus 237
Alcestis (character) 194
Alighieri, Dante 62
Anselm of Canterbury 50
Antonio (character) 143
Aquinas, Thomas 103, 145, 147, 316n89
Aristotle 35, 134, 237, 242
Arnold, Matthew 178, 180
Austin, John 146

B
Babbitt, Irving 36
Bagehot, Walter 111n236
Baker, Herschel C. 44n28
Bentham, Jeremy 172–73
Berdyaev, Nicolas 63
Bonaparte, Napoleon 327
Bonhoeffer, Dietrich 64–67
Borowitz, Eugene B. 134n2
Bramhall, John 145
Brandt, Richard 216n106
Brunner, Emil 134n2
Buber, Martin 34n2, 217
Bush, Douglas 35n4, 42n23, 48, 229n39

C
Cairns, Huntington 314n82
Calvin, John 64
Camus, Albert 36
Carlyle, Thomas 102, 327
Christophe, Paul 315n85
Cohen, Boaz 221n10
Coleridge, Samuel Taylor 134
Cox, Harvey 50, 66, 67n111
Crane, Hart 179n16

D
Devlin, Patrick 227, 235–36
Dewey, John 36
Dunbar, William 69

E
Edgeworth, Francis Ysidro 173
Emerson, Ralph Waldo 327

Erasmus, Desiderius 36, 45

F
Fletcher, Joseph 134n2
Forster, E. M. 229n39
Freehof, Solomon 3, 12n4, 13n5, 13n9, 26n67, 27n68, 110–11
Fromm, Erich 34n2
Frost, Robert 178
Fuller, Lon L. 139, 153n40, 236–39

G
Gauguin, Paul 179
Gilmore, Myron P. 35n4
Gilson, Etienne 147n28
Gordon, Y. L. 4
Greenspan, N. S. 221n10, 245n88

H
Hadley, Arthur T. 314n82
Hamlet (character) 20n42, 103, 266
Hardy, E. R. 315n85
Hart, H. L. A. 227
Hector 35
Hegel, G. W. F. 314
Heinemann, Yitzchak 151n37
Henson, H. H. 83
Hermans, Francis 44n28, 46
Hirsch, Mendel 34n2
Hirschberg, Harris H. 34n2
Hobbes, Thomas 145
Hobhouse, L. T. 316
Holland, Henry Scott 314n84
Hooker, Richard 36, 103, 145
Hunter, G. K. 35n3, 48
Hutcheson, Francis 215

I
Irwin, William A. 45n30

J
Jaeger, Werner 47n36, 48
James, William 59, 240n77
John of Salisbury 36
Julius Caesar 101

K
Kant, Immanuel 62, 71, 193, 216, 224, 239, 281n11
Kaufmann, David 114n1
Keats, John 68
Keynes, John Maynard 216
Kierkegaard, Søren 62, 229
Kingsley, Charles 70
Kohn, Hans 34n2
Kristeller, Paul Oskar 35n4

L
Lamont, Corliss 37
Lew, M. S. 2n3
Lewis, C. S. 147n31
Locke, John 171, 316
Luther, Martin 217

M
Mackinnon, M. D. 224n18
Mandeville, Bernard 215
Manetti, Giannozzo 48
Maritain, Jacques 46
Marx, Alexander 163n10
Melville, Herman 180
Mill, John Stuart 37, 44n27, 173, 207, 224, 227
Miller, Arthur 194n61
Milton, John 36, 47, 68, 220, 239
More, Henry 83–84

N
Neubauer, J. J. 75n141

Newman, John Henry 70–71, 77–78, 95, 150
Niebuhr, Reinhold 47n36, 173
Neitzsche, Friedrich 207

O

O'Brien, Gordon W. 44n28
Olan, Levi A. 45n29
Orwell, George 107

P

Pascal, Blaise 45
Paul of Tarsus 217
Pico della Mirandola, Giovanni 36, 45
Plotinus 49
Plutarch 220n4
Porphyry 49
Pound, Roscoe 227
Prometheus 45
Prospero (character) 64
Protagoras 42, 45
Proudhon, Pierre J. 315

R

Raskolnikov (character) 35
Raven, C. E. 59
Ross, Jacob 227n29
Ruskin, John 178

S

Sandburg, Carl 179n16
Schwarzchild, Steven S. 67n111
Shaftesbury, Earl of (Anthony Ashley-Cooper) 172, 215
Shinn, Roger L. 34n1
Smith, Adam 171, 215, 236
Socrates 237
Sonia (character) 35
Sophocles 45, 226–27, 237
Spencer, Theodore 44n28
Stephen, James Fitzjames 227
Swift, Jonathan 45

T

Tauler, Johannes 62
Tawney, R. H. 58, 68, 142, 316n89
Tchernowitz, Chaim 106n225
Tennyson, Alfred 39, 85
Toynbee, Arnold J. 46

U

Underwood, Kenneth W. 134n2
Urbach, E. E. 15n22

V

Vinogradoff, Paul 227
Voltaire 195

W

Whitman, Walt 179n16
William of Ockham 145
Woodhouse, A. S. P. 43–44
Wordsworth, William 47–48, 239

Maggid Books
The best of contemporary Jewish thought from
Koren Publishers Jerusalem Ltd.